Airborne Landing to
Air Assault

Airborne Landing to Air Assault

A History of Military Parachuting

Nikolaos Theotokis

Pen & Sword
MILITARY
AN IMPRINT OF PEN & SWORD BOOKS LTD.
YORKSHIRE – PHILADELPHIA

Dustjacket photograph. The main photograph shows Private Roland Smith of the 8th Parachute Battalion of the British army's 1st Airborne Division on 3 May 1943 at Bulford during preparations for the division's planned involvement in operations in continental Italy (the assault on Taranto). The photograph (H 29600) was taken by Lieutenant Spender, a War Office official photographer, and is from the collection of the Imperial War Museums (Public Domain).

First published in Great Britain in 2020 by
PEN & SWORD MILITARY
An imprint of
Pen & Sword Books Ltd
Yorkshire – Philadelphia
Copyright © Nikolaos Theotokis 2020

ISBN 9781526746993

The right of Nikolaos Theotokis to be identified as Author of this work has been asserted by him in accordance with the Copyright, Designs and Patents Act 1988.

A CIP catalogue record for this book is available from the British Library

Typeset in 10.5/13 Ehrhardt by Vman Infotech Pvt. Ltd.

Printed and bound in the UK by TJ International Ltd, Padstow, Cornwall.

Pen & Sword Books Ltd incorporates the imprints of Pen & Sword
Archaeology, Atlas, Aviation, Battleground, Discovery, Family History, History, Maritime,
Military, Naval, Politics, Social History, Transport, True Crime, Claymore Press, Frontline
Books, Praetorian Press, Seaforth Publishing and White Owl
For a complete list of Pen & Sword titles please contact

PEN & SWORD BOOKS LTD
47 Church Street, Barnsley, South Yorkshire, S70 2AS, England
E-mail: enquiries@pen-and-sword.co.uk
Website: www.pen-and-sword.co.uk

Or

PEN AND SWORD BOOKS
1950 Lawrence Rd, Havertown, PA 19083, USA
E-mail: Uspen-and-sword@casematepublishers.com
Website: www.penandswordbooks.com

Contents

List of Plates

1. A fully-equipped American paratrooper climbing into a transport plane hours before the Normandy landings on 6 June 1944. (Center of Military History, US Army)

2. As early as 1934, the USSR had twenty-nine paratroop and glider battalions. (www.quora.com/were-there-any-Soviet-paratroopers-during-ww2-)

3. Italian Air Force General Alessandro Guidoni. (Italian Air Force)

4. Major General William C. Lee. (1895–1948). (General William C. Lee Museum, Dunn, North Carolina)

5. A German paratrooper ready to exit from a Junkers Ju 52 for an operational jump in the early stages of the Second World War. (Bundesarchiv, Bild 101I584-2154-06A)

6. German paratroopers on the attack after landing in the drop zone. (https://mxdoc.com/queue/osprey-combat-oo1-british-paratrooper-vs-fallschirmjager-medhtml)

7. Some 10,000 German paratroopers and 750 glider-borne troops landed on the Greek island of Crete on 20 May 1941. (Arthur Conry/Wiki-Ed/ Wikimedia Commons / CC BY-SA 3.0)

8. Friedrich August Freiherr von der Heydte. (1907–94). (Bundesarchiv, Bild 183-H 26044)

9. On 22 June 1940, British Army's No. 2 Commando was turned over to parachute duties. (https://arnhemjim.blogspot.com/2012/ii/earlybritish-paratroop-training.html: 30 November 2012)

10. British paratroopers at the central training establishment in Ringway near Manchester in January 1941. (Imperial War Museum)

11. British airborne troops inside an Airspeed Horsa glider ready to take off from RAF Brize Norton, Oxfordshire, during the Second World War. (Public Domain)

12. Major John D. Frost was one of the first officers of the British Army to join the newly-formed Parachute Regiment in 1941. (Public Domain)

13. American paratroopers before jumping over Normandy on 6 June 1944. (US Army Signal Corps)

14. Chinese paratroopers, members of the uniformed Operational Groups (OGs). (http:// www.soc.mil/oss/operational-groups.html)

15. SAS recruits being trained in parachute jumping at Qabrit in Egypt during the Second World War (www.dailymail.co.uk/news/article-2076967/www2-sas-raid-deep-Rommel-territory-convinced-brass-help-win-war.html)

16. The founder of the SAS and its first commander, Lieutenant Colonel David Stirling, in 1942 in North Africa. (Imperial War Museums: E 21338)

17. Luftwaffe Major Erich Rudorffer (1917–2016) was shot down sixteen times during the Second World War, in nine of which he parachuted to safety! (Bundesarchiv, Bild 183-2007-1218-501/CC-BY-SA 3.0)

18. Captain Klavdia Y. Fomicheva. (1917–58) was one of the Soviet female pilots who parachuted to safety during the Second World War. (en.wikipedia.org)

19. RAF Group Captain Douglas Bader. (1910–82), who flew combat missions with artificial legs during the Second World War, was forced to bail out over France on 9 August 1941. (Public Domain)

20. Aleksander K. Gabszewicz. (1911–83) was a Polish pilot who had to bail out when his fighter plane was shot down in the first day of the German invasion of Poland in 1 September 1939. (Public Domain)

21. Canadian Flying Officer Vernon C. Woodward, of the Royal Air Force, dons his parachute before taking off in a Hawker Hurricane Mark I. (Public Domain)

22. USAAF Second Lieutenant. (later Major) Owen J. Baggett. (1920–2006). He is referred to as the only person ever to shoot down an enemy fighter with a pistol. (RallyPoint.com, 29 January 2018)

23. The US 187th Airborne Regimental Combat Team was dropped on 20 October 1950 25 miles north of Pyongyang, during the battle of Yongju. (Public Domain)

24. Over 100 C-119 Flying Boxcar transport aircraft drop the US 187th Airborne Regimental Combat Team at Munsan-ni, close the Demilitarized Zone, on 23 March 1951. (Public Domain)

25. The paratrooper commanders at Dien Bien Phu. (ECPAD)

26. Captured French soldiers from Dien Bien Phu. (Public Domain)

27. American soldiers are dropped off by US Army UH-1 Huey helicopters in South Vietnam in 1965. (Horst Faas/Associated Press)

28. US Army helicopters flying over combat patrols in South Vietnam in 1968. (Overseas Weekly Collection/Hoover Institution Library and Archives)

29. One of the British SAS units that was deployed during the Falklands War. (Newsrep. com/57879/sas-sbs-war-operation-corporate-part-4: 27 July 2016)

30. For many years after the Second World War the Red Army had the largest airborne force in the world. (https: //Maximietteita.blogspot.com/2017/02/history-of-soviet-airborne-forces-ww2.html?m=1)

31. Elements of the US Army's 82nd Airborne Division in a mass paratroop drop near Andrews Air Force Base in Maryland on 20 May 2006. (Public Domain)

Preface

There have been several publications on military parachuting and airborne warfare. A reader or a potential buyer of this book is therefore entitled to ask why there is a need for another. The purpose of this effort is obviously not to focus on military parachuting in relation to the major airborne units of the world, as has been done already in an exemplary way by numerous writers, but to concentrate on the impact of parachuting in warfare globally and the involvement of paratroopers and aircrews in combat missions throughout the world. It follows developments from the summer of 1918, when parachutes were used for the first time in combat by German and Austro-Hungarian pilots, until the autumn of 2018, when a relatively large-scale parachute drop was conducted in Mali, a landlocked country in West Africa, by the French army. Emphasis is given to the presentation not only of the major airborne and air-assault operations carried out by various armies around the world in the last 100 years but also of missions in which paratroopers were involved in an infantry role. An interesting disclosure in the book is also the degree of influence by certain models (British, French and Soviet) in the training of paratroopers and the raising of airborne units in many countries after the Second World War. Several cases of bailed-out pilots or airmen that occurred in the First and Second World Wars and various wars of the post-1945 period have also been included, as they also represent part of the history of military parachuting.

The parachute was not invented for military purposes, as many people still believe. The Chinese experimented with parachute-like devices as early as 1306 in an attempt to slow the motion of an object through the atmosphere by creating drag. In South East Asia, particularly in Siam (now Thailand) performers were using a two-umbrella system to jump from a height to the amusement of spectators in court celebrations or local fairs. The first known test of a purpose-made parachute was carried out in Venice in 1617 by the inventor and polymath Fausto Veranzio (also known as Faust Vrancic). He is regarded as the pioneer of the parachute as we know it today. Having examined Leonardo da Vinci's 1595 rough sketches of a parachute, the Croatian-born Veranzio designed (and probably tested personally at St Mark's Campanile, although there is no evidence for such a jump) his own parachute. The parachute was reinvented by the Frenchman Louis-Sébastien Lenormand. He was also the first man to make a witnessed decent with a parachute. This historic jump was performed from the tower of the Montpellier observatory in 1783. Lenormand's intended use for the parachute was to help trapped occupants of burning buildings to escape unharmed. Another Frenchman, the inventor and balloonist Jean-Pierre Blanchard, was probably the first person to use a parachute in an emergency, bailing out of a ruptured hot-air balloon in 1793. Blanchard had demonstrated his personally designed and constructed parachute eight years earlier as a means of jumping safely from a hot-air balloon. During the nineteenth century parachute was generally confined to carnivals and daredevil acts with jumps performed usually from hot-air balloons.

The first person to propose airborne troops, the American inventor and politician Benjamin Franklin, was inspired by a hot-air balloon ascent in 1783. His reasoning, penned in a 1784 letter, was that 5,000 balloons, carrying two men each, would cost less than five ships and would overwhelm the enemy.[1] Military parachuting developed in the early twentieth century primarily as a method of exit from balloons, observers being issued with parachutes during the First World War to escape the threat of fighter aircraft. Parachutes were later adapted for escape from aircraft. The origins of airborne operations are attributed to Italian troops in 1927. Battalion-sized units were dropped in the then Soviet Union by the Red Army in 1936. The same year the development of parachute troops began in Nazi Germany and in 1940 in the United States and Great Britain. Advances in helicopter technology since the end of the Second World War brought about increased flexibility to the scope of airborne warfare with air assaults largely replacing large-scale parachute operations.

Acknowledgements

No book of any nature would be possible without the assistance of several people, who either share the author's vision or who are experts in their own particular field. I could not have completed the project without the collaboration and support of a few notable people. To start with, I am indebted to Pen and Sword (P&S) for taking on this project. It is a great pleasure to acknowledge the encouragement and friendly assistance I have received from P&S in the persons of Rupert Harding and Stephen Chumbley. Without their creative enthusiasm and generous assistance this book would simply not have been possible.

I would like first and foremost to thank R. Harding, the commissioning editor. His wisdom and guidance throughout the process of publishing this book has been invaluable. He did a meticulous job checking through the text and offering suggestions to improve the book. While he saved me from numerous errors, I of course am entirely responsible for any of which have escaped detection. I also owe a great measure of gratitude to S. Chumbley, the copy editor, for turning the manuscript into something someone may actually wish to read. Without his knowledge, good sense, eye for detail and literary skills this book would have been much poorer. I owe my editors a great deal for providing sage counsel and generous patience and I am truly humbled even to have my name mentioned next to theirs.

I would be remiss if I did not praise the critical interest of colleagues and friends in various places whose questions and discussions sharpen the text considerably. Their suggestions and criticisms were invaluable.

Finally, I would like to acknowledge the precious contribution of my wife, Voula. It was she who encouraged me to devote the time and energy necessary for this book. Her patience and unbending support throughout this project really made much of the work of the project not only enjoyable but possible. I am also indebted to my son, Dr Georgios Theotokis, the military historian, for discussing this subject with me on numerous occasions prior or in the course of writing and above all for suggesting alterations and additions. It is to Voula and Georgios that this book is dedicated.

Glossary and Abbreviations

air assault: The movement of friendly assault forces by rotary-wing or tiltrotor aircraft to engage and destroy enemy forces or to seize and hold key terrain.

airborne: Troops specially trained to effect, following transport by air, an assault disembarkation, either by parachuting or touchdown.

airborne assault: The use of airborne forces to parachute into an area to attack and eliminate armed resistance and secure a designated objective.

airborne assault weapon: An unarmoured, mobile, full-tracked gun providing a mobile capability for airborne troops, which can be airdropped.

airdrop: The unloading of personnel or materiel from aircraft in flight.

airhead: A lodgement that, when seized and held, ensures the continuous air landing of troops and materiel, and provides the manoeuvre space necessary for projected operations.

air landing: A designation held by glider-borne infantry units of the British Army during the Second World War. The US Army's equivalent were the regiment-sized glider units.

air mobility: The rapid movement of personnel, materiel and forces to and from or within a theatre of operations by air.

air supply: The delivery of cargo by airdrop or air landing.

ARCT: Airborne Regimental Combat Team.

assault: A phase of an airborne operation beginning with delivery by air of the assault echelon of the force into the objective area and extending through attack of assault objectives.

beachhead: A designated area on a hostile or potentially hostile shore that, when seized and held, ensures the continuous landing of troops and materiel, and provides manoeuvre space requisite for subsequent projected operations ashore.

bridgehead: A position held or to be gained on the enemy side of a river, defile or other obstacle to cover the crossing of friendly troops. A defensive work covering the end of a bridge toward the enemy.

C-Day: The unnamed day on which a deployment operation commences or is to commence. Deployment is the movement of forces into an operational area.

chalk: A group of soldiers gathered to be transported by air for a mission.

close combat: A violent physical confrontation between two or more opponents at short range. The term has come to describe unarmed hand-to-hand combat, as well as combat involving fire arms and other weapons at short range.

CT (Combat Team): An infantry or battalion reinforced by the attachment of artillery, engineers or medical or other troops for a particular mission.

D-Day: The unnamed day on which a particular operation commences or is to commence.

Dakota: The nickname of the most common Allied transport aircraft of the Second World War. Capable of transporting twenty-eight paratroopers or 6,000lbs (2,722kg) of equipment, the US-built Douglas C-47 Skytrain aircraft was used for the drop of personnel and supplies by parachute during the Second World War as well as in the post-1945 period.

dispersion: The scatter of personnel and/or cargo on the dropping zone during an airborne operation.

dogfight: An aerial battle between fighter aircraft conducted at close range. It is formally known as ACM (Air Combat Manoeuvring).

dope on a rope: Derogatory term used for air-assault soldiers.

DZ (Dropping Zone): A specific area upon which airborne troops, equipment and supplies are airdropped.

ejector seat: A system designed to save a pilot of a military aircraft in an emergency. The seat is propelled out of the cockpit by an explosive charge, carrying the pilot with it. Once clear of the aircraft, the seat deploys a parachute.

flying ace: A military aviator credited with shooting down several enemy aircraft during aerial combat. The actual number of aerial victories required to officially qualified as an ace varied but it is usually considered to be five or more.

free fall: A parachute manoeuvre in which the parachute is manually activated at the discretion of the jumper or automatically at a pre-set altitude.

GIR (Glider Infantry Regiment): The designation of US Army's air landing regiments during the Second World War.

jumpmaster or **despatcher**: The assigned airborne-qualified individual who controls paratroops from the time they enter the aircraft until they exit.

H-Hour: The specific hour on D-Day in which a particular operation commences or is to commence.

HAHO (High Altitude High Opening): A parachute technique for insertion into hostile territory. The paratrooper, wearing an oxygen mask, exits the aircraft at an altitude of 33,000ft (10,000m), free falls for eight to ten seconds, and then deploys his parachute at around 29,000ft (8,500m). He then makes a flight to the ground by which time he will have travelled a distance of up to 19 miles (30km).

HALO (High Altitude Low Opening): Is a parachute technique according to which the jumper exits the aircraft at an altitude of 33,000ft (10,000m) and has his parachute open at around 2,500ft (760m). HALO allows special operations personnel to land together, even during nighttime missions behind enemy lines.

Irvin X-Type: The static-line parachute used by several paratrooper units during the Second World War.

KIA (Killed in Action): A casualty classification generally used to describe the death of combatants at the hands or because of hostile forces.

LALO (Low Altitude Low Opening): The traditional method of inserting airborne troops. The drops are made at low level (500–2,000ft/150–600m) by round canopy, static-line parachutes. Modern parachutes specially designed for low-altitude jumps can be used as low as 250ft (76m).

LZ (Landing Zone): The general area used for landing troops and materiel, either by airdrop or air landing during an airborne operation.

MIA (Missing in Action): Is a casualty classification assigned to combatants and prisoners of war who are reported missing during wartime or ceasefire. They may have been killed, wounded, captured or deserted.

NCO (Non-Commissioned Officer): A military officer who has not earned a commission. In most countries, NCOs include all grades of corporal and sergeant.

objective: The clearly defined, decisive and attainable goal toward which an operation is directed.

paradrop: The delivery to a place of personnel, equipment or cargo from an aircraft by parachute.

Paras: A colloquial name for the personnel of the British Army's Parachute Regiment. Their battalions are also known as 1, 2, 3 and 4 Para.

paratrooper: A soldier, regardless of branch, who utilizes a parachute as the primary method of transportation to the battlefield.

pathfinders or Landing Zone Control Party: Specially trained and equipped soldiers inserted or dropped into place during an air landing operation ahead of the main airborne force. Their tasks are to mark the dropping zones or landing zones, set up radio beacons as a guide to the aircraft carrying the main force and to clear and protect the areas until the main force arrives. Once the main force has landed, the pathfinders, normally a platoon-sized specially-trained and equipped unit, provides tactical intelligence and offensive roles for the main force.

PIR (Parachute Infantry Regiment): Designation of US Army's paratrooper regiments during the Second World War. In 1957, these units were renamed infantry regiments and six years later infantry regiments (airborne).

POW (Prisoner of War): A person who, while engaged in combat under orders of his or her government, is captured by the armed forces of the enemy.

raid: An operation by Special Forces to temporarily seize an area, to secure information, confuse an enemy, capture personnel or equipment, or to destroy capability culminating with a planned withdrawal.

raiding: A military tactical or operational warfare mission which has a specific purpose and is not normally intended to capture and hold a location but instead finish with the raiding force quickly retreating to a previous defended position prior to enemy forces being able to respond in a coordinated manner or formulate a counter-attack.

Rangers: Rapidly-deployable airborne light infantry organized and trained to conduct highly complex joint direct operations in coordination with or in support of other special operations units of all services.

recon or **reconnaissance**: A patrol, usually small, whose main mission is the gathering of information. Generally speaking, recce patrols tend to avoid contact with enemy forces.

Red Devils: British paratroopers were thus nicknamed by German forces in North Africa during the Second World War for the distinctive maroon beret worn by the men of the regiment in several missions. The Red Devils is also the name of the (free-fall) parachute display team which was raised by the regiment in late 1964.

SAR (Search and Rescue): The use of aircraft, surface craft, submarines and specialized teams and equipment to search for and rescue distressed persons on land or at sea in a permissive environment.

SEAL (Sea Air Land): US Navy forces organized, trained and equipped to conduct special operations with emphasis on maritime, coastal and riverine environments.

SFGA (Special Forces Group Airborne): The US Army's largest combat element for special operations consisting of command and control, Special Forces battalions, and a support battalion, capable of long-duration missions.

shock troops: Formations created to lead an attack. They are often better trained and equipped than other infantry and expected to take heavy casualties even in case of successful operations.

Special Forces: US Army forces organized, trained and equipped to conduct special operations with an emphasis on unconventional warfare capabilities. They are also known as the Green Berets.

special operations: Operations requiring unique modes of employment, tactics, equipment and training often conducted in hostile, denied, or politically sensitive environments.

static line: A fixed cord attached to a large, stable object. It is used to open parachutes automatically for paratroopers and novice parachutists.

static line cable: A cord used instead of a ripcord to open a parachute. The cord is attached at one end of the aircraft and temporarily attached to the pack of a parachute at the other; it opens the parachute after the jumper is clear of the plane.

stick: A planeload of paratroopers assigned for a training or operational jump.

T-5: A parachute utilized by Allied paratroopers during the Second World War. It consisted of a 28ft (8.5m) static line-activated canopy. It was capable of carrying one man and his assigned equipment safely to the ground from a drop altitude as low as 125ft (38m).

vertical envelopment: A tactical manoeuvre in which troops, either airdropped or air landed, attack the rear and flanks of a force, in effect cutting off or encircling it.

WACO (CG-4A): The most common type of glider used in operations by Allied forces during the Second World War. It was constructed of steel tubes, plywood and canvas; it had a wingspan of 84ft (25.6m), a length of 49ft (14.9m) and was capable of transporting fifteen combat-equipped men.

Chapter 1

The Origins of Military Parachuting

The first paratrooper-style descent was performed by US Army Captain Albert Berry, who in 1912 became the first person to successfully parachute from a powered aircraft. Some sources, however, give the credit for the first aircraft jump to another American, a civilian exhibition jumper called Grant Morton. Morton's jump was made from a Wright Model B aircraft over Venice Beach, California, in late 1911. The pusher-type biplane, a 1911 Benoist Type XII, flown by Anthony Habersack Jannus, had taken off from Kinloch Field, a balloon-launching field near St. Louis, Missouri, in the morning of 1 March. The propeller was behind the plane's two seats. The parachute was too bulky to be strapped to Berry's back so therefore it was packed inside a conical iron canister, mounted beneath the plane's lower wing.

Berry had a lot of experience parachuting from balloons, having made his first descent from one of them at the age of 16. The aircraft was heading towards the dropping zone, being the Jefferson Barracks Army Base, south of St. Louis, 18 miles (29km) from Kinloch Field. As they neared the barracks, Berry looked down and spotted an insane asylum: 'That's where we both belong!' he told Jannus.[1] When they were over the barracks' parade ground, cruising at 55mph, Berry climbed out of his seat. The aircraft was 1,500ft (457m) above the ground, when the daring military officer attached the parachute to the harness he was wearing. He lowered himself on a trapeze-like bar suspended in front of the wings and then jumped from the undercarriage. On dropping from the aircraft, Berry's weight pulled the parachute out of the canister.

When jumping from a balloon, a parachute opens ordinarily after a 200ft (61m) drop. That day, Berry went down 500ft before his parachute was opened by a static line.[2] According to a newspaper account, hundreds of watchers held their breath as Berry shot towards the earth, the parachute tailing after him in a long, shaky line. Berry later said that he was not prepared for the violent sensation that he felt when he broke away from the aircraft.[3] The historic jump was witnessed by 'hundreds of cheering soldiers'.[4] When the aeronaut landed, the soldiers 'lifting him in their arms', according to another report, 'half-carried him to the office of Colonel Wood, the commanding officer, who congratulated him . . .'. Nine days later, Berry decided to repeat his feat.[5] On 10 March, he jumped again – before the public this time. The plane flew lower, at 800ft (244m), to ensure that the crowd had a good view of him. Berry's two parachute jumps were admirable, but proved impractical – at least for some time. Jefferson Barracks went down in history as the base of the first experiments in aviation parachuting, but US Army Air Corps needed something not to require a circus act for a pilot in case of emergency.

Parachuting in the First World War

Although parachutes were successfully demonstrated several times in the early years of the twentieth century, it took quite a while for their use to be appreciated in military circles. Meanwhile, a new type of parachute, designed by an Italian named Pino, seemed very practical: the jumper could wear it in a pack like a knapsack. A small pilot chute would emerge from the top of the pack during the jump, thus facilitating the deployment of the larger chute.[6] A parachute of this type, designed by Käthe Paulus, a distinguished German female parachutist, was worn as a pack on the observer's back in German artillery observation balloons during the First World War. French and British observers had parachutes packed in conical containers attached to the balloon's basket and linked to the occupants by static lines. Balloonists had to bail out in case of attack by enemy aircraft or a technical problem. The 2nd Balloon Wing of the Royal Flying Corps recorded 106 (emergency) parachute descents in one year of operations during the First World War.[7]

In May 1916, five German balloons were attacked by British fighter planes and all went down in flames. There were no survivors, although the observers were all equipped with parachutes. On the other hand, there were cases on both sides where artillery observers survived four or five emergency jumps. Parachutes, although used with relative frequency by men who needed to escape from tethered balloons or from flaming Zeppelins, were considered impractical for aircraft by the top brass. German bomber crews were also issued with parachutes, but all references to this matter are vague, as records of German Air Force units disappeared at the end of the war. Some spies and saboteurs were dropped by parachute in enemy rear areas.[8]

As the war progressed, many aircraft pilots, having seen observers floating safely to earth from flaming balloons, wondered why parachutes were not available for them. Of the warplanes downed between 1914 and 1918, 32 per cent were forced to land with the pilot alive and often wounded. Another 23 per cent were destroyed in mid-air with the pilot killed. Thirty per cent went down in flames and a further 12 per cent crashed into the ground. The remaining 3 per cent were downed for other reasons.[9]

Even before the war, a parachute for aircrews had been developed in England by an engineer and businessman, Everard Richard Calthrop, who called it the 'Guardian Angel'. As early as 1913, when the parachute was patented, the Royal Flying Corps was informed of this invention and successful tests were carried out at the Royal Aircraft Factory at Farnborough. On 13 January 1917, after twenty drops with dummies, Captain C.F. Collett made a successful jump from a BE.2C aircraft cruising at 600ft (183m). He landed safely in an undisclosed dropping zone.[10] During the First World War, pilots and observers flew aircraft without carrying parachutes that would enable them to bail out in case of emergency. A number of Germans and Austro-Hungarians, though, began taking private-owned static-line parachutes with them. In the autumn of 1916, an Austrian pilot, whose name was never disclosed, was saved from a burning fighter plane by jumping out with a parachute bought with his own money. According to another story, in 1917 a German pilot, ignoring the prohibition, bought a personal static-line rig, wore it on combat missions and one day successfully bailed out of his unmanageable aircraft.

The question of supplying pilots of the Royal Flying Corps with parachutes was raised several times between 1915 and 1917. The point of view of the top brass was that possession of a parachute might impair a pilot's nerve when in difficulties. The pilot who knew that he had a chance to bail out would not go into a fight with the same 'do or die' determination as the one who knew that the issue must be to kill or be killed. The reason given to the public for not issuing parachutes to pilots was that the 'Guardian Angel' was not 100 per cent safe. They also claimed that the particular parachute was too bulky to be stored by the pilot and its weight would affect the performance of the aircraft.[11] Pressure was put on Calthrop not to publicize his invention. He had repeatedly offered his parachute to the Directorate of Military Aeronautics, only to be – just as repeatedly – turned down. Even when the Russian government ordered 100 Calthrop parachutes in 1917, they only got twenty sets. Meanwhile, the US Army Air Corps refused to provide parachutes to aircrews as long as the proper ones were being developed, as they claimed.

In Germany in 1917 an airship mechanic, Unteroffizier Otto Heinecke, developed a static-line parachute which could be placed under the pilot's seat.[12] A test of what was probably a production model was made by Heinecke at Adershooft near Berlin on 21 February 1918. The final tests were made by him in the same dropping zone on 1 May and again on 6 May 1917.[13] The parachutes issued to German and Austro-Hungarian pilots were not perfect and sometimes failed to operate safely. A third of the first seventy German airmen to bail out died – in some cases because the static line tangled and in others because the parachute caught on the fuselage or the harness broke free. Reports that German flyers were using parachutes began to circulate among the Allies in the spring of 1918. The capture of a bailed-out pilot on 1 April revealed that the German airmen had been supplied with Heinecke parachutes manufactured by Schroeder and Company in Berlin. A pilot named Vizefeldwebel Weimar had abandoned his stricken Albatross DVa and had landed safely among British troops in France before being taken prisoner.

On 27 June, Lieutenant Helmut Steinbrecher was hit in a dogfight over Warfusée, near Liège in Belgium, by a British flying ace, Captain Edward Barfoot Drake. He managed to land safely with his parachute. A day later, Lieutenant (later General) Ernst Udet was forced to bail out, when his Fokker D-VII was set on fire during a dogfight with French pilots. His parachute did not open until he was 250ft (76m) above the ground. He sprained his ankle on landing. Udet became a notable flying ace during the First World War, scoring sixty-two confirmed victories. He was the second-highest scoring after the legendary Manfred von Richthofen, also known as the 'Red Baron', one of the few German pilots who never wore a parachute. Udet had to bail out again eighteen years later. In 1936, while testing a prototype bomber, he had to abandon it in mid-air. Surprisingly enough, his parachute opened once again 250ft above the ground. As a result of this, Udet again suffered minor injuries on landing.[14]

By July 1918, German and Austro–Hungarian parachute escapes had become routine. On 22 August, Lieutenant Frigyes Hefty, a pilot of the Austro–Hungarian Air Corps, was forced to bail out over the Piave River in northern Italy when his Albatross D.III was hit during a dogfight with Italian Hanriot HD.1 fighters. While descending, Hefty realized that one of the enemy pilots had fired several shots at the canopy of his parachute. Despite that, the Austrian pilot managed to land safely and soon found himself surrounded by friendly (Hungarian) troops.[15]

The lives of many German and Austro–Hungarian airmen were saved by the introduction and use of parachutes during the First World War. The Germans were the first to realize it was enormous waste of personnel to place an airman in danger without a means of saving his life. Later, much later, the Allies reluctantly came to the same decision. The reluctance of Allied commanders to encourage the intensive development and universal use of such life-saving equipment is a very serious indictment indeed.[16] Allied engineers studied the Heinecke parachute and eventually realized that attached-type balloon parachutes should be adopted. In September 1918, a declaration from the Field Headquarters of the Royal Flying Corps gave authorization that 'all single-seaters are to be fitted with parachutes forthwith'. A conference on parachutes, which was held in Paris in early November, was attended by representatives from France, Great Britain, Italy and the United States of America. Participants reported that Great Britain and France had put parachutes in production after extensive tests and experiments and that a few had been already sent to the front. Large orders had been placed for production, but these had been cancelled after the signing of the Armistice.

Manually-Operated Parachutes

The first parachutes were of the automatic type. These static-line parachutes were either inflated prior to the jump or were pulled into the airstream from a container fastened to the balloon or aircraft. This type of parachute, however, soon proved inadequate for safe escape from moving aircraft. In 1908, Leo Stevens devised the first manual parachute. It could now be opened by the jumper with a ripcord – although the free-type parachute was not used on a large scale until 1920. Charles Broadwick (born John Murray), a pioneering American parachutist, had invented the coatpack chute. The Army purchased two sets for testing during the war but did not evaluate them. Shortly after the war, there was an effort to combine the best aspects of the then current parachute designs. The result was the parachute Type-A. It incorporated Charles Broadwick's coatpack, a ripcord that allowed a pilot to manually deploy the parachute instead of depending on a static line connected to the plane, and a small pilot chute that pulled the parachute from its pack.

In early 1919, at McCook Field, north of Dayton in Ohio, Major E.L. Hoffman of the Army Air Service accelerated the testing and examination of all American and foreign parachutes that could be obtained. It was clearly demonstrated that none of the existing parachutes was suitable for the Air Service. By 1919, the Type-A parachute was modified so as to be worn as a seat pack. It was named the Type-S. The pilot sat on the seat pack (parachute) as on a cushion. In 1919, the Type-S parachute gained US Army Air Service's approval after 1,500 'experimental jumps'.[17]

One of the better pack-on-the-back parachutes was submitted by Floyd Smith and it was similar to the Type-A soon developed by the Army Air Service. Another parachute was designed by a young balloonist and parachute jumper, Leslie L. Irvin, who owned a small parachute business in Buffalo, New York. Since it was static-line activated, Irvin's parachute had to be redesigned in order to become manually operated. Working with Irvin, Smith improved his design. On 28 April 1919, the two men demonstrated their parachute with Smith piloting a DeHavilland biplane. Irvin exited, while the plane, cruising at 100mph, was 1,500ft (457m) above the ground. After free-falling 500ft (152m), Irvin pulled on the cord and the parachute spilled out in 1.4 seconds. Upon landing, Irvin broke his ankle when an unexpected gust of wind swung him into the ground. Using Smith's design, Irvin became the first man to jump from an aircraft and manually open a parachute after an extended free fall.[18]

On 19 May, Master Sergeant Ralf W. Bottriell was the first Army man to jump with a manually-operated free-type Type-A parachute.[19] Between January 1918 and January 1919, he performed approximately 200 jumps from aircraft with various attached and free-type parachutes. Bottriell was in charge of the Parachute Section of Kelly Field, south of San Antonio, in Texas. On 19 May 1929, Bottriell broke the world's record for most parachute jumps, performing over 200 of them from powered aircraft.[20] On 11 July 1919, a British pilot, Lieutenant R.A. Caldwell of the Royal Flying Corps, was killed while demonstrating a British-made Guardian Angel parachute at McCook Field. His death, which was witnessed by many spectators, provoked renewed scepticism among pilots and encouraged critics who were still saying that parachutes were for the circus and not for aviators.

In the meantime, all parachutes continued to be snubbed by most US pilots on the grounds that all had been tested under experimental conditions and not in an actual emergency situation. It all changed when a military flyer, a fellow American, ran into trouble on 20 October 1922. That day, 27-year old Lieutenant Harold R. Harris was test-flying a Loening monoplane near Dayton in Ohio. While facing a certain crash, Harris managed to bail out and activate his Smith-designed manually-operated parachute only 500ft (152m) above the ground.[21] The pilot landed in the backyard of a house, suffering only bruises on his legs and hand. His stricken aircraft crashed three blocks away.[22] Harris entered aviation history as the first pilot to make an emergency jump from a powered aircraft and survive after using a manually-operated free-fall parachute. An early brochure of the Irving Air Parachute Company credits another pilot, named William O'Connor, as the first person to be saved by an Irving parachute. The jump was made at McCook Field on 24 August 1920.

In early 1924, after Harris' successful jump, a parachute became a required item for all Army and Navy flyers by order of the War Department.[23] A contract was signed with Irvin's company for the construction of the first 300 Type-A parachutes for the Army at a cost of $550 each.[24] The Air Service Type 'S' was the model on which a number of American and foreign parachutes were based during the next decades. When the Royal Air Force adopted parachutes after the war, they chose British and American designs.

The Air Ministry's first order was for 500 Guardian Angels together with 500 parachutes of other types.[25] Irving Air Chute[26] became the largest parachute manufacturer in the world. By 1939, forty-five foreign countries were using Irving parachutes, including Nazi Germany, since the latter had seized an Irving plant in Romania in 1941. It has been said that during the Second World War Irving parachutes saved over 10,000 lives.

In 1922, Irvin's company instituted the Caterpillar Club, an informal association of aviators, awarding a gold pin to those who successfully bailed out of disabled aircraft using an Irving chute. For his survival Harris was awarded the first membership in the club. Other famous members include James Doolittle and Charles Lindbergh. Lieutenant Colonel (later General) James H. Doolittle organized and led the first air raid on Tokyo and other Japanese cities during the Second World War. World-famous American aviator Charles Lindbergh, the first pilot to cross the Atlantic flying solo, had previously parachuted to safety four times – once as an Army student pilot, again as a test pilot, and twice as a contract pilot for the US Air Mail Service. Lindbergh conducted the first non-stop solo flight between North America and the European mainland in 1927. Three years earlier, while trained as a pilot in the Army, Lindbergh had to bail out, after colliding in mid-air with another trainee.[27] He joined the 110th Observation Squadron of the National Guard in St. Louis as a part-time pilot until October 1925. Three months before returning to civilian life, Lindbergh had been promoted to captain.[28]

In 1924, Lieutenant (later Colonel) John Arthur Macready of the US Army Air Service became the first pilot to bail out of a stricken aircraft at night. On 13 June, Macready was returning to McCook Field from Columbus, when his aircraft, a Fokker T-2, developed engine trouble. As no pilot had tried an emergency landing at night before, Macready decided to bail out, although no one had attempted a night parachute jump until then either. Before reaching the ground, his parachute tangled in a tree and the pilot required assistance to get to the ground. In 1929, the quick-release mechanism was patented in Great Britain and was subsequently manufactured in the United States by the Irving Chute Company. Prior to the introduction of this, jumpers risked serious injury by being dragged along the ground after landing or drowning in the event of a water landing as they struggled to free themselves.[29]

In 1934, two Americans, Stanley Switlik and George Palmer Putman, Amelia Earhart's husband, formed a joint venture and built a 115ft (35m) tall tower on Stanley's farm in Ocean County. It was designed to train airmen in parachute jumping. The first public jump from the tower was made on 2 June 1935 by one of the leading pioneers in aviation. Witnessed by a crowd of reporters and officials from Army and Navy, Earhart described the descent she performed as 'loads of fun'![30] Such towers were later constructed all over the world and are still in use for the training of paratroopers.

Chapter 2

The Four Pioneer Nations

By the end of the First World War the parachute had been introduced in the military of certain countries and plans were under way to mount what was later to become known as 'vertical envelopment'.[1] The Soviet Union led the way in the development of military parachuting and the establishment of the first operational airborne units. Soviet troops also made the first combat jump in military history.

The Soviet Union

In the mid-1920s, a flyer named Leonid G. Minov was the first military man to perform a parachute jump in the Soviet Union. He was later put in charge of the Red Army's first parachute training facility. In 1928, Minov was sent to the United Stated to test parachutes – although a Russian named G. E. Kotelnikov had been designing and testing parachutes in Tsarist Russia as early as 1911. Minov brought back from the United States a number of Smith/Irving parachutes which were copied by the Soviets for military purposes. Although the Air Force Major L. Minov had pioneered the use of the parachute in the Red Army, the real father of the Soviet airborne forces was Marshal Mikhail Tukhachevsky, the commander of the Leningrad military district, who had ordered the formation of the first paratroop units. Tukhachevsky sponsored the role of the emerging airborne forces in his theory of *gluboki boi* (deep battle) that became a characteristic element of Soviet military doctrine. In 1931, Tukhachevsky ordered that all aviators were to be trained to parachute. By 1937, air crews had also been trained as parachutists.[2]

On 2 August 1930, a demonstration drop was carried out in a field at Voronezh, south of Moscow. Forty-six paratroopers jumped from a Tupolev TB-3 transport aircraft. They were officers and other ranks from the 11th Rifle Division who had volunteered for parachute training. Until the end of the year, over 500 jumps were performed by Red Army personnel. In March 1931, a 24-man experimental airborne landing detachment was formed and assigned to the Leningrad military district.[3] Armed with rifles and light machine guns, they began jumping from three aircraft. In 1932, the detachment was upgraded with the 3rd Airborne Brigade (Special Purpose) being established in Leningrad in December.[4] Two more airborne brigades were formed later and assigned to the Kiev and Belarus military districts. For deployment in the Far East three airborne regiments, the 1st, 2nd and 5th, were established. The following year, during the autumn manoeuvres the Soviets dropped a small tank with a large parachute. By the end of 1933, the Red Army numbered a total of twenty-nine parachute and glider battalions. A 300-man machine-gun battalion was added to each airborne brigade in 1934.

On 1 March 1935, the future commander of the German paratroopers, Kurt Student, and a British general, A.P. Wavell, were present at the Red Army spring manoeuvres near Minsk. They witnessed thirty TB-3 transport aircraft dropping two battalions of over 300 paratroopers each. After securing the dropping zone, thirty more planes brought in reinforcements and sixteen artillery pieces. A light tank was also parachuted. In the same exercise, three gliders, carrying eighteen armed soldiers each, landed following an 1,170-mile (1,883km) flight.[5] A few months later, an entire division, including motor vehicles and artillery, was flown from Moscow to Vladivostok, a distance of over 4,000 miles (6,437km), as a demonstration by the Soviets of their air-transport capabilities.

In September 1936, during the autumn manoeuvres, a massive drop was conducted near Minsk. Twelve hundred men, lead by a general, 150 machine guns and eighteen field guns had been delivered by parachute. 'If I had not witnessed the descents', Wavell noted in his report, 'I could not have believed such an operation possible.'[6] However, he also noted that troops were only lightly armed and that it took them about an hour and a half to get organized and ready to fight. By 1938, the Soviets had six airborne brigades, one of which was assigned to the Far East. The 212th Airborne Brigade, fighting as infantry, was among the Red Army forces that defeated invading Japanese troops at the Battle of Khalkhin Gol in eastern Mongolia on 31 August 1939. On 30 November, Soviet paratroopers made the first combat jump in history, when they dropped behind enemy lines during the Soviet invasion of Finland. The first actual use in combat of Red Army paratroopers had come ten years earlier, when a fifteen-strong detachment was dropped to relieve the besieged Tadzhik town of Garm, which was under threat from Basmachi bandits.[7] On 28 June 1940, three Soviet parachute brigades, the 201st, the 204th and the 214th, were dropped from 170 TB-3 transport planes next to the northern Romanian cities of Bolgrad, Kahul and Ismail and captured them without encountering any resistance from Romanian troops.[8] In March and April 1941, five airborne corps (divisions, in fact, by Allied standards) were established on the basis of the existing airborne brigades.[9]

The Soviet Union pioneered the use of parachute troops during the 1930s, but few of the operational drops conducted by the Soviets during the Second World War were successful by Western standards. In September 1941, twenty-three paratroopers were dropped thirty minutes ahead of the Soviet seaborne landing forces in Odessa. They attacked a German communication complex and blocked the route for enemy reinforcements. On 24 October 1942, forty Soviet paratroopers raided the Maykop airfield in the northern Caucasus, destroying twenty-four German aircraft and damaging a further fifty-four. Fourteen of the raiders were killed in the operation.[10] The Soviets conducted two major airborne operations during the Second World War. Both were unsuccessful and incurred heavy losses. In Vyazma, situated between German-held Smolensk and Moscow, the plan was for a drop of 10,000 men to disrupt German forces, while the Red Army would advance from the east. Due to shortages of transport aircraft, however, only 2,081 men had been parachuted by 1 February 1942. There was very little fighter cover for the transport planes, many of which were shot down. As a result of this, the Red Army high command was forced to suspend the drops. For a month, the lightly-armed Soviet paratroopers fought in sub-zero temperatures against a numerically superior enemy, who was reinforced with armoured units. To rescue the remainder of the trapped paratroopers, the Soviet high command mounted a larger and more aggressive offensive towards Vyazma, involving both airborne and ground forces. Between 16 and 24 February, 1,525 paratroopers were dropped in the area of Zelanje. The commander of the 4th Airborne Brigade, Major General Alexei Levaskev, was killed when his transport was shot down by anti-aircraft fire. The operation was a disaster with the majority of the paratroopers being surrounded by vast numbers of German troops including armour. It took them months to fight their way out and link up with friendly forces.

At 18.00 hours on 25 September 1943, two brigades were to be parachuted in support of the Red Army ground forces advancing towards the Dniepr River on their way to Kiev. Because of the fierce anti-aircraft fire, most of the pilots dropped their sticks (planeloads) of paratroopers from higher altitudes than the designated 1,640ft (500m). As a result of this, most of the men became scattered over an area of 15 to 40 miles (24 to 64km) with less than 10 per cent of them landing in the designated dropping zones.[11] Dozens landed in the Dnieper River and many drowned, entangled in their parachutes. By the time the operation was called off, the 3rd Airborne Brigade in its entirety, but without its artillery, and roughly half of the 5th Airborne Brigade, had been landed – a total of over 4,500 men.[12] Many paratroopers landed on top of the moving German 19th Panzer and the 10th Motorized Divisions. Several of those captured were executed by the Germans. Seventy-five per cent of the paratroopers participating in the operation were either killed or wounded. The survivors kept fighting until 13 November, when they linked up with friendly forces. In late November, the survivors of both brigades, a total of 1,000 men, were returned to Moscow. After the disasters at Vyazma and Dniepr, the Soviets avoided any further massive drops, limiting themselves to small-scale tactical drops to aid partisans or disrupt the enemy rear. For many years after the war, the Red Army had the largest airborne force in the world. In 1989, the Soviet airborne troops were more numerous than all the other airborne forces on earth combined. This powerful and formidable force consisted of seven divisions, each having 7,000 blue-beretted men. The force was split, after the dissolution of the Soviet Union in 1991, between Russia, Belarus and Ukraine. A year later, the number of Russia's airborne divisions was reduced to four.

Italy

The Italians were among the first to experiment with parachutes for military purposes. Italy was also the first nation to form a real parachute unit, although the country's paratroopers were not involved in a large-scale airborne operation during the Second World War as long as Benito Mussolini was in power. Qualified paratroopers were also provided by the officers and other ranks of the 10th Regiment Arditi, who carried out small-scale airborne assaults in North Africa. Parachute units could also be found among the country's Carabinieri (Gendarme) forces and in the Italian air force (*Regia Aeronautica*). The initial collective drop from CA 73 troop carriers was performed by military personnel using static-line parachutes on 6 November 1927 at Cinisello Balsamo, near Milan. By the end of the year, a trained company of Italian troops was regarded ready for airborne warfare. Meanwhile, on 27 April, a *Regia Aeronautica* pilot, General Allesandro Guidoni, was killed on landing at Montecelio airfield while testing a new model of parachute.[13] The following year, Italian paratroopers performed a mass display jump in North Africa.

In early 1938, a parachute training facility was established at Castel Benito, near Tripoli in Libya, part of Italy at the time. The same year, in March, a 300-strong paratroop unit, the 1st Battalion of the Air, was formed in Tripoli by the Air Force Marshal Italo Balbo, the Governor-General of Libya.[14] The unit was recruited from the native population and officered by Italians. In Libya Italy's first airborne units were raised and stationed, being the Libyan Parachute Battalion and the 1st National Libyan Parachute Battalion of the Royal Corps of Colonial Troops.[15] When the accident toll rose to fifteen dead and seventy-two seriously injured during parachute training at Castello Benito, the re-organization of the National Libyan Battalion was decided, as well as its formation with Italian volunteers entirely. The two battalions then joined forces to form a regiment. In early 1938, a parachute battalion was established in Italy. On 1 July 1940, the 1st Royal Carabinieri Parachute Battalion was formed and was eventually deployed in North Africa. By the end of the year, the number of the Carabinieri parachute battalions had increased to three. The Italian air force also had formed a parachute unit.

Two parachute regiments were raised by the Army between April and August 1941 to be deployed in North Africa. One of these regiments was parachuted onto the Greek island of Cephalonia in what went down to history as the Italian army's first combat jump. On 30 April 1941, elements of the 6th Paratroop Regiment headed by Major Mario Zaninovich were dropped from Savoi-Marchetti SM82 transport aircraft that had took off from Otranto airfield. In the port area of the island's capital, Argostoli, there was not even a single Greek soldier – only a number of armed Gendarmes, who did not fire a single shot. Although the landing was unopposed, the losses for the invaders were considerable. A number of paratroopers drowned after falling into the sea, while others were injured on landing. On 1 May, seaborne Italian paratroopers landed and secured the nearby islands of Ithaca and Zakynthos (Zante). Meanwhile, the parachuting school had been re-established at Tarquinia, in the Lazio area near Rome. On 1 September 1941, the 185th Parachute Division was raised by the Army in Tarquinia. It was earmarked for the planned Axis assault on Malta. When the invasion was cancelled, the division was deployed in North Africa. At the same time, the 80th Infantry Division La Spezia was trained and equipped similarly to the German air landing (glider-borne) divisions. After the invasion of Malta was cancelled, the division was deployed in Tunisia, where it fought as infantry. In June 1942, the division's name changed to 185th Airborne Folgore (Thunderbolt). In North Africa, the Folgore Division participated in the Battle of El Alamein, near the Egyptian border, in November 1942. Fighting as infantry, they put up stiff resistance to British,

Greek and Free French forces.[16] In the end, Erwin Rommel's Afrika Korps, including the Italian paratroopers, were overrun by the Allies. Of the 5,000-strong Folgore division only 300 officers and other ranks returned to Italy.

On 8 September 1942, the 10th Arditi regiment was re-established to be assigned special purpose missions behind enemy lines.[17] Arditi commandos carried out missions in Egypt, Tunisia and Algeria between 1940 and 1944, as well as in Sicily during the Allied invasion in July 1943. On 17 December 1940, an 11-man Arditi detachment that was dropped by parachute at Gumbert in Egypt destroyed with explosives several captured Italian planes that were parked in an Allied airfield. On 16 February 1943, Arditi commandos parachuted near the Algerian town of Beni Mansur interrupted temporarily the flow of reinforcements and supplies to the Allied troops by blowing up parts of a railway line. They escaped with the exception of a wounded colleague who was captured by British troops.

In the spring of 1943, the 184th Airborne Division Nembo (Italian for 'Nimbus') was raised. It was deployed for operations against Italian resistance fighters near the border with Yugoslavia. The Nembo Division then fought against the Allies in Sicily.[18] The planned raising of a third parachute division (named Ciclone) was called off because of the Badoglio armistice of 8 September 1943. For ideological reasons, as they were either fascists or fanatically anti-communist, many Italian servicemen wanted to carry on fighting on the German side. It was then when a number of their paratroopers joined the German 4th Parachute Division.[19] The Nembo Division had been deployed in Sardinia since June with the 185th Parachute Division being, at the same time, in Calabria in southern Italy. On 9 July 1944, paratroopers of the Nembo Division distinguished themselves in the Battle of Filottrano on 9 July 1944.[20] One hundred and thirty-five of them were killed in the division's attack, alongside II Polish Corps, to capture and secure German strongholds in the area.[21] The victory in Filottrano opened the way to Ancona and its strategic port for the advancing Allied forces.

After the fall of Italy's fascist regime, two Italian parachute units were organized by the Allies and were dropped onto enemy-occupied territory in northern Italy to coordinate the local resistance in their attacks against German troops. Another Italian paratroop unit, named F Squadron, participated in operations of the British XIII Army Corps in north Italy, mostly in a reconnaissance role. On the night of 19/20 April 1945, 226 Italians from F Squadron and the Nembo parachute division were dropped behind German lines in areas south of Po river, near Ferrara and Modena. The drop, made from fourteen Douglas C-47 Skytrain (Dakota) transports of the United States Army Air Force, was not accurate as a number of men landed as far as 25 miles (40km) from their designated dropping zones. Fighting in small groups, the paratroopers carried out their main assignment by inflicting heavy losses on the German troops and capturing intact bridges that could be used for the Allied advance. Elements of F Squadron seized the little town of Ravarino, near Modena, and a nearby village (Stuffione), capturing in total fifty-one Germans and holding out until relieved by Allied ground forces. Sixteen Italian paratroopers who were surrounded in a farm by numerically superior German troops died (all but two) fighting to the last round of ammunition. In the operation, code-named Herring, which lasted seventy-two hours, 481 Germans were killed and a further 1,083 were captured or surrendered. The Italian paratroopers' casualties numbered thirty-one dead and twelve wounded. Operation Herring was the last combat drop in Europe during the Second World War. The Folgore Parachute Brigade is part of the post-war Italian army, made up of four parachute regiments, the 9th Parachute Assault Regiment ('*Arditi Incursori*') and an Alpini regiment whose officers and other ranks are qualified paratroopers.

The United States

On 14 August 2002, US President George W. Bush declared 16 July US National Airborne Day. In his speech Bush stressed that the history of his country's airborne forces began when Brigadier-General William M. Mitchell first conceived the idea of parachuting in combat. It all started in 1918, during the First World War, when Mitchell, an Army colonel at the time, devised a plan to actually drop troops by parachute from giant British Handley-Page bombers onto the French city of Metz on 17 October in an operation code-named 'Panic Party'.[22] The operation had to be cancelled because the war ended three weeks later. A later idea of Mitchell to assign infantrymen to the United States Army Air Force (USAAF) for drops behind enemy lines with cover provided to them by fighter planes was not put into effect.[23] Mitchell was considered by many at the time to have lost touch with reality.[24] Apart from some testing of parachutes for pilots, the US seemed to dismiss military parachuting.[25] In the autumn of 1928, Mitchell, who had risen in the meantime to the rank of general, unofficially launched a parachute training programme, during which six armed soldiers jumped from a Martin bomber over Kelly Field in Texas.[26] The paratroopers, after landing safely, had their weapons operational in less than three minutes.[27] The only country to pay attention to Mitchell's concept, however, was the Soviet Union. In 1930, the year Mitchell's book *Skyways* was published, the Red Army deployed a small section of paratroopers in manoeuvres for the first time in history.[28]

The matter did not go any further until the outbreak of the Second World War, when the concept of airborne warfare was sponsored by Franklin D. Roosevelt. In May 1940, the President had been reading about Hitler's airborne operations and wanted to know more about them. Major William Lee was sent to the White House to brief Roosevelt as no one at the War Department was more knowledgeable than him at the time about German airborne forces. Having observed Hitler's troops in the late 1930s during a formal tour of Europe, Lee believed in them as a model from the US Army. Roosevelt was so impressed that he ordered airborne planning and training to begin immediately. Lee was given the airborne project. He was authorized to form a test paratroop platoon at Fort Benning in Georgia and 'pioneer methods of combat jumping'.[29] In June, Lee called for volunteers from the 29th Infantry Division to form a paratroop test platoon. Forty-eight out of the 200 volunteers were accepted.[30] Major General W. Lee is often referred to as 'the Father of the US Airborne'.[31] Lee was the first commander of the Army's jump school that was established at Fort Benning in 1941. To honour their 'father', the American paratroopers yelled out 'Bill Lee!' as they made combat jumps in Europe and the Pacific during the Second World War.[32] Lee also wrote US Army's airborne doctrine.

Lieutenant William T. Ryder became the test platoon's leader. Ryder helped pioneer Army airborne training, equipment and tactics alongside Lee and other officers like James Gavin, William Yardborough, Art Gohram and Bud Miley. He is considered the first American paratrooper. He had exited the aircraft, a Douglas C-33, ahead of a ten-man 'stick' (a planeload of parachutists), on 16 August 1940, when the test platoon performed their first jump. A different date for the first jump is listed elsewhere.[33] The first enlisted man to jump was Private William N. King.[34] The platoon's first mass drop was conducted on 20 August. The test platoon became the nucleus of the 501st Parachute Infantry Regiment (PIR). On 25 March 1942, the 82nd Airborne Division (82nd Airborne) was activated. The 101st Airborne Division (101st Airborne), formed from a nucleus from the 82nd, followed on 15 August 1942. The 82nd Airborne's nickname is the 'All Americans' (AA). It derives from the fact that the unit's forerunner, the 81st Infantry Division, when it was formed in 1917, had conscripts from all forty-eight (at that time) states.[35] The 101st Airborne also has a famous nickname – 'Screaming Eagles'. In the spring of 1943, two more divisions were activated, the 11th Airborne and the 17th Airborne. A fifth, the 13th Airborne, was raised in the summer of 1944, but never saw active service as a division.

There were also thirteen independent units, starting with 503rd PIR, which was formed in February 1942. Nine PIRs, the 504th, 501st, 502nd, 505th, 506th, 507th, 508th, 509th and 513th, were raised (in this order) until the end of 1942 and three more, the 511th, 517th and 515th, came into being between January and May 1943. Three independent battalions were raised in 1942. These were the 550th Airborne Infantry Battalion (in July), the 551st Parachute Infantry Battalion (in November) and the 555th Parachute Infantry Battalion (in December). The all-black 555th Parachute Infantry Battalion remained in the United States throughout the war. The US Army's airborne forces also included four Glider Infantry Regiments (GIRs). These units, which fought in Europe and in the Pacific during the Second World War, were the 327th GIR (formed in March 1942), the 325th GIR (5 August 1942), the 401st GIR (16 August 1942) and the 194th GIR (April 1943). Rivalry between US Army's parachute and glider elements developed during the Second World War, because of the extra pay provided for paratroopers for participating in hazardous missions. The glider-borne officers and other ranks were not authorized extra pay, although their missions were just as dangerous. In 1941 the US Marines Corps acquired qualified paratroopers. A regiment was made up of Para-marines, as they were called. However, they were destined not to see combat as airborne troops during the Second World War. In the last stage of the war, the Para-marines were employed in a traditional role, participating in amphibious landings in the Pacific.

On 8 November 1942, the 2nd Battalion, 509th PIR, conducted America's first combat jump, leaping from Dakota transports near Oran in Algeria during the Allied invasion of North Africa. The men were led in the historical jump by their regimental commander, Lieutenant Colonel Edson D. Raff. During the Second World War,

American paratroopers fought with distinction as airborne, amphibious and land troops in North Africa, in Europe and in the Pacific theatre.

In the post-war period, American airborne units saw action in Korea, Vietnam, Grenada, Panama and Iraq. The officers and other ranks of the Army's Special Forces (Green Berets) and the Navy's Sea Air Land (SEAL) unit, which were formed in 1952 and 1962 respectively, are also qualified parachutists. Since 1958, the 82nd and the 101st Airborne Divisions have been part of the re-activated XVIII Airborne Corps designed for rapid deployment anywhere in the world. In January 1969, the 82nd Airborne Division was equipped with its first (of a total of fifty-one) M551 Sheridan light tanks. Ten of these armoured reconnaissance/airborne assault vehicles were dropped by air for the first time in combat during the US invasion of Panama in 1989.[36] The 82nd has always a battle-ready task force ready to jump anywhere in the world in only 18 hours.[37] Since October 1974, the 101st Airborne Brigade has been trained for air assault, its troops being landed behind enemy lines by helicopter. Also part of the airborne forces are the 75th Ranger Regiment, the Alaska-based 173rd Brigade Combat Team and the special operations capability units of the Army, the Marine Corps and the Air Force. The USAF's Combat Control Team (CCT) was raised in 1953 and its 360 scarlet-bereted men provide expert airfield seizure, airstrike control and communications capabilities. The US Army's Delta Force, which was formed in 1977, is normally assigned anti-terrorist missions worldwide.

France

On 6 June 1940, the British Prime Minister, Winston Churchill, wrote a message for the attention of the War Office. It reads: 'We ought to have a Corps of at least 5,000 paratroops including a proportion of Australians, New Zealanders and Canadians together with some trustworthy people from Norway and France . . .'[38] Such 'trustworthy people' were, also, at the time, elements of France's paratroop units, who had taken refuge in England following their country's occupation by the Germans. The first uniformed man to perform a parachute jump in France was a soldier named Constant 'Marin' Dyclos. The drop, carried on 17 November 1935, was not related to any project or activity of his country's armed forces. It was the first of the twenty-three tests or exhibition parachute jumps unofficially performed by this pioneer of French military parachuting. In France, the military dabbled briefly with the airborne concept in 1937, when two Air Force companies became the country's first parachute units. Two years earlier, an Air Force officer, mentioned as 'Captain Geille', had been trained in the Soviet Union as airborne instructor, but the airborne experiment had been dismissed by the French General Staff as 'a circus act'.[39] At the opening phase of the Second World War, the two paratroop companies, called *Groupes d' Infanterie de l'Air* (GIA), were deployed in eastern France in a patrolling role. In June 1940, when the French army was defeated, the remnants of the two companies were withdrawn either to England or to the French colonies in North Africa. In Algiers, these men formed the nucleus for the 1st *Régiment De Chasseurs Parachutistes* (RCP) and the *Battalion de Shoc* (Shock Battalion) that was established in 1943.

In the meantime, in 1941, a Free French (FF) officer in England and Egypt, Captain (Commandant) Georges R.P. Bergé, organized the training of French agents who were sent to France on espionage or sabotage assignments. He also led the first French mission that was parachuted to their German-occupied country. On 15 March 1941, five Frenchmen, headed by Bergé, made a blind drop at midnight, landing near the town of Vannes in north-western France. Of the agents involved in the operation, further two went missing, one was left behind and the remaining two, including Bergé, returned to England on board a Royal Navy submarine, HMS *Tigris*.

Free French volunteers were associated with the British Special Air Service (SAS) in late 1941, when Bergé is mentioned by David Stirling, the SAS's founder and first commander, as one of the co-founders of the unit. In March 1942, the FF contingent, having grown in numbers, was integrated into SAS as the unit's 3rd Squadron. Though these Frenchmen were part of the SAS and wore the same uniform and insignia, in fact they formed a separate section within the brigade because of language difficulties. These men were, nevertheless, engaged in clandestine operations in occupied France, including raids on Axis installations on the Greek island of Crete, as well as in Syria, Libya and Tunisia.

In June 1942, an SAS party parachuted into the German-occupied island of Crete. It was made up of four Frenchmen, one Englishman, Captain George Jellicoe of the Special Boat Squadron (SBS), and a Greek officer, identified as Lieutenant Costis. The SAS party attacked the German airfield at Heraklion in the midnight of 13/14 June and destroyed twenty-one aircraft. German patrols, possibly acting on intelligence provided by an informer, surprised the French.[40] One of them was killed during the exchange of fire and a further three were captured. Jellicoe and Costis managed to escape.[41] Later, a second French squadron, the 4th, was formed. In mid-March 1943, the two squadrons were handed over to the FF Army and became part of the newly-formed and North African-based 1st RCP. The two units re-joined the SAS Brigade prior to the Allied landings in Normandy in June 1944.

The first Allied soldier to land in France was FF SAS Captain Pierre Marienne, who landed near Vanne in Southern Brittany on 5 June 1944, on the eve of the Normandy landings, at the head of a seventeen-man parachute force. One of them, the Brittany-born SAS Corporal Émile Buétard, killed by enemy fire near Plumelec, was the first Allied casualty of the Normandy invasion. During D-Day Normandy, elements of the SAS's FF squadrons created diversions in Brittany in north-west France. On 6 June, 160 men of 4 SAS landed by parachute in the Vannes area of Brittany and began interrupting the enemy forces in cooperation with the local Resistance and a company of gendarmes. Between 6 and 9 June, 116 men of 4 SAS were parachuted into northern Brittany to prevent the movement of German forces from western Brittany to Normandy. On 16 July, sixty-five men of 3 SAS were parachuted in the Nantes/Saumur area of western France. Their assignment was to disrupt rail communications, gather intelligence and lead the local Resistance in attacks against German troops. On 5 August, eighty-nine men of 3 SAS were dropped around Finnisterre in Brittany. They hindered enemy movement towards Brest and prevented the destruction of the viaducts at Morlaix and Plougastel by the Germans. On 15 August, fifty-seven men of

3 SAS were dropped between the Rhône and Loire Rivers to disrupt enemy movements. They were the first Allied soldiers into Lyons, where they became involved in fierce house-to-house fighting.[42] On 29 August, 314 men of 4 SAS were parachuted into the area of Burges in central France. They inflicted damage on the retreating enemy and forced some 2,500 Germans to surrender.[43] FF units were assigned missions to other parts of the country, as well as in Holland and Belgium. The FF shock battalion was dropped near Le Muy in southern France on 15 August 1944, acting as a pathfinder during the Allied air and sea landings in the area. Between 24 December and 25 January 1945, 186 men of 4 SAS operated around St. Hubert and Houffalize in the Belgian Ardennes. Mounted on thirty-one jeeps, the French SAS fought to support the left flank of the US VIII Corps.[44]

After the war, the SAS's French paratroopers were integrated into France's Colonial Marine Force that was stationed in Algiers. Paratroop battalions of the Colonial Marine Force and the French Foreign Legion fought against the Viêt Minh communist rebels in Indochina from 1946 to 1954. The 2nd Marine Airborne Regiment jumped with the British 3rd Battalion, Parachute Regiment, in Egypt during the Suez Crisis in 1956. The same year, France's two parachute divisions, the 10th and the 25th, were employed as a strike force during the Algerian conflict. In 1962, the two divisions were disbanded and their regiments merged into the *Division Légère d'Intervention* (Light Intervention Division). Nine years later, this division became the 11e *Division Parachutiste*. French paratroopers were deployed later on in Tunisia, Chad and Congo (Zaire at the time) to rescue French nationals or safeguard France's interests. In 1999, the 11th Parachute Division was reduced in size to brigade. Attached to the 11th Parachute Brigade are two Army parachute regiments (1st Parachute Chasseur and 1st Parachute Hussar), two Marine Infantry Parachute Regiments (3rd and 8th) and the French Foreign Legion's 2nd Foreign Parachute Regiment (2e REP) To the 11th Parachute Brigade belong, also, an engineer (17th) and an artillery (35th) parachute regiments. Qualified paratroopers are, on the other hand, the Fusilier Commandos of the Air (F C de l'Air), a French Air Force equivalent to the British RAF Regiment. In the twenty-first century French airborne units have merged with marine commando, alpine and Special Forces units to create the *Commandements des Operations Spéciales*, an equivalent of the US SOCOM (Special Operations Command).

Chapter 3

The German Paratroopers

As early as 1921, General Hans von Seeckt, Commander-in-Chief of the German Army (Reichswehr) from 1920 until 1926, wrote how the use of relatively small but highly skilled mobile armies in co-operation with aircraft would matter most in future warfare.[1] How completely justified Seeckt was in his ideas is evident from the successes which awaited the German war machine from 1939 to 1942. The *Fallschirmjäger*, the paratrooper branch of the Luftwaffe, the German air force before and during the Second World War, proved a principal component of this formidable machine. They went down in history as the first paratroopers to be committed in large-scale airborne assaults. Due to the Versailles Treaty's military restrictions on Germany, paratroopers were organized and trained initially as part of a Prussian police unit. In April 1935, a parachute battalion was formed from volunteers in the *Landespolizeigruppe* (State Police Regiment) 'General Göring'. Six months later, when the regiment was transferred to the Luftwaffe, the parachute battalion became the cadre for the country's future airborne forces.[2] In 1936, the German Army started experimenting with airborne warfare after establishing a paratroop company. In March 1938, the Army paratroop company was enlarged to the size of a battalion with Major Richard Heidrich assuming command. However, they were transferred to the Luftwaffe when it was decided that the air force should have control of all parachute troops.

Hermann Göring, the Luftwaffe's commander, was a strong advocate of the forming of paratroop forces in Germany.[3] Also present at the Red Army manoeuvres in the summer of 1935, during which a massive parachute drop was conducted, was another German officer, Colonel Kurt Student, who was thus also introduced to the concept of airborne operations. In July 1938, Student was appointed commander of the Luftwaffe's paratroop units. One of the first orders he received from Göring was to establish an airborne division by 17 September. The 7. *Fliegerdivision* (7th Air Division) was created to seize objectives using parachute and glider-borne troops. An Army unit, the 22nd Infantry Division, was trained to carry out air-landing missions as an integral part of Germany's first airborne formation. In January 1939, the Army's paratroop battalion was transferred to the Luftwaffe's 7th Air Division. Three months later, on 20 April, the German paratroop forces appeared for the first time in Hitler's birthday parade. They marched in Berlin in review past Hitler under the command of Colonel (later General) Bruno Bräuer.[4] The first airborne school was established at Stendal, a town in the Altmark region of Saxony.[5] Twenty-four officers and 800 other ranks volunteered for parachute training. Many of them were already members of the Hitler Youth or the Nazi Labour organization. Their average age was only 18. Constant training and indoctrination quickly fostered an esprit de corps that instilled fierce loyalty, high morale and an aggressive self-confidence in the men, deemed the 'parachutists' spirit'.[6]

Student pushed ahead with his dream of a parachute force whose military standards and morale far exceeded those of ordinary fighting men. Some 450 three-engined Junkers Ju 52/3M transport aircraft were provided for parachute drops. Each aircraft could carry eighteen fully-equipped paratroopers. Nine soldiers could be transported to the landing zone with each of the DFS 230 gliders provided to Germany's airborne forces. Three different parachutes were developed for the *Fallschirmjäger*, the RZ1, the RZ16 and the RZ20. The canopy was round with a diameter of 29ft (8.5m). It was connected to a 23ft (7m) static line that was hooked on a cable inside the aircraft. After 1943, the requirements for the award of the paratrooper's insignia after the completion of basic training included at least one jump at night. Regular training in night jumping begun in 1942. The jumping altitude was normally just over 330ft (100m). Tests had been carried out at lower altitudes, but the results had been discouraging as jumping injuries rose to an average of 20 per cent.[7] German paratroopers were only able to jump with a surface wind of less than 14mph. The relatively heavy losses from jump casualties during combat missions on the island of Leros in the autumn of 1943 and in the Ardennes in December 1944 have been attributed entirely to the high surface wind. On several occasions, German paratroopers were scattered widely after jumping, either because of the wind or owing to pilot/jumpmaster's miscalculation. In Maleme, during the invasion of Crete, entire companies were dropped into the sea. Of the personnel of a parachute unit assembling after a jump, more than 10 per cent were injured in jumping.[8]

The first operation of Germany's parachute and air landing troops had been planned to be an airborne assault on the Sudetenland in September 1938. Although this part of Czechoslovakia was given to Hitler by Great Britain and France without a shot being fired, the triumphant landing of 250 Junkers Ju 52s, packed with paratroopers, was ordered as an additional show of strength. The parachutists who later made combat jumps were armed only with 9mm automatic pistols, knives and hand grenades. The remaining weapons and ammunition were parachuted in canisters fitted with special smoke markers for quick recovery and distribution. Since heavy casualties were sustained in Crete because the paratroopers could not reach their weapon containers or because they had to leave cover in order to unpack them, after 1942 regular training was given in jumping with the weapons attached to the soldier.[9]

At the beginning of the war the 7th Air Division consisted of three parachute regiments – each with three battalions and other combat and support units. The Sturm Regiment consisted of three battalions and was trained both for parachute and air-landing operations. In April 1940, the formation took part in the invasion of Denmark and Norway, successfully seizing several airfields. The 7th Air Division was brought up to full strength in 1941. It was then renamed the 1st Parachute Division (1. *Fallschirmjäger* division) and existed as a fighting formation until the German surrender in Italy on 2 May 1945, one week before the end of the Second World War in Europe. The 2nd

Parachute Division was raised in early 1943, but by then only 50 per cent of the men in the 1st Parachute Division and 30 per cent of the men in the 2nd Parachute Division were qualified paratroopers. In May, the division became part of the XI Air Corps along with the 1st Parachute Division. It fought in the Ukraine in late 1943 and in France a year later. The 3rd and 4th Parachute Divisions were formed in late 1943, the 4th being reinforced with Italian paratroopers from the 184th Airborne Division Nembo. The 3rd, raised in October 1943, fought during the Normandy campaign. The 4th, formed in November 1943, saw combat exclusively on the Italian front. The 5th, 6th and 7th Parachute Divisions were formed in France in February, June and August 1944, and fought on the Eastern Front as regular infantry. The 8th, 9th and 10th Parachute Divisions were paratroops in name only, as they were hurriedly formed in 1945 from a disparate collection of Luftwaffe personnel. Poorly trained and mostly ill-prepared for combat, they fought on the rapidly collapsing Eastern Front as well as within Germany. The 8th Parachute Division fought in the Netherlands and the 9th in the Battle of the Seelow Heights and the Battle of Berlin.

The Germans only carried out airborne operations on a large scale twice during the Second World War: once in May 1940 in Holland, and again in May 1941 in Crete. These two operations constituted the first large-scale airborne assaults in the history of warfare. During the assault on Crete, it was impossible for the airborne troops to achieve victory by themselves. Since it had not been possible to transport the 22nd Infantry Division to Greece from Romania in time, another infantry formation, the 5th Mountain Division, being already in Greece, had to be employed. On the other hand, in other operations, including the capture of the Eben Emael fort in Belgium on 11 May 1940, the airborne forces accomplished their objectives without assistance from other units. The common characteristic of all these earlier operations is that they were limited to capture the objectives and holding them until the ground forces arrive.[10]

Early Operations

During the German invasion of Poland in 1939, the *Fallschirmjäger* were sent to occupy several airfields between Vistula and Bug rivers.[11] During the invasion of Denmark, on 9 April 1940, German paratroopers made landings and captured two airfields at Aalborg north of Aarhus. It was the first airborne assault, albeit unopposed, in history.[12] That same month, airborne forces took part in the invasion of Norway. On 8 April, airborne troops landed at Oslo and Kristiansand airports and at Sola airfield near Stavanger, the capture of which was the first opposed attack the *Fallschirmjäger* were involved in, and indeed the first of its kind ever.[13] However, in Norway the German paratroopers also suffered their first defeat, when a 185-strong unit was destroyed by the Norwegian Army after a five-day battle. They had been dropped onto the village and vital railway junction of Dombås on 14 April from fifteen Junkers Ju 52 transports.[14] Of the aircraft involved in the drop, seven were shot down by enemy fire and another one made an emergency landing in Sweden, where it sank through a frozen lake. Due to poor weather conditions, the paratroopers were scattered over a large area stretching from 12 miles (20km) to the west to 11 miles (18km) to the north-east. The men took heavy fire while descending to the ground, as a battalion of the Norwegian army was deployed in the area. Fifteen paratroopers were killed during the drop and thirty-four were wounded or injured on landing. The commander of the paratroopers, Lieutenant Herbert Schmidt, managed to assemble about sixty-three of his men. After failing to fight their way through towards Dombås, the *Fallschirmjäger*, having their commander wounded in a firefight with Norwegian troops, fulfilled part of their mission by blowing up the railway line connecting Oslo with Trondheim in four places. They were eventually surrounded by better-armed troops in a farm near Lindse in southern Norway. On 19 April, the paratroopers surrendered. They had lost twenty dead and as many wounded. The *Fallschirmjäger* were sent by the Norwegians to a prisoner of war camp at Lom in southern Norway, but they were freed in early May by elements of the Luftwaffe's General Hermann Göring Regiment. Many of them volunteered for a combat jump conducted on 16 May onto the isolated Narvik front in north Norway, where they fought alongside the 3rd Mountain Division.

On 10 May 1940, German airborne forces mounted a spectacular raid on the most powerful fortification in the world at that time, Eben Emael, the single most important anchor in the Belgian defence line. The fortress was guarded by 1,200 Belgian troops and its strategic position was paramount as its strong multiple-gun emplacements dominated three important bridges, over the Albert Canal, leading to the Belgian heartland. The assault on Eben Emael was part of a larger airborne operation involving parachute and glider-borne units.[15] Besides the fort, airborne units were also tasked with capturing and holding three vital bridges in the region and three airfields in the general area. The attack was made by eleven gliders, nine of which landed on the top of the mighty fortress. Using grenades, demolition charges and flamethrowers, the raiders, members of the 7th Air Division's 85-strong *Sturmgruppe Granit* (Assault Group Granite), disabled the garrison and outer defences such as artillery casemates and pillboxes. Despite being at a numerical and firepower disadvantage, the airborne assault group had captured the fortress by the following morning, when the main German force made contact. Six Germans were killed and twenty were wounded. While Eben Emael was under attack, forty-three DFS.230 gliders with eleven officers and 427 men on board landed to capture three river crossings on the Albert Canal and the fortress. By midnight, two of the bridges were captured intact with the third, at Kanne, being blown up by its guards. The assignment of the German airborne force included the protection of the bridges against Belgian counter-attacks until they were relieved by elements of the 18th Army. Meanwhile, three airfields, at Valkenburg, Waalhaven and Ypenburg, had been captured and held by parachute units as well. The successful employment of the airborne forces on 10 May 1940 in Belgium enabled the Panzer divisions to sweep across the Low Countries and made the eventual conquest of France relatively easy.

Two thousand troops of the 7th Air Division and 12,000 men of the air-transported 22nd Mountain Division were committed to the German invasion of Holland.[16] A major airborne operation was mounted to capture the Moordijk bridges and then Rotterdam and the Dutch capital of The Hague, including the nearby airfields. Nevertheless, the surrender of Rotterdam was the result of the bold actions of paratroop units and the air attack against the city's defended positions.[17] Four battalions, reinforced by two air-transported regiments, captured three Dutch airfields plus several bridges over rivers that lay across the Germans' approach to The Hague and to Rotterdam. In each case, the airborne units held their positions until the main assault forces arrived overland. Another parachute battalion, supported by two glider-borne regiments, landed near The Hague with the mission of decapitating the Dutch government and military high command. This particular force failed to achieve its goals, but did cause considerable disruption to the defenders. The 22nd Mountain Division was forced to land many of its aircraft on exposed motorways, because the 7th Air Division failed to secure designated airfields and several transport planes were hit by Dutch infantry and artillery fire.[18]

Twelve Heinkel He 59 seaplanes, packed with two platoons of airborne troops, landed in the heart of Rotterdam. They unloaded assault teams that captured the Willemsburg, a bridge over the Nieuwe Maas, and formed a bridgehead. At the same time, the military airfield of Waalhaven, positioned south of the city, on the island of Ijsselmonde, was also attacked by German airborne forces. The Dutch defenders were eventually overwhelmed. The *Fallschirmjäger* then occupied the vital bridge on the island of Dordrecht, where the city garrison held out, the paratroopers suffering heavy casualties.[19] The long Moerdijk bridges over the Holland Diep estuary were captured with a bridgehead being established on the southern side. On 14 May, Göring worried about the fate of his surrounded airborne troops, but all of a sudden, the following day, after a hellish bombing by the Luftwaffe, the Dutch surrendered.

During the Greek campaign, in April 1941, the *Fallschirmjäger* performed their last strategic jump of the war.[20] On 26 April 1941, the Germans mounted a small-scale airborne assault on the Isthmus near Corinth, as they wanted to protect the Italian-Romanian oil link by holding the canal.[21] The *Fallschirmjäger* were to capture the bridge that crossed the canal, so German forces could pursue Allied troops further south in the Greek mainland.[22] One group of paratroopers was accidentally dropped into the sea where they all drowned. Demolition charges were also accidentally detonated due to carelessness, leading to the bridge being damaged and heavy casualties. The German paratroopers suffered 63 killed and 174 injured, although the defenders' resistance was limited.[23] The actual tactical success of the mission was limited to the capture of the Isthmus. Makeshift repairs were made to the bridge, making it useable again by the end of the day.

The Battle of Crete

The last major parachute assault came in mid-1941. It was also to be the first ever employment of airborne forces on such a scale. With Greece and Yugoslavia militarily eliminated, the Germans had to attack one last objective: Crete, the southernmost Greek island in the Aegean. The operation, code-named *Merkur* (Mercury), was ordered, because Hitler wanted to secure the Romanian oil fields from the threat of air raids.[24] Allied planes based on the island could also hit targets in North Africa.

Hitler viewed Crete as a sizeable base from which Luftwaffe could dominate the Balkans, the eastern Mediterranean, North Africa and the Suez Canal. In view of the forthcoming invasion of the Soviet Union, the Germans' southern flank could also be protected.[25] On the other hand, possession of Crete by the Allies would have given them an ideal base to supply arms to resistance forces throughout Axis-occupied mainland Greece.[26] Due to the strength of the Luftwaffe and Germany's weakness when compared to the Royal Navy, airborne assault emerged as the most appropriate means to conquer Crete. This was a risky operation as airborne forces were without heavy weapons, while the island was controlled by Allied and Greek troops, most of whom were combat-tested, as they had fought against German forces on the Greek mainland before being evacuated.

The Germans were expecting to confront no more than 5,000 second-rate and poorly-armed troops to defend Crete, but in fact General Bernard C. Freyberg, the commander of the Allied forces on Crete, deployed about 28,000 British, Australian and New Zealand troops plus 14,000 ill-equipped Greeks and the island's Gendarmerie forces. Many of Freyberg's troops had fled from the Greek mainland without their heavy equipment, but their morale remained high.[27] The German paratroopers jumped into a hornet's nest of resistance in Crete.[28]

The Germans planned to seize Crete by a combined air and sea attack spearheaded by General Alexander Löhr's 7th Airborne Division. This was a risky operation as airborne forces were unable to bring heavy weapons with them, while the British naval presence thwarted the planned maritime support for the invasion.[29] In total, 716 aircraft, including 480 bombers and 72 gliders, were ready for the operation. The airborne forces would be parachuted or land by glider on 20 May 1941 and the 5th Mounted Division was to be air-transported the following day.[30] The key points of the islands were the airfields of Maleme, Rethymno and Heraklion, as well as the port of Souda Bay, near Maleme. The principal objective was to capture three airfields for the ensuing arrival of the air-transported reinforcements. Shortages of transport aircraft forced the Germans to plan a two-wave attack. The morning assault would strike Maleme airfield, on Crete's western side; transport planes would return in the afternoon with a second wave of parachute and glider-borne troops to attack Rethymno and Heraklion, situated in the central part of the island. The airfield and the town of Rethymno were the objectives for the 3rd Parachute Regiment. The capture of Heraklion, Crete's largest airfield, and the nearby town were assigned to the 1st Parachute Regiment. The airborne assault on Crete was preceded by 280 bombers, 150 dive-bombers and 180 fighters.[31] On their way to the island, German seaborne forces were severely mauled by the Royal Navy – at the cost of two cruisers and three destroyers sunk, and other units, including the battleship HMS *Warspite*, severely damaged. Almost half of the German amphibious forces were lost and the rest were driven back. Without adequate air defences – Crete being too far from support from Britain's air bases in North Africa, while covered from German airfields in occupied mainland Greece – the island could not be held against a massive attack by an airborne army.[32]

On the morning of 20 May, the first wave of *Fallschirmjäger*, belonging to the 2nd Parachute Regiment, were dropped on and around Maleme. They were tasked with capturing the airfield and the nearby village. They also had to seize the port of Canea and secure a vital road junction. Casualties were heavy among the first wave of 3,000 Germans who landed by parachute or glider, but many more continued to pour in. Generalmajor Eugene Meindl was seriously wounded shortly after landing, leaving his men of the Maleme task force without their commander.[33] By the end of the day, German forces around Maleme, Rethymno and Heraklion had failed to secured their objectives. The 42,000 Allied defenders, in overwhelming numbers, did not press their initial advantage. Throughout the crucial first phase of the battle, the defenders focused on the seaborne threat rather than the actual airborne assault. Consequently, the bulk of Freyberg's forces defended the beaches with most of the anti-aircraft guns covering the Souda Bay–Canea sector. Only one infantry battalion, the 22nd, held the crucial Maleme airfield, as most of the 5th New Zealand (NZ) Brigade had been deployed to the coastal area. The Germans threw all their resources into an attack on Maleme, while Freyberg's attention remained the coastal defence of Souda, where the Allies reserves were stationed. Despite heavy losses, the invaders managed to secure tenuous footholds west of the airfield and in a valley south-east of Canea. The turning point came at Maleme, when during the night of 20/21 May the 22nd NZ Battalion withdrew from the hill overlooking the airstrip.[34] The battalion's withdrawal enabled the Germans to capture the airfield. With the New Zealanders off the heights, reinforcements could fly in. The landing of planes transporting the 5th Mountain Division began late on 21 May, although the airstrip was still under Allied artillery fire. From the seized airfield, the Germans were also able to support a new amphibious attack on Crete. By then, 30,000 German troops had landed the island.[35] After seven days of bitter fighting, the Allied forces were defeated. The German emerged victorious, but at a terrible cost: 4,054 dead and 2,800 wounded, including both airborne forces and aircrew. A casualty figure of 5,670 is given for the Germans by Mark Mazower.[36] Of 8,674 paratroopers deployed, 3,674 were killed or wounded.[37] This is a casualty rate of 44.3 per cent. In percentage terms, the losses in Crete greatly exceeded those sustained by the German airborne forces in their previous operations in the Second World War. The Luftwaffe also lost 350 aircraft – half of which were Junkers Ju 52 transports.[38] According to another source, twenty-two German aircraft were shot down in Crete and a further 150 damaged.[39]

Field Marshal Albert Kesserling later commented on the near-suicidal use of Germany's airborne forces in Crete.[40] Lightly-armed troops that were previously employed to seize bridges, strongpoints and road junctions were assigned to capture an entire heavily-defended island. The airborne forces should have landed in a single area, away from the occupied objectives with effective defensive fire, and then capture the decisive points (the airfields and seaport) in conventional infantry attacks. Surprisingly, the Germans not only avoided annihilation in Crete, but they captured the island. Although outnumbered five to one, the invaders inflicted an even higher – 47.3 per cent – casualty rate on the defenders. More than 1,700 Allied soldiers lost their lives in the battle.[41] The total figure of dead, wounded or captured is 13,000. Over 2,000 British were killed or wounded in the area of Crete during naval operations related to the German invasion. Nearly 12,000 Allies had to surrender to the Germans and another

800 were either killed or wounded at sea during the evacuation from the island, and in all 16,500 Allied troops were evacuated, mostly to Egypt. Crete represented a severe tactical blow to the Allies.[42] At the same time, the first large-scale airborne operation in history had been a success and the whole world took notice. In his 1941 report on Crete, the US Military Attaché in Egypt, Major Bonner Fellers, wrote that for the first time in history airborne troops, supplied and supported by air, had landed in the face of the enemy and defeated him.[43] This German victory was to give the final push to increase both British and American airborne capabilities.[44]

The conquest of Crete, the largest and most spectacular German airborne assault of the Second World War, was also the turning point for the Germans: the loss of 4,000 men killed, most of them paratroopers, dampened Hitler's enthusiasm for such operations. In ten days, nearly half of Germany's airborne troops had been killed or wounded in Crete. Since everything Hitler possessed in the way of airborne forces had been committed in the attack of Crete, too few qualified troops remained to carry out large-scale operations during the Russian campaign. Air transportation was also insufficient for such operations in the future. Furthermore, Hitler had concluded that airborne operations could lead to success, only when they came as a complete surprise.[45] As surprise attacks of this nature now seemed impossible after Crete, he reached the conclusion that the days of successful airborne operations were over.[46] Hitler wrongly ascribed the disaster to the loss of the element of surprise and banned further parachute operations.[47] Although the *Fallschirmjäger* remained a potent and professional force, the ban of their employment in accordance with their special skills lasted until 1943, when it was clear the Allies considered airborne operations as a viable form of warfare. Hitler also believed that the enemy would not engage in large-scale preparations for airborne operations.[48] This seemed to be the case, as the US Army, at the time of the invasion of Crete, had only a single parachute infantry battalion.[49] But two years later, on the eve of the Allied invasion of Sicily, the US airborne forces had grown to four divisions with a fifth activated a month later. When Hitler was proved wrong on this matter, the Wehrmacht itself was no longer in a position to mount such operations. The main essential, air superiority, was lacking for the Germans in the last year and a half of the war. Airborne units were available, but they were constantly committed in ground operations. The lack of transport planes had negative effects not only in their training but most importantly in the planning and carrying-out of large-scale airborne operations.[50]

Later Operations

By late 1941, the main airborne force was sent into action as infantry in the Soviet Union. These elite troops were withdrawn to the Mediterranean area in early 1942 for a planned airborne assault on Malta, which was never carried out. A parachute brigade was then formed and sent to North Africa to support the Afrika Korps' advance into Egypt. When the Allies landed in North Africa in November 1942, every available *Fallschirmjäger* unit was flown into either Tunis or Bizerta to confront the Anglo-American forces as infantry. By the time of the Normandy landings, the newly-created

Fallschirmkorps (Parachute Corps) I and II were deployed close to the 'Atlantic Wall'. In July 1943, in Sicily, south of Catania, British paratroopers jumped into an area where *Fallschirmjäger*, brought in as reinforcements, had jumped a short while before. One account mentions a complete victory by the British troops with heavy casualties among the German paratroopers, while another speaks of the annihilation of the British paratroopers.[51] The German paratroopers who fought as infantry in Russia, North Africa, Sicily, and Italy – especially at Monte Cassino in 1943 – and later in France, Belgium and Holland proved formidable opponents. When Italy switched to the Allied camp in September 1943, the German 2nd Parachute Division was deployed in Rome to participate in the capture of Italian troops. A battalion was dropped on the island of Elba, which was seized without a shot being fired. Another battalion landed on the Italian Army headquarters at Monte Rotonto in central Italy, after the nation's government collapsed, capturing the Italian general staff. Then came the glider-borne rescue of Benito Mussolini, the deposed Fascist dictator of Italy, from pro–Allied hands. He was hidden away in a heavily guarded and isolated resort at Gran Sasso in central Italy, on the top of a mountain that was normally accessible only by cable car. A total of 108 air-transported German commandos would face 150 Italian soldiers who knew the surroundings and could use the hotel as a strongpoint. On 12 September 1943, twelve gliders landed as close as 50ft (15m) to the hotel in which Mussolini was held. The German raiders, led by Major Otto Skorzeny, stormed in. After the surrender of the Italian troops, Mussolini was flown out in a light aircraft.

Following the Italian surrender on 8 September 1943, the Germans moved swiftly to occupy the Greek-inhabited islands of the Dodecanese, which had belonged to Italy since 1912. The British sought to intervene and cooperate with pro–Allied Italian forces stationed on the islands in an attempt to prevent this. On the morning of 3 October, a battalion of the 2nd Parachute Division was dropped west and south of Antimachia airfield on the island of Kos, while an amphibious battalion of the elite Brandenburger Division was landing from the sea.[52] The island had been secured a few days earlier by 120 British paratroopers, who landed unopposed, as the 4,000-strong Italian garrison did not put up any resistance. At 15.30 the 5th Battalion of the Brandenburgers parachuted in the centre of the island. Kos was secured by the airborne and seaborne forces even before the arrival of reinforcements, including air-transported units of the 22nd Infantry Division. On 12 November 1943, German forces, spearheaded by one battalion of the 2nd Parachute Regiment landing by parachute, invaded Leros. The island was captured by the Germans after a four-day battle mainly against the seaborne British troops that had landed to the island.

When the Allied forces invaded Normandy in June 1944, the German 2nd Parachute Division was sent to Brittany. Meanwhile, battalions of the division's 6th Regiment were deployed around Saint Lô and in the Carentan area of the Cotentin Peninsula, near the drop zones of American paratroopers. The regiment was heavily engaged in the subsequent battles, at Carentan and Saint Lô. On the night of 10/11 June, elements of the US 101st Airborne Division forced a passage across the causeway into Carentan. The *Fallschirmjäger* had to retreat, because of ammunition shortages. Two days later, surviving elements of the regiment were caught in the Falaise Pocket and destroyed by

21 August. Meanwhile, II *Fallschirmjägerkorps* (II Parachute Corps), commanded by General Eugen Mendl, and the 352nd Infantry Division had failed to hold Saint Lô, when it was assaulted by the XIX Corps of the First US Army.[53] When US VIII Corps attacked Brittany, the German 2nd Parachute Division fell back to the city of Brest, in western France. General Hermann B. Ramcke, the divisional commander, ordered his men to strengthen the positions already held by poorly-trained and equipped infantry units.[54] The Germans, surrounded by US forces, were cut off. On 13 September, after days of fierce fighting, Ramcke rejected a US proposal to surrender his troops with honour.[55] Five days later, the defenders were forced to surrender and Brest was liberated. Ramcke attempted to escape but was captured by the Allies the next day.

On the morning of 26 August 1944, 400 German paratroopers were dropped to relieve a Wehrmacht force that was encircled at Otopeni airfield near Bucharest, Romania's capital, but the *Fallschirmjäger* were almost wiped out by Soviet infantry and Romanian paratrooper units. In September 1944, 1. *Fallschirm Armee* (1st Parachute Army) was raised by General Student, who also assumed command. Not all personnel were trained parachutists. The 30,000-strong formation was headquartered in Nancy, France. Two parachute divisions, the 6th and the 7th, were the formation's spearhead. During the Allied airborne invasion of the Netherlands (Operation Market-Garden), units of the 1st Parachute Army considerably delayed the Allied advance across the south of the country.[56] On 18 November, the command of the formation passed to General Alfred Schlemm.

In December 1944, German paratroopers took part in an ill-fated small-scale airborne assault during the Ardennes offensive. At 03.00 on 17 December, some 1,300 *Fallschirmjäger*, most of whom were poorly-trained and inexperienced, were dropped from 112 Junkers Ju 52s north of Malmedy, at the rear of the American forces.[57] It was the first night combat jump in the history of the German airborne forces. Their objective was to seize the crossroads at Belle Croix and hold it for approximately twenty-four hours until relieved by the 12th SS-Panzer Division. Because of bad weather and pilot/jumpmaster errors, only a fraction of the airborne force landed near the intended dropping zone. Paratroopers were scattered all over the Ardennes with a number of them landing across the border, on German soil, as far away as Bonn.[58] By noon, Colonel Friedrich August Freiherr von der Heydte, who led the operation, managed to gather 300 of his men. They were lightly armed and had enough ammunition for only a single fight. The force was too small to capture the crossroads, so their commander, who had been injured on landing, decided to wait for the panzer division. After three days, he ordered his men to withdraw in small teams towards the German lines. A third of them were able to make it. Many German paratroopers were killed in the process, after being encircled or ambushed by American troops. Others, including von der Heydte himself, were forced to surrender.

Three months later, units of the 1st Parachute Army were among the German forces that failed to halt the Allied advance in the Reichswald, a forested area close to Germany's border with Holland. On 10 March 1945, the rearguard of the 1st Parachute Army evacuated a bridgehead on the west bank of the Rhine, near Wesel, and had the bridge blown behind them. Prior to Operation Varsity, the Allied airborne assault on

German soil (east of the Rhine), the formation's II Parachute Corps was deployed to the north.[59] Referring to the Reichswald battle, Field Marshal Bernard Montgomery commented later that 'the enemy parachute troops fought with fanaticism unexcelled at any time in the war'.[60] In mid-April 1945, elements of the 1st Parachute Army were among the German forces encircled by the Allies in the Ruhr, east of the Rhine. During a battle that followed between 1 and 18 April, 250 Germans were killed and over 317,000 were captured, including 25 generals. Of the German parachute divisions that fought during the Second World War, the 2nd was surrounded and destroyed in Brest as early as September 1944. The 1st Parachute Division lasted as a fighting unit until the German surrender in Italy on 2 May 1945, one week before the end of the war in Europe. Two divisions, the 3rd and the 4th, surrendered to Allied forces in April 1945. Two more divisions, the 5th and the 8th, were destroyed in the Ruhr Pocket, also in April 1945. The 6th and the 7th Parachute Divisions surrendered to the Allies at the war's end in May 1945. The 9th Parachute Division was destroyed, during the Battle of Berlin between April and May, and the 10th Parachute Division surrendered to Soviet forces in May 1945.

Chapter 4

The British Paratroopers

The last of the world's major military powers to acquire airborne forces was Great Britain. It occurred in the summer of 1940, although an ambitious plan for the establishment of a paratroop division had been discussed at the highest levels in London, without further progress, as early as 1917. Nineteen years later, there was a warning by General (later Field Marshal) Archibald P. Wavell of the threat to the Empire's global interests from Soviet airborne forces. He had submitted a report after witnessing a massive parachute drop near Kiev as a guest of the Red Army. No measures were taken in London as the Committee of Imperial Defence regarded the danger of an airborne raid by an enemy force for Great Britain as 'negligible at the time'.[1] The issue of forming paratroop units in Great Britain was raised again on 22 June 1940, when the Prime Minister Winston Churchill ordered the formation of 'a corps of at least five thousand parachute troops', having been impressed by the successes of the *Fallschirmjäger* after the outbreak of the Second World War. Things started moving fast because, as a senior officer put it, the British had to cover in six months the ground the Germans had in six years.[2] By the beginning of July, the establishment of a parachute training centre in Ringway, near Manchester, had been decided. Major J.F. Rock, Royal Engineers, became the first commander of the British airborne forces. The parachute training centre, also known as the Central Landing Establishment, was ready to function by August. It was put under the command of a Royal Air Force (RAF) officer, Group Captain L.G. Harvey. Another RAF officer, Squadron Leader L.A. Strange, took charge of the 'air side' of the parachute training with Rock being responsible for the military requirements of airborne warfare. Fourteen pilots, including the already famous Flight Sergeant (later Wing Commander) William Brereton, were called upon to help with the training, as they had been put through an experimental course in parachuting before the war. The 'ground part' of the training in Ringway became the responsibility of nine Army non-commissioned officers (NCOs) belonging to the Army Training Corps. Things changed in October 1941, when it was decided that the instructors in Ringway should belong to the physical training branch of the RAF. Until the end of the war, some 60,000 Europeans recruited by the Allies for parachute training went through courses at Ringway.

On 10 August, Churchill was informed that although 3,500 volunteers had been selected to train as airborne troops, only 500 could actually begin training due to limitations in equipment and aircraft. Officers, NCOs and men of the airborne forces were initially drawn from various units of the British Army. They had been carefully chosen. On several occasions the interviewing officers had rejected three-quarters of the applicants. Of those who remained almost all had already seen active service. They were entitled to extra pay for being parachutists; four shillings a day for officers and two shillings for other ranks. Some time in 1942 the extra pay was made equal – two shillings for all ranks. The preliminary exercises were carried out by Army instructors at a depot at Hardwick, near Chesterfield, in Derbyshire. After a fortnight there, the recruits had to go to Ringway for parachute training. They had to do two jumps from a balloon and five more from an aircraft before being regarded as qualified parachutists and receiving the coveted blue parachute wings. The RAF had provided a number of British-made Armstrong Whitworth Whitley medium bombers for conversion into aircraft for paratroopers. They were jumping from the rear of a Whitley or from a hole in its fuselage. Other types of British aircraft, such as Stirlings and Halifaxes, were also used for parachute drops. Thirty-three Douglas Dakota transports that were brought from the United States in the summer of 1942 gradually took the place of the outworn Whitleys, although these planes, with the convenient side exit for the paratroopers, were never in enough numbers to cover operational needs. The parachutes – in use at the time and long after the end of the Second World War – had been invented by Raymond Quilter and Leslie Irving.

The first parachute drop was made from a Whitley on 13 July 1940. Twelve days later a recruit fell to his death, when his parachute failed to open. A unit made up of qualified parachutists was formed under the informal name No. 2 Commando. The first demonstration drop was performed on Salisbury Plain, near Shrewton, on 18 November, when fifty officers and men parachuted before a number of British and Allied officials. By the end of the year, the 500-man No. 2 Commando was renamed 11th Special Air Service Battalion. In September 1941, the unit, under a new name now, that of 1st Parachute Battalion, moved to Hardwick to become part of the 1st Parachute Brigade. It was to consist of four parachute battalions. The three were ready – being the 1st Battalion, the 2nd and the 3rd, commanded by Lieutenant Colonels E.E. Down, E.W.C. Clavel and G.W. Lathbury. Lieutenant Colonel M.R.J. Hope-Thompson took command of the 4th Battalion, when it was formed later on. The commanding officer of the new unit was Brigadier R.N. Gale. The brigade was part of an airborne division composed of parachute and glider-borne troops, which Major General F.A.M. Browning, a former Guardsman, had been ordered to raise. In March 1942, the 1st Parachute Battalion moved to Bulford on Salisbury Plain. The lanyard on the uniform was different in colour from battalion to battalion in order to facilitate distinction. It was green for the 1st, yellow for the 2nd, red for the 3rd and black for the 4th Battalion. Browning wanted a distinct 'headdress' for his paratroopers.[3] Three colours were considered – red maroon, blue and green. The red maroon was finally chosen. According to legend, it was the choice of Browning's wife, the famous novelist Daphne du Maurier. When the 5th and the 6th Battalions were formed, their officers and men did not wear the red beret. As they were drawn from Scottish and Welsh units, they were allowed to have instead the Baltimore bonnet and the black flash of the Royal Welsh Fusiliers. The 5th Battalion was also allowed to maintain its bagpipe band. In addition to the blue parachute wings and the red beret, the Pegasus badge was introduced. The flying horse of the Greek mythology, linked with Bellerophon, the first mounted warrior, was an idea conceived by Major Edward Seago. According to another source, Pegasus was chosen as a fitting emblem for the airborne forces again after a suggestion by Daphne du Maurier.[4]

In October 1941, two battalions based in India became part of the 1st Airborne Division. These were the 156th Battalion and the 10th Battalion. The first was drawn from British volunteers from the ranks of the twenty-seven British battalions serving in India in the early period of the war. The battalion was organized in six companies. A parachute training school was established at Willingdon Airport, near Delhi. Shortly before Christmas, two more battalions were formed, being the 152nd Indian Parachute Battalion and the 153rd Gurkha Battalion. In October 1942, the 156th Battalion was ordered to move to the Middle East. They were stationed initially in Qabrit, north of Suez, in Egypt and later in Ramat David, south-east of Haifa, in Palestine. The 10th Battalion was formed in January 1943, basically from volunteers from the Royal Sussex Regiment, and carried out their training in Palestine. Three parachute battalions, the 156th, the 10th and the 11th (raised in March 1943), made up the Middle East-based 4th Parachute Brigade. The 10th Battalion moved to North Africa at the same time as the 156th and in due course went with it to Italy.[5] On 10 October 1941, the 31st Independent Brigade, after coming from India, was named 1st Airlanding Brigade. By the end of the year, the Glider Pilot Regiment (GPR) was formed. It was equipped with Hotspur and Waco gliders, initially, with the more advanced Horsa and Hamilcar to be provided sometime later. The GPR, commanded by Major George Chatterton, a former RAF pilot, adopted a special set of wings for the pilots of the unit. After the formation of two parachute brigades and the air landing brigade, Great Britain's 1st Airborne Division was operationally ready for combat. In August 1944, the 52nd (Lowland) Infantry Division was trained to become an air-transported unit.[6]

On 23 October 1943, the War Office authorized the raising of a second airborne division.[7] It was numbered the 6th and consisted of the 3rd and the 4th Parachute Brigades and the 6th Airlanding Brigade. The 6th Airborne Armoured Reconnaissance Regiment, the 53rd Airlanding Regiment, Royal Artillery and the 21st Independent Parachute Company (Pathfinders) became part of the new division, which was stationed in Figheldean, Wiltshire.[8] The first commander of the 6th Airborne Division was Major General Richard N. Gale.

Operation Colossus

An aqueduct at Tragino in Southern Italy was the target chosen by the British for the first combat mission of their newly-formed airborne forces. The codename given was Operation Colossus. The aqueduct, which had been constructed close to the town of Calitri, carried the water supply for two million inhabitants of Apulia province. It also supplied water to ports used by the Italian military, such as Taranto, Bari and Brindisi. The aqueduct's location, being quite far from the coast, didn't favour the employment of a seaborne raiding party. It seemed also too strongly constructed to be destroyed by aerial bombing. It was decided therefore that this was a suitable mission for airborne troops. In December 1940, a raiding party, made up of seven officers and thirty-one other ranks, was selected. They had to go through a special six-week training programme, mostly at Ringway. The party, code-named 'X' Troop, was headed by Lieutenant Colonel T.A.G. Pritchard. A fatal accident happened during a preparatory drop. After falling with his parachute into an ice-covered pond because of strong winds, one trooper drowned. On 7 February 1941, the raiding party arrived in Malta after traveling by night on six Whitleys. The aircraft covered the 1,600-mile (2,575km) distance flying partly over occupied France. The operation started on 10 February. One officer and five other ranks were on each plane. The first Whitley reached the dropping zone, being some 500 yards (427m) from the target, at 21.42. The drop was made from 400ft (123m). Six paratroopers landed in a valley some two miles (3.2km) from the aqueduct, because Whitley No. 6 couldn't locate the dropping zone. Two other planes failed to drop their containers due to a technical problem with the release mechanisms, leaving the raiding party short of explosives and ammunition.

The aqueduct was blown up, according to plan. The paratroopers also destroyed with explosives a nearby wooden bridge on the Ginestra River. After leaving one of their men who had broken his ankle on landing with a local farmer, the paratroopers headed towards the nearest coast, being some 50 miles (80km) away. A submarine, HMS *Triumph*, should have been waiting to pick them up, but it never happened. The submarine had to abandon the area as an Italian search for a missing plane was conducted there. They had been searching for an RAF Whitley, which had developed engine trouble after bombing the Foggia railway station as a diversion for the 'X' Troop mission. The pilot had informed his airfield in Malta that he was ditching in the mouth of the River Sele, being coincidentally the rendezvous point for the paratroopers. It was regarded too risky for HMS *Triumph* to surface, as an Italian aircraft was also taking part in the search. Therefore, it was decided at headquarters in England for the submarine to abandon the area and the British paratroopers to be left in their fate.

The 'X' Troop men had left the area at 01.00. Splitting into three groups, they headed towards the coast. When they were informed that the rendezvous with the submarine had been called off, they spent the night hiding in various places. The two groups were soon located by Italian Army and Carabinieri (gendarme) detachments and, after a brief exchange of fire, were forced to surrender. The third group, headed by Pritchard, surrendered to the Carabinieri, as the British were heavily outnumbered and short of ammunition. The presence of women and children in the area was another reason for Pritchard's decision to surrender without a fight. The paratroopers were regarded as spies by a blackshirted Fascist paramilitary leader, who was determined to have them shot. Fortunately, the Army general who commanded the region intervened in time and on his orders the British were treated as prisoners of war. They were chained to each other and were led off to captivity with the exception of Fortunato Picchi. He was a civilian of Italian origin, who was working at the Savoy Hotel in London before joining the raiding party as interpreter. Although tortured by the blackshirted militia, Picchi didn't give away any information about Great Britain's newly-formed airborne forces. For this reason he was court-martialled and shot by the Italians. The thirty-six British paratroopers were imprisoned until the Italian surrender in 1943. They were then freed and repatriated. Lieutenant Anthony Dean-Drummond didn't wait that long, as he managed to escape and return to England. By the end of 1942, Dean-Drummond was an officer, this time in the 1st Airborne Division. Corporal Alfred Parker also escaped initially from the Italians and later, when recaptured, from the Germans. After his second escape, he managed to reach Allied-controlled North Africa. From there Parker's repatriation was a matter of days.

Operation Colossus had a negligible effect on Italy's war effort in Albania and North Africa, as it didn't create a serious interruption to the water supplies to Taranto and the other ports. The morale effect in Britain, however, was great, where the raid on Southern Italy was hailed with joy and enthusiasm, as the country now possessed airborne forces capable of hitting enemy targets in distant locations. The Tragino raid also affected the morale of the population in Italy, as it left wide open the possibility of another strike by British paratroopers. Above all, the destruction of the Tragino aqueduct caused additional headaches to the warlords of the Axis alliance, as they didn't know much, at the time, about the strength and the capabilities of the Great Britain's newly-established airborne forces. Operation Colossus, on the other hand, provided the military in Great Britain with valuable experience, both technical and operational, that helped in the planning and execution of the next mission, Operation Biting. The success of the Tragino raid prompted the War Office to expand the existing airborne force. In July 1942, permission was granted to form another parachute brigade. Ernest E. Down, promoted to brigadier, became its first commander. The 4th Parachute Battalion, transferred from the 1st Parachute Brigade, was one of the formation's three battalions. It was formed in January 1942. The other two were line infantry battalions converted to parachute ones, as the 5th and 6th. These were the Queen's Own Cameron Highlanders and the Royal Welch Fusiliers, which became the brigade's 5th and 6th Parachute Battalions, in May and August 1942 respectively. The new brigade became initially part of the 1st Airborne Division. It remained in Great Britain until April 1943, when it left for North Africa. After the Allied invasion of Italy, the brigade became an independent formation.

The Bruneval Raid

The stakes of the next operation involving British airborne troops were much higher than those of the Italian operation almost a year ago. The target this time was a *Würzburg Riese* (Giant Würzburg) radar station in German-occupied northern France. It had been established in 1940 near the village of Bruneval, two miles (3.2km) north of Le Havre. It was designed to give the Luftwaffe and the German Army early warning on the approach of enemy aircraft and ships. The paratroopers didn't have to just blow up the target, as the objective in the first mission had been. This time, they had to seize a heavily-guarded coastal area, dismantle the apparatus and bring the radar dish and key components of the device back to England. They also had to photograph the parts of the installation that couldn't be removed. At the time, such radar installations were being operated by the Germans along the coast of Western Europe. If one was captured, scientists in Great Britain could assess its operational capabilities by examining key components. The success of the mission could mean a lot to the British in the light of 'the ceaseless warfare waged between the bombers of the RAF and the defence of occupied Europe', as any knowledge on this radiolocation apparatus would be precious from a strategic point of view.[9] The fact that a radar expert had to parachute in the area, dismantle the apparatus and take away its components considerably increased the mission's degree of difficulty. The German defences in and around the Bruneval installation were heavy. There were the signallers and the covering troops who were on duty day and night at the radar post itself. In addition, thirty men were stationed in nearby barracks and a hundred more at La Presbytere, a farm-type building situated some 300 yards (274m) to the north. There was also a garrison of forty men in the village down the road. They were manning the defences on the coast from which the British evacuation had to be made. At the time of the airborne assault, a total of 130 German soldiers were stationed in the Bruneval area.

It all started on 8 January 1942, when Admiral Lord Louis Mountbatten, chief of Combined Operations, informed the commanders of the 38th Wing RAF and 1st Airborne Division that the Chiefs of Staff Committee had approved a proposal for the Bruneval raid. At the time, the 1st Airborne Division was composed of only two battalions, of which only one was combat-ready. Major General F.A.M. Browning, the division commander, decided to use the 'ill prepared' 2nd Parachute Battalion for the mission and keep the fully-trained 1st Parachute Battalion for a larger operation in the future. 'C' Company was selected, although there was a problem there, as a number of men, including the commander of the assault force, Major John Frost, were not qualified parachutists. The operation therefore had to wait until these men, plus the RAF radar expert, had gone through a crash course in parachuting at Ringway. They completed the training successfully within five days. The raiding party consisted of 120 officers and other ranks, divided into three groups. The first group was made up of fifty men, who were to attack the radar and the nearby building. They were to drop first, followed after a short interval by the forty-strong second group, including the radar expert and a section from the 1st Parachute Field Squadron, Royal Engineers. Their task was to dismantle the radar set, bring to England parts of the apparatus and take pictures of the key parts that couldn't be removed. The third group, to be parachuted last, consisted of thirty men, who were to deal with any German counter-attack launched in the radar area or on the evacuation beach. Assault landing craft from the landing ship HMS *Prins Albert* were to pick up the paratroopers and the components of the radar. Onboard the craft were to be thirty-two officers and men of the Royal Fusiliers and the South Wales Borderers to provide covering fire during the embarkation. Two Royal Navy destroyers were to provide support and escort the paratroopers in their trip back to England.

After a special session in Inveraray in Loch Fyne in Scotland, the raiding force carried out a practice drop. The night of Sunday, 23 February, was spent on the shores of Southampton Water in a final exercise. They were ready, but the weather was not suitable – so they had to wait for it to improve. On the night of 27 February, after a period of intense training and several postponements because of bad weather, Operation Biting, as the raid was code-named, was on. One by one the Whitleys with the raiding force on board took off. When the lights of the French coast could be seen from the cockpits, anti-aircraft shells began to burst around the planes. In their effort to avoid the enemy fire two Whitleys dropped their paratroopers away from the dropping zone. The British were parachuted not far from the installation. On reaching the ground, Frost and his 'stick', a term used for those jumping from the same plane (plane load), reportedly performed a 'natural function' as a gesture of defiance.[10] It took the men of the first group ten minutes after landing to collect weapons from the containers. They then headed towards the lodging and the radar station. The two buildings were shortly surrounded by the British. Major Frost, before storming in, blew his whistle. Explosions, yells and the sound of automatic fire broke the silence of the quiet night. At the head of four men, Frost dashed into the villa, shouting 'Hands up!' in German (*Hande hoch*). On his way upstairs, he gunned down the only German inside. He was leaning from a window firing at the British, who were entering the building that housed the radar. Leaving two men in the villa, Frost with the rest made off to the radar. There he found that the Germans manning the radar had been killed or captured. It was then when fire was opened from Le Presbytere. One paratrooper was killed. Frost and his men formed a defensive perimeter round the radar installation. In the meantime, the sappers had arrived and were getting on with their task. RAF Flight-Sergeant C.W.C. Cox inspected the installation and then started dismantling the parts of the radar set to be taken back to England. The radar array and certain components of the apparatus were put on trolleys and taken to the evacuation beach. On their way to the coast, the paratroopers came under fire from a pillbox situated on the edge of a cliff. Some men were hit. Rushing to reach their colleagues, those who had been dropped at the wrong place, almost 2½ miles (4km) away, were able to attack the pillbox from behind and silence it by killing its occupants. They also helped their colleagues of the second group to clear the evacuation beach from the German defences.

By 02.15, the beach was in British hands. The radar components were lying on the beach next to the wounded. When the landing craft finally arrived, the wounded and the captured radar equipment were put into one of them with paratroopers scrambling aboard the other five. In the meantime, Germans were approaching the shore shooting and throwing grenades. There was no time for the British to make sure that everyone had been taken. Eight men were left behind. Two of them were dead and six had had not made it to the beach. Eventually, two of the six who arrived later were picked up by one of the motor gunboats. The raiders were taken from the open landing craft into the gunboats which then made off for England with the landing craft in tow. At dawn, the flotilla was not more than 15 miles (24km) from the French coast. Then it was met by a squadron of Spitfires, providing cover throughout the passage home. The raiding force suffered relatively few casualties. Two paratroopers were killed, six wounded and six captured. The German casualties were five killed, two captured and three missing. The radar components brought to England, along with a captured German technician, allowed British scientists to understand the enemy advances in radar technology and create countermeasures to neutralize them. Churchill applauded the raid and guaranteed further wartime operations for the paratroopers, and Major Frost was awarded the Military Cross.[11]

North Africa

The summer of 1942 found British airborne units training with US Army's 509th Parachute Infantry Regiment (PIR), which arrived in England in mid-July. The programme included tactical jumps from 350ft (107m) and extensive night training. British paratroopers were then deployed to North Africa – some 1,500 miles (2,400km) away from England – when Allied forces invaded French Morocco and Algiers. On 9 November 1942, twenty-nine Douglas C-47 Skytrain (Dakota) transports, loaded with British paratroopers, took off from St. Eval airfield in Cornwall. On its way to North Africa, one Dakota made an emergency landing into the sea. An officer drowned trying to rescue one of the men. The rest were picked up by an American ship on her way to New York. After a refuelling stop in Gibraltar, the planes landed in Maison Blanche airfield near Algiers. It was the 1st Parachute Brigade – less the 3rd Parachute Battalion. On the same day, the brigade was joined by the 2nd Battalion of the (American) 509th PIR, which was forthwith attached to the formation. The British airborne operations started a few days later, when the 3rd Battalion carried out their first battalion-sized parachute drop onto Bone airfield, between Algiers and Tunis. On 15 November, a 350-man force parachuted into Bone, being a target for the enemy, too, as the drop was observed by a formation of Ju-52s with German paratroopers on board.[12] Seeing that the British had landed and seized the airfield, the German planes turned around and headed back towards Tunis.

In the Bone jump thirteen paratroopers were injured, one of them fatally, being throttled in mid-air by a rigging line which twisted around his neck.[13] In addition to that, four men were slightly wounded by the accidental discharge of a Sten gun. The drop was accurate, although a number of containers with arms and ammunition fell a mile short. The important thing was that both the two mortar platoons and the headquarters contingent landed on the field or close to it. The British occupied the airfield which was found to be deserted. The following day, a force from No. 6 Commando arrived to relieve the paratroopers. In the meantime, a squadron of RAF Spitfires had landed and started using the airfield. On 15 November, the 2nd Battalion of the American 509th PIR parachuted at Tebessa, capturing their objectives and securing the area. The following day, the British 1st Parachute Battalion was dropped accurately around the airfield of Souk el Arba. On 15 November, the battalion took part in an air raid, followed by the capture of a vital road junction at Beja, 90 miles (145km) west of Tunis. They also captured Matcur, after attacking a German armoured column and an Italian tank position. Nine days later, the 2nd Parachute Battalion, commanded by the (newly-promoted) Lieutenant Colonel John Frost, carried out a parachute drop onto Dapienne airfield, 30 miles (48km) south of Tunis. One man was killed and six injured in the jump. As the airfield was deserted, Frost decided to march 10 miles (16km) further on and capture Oudna airfield. The airfield was also taken without a shot being fired, but the paratroopers found themselves cut off from friendly forces. The Germans returned with tanks and infantry forces to claim the airfield. The British paratroopers, who were also at the mercy of the Luftwaffe, had only two anti-tank rifles and a few Gammon bombs in their possession. It was impossible to stand against tanks.

When the Germans attacked on 31 November, retreating seemed the only alternative for the British. The retreat was over when the battalion eventually reached the French outposts in Medjez el Bab. The cost of the brief seizure of a deserted airfield was heavy for the British: sixteen officers and 250 other ranks killed, wounded and missing.[14]

The British airborne forces were later deployed in North Africa in small-scale missions usually in cooperation with infantry and armoured units. On 10 December, men from the 2nd Parachute Battalion and a Lancashire Fusiliers company ambushed a 400-man German column in the desert. The ambush turned into a massacre for the surprised enemy. After Christmas, British airborne forces were used as infantry. In February and March 1943, the parachute brigade served in the front lines until the end of the Tunisian campaign. They fought notable actions at Bou Arada and at Tamera Valley. It was there, at Tamera Valley, where they earned the nickname '*Die Roten*' ('The Red Devils'). From 8 March to 18 March 1943, the 1st and 2rd Battalions held their positions at Tamera Valley although outnumbered and completely surrounded by German forces, including paratroopers. They also captured about 300 Germans. The British casualties (killed, wounded and missing) were 150 men. On 15 April 1943, the 1st Parachute Brigade was relieved by the American 9th Infantry Division. By then, because of the casualties, the average strength of a company in any battalion was no more than sixty men.[15] The brigade's casualties during the North African campaign were 1,700 killed, missing and wounded. The lack of anti-tank weapons was later given as the main reason for the casualties. Among the famous units the British paratroopers fought in North Africa were the Hermann Göring Parachute Regiment, the 10th Panzer Grenadiers, Witzig's parachutists and the Austrian Mountain Division. In North Africa the British paratroopers took 3,500 prisoners.

Norway

A daring commando operation involving gliders for the first time by the British Army was decided in London, whilst the airborne forces were engaged in the North African campaign. The target this time was a heavy water plant in southern Norway, some 400 miles (650km) from Great Britain. The Vermork Norsk hydroelectric power station in Telemark had to be sabotaged because it was reportedly linked with Nazi Germany's nuclear programme. The use of paratroopers was rejected because a wide disperse in the drop was possible, whereas the gliders could – it was hoped – deliver the commandos close to the objective.[16] In winter time, sixty-four German soldiers were guarding the plant and the dam next to it. They were stationed in the nearby village of Rjukan. The operation was code-named Freshman. On the night of 15 November 1942, two Handley Page Halifax bombers took off from the RAF airfield of Skitten in Scotland, towing a Horsa glider each. Thirty-four paratroopers who had volunteered for the mission were on board the two gliders. All were sappers from the Royal Engineers units attached to the 1st Airborne Division. Their task was to demolish the plant with explosives and then escape over the Norwegian border into neutral Sweden. The paratroopers had gone through a special training course in Wales. Norwegian Special Operation Executive (SOE) agents had already parachuted into Telemark to assist the arriving commandos.

The two aircraft-glider combinations managed to cross the Norwegian coast, but neither was able to reach their objective. The first glider was released north-west of Rjukan village some 25 miles (40km) from the target. The glider then crash-landed in a mountainous area overlooking Fyljesdal with the tow aircraft already returning to base. Out of the seventeen men on board the glider three were killed outright with the survivors being captured by the Germans twenty-four hours after the crash. The second pair both crashed into a mountain at Hestadfjell in a hell of high winds and rain. The glider had been released just before the tow aircraft crashed. The six-man aircraft crew and some of the paratroopers on board the glider were killed instantly.[17] Those who survived were taken prisoner. They were later shot as a result of Adolf Hitler's Commando Order, which stated all commando personnel were to be executed upon capture. At the end of the war, those responsible for the executions were tried and condemned to death. In May 1945, when the 1st Airborne Division was deployed in Norway, the executed paratroopers were buried with full military honours. Although Operation Freshman had been a failure, with forty-one British killed in plane and glider crashes or executed by the Germans, it 'demonstrated the range, flexibility and possibilities of airborne and glider operations' in warfare.[18] It also highlighted equipment problems that were rectified for later missions.

Greece

British paratroopers were deployed in Greece in October 1944, whilst German troops were still in Athens preparing their withdrawal from the country. A force, including tank units and RAF personnel, arrived in the Greek capital on Churchill's orders at a time they all were badly needed in Italy to fight against the Germans. The Prime Minister wanted to prevent the communist guerrillas from taking power in Greece by the force of arms. He was determined to defend Great Britain's 95 per cent influence over post-war Greece, a promise Joseph Stalin, the Soviet leader, had made to Churchill in Moscow in early October.[19] The British airborne operations had started on 14 September 1943, when three platoons of the 11th Parachute 'Brigade' parachuted on the Italian-occupied Dodecanese island of Kos. They belonged, in fact, to a parachute battalion, which was 'baptised' a brigade to deceive the enemy. The 11th Parachute Battalion was formed in Qabrit and was stationed in Transjordan. It remained in Kos until mid-December. They were gone by the time Germans launched an attack, involving paratroop forces, to capture Kos and other Dodecanese islands.

In early September 1944, the 2nd Independent Parachute Brigade (IPB) was deployed in Italy. Then they were ordered to start preparations for an airborne landing in Greece. On 24 September, an SAS detachment was parachuted on the area of Araxos, east of the port of Patras, in the Peloponnese and seized the local airfield. Now it was the 2nd IPB's turn to take action. The 4th Battalion was ordered to secure a dropping zone for the rest of the formation at Megara, some 7½ miles (12km) west of Athens. On 12 October, 'C' Company, headed by Lieutenant Colonel H.B. Coxen, took off from Brindisi airport in southern Italy. Their destination was German-occupied Greece. The German withdrawal from Athens started in the morning of 12 October.

At about noon, the 4th Battalion was dropped on Megara and seized the local airfield. As a result of a strong wind blowing at the time of the jump, a medical officer and forty other ranks were injured on landing.[20] On 15 October, a British parachute force entered the city of Athens.[21] Two days later, a paratroop detachment sailed from Megara to the port of Piraeus in order to set up a defensive perimeter on the arrival of Royal Navy ships and the disembarkation of the British Army's tanks and infantry. By 18 October, two British brigades were guarding the city centre of Athens, the 2nd (Parachute) and the 23rd (Armoured).

On 6 October, 'C' Company, commanded by Major George Jellicoe, an SBS officer, was ordered to occupy a mountainous area above the town of Kozani, in northern Greece. The Germans were still holding out, whilst other units of theirs were heading towards the Greek-Yugoslav border. After a fierce fighting, the position was secured and all attempts to retake it by the enemy were defeated.[22] The last German soldiers crossed the border into Yugoslavia in early November. On 29 October, an eleven-man paratroop detachment was dropped into Chalkidiki in northern Greece. A few hours later, they were established in a suburb of Thessaloniki, Greece's second city, which was already in the hands of the Communist 10th 'Division'.[23] On 4 November, the 5th Parachute Battalion and No. 9 Commando arrived at Thessaloniki by sea to reinforce the British presence in a city that was 'entirely controlled by the communists'.[24] The 5th Parachute Battalion then moved on to Eastern Macedonia and Thrace, where a single troop of No. 9 Commando was established in the town of Drama. By the end of the month, the whole area from Drama to the Bulgarian border was 'alight with civil war'.[25] The British paratroopers were then ordered to leave northern Greece right away and come by sea to Athens, where the situation was getting worse every day.

The so-called Battle of Athens started on the night of 4 December, when the communist rebels, aiming at seizing power and establishing one-party rule in Greece, attacked a city-centre gendarmerie station. The gendarmes held out until 15.00, when a British parachute patrol came to their rescue. The communists then tried to seize the Military Academy, defended by 240 cadets, their military instructors and a detachment of British paratroopers. On 10 December, they were ordered to withdraw, as they had to reinforce the defence of the Old Palace. The 5th Parachute Battalion spent a whole day to force their way from Constitution Square, at the city centre, along the road towards the Acropolis and another road leading to the coast of Faliro. The paratroopers suffered heavy casualties, including Lieutenant Conway who was killed and Major Hunter who was very badly wounded. The paratroopers were ordered to hold and secure Acropolis and other points in central Athens. During the night 'B' Company was established upon Acropolis, which it was found unoccupied. The communist rebels then made an attempt to pass men through the sewers and blow up the British headquarters at the Great Britain Hotel. They were defeated by men of the 2nd Parachute Field Squadron, Royal Engineers, commanded by Major Dennis Vernon.[26] On Boxing Day, the 5th Parachute Battalion, supported by tanks of the British 23rd Armoured Brigade, attacked a communist rebel stronghold and reached Piraeus Street, connecting Athens with the port. They joined the 6th Parachute Battalion there, which was already involved in mopping-up operations. From 2 to 5 January 1945, British paratroopers managed to advance to Attiki Square. On 4 January, the 2nd IPB maintained its advance and after three days of fierce fighting forced the communist rebels to withdraw from the Greek capital. From 5 to 14 January, British paratroopers supported the Greek army and police's newly-organized forces to pursue the communist rebels. It was then when the rebels asked for a ceasefire.

The 'First Round' (Πρώτος Γύρος) of the Greek civil war thus ended. The second round, when the fighting scattered in many parts of the war-torn country, followed from 1946 to 1949. The National forces, relying a great deal on US assistance, won in the end, keeping Greece outside the Communist bloc. On 6 January 1945, London was formally informed on the British military casualties in Greece, including those of the 2nd IPD. In thirty-three days of fierce fighting, 204 (officers and other ranks) were killed, 664 missing and 947 wounded – a total of 1,815 men.[27] Meanwhile, British airborne forces had taken part in significant operations in Sicily, the Italian mainland, France, Holland and Belgium, as well as later on in Germany.

In the post-war period, British paratroopers were deployed during the Suez crisis in 1952, the Northern Ireland conflict, the Falklands War, the Gulf War, and in Iraq and Afghanistan. Britain's airborne forces are headed by the Special Forces Support Group (SFSG), which was established on 3 April 2006. The 1st Battalion of the Parachute Regiment is permanently under the command of the Special Forces director in the SFSG. The other two battalions of the Parachute Regiment, the 2nd and the 3rd, as well as the Territorial Army's reserve battalion, are the parachute infantry component of the British Army's rapid response formation, being the 16th Air-Assault Brigade. The formation's origins can be found in the 16th Independent Parachute Brigade that was raised in February 1948 and was numbered 16th to commemorate the two wartime airborne divisions – the 1st and the 6th. The 16th Air-Assault Brigade, which was formed on 1 September 1999, emerged after the amalgamation of the 5th Airborne Brigade with the 24th Airmobile Brigade. Also fully airborne are the 22nd Special Air Service (22nd SAS) Regiment and the 7th Parachute Regiment Royal Horse Artillery. Qualified paratroopers can be found in the RAF Regiment (Number II Squadron), as well as in units of the Royal Marines (RM), such as the Patrol Troop, the 43 Commando Fleet Protection Group (formerly Commacchio Group, RM) and the RM's Mountain and Arctic Warfare Unit.

Chapter 5

Other Allied Paratroopers

The Poles

In Poland, military parachuting started in the mid-1930s, but the country's first airborne unit was formed in Great Britain five years later during the Second World War. It all started in 1936 with the establishment of a parachute school at Legionowo, near Warsaw. In September 1939, developments were cut short by the German occupation. With the collapse of their country a cadre of Polish parachute instructors escaped to England, where Poland's army-in-exile was formed in 1941. On 23 September 1941, an airborne unit was created in Scotland by the Polish High Command.[1] It was named 1st Independent Parachute Brigade (IPB) and placed under the command of Major General Stanisław F. Sosabowski. The brigade was made up mostly of volunteers from the Polish army-in-exile. They were reinforced, in the process, by Poles who had escaped from their occupied country and Polish immigrants who had come to Great Britain from the United States and other parts of the world. The 1st IPB was based initially close to British Army's parachute training centre at RAF Ringway, near Manchester, and later at Upper Largo, Fife, in Scotland. A cadre of instructors who had escaped from their country made up a Polish section at Ringway. The Poles remained there until a facility with two jump towers was set up for them at Upper Largo. A special facility for the training of the *Chichociemi* ('The Silent Unseen' in Polish) was established at Inverlochy Castle, also in Scotland. They were Polish volunteers specially trained in covert missions, who were eventually parachuted into occupied Poland.[2]

The 1st IPB's mission was to drop into occupied Poland and assist in the country's liberation. General Władysław Sikorski, Poland's prime minister-in-exile and commander-in-chief of the Polish Army, shared Sosabowski's strategic conclusion that the role of the Polish airborne forces would be critical in an Allied offensive for the liberation of Poland. This is why the unit was kept in reserve for so long. By September 1943, the 2,500-strong brigade was fully organized. There were three battalions with three companies each. The brigade, also, had two batteries (one artillery and one anti-tank) and three support companies (one engineer, one signal and one medical), all airborne. In early March 1944, the Poles were pressured by the Supreme Allied Command to reconsider the role of the Polish airborne forces and release them for combat in north-west Europe.[3] The pressure of the British government on the Poles eventually paid off and the Polish airborne unit was made available for combat in the Western Front.

In July, the brigade was transferred to England and became part of the First Allied Airborne Army. A frustration period of inaction followed for the Poles although they were slotted to take part in various operations. All of these had to be called off because of the speed of the Allied advance both in France and in Belgium. On 27 July 1944, the Polish government-in-exile, aware of the imminent uprising in Warsaw, urged for the dropping of the brigade in the vicinity of the Polish capital.[4] The request was denied by the British government on the grounds of 'operational considerations' and the difficulties in 'coordinating' with Soviet forces.[5] On 1 August, when the Warsaw uprising started, the Poles were unable to intervene. The death of Sikorski in a plane crash and the collapse of the Warsaw uprising had left Poland's government-in-exile powerless and isolated. The reason for the operational independence of the Polish brigade diminished. The Polish airborne brigade was attached to the British 1st Airborne Division and took part in the assault to capture the Rhine crossings at Arnhem in Holland.

In 1945, the 1st IPB was attached to the Polish 1st Armoured Brigade. Polish paratroopers undertook occupation duties in north Germany until the unit was disbanded in June 1947. Most of the Poles, officers and other ranks, decided to remain in exile rather than hazard returning to the new Communist Poland. On 31 May 2006, the Polish airborne brigade was awarded the Military Order of William, the Netherlands' highest military award, for their 'distinguished and outstanding acts of bravery, skill and devotion to duty', during Operation Market-Garden. The award is now worn by the British 6th Airborne Division, which inherited the battle honours of the Polish unit. Poland's 6th Air-Assault Brigade is the present-day successor to the wartime brigade. On 4 August 1995, Grom, a Polish Special Forces unit, adopted the name and the traditions of the *Chichociemi*.[6]

The Belgians

Belgium's first paratroop unit was established in England during the Second World War. In January 1942, the first Belgian parachutists were trained at RAF Ringway, near Manchester. They were volunteers from the Belgian Army units which had escaped to England after their country was invaded by the Germans. A month later, a whole Fusilier unit, 'A 'Company, went through parachute training voluntarily. On 8 May 1942, the Belgian Independent Parachute Company was established at Malvern Wells, Worcestershire. The unit, commanded by Lieutenant Freddy Limbosch, was comprised of officers and other ranks from the Fusiliers' 1st and 2nd Battalions, volunteers from other units of the Belgian forces and civilians who had escaped from occupied Belgium and volunteered for parachute training. The Belgians wore the maroon beret and the parachute wings of the British paratroopers. When they were later incorporated into the British SAS Brigade, they adopted the SAS-pattern parachute wings, as well as and their famous motto 'Who Dares Wins'. A downward-pointing flaming sword and a crusader shield were pictured in their cap badge.[7] Initially, the unit was attached to the 8th Parachute Battalion of the British 6th Airborne Division (autumn 1943).

In February 1944, the Belgian paratroopers, after a month of intensive training at Inverlochy Castle (Fort William), moved to Loudoun Castle Camp, near Galston (Ayrshire) in Scotland. A little later, the unit was incorporated into the British SAS Brigade and became 5 SAS Squadron, also known as the Belgian SAS Squadron. During the war, they conducted reconnaissance and sabotage missions, after being parachuted into German-occupied France, Belgium and Holland. Between 31 July and 15 August 1944, a 22-man Belgian detachment was dropped into an area near Le Mans, in north-west France (Operation Shakespeare) to harass the retreating Germans. They also assisted in the rescue of 150 downed Allied airmen.[8] On 6 August 1944, forty-one Belgians of the SAS were parachuted into the Ardennes to gather intelligence. They were the first Allied unit to set foot on Belgian soil in the Second World War. On 17 August, French and Belgian paratroopers, 120 in all, divided into twenty-five parties, were dropped onto twelve dropping zones north-west of Paris. The operation ended up disappointingly as the SAS force was parachuted too late to catch up with the German retreat.[9]

On several occasions, the Belgian paratroopers fought as motorized reconnaissance in armoured jeeps with the exception of Operation Regent in which they were deployed as assault troops. The operation was conducted between 27 December 1944 and 15 January 1945 by the whole of the Belgian Independent Parachute Company. The jeep-mounted force was tasked with supporting British armoured units in the Ardennes during the Battle of the Bulge. The Belgians operated in the wooden terrain between St. Huber and the Burl area. In April 1945, Belgian paratroopers, consisted of three reconnaissance squadrons, were deployed in the north of Holland and in Germany. Between May and July 1945, they were the only Belgian unit on active deployment. In the final stage of the war, the Belgian SAS Squadron was involved in counter-intelligence missions in Germany and Denmark. They were also tasked with the location and arrest of top-ranking Nazis and war criminals. On 21 September 1945, 5 SAS was transferred by the British to the newly-reformed Belgian Army. They were named 1st Parachute Regiment and served independently as a highly mobile unit. Seven years later, the regiment was reduced to a battalion and became part of the Commando Regiment (CR). In memory of their wartime links with the British the paratroopers (the Para-commando Battalion, in fact) of the CR kept wearing the maroon beret with the SAS wings. The Belgian paratroopers' most memorable operation in the post-war era was the rescue of European nationals in Stanleyville, Congo in 1964. In 2010, the paratroopers' banner, flag and insignia were officially handed over to the newly-formed Special Forces Group (SFG). A year later, Belgium's 1st Parachute Regiment was formally disbanded.

The Canadians

The man behind the creation of Canada's airborne forces was Colonel E.L.M. Burns.[10] With tension in the Pacific growing in 1941 and the German U-boats venturing in the Atlantic and the Gulf of Saint Lawrence, close to Quebec City, he believed that airborne troops could play a key role in defending or even recapturing remote areas in case of enemy activity or attack on either coast of Canada. Burns' requests, made to his superiors at the initial stages of the Second World War, were finally granted. The unit was conceived as a rapid deployment force. On 1 July 1942, men from various units of the Royal Canadian Infantry Corps who already had infantry experience volunteered for parachute training. Since Canada didn't have an airborne training school, members of the initial cadre had to go abroad – either to Ringway, near Manchester, in England or to Fort Benning, Georgia, in the United States. A training facility, which was established at Camp Shilo, Manitoba province, in central Canada, became operational on 5 April 1943. The officers and other ranks who successfully concluded the four-month course formed the 1st Canadian Parachute Battalion. The unit, also known in Canada as 1st Can Para Battalion, was comprised of a headquarters, a HQ company, and three rifle companies. They were stationed at Camp Shilo.

Major H.D. Proctor was the battalion's first commanding officer. He was killed on 7 September 1942 in the United States during a drop of Canadian trainees, when his canopy was hit by an aircraft. Lieutenant Colonel G.F.P. Bradbrooke took his place as commander of the 1st Can Para. Later in the year, a second parachute battalion was formed. It was later integrated with the First Special Service Force (FSSF), a US–Canada shock unit, also known as the 'Devil's Brigade'. On 8 July 1943, thirty-one officers and 548 other ranks of the 1st CaPaBa left for England aboard the *Queen Elizabeth*, an ocean liner turned troopship. They were based at Carter Barracks in Bulford, near Salisbury, as part of the British 6th Airborne Division. The Canadians were placed under the command of the 3rd Parachute Brigade as one of the unit's three battalions, the other two being the British 8th and 9th (Parachute). Initially, there was an adjustment issue for the Canadians who had been trained in the United States, as they had to rely now on one parachute as the British and not on two as the Americans. They also had to jump through a hole in the floor of a converted Stirling bomber rather than through the side door of a Douglas Dakota transport. On 19 November 1943, the Canadian paratroopers were proved combat-ready after completing a 50-mile (80km) march with full gear within eighteen hours. Until May 1944, the battalion had to undergo extensive training in preparation for the airborne phase of the forthcoming Allied assault across the English Channel.

The 1st CaPaBa's service in the European theatre included the airborne invasion on D-Day. Eight days after the Normandy landing there was a change of command in the battalion. Major Jenov Albert Nicklin replaced Colonel Bradbrooke, who was appointed to the General Staff at the Canadian Military Headquarters in London. In France, after the initial drop on D-Day, the Canadian paratroopers spent eighty-eight days in combat. The officers and men of the parachute battalion were the only Canadians to participate in the Battle of the Bulge in December 1944–January 1945.[11] They had also advanced deeper than any other Canadian unit into enemy territory. Two months later, during the Rhine crossings, the Canadians parachuted again. In this operation, code-named Varsity, Corporal Fred Topham earned the battalion's only Victoria Cross, the highest and most prestigious award for gallantry in the face of the enemy than can be awarded to British and Commonwealth forces. After Varsity the battalion was tasked with racing to the Baltic. They had to fight as light infantry all the way across Germany until they met the advancing Red Army at the Hanseatic city of Wismar in north Germany on the Baltic Sea, 28 miles (45km) east of Lübeck. The Canadians reached Wismar two hours before the Red Army. Six days later the war in Europe ended.

Major Nicklin, the commander of the 1st CaPaBa, was killed on German soil in the final stage of the war. On 24 March 1945, during Operation Varsity, his parachute became tangled in a tall tree. Nicklin was fired upon and killed by German soldiers while he was trying to free himself.[12] The Canadian paratroopers reached Wismar under their new commander, Lieutenant Colonel Fraser Eadie. Some 128 officers and other ranks were killed or died of their wounds during the Second World War and further 310 were wounded. This figure doesn't include the Canadians who were on loan to the British Army. Two of them were killed and further eight were taken prisoner at Arnhem, fighting with the King's Own Scottish Borderers Regiment, a unit of the British 3rd Parachute Brigade. From 6 August to 2 September 1944, the 1st CaPaBa, as well as the British airborne units, had been supported in their fight in northern France by a Canadian artillery detachment, the 1st Centaur (Field) Battery, commanded by Major D.M. Cooper.[13] The parachute battalion was the first Canadian unit to return home from Europe. On 30 September 1945, after the end of the war in the Pacific, the 1st CaPaBa was disbanded. Two years later, the Canadian Special Air Service Company was created. During the Korean War an airborne brigade, the Mobile Strike Force (MSF), was established to defend Canada's northern territories. In 1958, the MSF was reduced to three companies. Ten years later, the Canadian Airborne Regiment (CAR) was formed – only to be disbanded in disgrace in 1995 after the beating of a local teenager to death in Somalia by two Canadian paratroopers. In 2006, the 250-strong Canadian Special Operations Regiment (CSOR) was raised. CSOR's officers and other ranks are static-line and freefall parachutists.

The Greeks

Greece's first parachutists were trained in the Middle East by the British, during the Second World War. They were members of the Sacred Squadron (Ιερός Λόχος), a Special Forces unit, composed entirely of Greek officers and military cadets who had escaped from their German-occupied country. They were named after two formations that went down to Greek history. The original Ιερός Λόχος was organized by the Theban general Epaminondas (371–338 BC). Another formation bearing the same name was raised in February 1821 by Alexandros Ypsilantis at the initial stage of the Greek War of Independence.[14] The third Sacred Squadron was established in Palestine in August 1942. The Sacred Squadron was trained by the British at Qabrit, near Suez, in Egypt. They could sweep deep into the desert. They could, also, convert to seaborne raiders, while others, the majority of them, could eventually 'fall from the sky dangling from parachutes'.[15] Between February and May 1942, the Sacred Squadron, commanded by Colonel Christodoulos Gigantes, fought against the Germans as mechanized cavalry mainly in Tunisia. In February 1943, the squadron came under the command of the British Raiding Forces. Colonel David Sterling, the founder and first commander of the SAS, wanted the Greeks to be part of his para-commando unit. He believed that 'their knowledge would be an asset to any SAS operation in the Balkans'.[16]

The parachute training for the squadron started in July 1943 at Ramat David, an RAF airfield in Palestine. The instructors were British and the jumps were made from Hudson and Wellington aircraft. Two trainees lost their lives in parachute accidents.[17] Six hundred members of the 1,000-strong Sacred Squadron completed the five-week course and made the eight jumps required for qualification. Some of them were trained at Qabrit, in Egypt, also by the British. The Greeks who became qualified parachutists were awarded the SAS wings. On 30 October 1943, a few weeks after the Italian armistice, twenty Douglas Dakota transports dropped 200 Sacred Squadron paratroopers onto the Eastern Aegean island of Samos. The Sacred Squadron commander, Colonel Gigantes, although he didn't have any parachute training, was one of them! As the Allies were unable to provide back up to them, the Greeks had to withdraw a few days later, when the enemy launched an offensive in the Dodecanese Islands, involving fighter planes and paratroop forces. The German offensive had already led to the capturing of the islands of Kos and Leros. The Greek paratroopers crossed the channel on fishing boats and returned to the Middle East through Turkey. From October 1943 to May 1945, the squadron carried out amphibious operations that led to the liberation of several islands, including Chios, Lemnos, Naxos, Milos, Symi, Nisiros, Tilos and Rhodes.[18] Chios, an island in eastern Aegean, was Greece's first area liberated by Greek soldiers. In early October, after the German withdrawal from Athens, a Sacred Squadron unit was deployed in the Greek capital. Two months later, they fought along with British forces, including paratroopers, and prevented communist guerrillas from seizing power in Greece. The casualties for the Sacred Squadron during the Second World War were twenty-five dead, three missing in action and fifty-six wounded. Further twenty-nine men were taken prisoner.

The squadron was disbanded in April 1945. The unit's traditions were carried on in the post-war era by the forty Mountain Raider Companies (LOK), which were formed in 1946. They fought with distinction during the 'second round' of Greece's Civil War (1945–9). In 1955, a parachute training school was established at Aspropyrgos, near Athens. The 2nd Parachute Regiment (SAL) was formed in 1967. Units made up exclusively of paratroopers, besides the 2nd Parachute Regiment, are the long range recon patrol Special Paratrooper Detachment (ETA), the Zeta squadron, specializing in amphibious missions, and Greek Navy's Underwater Demolition Command (DYK). Qualified parachutists serve, also, in the raiding, marine and airmobile forces. A brigade, identified as the 71st Airmobile, made up of red-beret troops, has indirect links with the country's Special Forces. The brigade was established in January 1998 on a Rapid Reaction Force role. It was later transformed into an air-assault formation.

The Australians and New Zealanders

At the outbreak of the Second World War, Australia didn't have an operational airborne capability. Things started moving in November 1942, when a parachute training facility was established at Laverton, Victoria.[19] In August 1943, the 1st Parachute Battalion was raised, followed by two airborne units – an artillery battery and an engineer troop.[20] By then, the parachute training facility had been relocated to Richmond, New South Wales. In September, Major John Overall was appointed commanding officer of the 1st Parachute Battalion.[21] The Australian Army's airborne battalion didn't see any combat, although it was warned for action a number of times in 1945. A section of the 4th Field Artillery Regiment was the only unit of Australia's airborne forces to conduct an operational jump during the war.[22] They and their guns were dropped onto Natzab in Dutch New Guinea on 5 September 1943 in support of the US 503rd Parachute Infantry Regiment. The Australians provided thirty-four volunteers for the operation as well as two field guns. The volunteers received training from the American paratroopers. The intensive course concluded with a practice jump on 30 August, during which three Australians were injured.[23] The 1st Parachute Battalion did not take part in the landing of Australian troops on Balikpapan in Borneo on 1 July 1945.[24] Australian paratroopers were deployed as elite infantry in the operations that led to the liberation of Singapore.[25] The Australian Army's 1st Parachute Battalion was disbanded in early 1946.[26] Five years later, an airborne platoon was formed as part of the 6th Royal Australian Regiment (RAR). By September 1951, a parachute training establishment was set up at Royal Australian Air Force Williamtown, near Port Stephens in New South Wales. In July 1957, Australia's 1st Special Air Service Company was formed. By September 1964, the unit was awarded regimental status. A year later, two SAS units were deployed in Borneo – the 1st Squadron in Brunei and the 2nd Squadron in Sarawak. Australian SAS units were later involved in the Vietnam War. An operational parachute jump was made on the night of 15/16 December 1969 some 9 miles (15km) north-west of Xuyen Noc by the Australian 3rd Squadron. In Vietnam, the Australian SAS units served in rotation from 1966 to 1971. In 1974, an airborne company was formed. It became part of the 6th RAR. On 5 May 2003, the Special Operations Command (SOCOMD) was established to unite the Australian Special Forces. Meanwhile, the SAS has basically developed into a crack counter-terrorist unit.

The South Africans

The first serviceman to perform a display parachute jump in South Africa was Colonel Sir Pierre van Ryneveld, Director of Air Services, in 1926.[27] The country's first paratrooper unit was an Air Force platoon consisting initially of fifteen South Africans who had been trained as parachutists in Great Britain after the outbreak of the Second World War. Before long, the unit grew to the size of a company.[28] On 1 August 1943, the South African Air Force Regiment, made up of armoured and airborne units, was established. Thirty-six officers and other ranks were the first to volunteer for training at the 75th Air School at Lyttelton in Gauteng Province. For parachute training they were sent to a British-ran establishment at Ramat David in Palestine. But they never went through any parachute training course, being posted as reinforcements to the South African 6th Armoured Division, which was deployed in Italy.

Twenty-six South African officers, including Captain Ossie Baker, were eventually trained in parachuting and fought with the British 2nd Independent Parachute

Brigade against the Germans in Italy, Greece and southern France. Scottish-born Captain David McCombe, who had been sent to England during the war to be briefed on airborne warfare, eventually joined the British Army. He was wounded fighting in Arnhem in September 1944 as an officer of the British 1st Airborne Division. Seventeen years after the end of the war, on 1 April 1961, South Africa acquired its first airborne battalion.[29] Commandant Willem Louw was the commanding officer. During the years of conflict, in which South Africa was involved in Namibia (South-West Africa) and Angola, the South African Army built a competitive airborne force in the shape of the 44th Parachute Brigade.

Inter-Allied and Joint Allied Units

Qualified parachutists could be found in inter-Allied and joint Allied formations during the Second World War. Such units included the British No. 10 Commando and the Australian Z Special and M Special. No. 10 (Inter-Allied) Commando was an elite unit of the British Army that was raised on 2 July 1942.[30] Their headquarters was at Eastbourne, 19 miles (31km) east of Brighton, and the senior officers were British. The men were all volunteers from various western, central and eastern European countries, including Germans and Austrians who had escaped from Nazi Germany.[31] By the end of the war, No. 10 Commando had: three Belgian (Nos 4, 9 and 10), two French (Nos 1 and 8) and one Dutch (No. 2), Norwegian (No. 5), Polish (No. 6) and Mediterranean or Yugoslavian (No. 7) Troops. A unit made up of Germans, Austrians and Eastern Europeans was identified as Troop X or Troop 3. In May 1943, the first No. 10 Commando volunteers went through a parachute course at Ringway. The unit served in the Mediterranean, Scandinavia, Burma and Eastern Europe mostly in small numbers attached to other formations. In mid-1944 the Dutch Troop was divided between three parachute divisions – the British 6th and the American 82nd and 101st. By the time of the D-Day landings, the two French Troops were attached to the 1st SAS Brigade. By the night of D-Day, on 6 June 1944, detachments of No. 10 Commando had crossed the River Orne and were dug in, guarding the left flank of the British 6th Airborne Division.[32] In the night of 2/3 September, a No. 3 Troop team parachuted near Saint-Valery-en-Caux in Normandy on a reconnaissance mission. Also, in September No. 10 Commando elements took part in small scale parachute operations. On 4 November, Belgian and Polish Troops joined the SAS Brigade in Italy. No. 10 (Inter-Allied) Commando was disbanded on 4 September 1945.

Z Special was a Joint-Allied unit specializing in reconnaissance and sabotage missions. It was formed in Melbourne, Australia in June 1942 and operated behind the Japanese lines in Borneo and the islands of the former Dutch East Indies.[33] In Z Special, being a predominantly Australian unit, British, Dutch, New Zealanders and Indonesian volunteers also served. Many of them were trained in parachuting. The unit carried out a total of eighty-one covert missions in the South-Western Pacific theatre of operations with detachments inserted by parachute or submarine to provide intelligence and conduct guerrilla warfare.[34] A notable mission involving a parachute drop was Operation Python. On 25 March 1943, eight Z Special members were dropped into a high plateau to assist stranded American airmen who had been downed over Borneo. On 30 June 1945, another detachment parachuted onto an enemy-held territory near Semoi in east Borneo. Three operatives landed inside a Japanese camp. One of them was killed during the exchange of fire with Japanese soldiers and the other two were captured. Both men, a New Zealander and a Malian, were tortured and later beheaded.[35] Z Special was disbanded in 1946. Paratroopers could, also be found in M Special, another Joint-Allied unit made up of volunteers from Australia, New Zealand, Holland and Great Britain. They fought against the Japanese between 1943 and 1945 in Dutch New Guinea and the Solomon Islands. Small teams from this unit landed behind enemy lines by sea, air or land mainly for reconnaissance and intelligence gathering. M Special was disbanded on 10 November 1945.

Chapter 6

Allied Airborne Operations in Europe (I)

Sicily

British and American airborne units were the spearhead of the Allied forces that invaded Sicily in July 1943 – regarded by the operation planners as a stepping stone between Africa and Hitler's 'Fortress Europe'.[1] According to the plan, a British airborne division and two American parachute units, being a regiment and a battalion, were to be dropped on the island before the sea landings. The paratroopers had to seize vital bridges and keep the enemy away from the invasion beaches. A shortage of transport planes and trained pilots prevented the deployment of more parachute troops in the operation.

The British 1st Airborne Division, commanded by Major General George F. Hopkinson, was to conduct three brigade-scale airborne operations. The Ponte Grande road bridge, south of Syracuse, was to be captured by the 1st Airlanding Brigade, the port of Augusta was to be seized by the 2nd Parachute Brigade and, finally, the Primosole Bridge over the Simeto River was to be taken by the 1st Parachute Brigade.[2] The first bridge, over the Anape River, was to be captured by glider-borne forces. The second bridge, on the outskirts of Catania, a major city of Sicily, was to be taken in an airborne assault. A third bridge, spanned the Leonardo River and named Ponte del Malati, was assigned to No. 30 Commando, a special Royal Marines unit. The attack on the town of Augusta by the British 2nd Parachute Brigade, scheduled for the second phase of the operation, was cancelled and the unit remained at Sousse, Tunisia, in a reserve role.[3] The objectives were overrun so fast in Sicily that the deployment of a second airborne brigade in the operation was regarded as unnecessary by the Allied high command.

Due to the shortage of planes and pilots, only one full regiment of the American 82nd Airborne Division (82nd Airborne) was able to jump. This was the 505th PIR, reinforced by a battalion of the 504th PIR. The rest of the 504th PIR was scheduled to parachute in and fortify the beachhead on Day 2 of the operation. The 505th PIR plus a battalion of the 504th PIR had to take the high ground near Ponte Olivo airfield, north-east of Gela, in what it was to be the first mass regimental combat jump in United States' history. The 1st and the 2nd Battalions of the 505th PIR were to land behind enemy lines and seize a vital road junction. The paratroopers, both British and American, had been told that Sicily was defended by Italian soldiers, some German troops and a few small Italian tanks. In fact, several highly trained German divisions, consisting of 30,000 men and 120 tanks, were deployed on the island. The Allied high command knew about this, but withheld the information from the invading commanders. It did so to prevent the Axis from realizing that some of their codes had been cracked by Allied intelligence.[4] By June 1943, the whole of the 1st Airborne Division, consisting of two parachute brigades and the 1st Airlanding Brigade, was concentrated at Susse. Paratroopers weighted down by as much as 150lbs (68kg) of weapons and equipment climbed through the aircraft doorways with a push from the man behind.[5]

The first C-47 transports loaded with American paratroopers began to take off from airfields in Tunisia at 09.10 on 9 July 1943. Within fifteen minutes the Regimental Combat Team (RCT) was airborne. It was made up of the 505th PIR, a battalion of the 504th PIR, the 456th Parachute Field Artillery Battalion and other supporting units of the 82nd Airborne Division. In the early morning hours of 10 July, the RCT flew right over a coastal artillery battery on its way to the dropping zone (DZ). The jump, which began at 09.30, was made from less than 400ft (123m).[6] A total of 2,000 American paratroopers landed on Sicily that night. Strong winds of up to 45mph blew the troop-carrying aircraft off course. High winds on the 505th PIR's DZ caused a large number of men to be scattered widely all over the island. After daylight, 400 men of the 505th had made their way to the command post (CP). Colonel James M. Gavin, the commander of the regiment, made it to the CP after three days. By 14 July, about two-thirds of the 505th PIR had managed to concentrate, while half the US paratroopers failed to reach their rallying points.[7] Despite the wide scattering of the air assault, the objectives were seized and the units linked up with the American 1st Infantry Division on 11 July. On 10 July, as elements of the 2nd Battalion, 505th PIR, approached a coastal artillery battery, the Italians opened up with rifle fire. The paratroopers used their 75mm howitzer and after firing a couple of rounds forced the Italians to raise the white flag. The Americans captured sixty enemy officers and other ranks. At about noon, the same battalion invaded Santa Croce Camerina. The 2nd Battalion next cleared out Vittoria, as well as other locations in the area.[8]

The British airborne force took off from six airstrips in North Africa at 18.00 on 9 July. It was carried by 105 C-47 and eleven Albemarle transport aircraft. In addition, Halifaxes and Stirlings towed eight Waco and eleven Horsa gliders having on board men and anti-tank guns of the Royal Artillery. Four aircraft, for mechanical reasons, failed to take off or had to turn back before they reached Malta. The formation, having turned north-east after Malta, was subjected to heavy anti-aircraft fire. Some planes were hit and went down in flames. Of the 147 gliders taking part in the attack on Ponte Grande Bridge, only twelve landed on target. Sixty-nine gliders were released too early by the towing aircraft and crashed into the sea, drowning 252 men. Among those who fell into the sea was Major General G.F. Hopkinson, who was eventually picked up by the landing ship HMS *Keren*. Of the remainder, fifty-nine gliders landed up to 25 miles (40km) away. Only one Horsa, transporting a platoon of the 2nd Battalion, landed near the bridge. Half of the men, headed by Lieutenant Luis Withers, swam across the river and took up positions on the opposite bank. Two hundred yards (180m) from there, a Horsa exploded on landing, killing all on board. Three of the other gliders landed within two miles (3.2km) of the bridge.

The Ponte Grande Bridge was captured by the British airborne force following a simultaneous assault from both sides. An Italian counter-attack was launched by 11.30. Four hours later, when German troops approached the bridge, only fifteen paratroopers were not wounded. With their ammunition gone, they had to surrender. The bridge was recaptured by the British at 04.40.[9] By the end of the day, it was known at Susse that the glider attack on the Ponte Grande bridge, though costly, had been successful. The British, although suffering heavy casualties, being confronted by seven Italian battalions, managed to hold the bridge until 15 July, when the British 5th Infantry Division made contact. The casualties of the 1st Airlanding Brigade during the invasion were 313 killed and 174 missing or wounded/injured. They also had fourteen glider pilots killed and a further eighty-seven wounded or missing.[10] Elements of the brigade who had landed elsewhere in Sicily destroyed communications links and captured artillery batteries.

On 10 July, the British 1st Parachute Brigade, commanded by Brigadier Gerald W. Lathbury, was dropped on four DZs close to the Primosole River on the southern edge of the Catanian plain. The start of the operation was a disaster, as thirty-four of the 105 aircraft were shot down by enemy fire and further ten were damaged and forced to abort the mission. Two Dakotas were downed by friendly fire and five more were damaged and forced to turn back. Of the surviving aircraft, only thirty-nine managed to drop their paratroopers within five miles (8km) of the correct DZ. Of the nineteen Waco and Horsa gliders transporting men and anti-tank guns, only four arrived intact and those not shot down en route were wrecked on their attempt to land. Many paratroopers were scattered over a large area with some of them landing not on Sicily but also on the Italian mainland, partly because of the strong wind and partly because of the evasive action taken by the pilots.[11] Only the equivalent of two companies was dropped in the correct locations. Many British landed on a DZ which had been used earlier by *Fallschirmjäger* of the 1st Parachute Division, as the Germans had chosen the date of the Allied invasion to reinforce the garrison of Catania with some elite troops. The German paratroopers attacked at dawn and shortly the two forces were engaged in a bitter fight.[12] Some British paratroopers landed inside an area where the German *Fallschirmjäger* had set up camp. They were killed or taken prisoner. Because of the fight, the landing of a British glider force, carrying artillery pieces and heavy equipment, had to be called off, although a number of them managed to touch down. Despite these setbacks and the tough defence by German and Italian forces, some 250 British captured the bridge intact. They resisted attacks from the north and south, holding out until nightfall against infantry, armour and attacks by aircraft. With casualties mounting and supplies running short, the paratroopers had to withdraw. The following day, British forces with armoured support tried to re-capture the bridge. They succeeded on 12 July.

Although the three bridges had been seized by British airborne forces for the use of the Eighth Army, it was not found possible to attack Catania from the coastal plain, as the Germans had been able to concentrate their defences there. The British decided not to press it in this area and to move instead inland around Aetna. The cost of the assault on Sicily for the 1st Airborne Division was 454 dead, 240 wounded/injured and 102 missing.[13] The losses by the 1st Airlanding Brigade were the worst of all the British units involved. They amounted to 313 killed and 174 missing or wounded/

injured. In the American sector, the port of Licata had been captured by the morning of 10 July. A company of the 1st Battalion, 505th PIR, accomplished the main objective of the entire 82nd Airborne Division, when Captain Ed Sayer and 250 men captured three small hills, thus taking control of a route that could be taken by German armour to reach the landing beaches. Many men lost their lives in the fighting and Sayer's exceptional bravery earned him the Distinguished Service Cross.

On 11 July, the remaining three battalions of the 504th PIR, commanded by Lieutenant Colonel Reuben Tucker, were ordered to parachute in and reinforce the centre of the sector along with the 376th Parachute Field Artillery and other supporting units. The 144 C-47s arrived in the area at the same time as an Axis air raid. The first planes started dropping their loads when a nervous Allied naval vessel fired on the formation. Immediately, other naval vessels and troops on shore joined in, shooting down friendly aircraft. It was one of the greatest friendly-fire tragedies in contemporary history. Twenty-three planes were destroyed, thirty-seven more were damaged and almost 400 casualties were confirmed. Among these was Brigadier General Charles L. Keerans, the 82nd Airborne's deputy commander. The American 325th GIR, part of the 82nd Airborne, was in North Africa, scheduled to be transported in Sicily. After what happened to the 504th PIR, 82nd Airborne's commander, Major General Matthew B. Ridgway, cancelled the operation. On 13 July 1943, the 504th PIR moved out, spearheading the 82nd Airborne's drive north-west along the southern coast of Sicily. It became part of Lieutenant General George S. Patton's Task Force 323, consisting mainly of the American Seventh Army.

Patton rushed towards Palermo in an effort to reach Messina, a port close to the Italian mainland, before the British forces.[14] Empedocle and Agrigento were captured and on 21 July the attack turned north with the 505th PIR and the 504th PIR marching as far as Trapani. The 3rd Battalion, 505th PIR, took the city's surrender and the long march was over. On 3 August, the capture of Centuripe, an isolated pinnacle of rock, by American paratroopers proved critical. The position was defended by German elite troops such as the Hermann Göring Division and the 3rd Parachute Regiment. In six days across Sicily the 82nd Airborne Division captured 23.191 prisoners with the majority of them being Italians. By the end of the campaign, the number of the Axis soldiers captured by the Allied forces rose to 132,000. Meanwhile, the Germans had pulled back in a fighting retreat to the north-eastern end of Sicily in preparation for their evacuation across the narrow strait between Sicily and the Italian mainland. The casualties (dead, missing and wounded) during the Allied invasion were 24,000 for the Germans and 8,000 for the Italians. On 20 August, the conquest of Sicily was complete. Two days later, Dakota planes began airlifting the American paratroopers to Kairouan in Tunisia.

The widespread landing in Sicily of airborne troops, both American and British, had a positive effect, as small isolated units, acting on their own initiative, attacked vital points and created confusion.[15] More than a thousand men of the 504th PIR had been dropped in isolated groups on various parts of the island. They carried out demolitions, cut lines of communication, established road blocks and ambushed German and Italian motorized columns. A positive thing about the scattering of the parachute troops was that the German command believed that the number of Allied troops dropped in Sicily was very much larger than it actually was. They caused such confusion over an extensive area that initial German reports estimated the number of American parachutists dropped to be 'over ten times' the actual number. American General Dwight Eisenhower, the supreme commander of the Allied forces in Europe, was not satisfied with the performance of the airborne units in Sicily and seemed prepared to have their role in future operations revised.[16] However, General George Marshall, the Army Chief of Staff, believed otherwise. He persuaded Eisenhower to set up a review board and withhold judgement until the outcome of a large-scale manoeuvre could be assessed. The exercise, which took place on 7 December 1943 near Fort Bragg in North Carolina, was judged by observers to be a great success. As a result of this exercise, in which the 11th Airborne Division was the main participant, division-sized airborne forces were deemed to be feasible, and Eisenhower permitted their retention.[17]

Mainland Italy

On 25 July 1943, Benito Mussolini was overthrown by King Vittorio Emmanuelle III and Italy eventually switched over to the Allies. Thirty thousand German troops were deployed in Italy at the time. The German forces immediately swooped upon Italian positions and made sure there was no uprising against them. The British 1st Airborne Division was to participate in an operation to seize intact the Italian ports of Taranto, Bari and Brindisi. The shortage of air transport meant that the division's two available brigades had to be transported by sea. The 4th Parachute Brigade had the 10th and the 156th Parachute Battalions available to take part in the landings as the 11th Parachute Battalion was left in Palestine. The 1st Parachute Brigade was held in reserve because of the heavy casualties sustained in Sicily. On 9 September, the same day as the amphibious landings at Salerno by the American Fifth Army, the British airborne division took part in an amphibious assault against Taranto.

Airborne troops didn't take part in the initial assault, remaining at the disposal of the Allied high command. The American paratroopers were settled in close to airfields in Sicily, while plans were made for the 82nd Airborne Division (82nd Airborne) to jump on or near three airfields east of Rome. The operation was called off at the last moment. The 1st and 2nd Battalions of the 504th RCT were trained in Sicily for a drop at Capua, but it had to be cancelled because the enemy, having been tipped off, was waiting on the DZ. In the end, the 504th RCT was picked to spearhead the first airborne operation in mainland Italy. On 13 September 1943, two battalions, the 1st and the 2nd, of the 504th RCT and Company 'C' of the 307th Airborne Engineers were dropped next to the beaches of Salerno Bay to support a shrinking Allied beachhead at Paestum. The assault force took the high ground at Altavilla. The operation at Salerno was not only a success but also a good example of mobility for an airborne unit. Within six hours of notification the 504th RCT, commanded by Lieutenant Colonel Reuben H. Tucker, developed and disseminated its tactical plan, prepared for combat, loaded aircraft and jumped onto its assigned DZ.

The 504th RCT's 3rd Battalion and the regiment's glider units arrived in the Italian mainland by sea. Troops of the 319th Glider Field Artillery Regiment landed on a coast near Maiori on 14 September and the regiment's 105mm howitzers, after quickly establishing their positions, opened fire against the Germans in support of a US Army Ranger' unit. Although outnumbered by the battle-hardened enemy forces, the 319th Glider Field Artillery Regiment held out for ten days until it was reinforced by the Fifth Army. On 15 September, the 325th GIR and the 504th RCT's 3rd Battalion landed at Paestum, 18 miles (29km) south of Salerno. They quickly advanced inland to seize the Ghiunzi Pass and a vital railway tunnel. Between 17 and 20 September, elements of the 325th GIR took up a position north-east of Albanella in support of the 504th RCT. Despite German attempts to throw the Americans off the mountain, the later held their ground. On 23 September, the 320th Glider Field Artillery Regiment landed on Paestum where it remained in divisional reserve. The 319th Glider Field Artillery Regiment had been assigned to support the 505th PIR near the Volturno River. Meanwhile, in Altavilla the enemy counter-attacked inflicting heavy casualties on the two battalions of the 504th RCT. The 3rd Battalion, then being held in reserve, rejoined the rest. The regiment repulsed the Germans and forced them to retreat from Salerno. On 4 January 1944, the 504th RCT, severely understrength, was pulled back to Naples. It was replaced in the front by the inexperienced 507th PIR. From 8 to 12 February, the 3rd Battalion, 504th RCT, took part in a sea-landing operation on Red Beach, behind the coastal town of Anzio. The campaign in Italy had been costly for the 504 RCT as over 1,100 casualties were sustained. Just under 600 of these were suffered during the fighting at Anzio alone. Two of the three battalion commanders had become casualties.

On 14 September 1943, it was the 505th Regimental Combat Team's (RCT's) turn. The 505th PIR and Company 'B' of the 307th Airborne Engineers parachuted next to Salerno Bay, making their second combat jump. Then, they marched towards the mountains and relieved the 504th RCT at Castel San Lorenzo, a little village east of the bay. By then, the Allied beachhead had been expanded and consolidated. On 1 October, the 505th RCT, supported by tanks of the British 23rd Armoured Brigade, captured Naples although it is believed by some that the 504th RCT had entered the city first. Major Edward C. Krause, commander of the 3rd Battalion, 505th PIR, has been mentioned as the man who raised the American flag on a central government building. The division's units were tasked with policing Naples, inhabited by a million people, and the nearby hills.

In 4 October, the 2nd Battalion, 505th PIR, was officially attached to the (British) 22nd Armoured Brigade. The battalion's mission was to seize five canal bridges on its way to the town of Arnone. The American paratroopers achieved all of their objectives quickly and efficiently, but sixty men were killed in the process and more were wounded. At night, the battalion was relieved by a British infantry regiment and was transported to Naples, where it resumed policing duties along with other units of the 505th PIR. On 31 November, the 82nd Airborne (minus the 504th PIR which remained) sailed to Northern Ireland.

Meanwhile, on 9 September 1943, at around midnight, Royal Navy warships entered the port of Taranto in southern Italy, transporting the British 1st Airborne

Division. This unorthodox operation ended up successfully although a minelayer with 200 men of the 6th (Royal Welch) Battalion on board hit a mine. The explosion was massive and the ship, HMS *Abdiel*, sank in three minutes. Many of the men didn't survive, including the commanding officer, Lieutenant Colonel J. Goodwin. A total of seven officers and fifty-one other ranks lost their lives. Four officers and about 150 men had to be taken to hospital with injuries. The other seaborne parachute battalions got ashore without difficulty. The 4th Battalion moved quickly through the town and took up positions to the north-west. The 5th Battalion occupied a small village 12 miles (19km) east of Taranto. The 1st, 2nd and 3rd Battalions formed part of the perimeter defence. Their first objective was the airfield of Gioia del Colle 30 miles (48km) inland. On their way to the airfield, near Castellaneta, the British came up against a roadblock defended by elements of the German 1st Parachute Division.[18] During the assault on the roadblock, the divisional commander, Major General George F. Hopkinson, was mortally wounded in the head by a burst of machine-gun fire. Major General Ernest E. Down took his place as commander of the 1st Airborne Division.

The following day, the 156th Battalion, now part of the 4th Parachute Brigade, seized a position overlooking the airfield of Gioia. The airfield and the nearby town of Gioia were captured by the 156th and the 10th Parachute Battalions. The 156th Parachute Battalion then advanced as far as San Basilio, launching a successful flank attack against the German paratroopers who were defending the town. Two days later, the 10th Parachute Battalion reached Bari. By 13 September, the 1st Airborne Division was more than 20 miles (32km) from Taranto. The capture of Gioia airfield was strategically important, as it could be used as a base for fighter-bombers to cover the beachhead at Salerno. The Germans, deceived by the number of the British patrols, evacuated the area the night of 16/17 September. By 19 September, the 4th Parachute Brigade had reached Foggia, the northernmost point of its advance. It was then relieved by the 1st Airlanding Brigade and ordered back to Taranto. Nine days of fighting cost the 4th Brigade eleven officers and ninety other ranks (killed, wounded and missing). The 1st Parachute Brigade initially remained in reserve. Then, they had to move first to Castellaneta and then to Altamura, from where they were withdrawn at the end of September. At the beginning of October, Captain John Timothy, of the 2nd Parachute Battalion, was ordered to drop with seven other ranks in the area north of Pescara. There he made contact with escaped Allied prisoners and directed them to the British lines.

When the 1st Airborne Division quitted Italy in November, it left behind the 2nd IPB, under the command of Brigadier C.H.V. Pritchard. The advantage of leaving General Harold R. Alexander with a brigade of trained parachute troops was obvious. The brigade was in action at the River Sangro in November fighting on the left flank of the Eighth Army. Thereafter, the brigade fought for four months on the Adriatic front, steadily losing men who could not be replaced. December came with frost and snow. Those taking part in patrols clad themselves in white sheets, for camoflague in the deep snow. At the end of March 1944, the 4th, 5th and 6th Parachute Battalions were ordered to withdraw to Naples. The 1st Parachute Brigade then moved to the Monte Cassino sector. The three battalions patrolled the Rapido River under the eyes of a watchful enemy entrenched on Monastery Hill. On one occasion, Major General Down, on a visit to the brigade, became the target of phosphorus shells launched from the hill and was slightly burnt.[19] By the end of May, the brigade was withdrawn from the line for a short rest at a camp south of Salerno. Three officers and fifty-seven other ranks from the 6th Parachute Battalion were dropped one hour before the last night of June to prevent the Germans, then withdrawing to the Pisa-Rimini line, from carrying out large-scale demolitions. To disguise the small size of the force, Brigadier Pritchard made extensive use of dummies. The success achieved was considerable. The Germans were deceived. One of their brigades was moved to deal with what they thought to be a serious threat to their communications and one division remained where it was and was not brought up to reinforce the troops then heavily engaged with the Eighth Army.

Normandy

Allied plans for D-Day in Normandy included landings on both flanks of the invasion zone by British and American airborne divisions. On 6 June 1944, several hours before the beach landings some 1,200 aircraft transported three divisions behind enemy lines. The American 82nd and 101st Airborne Divisions were assigned objectives on the Cotentin Peninsula, while the British 6th Airborne Division was tasked with capturing two bridges over the Caen Canal and the River Orne.[20] The Free French 4th SAS Squadron was assigned objectives in Brittany. In the early morning hours of 6 June, a number of dummy parachutists were dropped into an area south of Carentan in Normandy to fool the Germans into thinking that an airborne landing was taking place.[21] Elements of the French 4th SAS Squadron landed by parachute in the Vannes area of Brittany to interrupt enemy movements and organize the local Resistance. Between 6 and 9 June, 116 men of 4th SAS were dropped into northern Brittany to establish a 'base' near Saint-Brieuc and prevent the movement of German forces from western Brittany to Normandy.

The primary objective of the British 6th Airborne Division on day one of the Normandy landings was to secure the left flank of the Allied invasion zone by occupying and dominating the high ground between the River Orne and the River Dives. First, they had to capture intact two strategically-important bridges over the Caen Canal and the River Orne. These were, according to intelligence reports, well-guarded by the enemy and wired for demolition. The German forces stationed in the area included two infantry regiments and one armoured regiment. A small force of glider-borne troops in a coup-de-main operation was to secure the bridges for use by ground forces after the completion of the Allied landings. The 6th Airborne Division, commanded by Major General Richard Nelson Gale, had to destroy several other bridges in order to deny their use to the enemy.[22] The division's objectives also included the destruction of a German gun battery at Merville before the landing of troops on the nearby Sword Beach. Furthermore, the British paratroopers had to prevent German reinforcements approaching the landing areas from the east, destroy bridges crossing the River Dives and dig in around Ranville.[23] Having achieved their objectives, the 6th Airborne Division had to create and hold a bridgehead around the captured bridges.

The objective of the first mission involving British airborne forces was to capture the road bridges in Normandy across the River Orne and the Caen Canal. These bridges were the only exit eastwards for the British 3rd Infantry Division and the 1st (British Army) Commando Brigade after their landing on Sword Beach. Once captured, the two bridges had to be held against any counter-attack until the airborne force were relieved by troops advancing from the beaches. The mission was vital to the success of the main British landing in Normandy. If the Germans retained control over the bridges, the latter could be used by their armoured divisions to attack the invaders on the beaches. Assigned to the coup-de-main operation, was a company of the 2nd (Airborne) Battalion, Oxfordshire and Buckinghamshire Light Infantry (OBLI), part of the 6th Airlanding Brigade, 6th Airborne Division. The assault group, led by Major John R. Howard, comprised of six infantry platoons and an attached fifteen-man sapper platoon. The platoons, split into two forces, were to attack the bridges simultaneously. Infantry were to overcome the troops on guard duty and the engineers were to locate and disarm any demolition charges. If the bridges were destroyed by the enemy, the British airborne forces would be left cut off from the Allied ground forces.

The coup-de-main force took off from RAF Tarrant Rushton in Dorset at 22.56 on 5 June. It was 'D' Company of the 2nd OBLI, reinforced with two platoons from 'B' Company and a platoon of the 249th (Airborne) Field Company, Royal Engineers. They were on board six Horsa gliders that were towed by Halifax bombers. Glider No. 3 had to return to England, because the tow rope had parted too early. Gliders Nos 1 and 2 were released by the towing bombers seven minutes after midnight on 6 June. Number 1 glider crashed close to the canal bridge 16 minutes after midnight. Number 2, landing some distance away from No. 1, broke in half and came to halt at the edge of a large pond. One of the men fell into the water and drowned, becoming the first casualty of the Allied invasion of Normandy.[24] Only 100 men of the coup-de-main force made it to the rallying point, but their machine guns, mortars and signals equipment were missing.[25] Using sub-machine guns and grenades, the British cleared the area. By 00.21 the German resistance on the west bank of the Canal Bridge was over. After a brief exchange of fire, both bridges were captured by the airborne force and were later defended against tank, infantry and gunboat counter-attacks. On 7 June, at 13.30, the first men of the advancing British 1st (Army) Commando Brigade arrived at the bridges from Sword Beach. Of the 181 men of the coup-de-main force involved in the capturing of the bridges, two were killed and an additional fourteen wounded. Operation Tonga followed, dropping the 6th Airborne Division's parachute brigades near Caen to the east.

On 5 June, between 23.00 and 23.20, six Albemarle transport aircraft took off from England carrying the pathfinders of the 22nd Independent Parachute Company, who were to mark out the three DZs for use by the division's paratroop forces.[26] The pathfinders landed in the area between the rivers Orne and Dives, having among them Brigadier Nigel J. Poett, commander of the 5th Parachute Brigade. Due to a combination of heavy clouds and poor pilot navigation, only one pathfinder group was dropped correctly.[27] Without realizing the error, the pathfinders set up radio beacons and markers that caused a number of airborne troops to drop in the wrong area.

The team assigned to mark out the DZ area for the force tasked with destroying the Merville battery was bombed by RAF Lancasters which missed the artillery battery and hit the area the pathfinders were in.

The division's main airborne force for the operation, code-named Tonga, was divided into three groups. The first was made up of 239 Dakota and Stirling aircraft, as well as seventeen Horsa gliders, transporting the 3rd and the 5th Parachute Brigades. The second group consisted of Horsa and Hamilcar gliders, carrying the divisional headquarters and an anti-tank battery. The third group was formed of three Horsas transporting sappers and men from the 9th Parachute Battalion. The first group was scheduled to land at 00.50 on 6 June and the second group at 03.20. The third group was intended to land close to the Merville battery at 04.30. At 00.50 the first aircraft carrying the division's parachute units appeared overhead and the paratroopers started descending towards the DZs. Because of the clouds and pilot errors the 5th Parachute Brigade was dropped incorrectly and widely scattered. The 7th Parachute Battalion had so many missing that by 03.00 only about 40 per cent of the men had been accounted for. Relatively few supply containers had been found by the airborne troops, meaning that the men possessed few heavy weapons and radio sets. However, the 7th Parachute Battalion managed to rendezvous with the 2nd OBLI and establish a defensive line against German counter-attacks.

The first German responses to the capture of the bridges came between 05.00 and 07.00 in the form of isolated and often uncoordinated attacks by tanks, armoured cars and infantry.[28] Despite the fact that the parachute troops had been widely scattered, the units managed to secure their objectives. The coup-de-main force had been reinforced and the Caen Canal and the Orne River bridges had been held. The 7th Parachute Battalion's losses during the defence of the bridges amounted to eighteen dead and thirty-eight wounded. As the day progressed, a battalion of the 192nd Panzer Grenadier Regiment counter-attacked in the Bénouville area. The coup-de-main force and the 7th Parachute Battalion held their positions, knocking out thirteen of the seventeen tanks that tried to get through to the Caen Canal Bridge. The British paratroopers moved forward into Bénouville and cleared it of Germans in house-to-house fighting. By midday, most of the missing men from the 7th Parachute Battalion had arrived at the bridges.[29] Despite the ferocity of the German attacks, the bridges were held until 19.00, when the leading elements of the British 3rd Infantry Division arrived in the area and began to relieve the airborne troops. The actions of the 6th Airborne Division had severely limited the ability of the German defenders to communicate and organize themselves, ensuring that the seaborne troops could not be attacked by the vital first few hours after landing, when they were most vulnerable.

The 5th Parachute Brigade's other two battalions, the 12th and the 13th, were badly scattered when they were dropped at 05.00. When both units moved out from their rendezvous points, neither had more than 60 per cent of their strength, although individual troops and small groups would join up with the battalions throughout the day. Both of the battalions had been tasked with securing the area around the DZ and the two bridges captured by the coup-de-main force. The 12th and the 13th Parachute Battalions managed to secure the village of Le Bas de Ranville and the town of Ranville respectively. Both objectives were achieved during the night against fierce resistance by the enemy. The 12th Parachute Battalion was bombarded with heavy mortar and artillery fire and repelled two counter-attacks by the 125th Panzer Grenadier Regiment. The 3rd Parachute Brigade was scattered throughout the area due to weather conditions and pathfinder error in the marking of the DZ. The 8th Parachute Battalion, tasked with destroying two bridges near Bures and a third by Troarn, was widely scattered with a number of paratroopers landing in the operational area of the 5th Parachute Brigade. When the commanding officer, Lieutenant Colonel Alastair S. Pearson, arrived at the battalion rendezvous point at 01.20, he found only thirty paratroopers. By 03.30, this number had increased to just over 140. Having achieved its objective, the battalion moved north and took up position near Le Mesnil to widen the bridgehead formed by the division.

The 9th Parachute Battalion, tasked with destroying the Merville gun battery, was scattered throughout the area. Lieutenant Colonel Terence Otway, the commanding officer, landed 400 yards (370m) away from the DZ in a farmhouse being used as a command post by a German battalion. After a brief exchange of fire with the enemy, Otway and other scattered paratroopers disengaged and rushed to the DZ.[30] As the gun battery had to be destroyed by no later than 05.30, Otway set off for there at the head of only 150 paratroopers.[31] They linked up at the battery with the survivors of the pathfinder group who had been hit earlier by a RAF raid in the area. The force was ready by 4.30, when two gliders carrying the sappers landed close to the battery. When the battery was captured, the paratroopers disabled the artillery pieces with explosives. The 9th Parachute Battalion had achieved its primary target at a heavy cost: fifty dead and twenty-five wounded. The battalion then secured the village of Le Plein by expelling the platoon-size German garrison.

The 1st Canadian Parachute Battalion (1st CaPaBa) was allotted as its primary task the demolition of two bridges at Varaville and Robehomme. The battalion was transported to France in fifty aircraft and landed an hour in advance of the rest of the 6th Airborne Division in order to secure the DZ. In addition, the Canadian paratroopers were to protect the left (southern) flank of the British 9th Parachute Battalion during their attack on the Merville battery. The Canadians landed between 01.00 and 01.30 and were also scattered throughout the operational area. One group of paratroopers landed 10 miles (16km) away from their DZ. A number of Canadians were dropped in flooded areas around Varaville, and some of them drowned where they were dragged under the water by the weight of their equipment. After the demolition of the Robehomme Bridge, the 1st CaPaBa moved to the area of Varaville, where they destroyed a gun emplacement and demolished a bridge over Dirette Stream. A small group assaulted the fortifications outside Varaville that were manned by approximately 100 Germans. The casualties were heavy for the Canadians, but by 10.00 the enemy garrison had surrendered. By midday, the battalion had achieved all their objectives. During the invasion in Normandy and the consequent advance towards the River Sein, the 1st CaPaBa suffered 367 casualties. Of these casualties five officers and seventy-six men were killed or died of wounds.

Next to come was the third airborne operation. Its objective was to airlift forces of the 6th Airborne Division on the left flank of the British invasion beaches. Assigned to the operation were the 6th Airlanding Brigade, the division's reconnaissance regiment and one of the division's howitzer batteries. The combined force crossed the English Channel in 256 gliders towed by bombers and started arriving in two landing zones (LZs), one to the east of Saint-Aubin-d'Arqenay and the other to the north of Ranville, at 21.00. Only ten gliders missed the LZs. Casualties were light with the exception of a man who was fatally wounded by a sniper. Within ninety minutes the glider-borne troops had gathered at their rendezvous points. By midnight, the entire 6th Airborne Division had been fully deployed on the eastern flank of the invasion beaches, with the exception of the 12th Battalion, part of the 6th Airlanding Brigade, that was due to arrive by sea later in the day. The division ended the day with the 3rd Parachute Brigade holding a four-mile (6.4km) front, having the 9th Parachute Battalion at Le Plein, the 1st CaPaBa at Les Mesnil and the 8th Parachute Battalion south of Bois de Bavent. The 5th Parachute Brigade had the 12th Parachute Battalion occupying Le Bas de Ranville and the 13th Parachute Battalion holding Ranville. The 7th Parachute Battalion had been placed in reserve. The 6th Airlanding Brigade was poised to commit its two battalions to extend the bridgehead.

At 15.00 in 7 June, the 2nd OBLI was engaged in fierce house-to-house fighting at Escoville, three miles (4.8km) to the south of Ranville. The fighting cost eighty-seven casualties to the unit including the commanding officer. At 18.30 on 8 June, the 12th (Airborne) Battalion, Devonshire Light Infantry (12th Devons), took over the defence of Bas de Ranville from the 12th Parachute Battalion. A bridgehead was forced by the 6th Airborne Division, whose units successfully repulsed a number of German counter-attacks. By now the division's objectives were achieved despite the problems encountered. The capture of Bréville became essential to secure British positions and protect the newly-established Allied beachhead. The units assigned were the 12th Parachute Battalion and the 22nd Independent Parachute Company, supported by a company from the 12th Devons, a tank squadron from the 13th/18th Royal Hussars and five regiments of the Royal Artillery. The attack against Bréville started on 12 June at 22.00, when elements of the 12th Parachute Battalion, led by Lieutenant Colonel Johnny Johnson, advanced against the enemy positions. The attack cost the battalion 126 killed. Of the 564 Germans defending the village, only 145 were alive when it fell. This battle was one of the most important of the invasion. Had the division failed in Bréville, the Germans would have been in position to attack the landing beaches.

On 23 July, a 16-year-old paratrooper was shot dead by a German sniper near Le Mesnil. Private Robert Johns, of the 13th Parachute Battalion, was the youngest of the soldiers parachuted into Normandy.[32] The 6th Airborne Division held the area between the rivers Orne and Dives until 14 June, when the 51st (Highland) Infantry Division took over the southern part of the Orne bridgehead. The paratroopers held the left flank of the British invasion sector until going onto the offensive on the night of 16/17 August. Their objective this time was the mouth of the River Seine, 45 miles (72km) away. To assist them in carrying out their mission the division was reinforced by the 1st and the 4th SAS, the 1st Belgian Infantry Brigade and the Royal Netherlands Motorized Infantry Brigade. In nine days of fighting the 6th Airborne Division had advanced 45 miles (72km) and captured 400 square miles (1,036km²) of territory. By the end of the month, the combined force reached their objective at the river Seine.

Victory came at a high price. Since landing, the 6th Airborne Division's casualties were 4,457 of which 821 were killed, 2,709 wounded/injured and 927 missing.[33] Between 5 and 7 June, the division's casualties were 800 men out of the 8,500 deployed. German losses were estimated to be 400 dead and a further 1,400 captured.[34] In addition, fourteen German tanks were lost in the fighting around the Orne River and the Caen Canal bridges. The attacks against the British airborne forces had not been of sufficient strength to achieve a decisive result, according to their commander, Lieutenant General Gale. The Germans seemed to attack 'indiscriminately and in pursuit of no definite plan'.[35]

The combat assaults in June 1944 in Normandy involving the American divisions, the 101st Airborne and 82nd Airborne, were code-named Albany and Boston respectively. Each mission consisted of three regimental-size air drops. The 504th PIR, 101st Airborne, was not combat-ready as it had recently returned from the Italian front. Two new regiments, the 507th and the 508th, were attached to the division. The only unit with combat experience was the 505th PIR. The division's 325th GIR was reinforced by the addition of the 1st Battalion, 401st GIR, bringing it up to the strength of three battalions. On 7 June 1944, the 325th GIR would arrive by glider near St Marie-du-Mont and Sainte-Mère-Eglise. The 1st Battalion, 401st GIR, would come in by sea with the American 4th Infantry Division. The 101st Airborne's objectives were to secure the four causeway exits behind Utah Beach between Saint-Martin-de-Varevile and Pouppeville and ensure the exit route for the American 4th Infantry Division from the beach later that morning.[36] In addition, the division had to destroy a German coastal artillery battery at Saint-Martin-de-Varevile and the highway bridges over the Douve River at Saint-Come-du-Mont. It also had to capture the footbridges spanning the Douve River at La Porte and later secure the southern flank of the American VII Army Corps.[37] German forces opposing the operation included the 6th Parachute Regiment that was deployed to Carentan during D-Day.

Between 00.48 and 01.40 some 6,928 paratroopers made their jumps from 443 Douglas C-47 Skytrain transports into an intended objective area of roughly 15 square miles (39km²) in the south-eastern corner of the Cotentin Peninsula of Normandy five hours ahead of the D-Day landings. The DZs of the 101st Airborne were east and south of Sainte-Mère-Eglise. The 501st PIR DZs were north and east of Carentan. The main combat jumps were preceded at each DZ by three teams of pathfinders who arrived thirty minutes before the main assault to set up navigation aids including Eureka radar transponder beacons and marker lights to aid the C-47s in the dark. To achieve surprise, the parachute drops were routed to approach Normandy at low altitude from the west. The paratroopers were badly scattered by bad weather and enemy ground fire, with some troops being dropped as far as 20 miles (32km) to the north. The division's parachute artillery lost all but one of its howitzers in the drop. The 2nd Battalion, 502nd PIR, jumped on the wrong DZ with its commanding officer, Lieutenant Colonel Steve A. Chappuis, landing virtually alone on the correct DZ. The 101st Airborne destroyed two bridges along the Carentan highway and a railway bridge just west of it. They gained control of the La Barquette locks and established a bridgehead over the Douve River, which was located north-east of Carentan. They established a defensive line between the bridgehead and Valognes, cleared the area of the DZs to the unit boundary at Les Forge and linked up with units of the (American) 82nd Airborne. At 06.30, elements of the 1st Battalion, 502nd PIR, led by their commander, Lieutenant Colonel Patrick J. Cassidy, captured Saint-Martin-de-Vareville. The 101st Airborne, reinforced by 2,300 glider troops arriving by sea, achieved most of its D-Day objectives, but required four days to consolidate its scattered units and complete its mission of securing the left flank.

The second wave included the drop of the 506th PIR. The regiment was badly dispersed by the clouds and the intense anti-aircraft fire. Three of the eighty-one Dakotas were downed before or during the jump. Despite the opposition, the 1st Battalion, 506th PIR, was dropped accurately, but the regiment's 2nd Battalion landed incorrectly west of Sainte-Mère-Eglise. The 3rd Battalion, 501st PIR, was scattered, too. A company-sized team, headed by the divisional commander Major General Maxwell D. Taylor, reached the Puppeville exit at 06.00. After a six-hour house-clearing battle with enemy forces the American paratroopers secured the exit shortly before the 4th Division troops arrived to link up. The third wave also encountered severe flak, losing six aircraft. The drop was accurate as ninety-four of 132 'sticks' landed on or close to the DZ, part of which was exposed to machine-gun and mortar fire by the enemy. Among those killed at the DZ were two of the three battalion commanders of the 506th PIR. The surviving battalion commander, Lieutenant Colonel Robert A. Ballard, gathered 250 troopers and advanced towards Saint Com-du-Mont to complete his mission of destroying the highway bridges over the Douve. Less than half a mile from his objective, he was stopped by enemy forces. On 7 June, the 1st Battalion, 401st GIR fought several engagements in an effort to join 506th PIR's march on St Come-du-Mont, which they managed to do just before midnight near Angoville-au-Plaine. On 8 June, the 1/401st GIR spread out along the west bank of the Douve. Company 'C' led the battalion's assault across the river sometime after dark and then linked up with the 506th PIR.

The commander of the 501st PIR, Lieutenant Colonel Howard R. Johnson, gathered 150 troops and at 04.00 captured the main objective, the La Barquette lock. The bridgehead was reinforced by scattered paratroopers arriving from various destinations. At 04.30 a platoon of the 3/506th PIR, seized two footbridges near La Porte. A battery of four guns, near Sainte-Marie-du-Mont, was seized next by units of the 506th PIR, including the 1/401th GIR. At the end of D-Day, Major General Taylor had the operational control of approximately 2,500 of his 6,600 men. Two glider airlifts had brought in scant reinforcements. The 327th GIR had come across Utah Beach. The first reinforcement mission after the main parachute assault was code-named Chicago. Fifty-two C-47s, acting as tugs for an equal number of CG-4A Waco gliders, approached the LZ. On board the gliders were 155 men, sixteen anti-tank guns and twenty-five small vehicles. On its way, the formation drew ground fire resulting the going down of a C-47 and its glider near Pont l'Abbe. The first gliders were released under enemy fire at 03.54 from a flight altitude of 450ft (140m) Only six of them landed within the LZ. Most gliders ended up in fields to the east as far as two miles (3km) away. Even those that landed on target experienced difficulty with heavy cargo such as jeeps shifting during landing, crashing through the wooden fuselage and in some cases crushing personnel on board. Total casualties were five dead, seventeen injured and seven missing. Among the dead was the deputy commander of the 101st Airborne, Brigadier General Don Pratt.

The 101st Airborne Division had accomplished its most important mission of securing the beach exits. Two regiments, the 507th and the 508th, managed to hold La Fière Bridge after a bloody battle against numerically superior enemy forces, supported by tanks and artillery, that lasted several days. The American paratroopers then captured Montebourg Station. Saint-Côme-du-Mont had to be seized, as it was part of the division's original mission. The town was defended by a force including elements of the 6th Parachute Regiment. On 7 June, the understrength 1st and 2nd Battalions of the 506th PIR spread out in skirmish line in the dark. The American paratroopers, when attacking supported by six Sherman tanks, were subjected to persistent sniper fire. In the evening of 8 June, German troops started withdrawing without orders and in a few hours Saint-Côme-du-Mont was in American hands. On their way to Carentan German paratroopers demolished a railway bridge and a causeway. On 9 June, the 101st Airborne was ordered to take Carentan. The city was encircled the following day by the 502nd PIR and the 327th GIR, including the 1/401st GIR, and captured in the morning of 12 June. The German paratroopers defended the city against a bayonet charge by American paratroopers, developing into hand-to-hand combat. After fruitlessly attempting to repel the Americans with counter-attacks, the German paratroopers withdrew in the night of 11/12 June, being short of ammunition. On 13 June, the Germans launched a fierce counter-attack in an attempt to retake the town. Elements of the 501st PIR, the 506th PIR and the 327th GIR managed to hold Carentan with the support of elements of the American First Army's 2nd Armored Division. From 13 to 18 June, the division held its positions at Saint-Sauveur-le-Vicomte, thus helping the Allied forces to cut off the peninsula and isolate Cherbourg. The port town of Cherbourg fell into Allied hands on 29 June. Until 3 July, static warfare, including aggressive patrolling and the mopping-up of German strongholds on two hills by elements of the 505th PIR, were the characteristics of the division's activity. D-Day casualties for the 101st Airborne were calculated in August 1944 as 1,240: 182 killed, 338 wounded/injured and 501 missing presumed killed or captured. Casualties through 30 June were reported as 4,670: 546 killed, 2,217 wounded and 1,907 missing.

Operation Boston was the parachute combat assault in the Normandy landings involving the American 82nd Airborne. There was the 505th PIR, but not the 504th PIR, as the latter had not arrived in England in time to train for the invasion in northern France and had been replaced in the mission by two untested American regiments, the 507th PIR and the 508th PIR. There was also the 501st PIR minus its 3rd Battalion which was placed in division reserve. The division's fourth regiment, the 325th GIR, was scheduled to fly in on 7 June and half of the 327 GIR was to land by boat on 8 June. The regiment was reinforced by the 2nd Battalion, 401st GIR. Because of its experience, as it had made combat jumps in Sicily and the Italian mainland, the 82nd Airborne was assigned to the riskier of the missions involving American parachute forces in Normandy. The division's objectives were to capture the town of Sainte-Mère-Eglise, a crucial crossroads behind Utah Beach and block the approaches into the area from the west and the south-west. They were to seize causeways and bridges over the Merderet River at La Fière and Chef-du-Pont, destroy the road bridge over the Douve River at Pont l'Abbe (now Etienville) and secure the area west of Sainte-Mère-Eglise in order to establish a defensive line between Gouversville and Renouf.

To complete its assignment the 82nd Airborne divided itself into three forces. The three parachute regiments and support elements, commanded by Brigadier General James M. Gavin, made up 'Force A'. The glider regiment and the artillery battalions, commanded by Brigadier General Matthew B. Ridgway, formed 'Force B'. The remaining combat elements, division support troops and attached units, commanded by Brigadier General George P. Howel, were 'Force C', scheduled to land by sea. Pathfinders, parachuted at each of the division's three DZs thirty minutes earlier, set up navigation aids. To achieve surprise, the massive parachute drops were routed to approach Normandy at low altitude from the west. Some 6,420 paratroopers jumped from nearly 370 C-47s into an intended objective area of roughly 10 square miles (26km^2) located on either side of the Merderet River on the Cotentin Peninsula. The paratroops were organized into sticks – a planeload of troops numbering 15–18 men. The drops were scattered by bad weather and German anti-aircraft fire over an area three to four times as large as that planned. Two inexperienced units of the 82nd Airborne, the 507th PIR and the 508th PIR, were given the mission of blocking the approaches west of the Merderet River, but most of their paratroops missed their DZs entirely. During the action Private Joe Gandara of the 507th PIR earned the Medal of Honor for single-handedly attacking three German machine-gun emplacements. Elements of the 507th PIR were involved in the Battle of Graignes. Lieutenant Colonel George V. Millett, commander of the 507th PIR, was captured by the Germans near Amfreville on 9 June. He was replaced in command of the regiment by Lieutenant Colonel Edson Raff. The 507th PIR continued to fight in the Battle of Normandy, sustaining heavy casualties. The 508th PIR jumped at 02.15. Its immediate objectives were to capture Sainte-Mère-Eglise, secure crossings at the Merderet River, near La Fière and Chef-du-Pont, and establish a defensive line north from Neuville-au-Plain to Breuzeville-au-Plain. There they were to tie with the 502nd PIR of the 101st Airborne. Like most of the paratroop units the 508th was dropped in the wrong location. A 508th platoon leader, 1st Lieutenant Robert P. Mathias, was the first American officer killed by German fire on D-Day in Normandy. Of the 2,056 paratroopers of the regiment who participated in the D-Day landings only 995 returned. The regiment had suffered 1,061 casualties including the commanding officer, Lieutenant Colonel Herbert F. Batcheller.

The veteran 505th PIR jumped accurately and captured its objective, the town of Sainte-Mère-Eglise. By 01.00, the square of Sainte-Mère-Eglise was filled with German soldiers, when two 'sticks' were dropped in error directly to the village. They belonged to the 1st and 2nd Battalions, 505th PIR. Private John M. Steele, of the 2nd Battalion, landed on the steeple of the church. He remained hanging for two hours slightly wounded before the Germans took him prisoner. He managed to escape when the Americans attacked the village. The 319th GIR and the 320th GIR landed on the evening of D-Day near Sainte-Mère-Eglise. The first 148 men of the 325th GIR arrived in a pre-dawn flight of fifty-two Wacos on 7 June.[38] In a second wave later thirty-two Horsa gliders landed carrying more soldiers and more guns, medical staff, vehicles, equipment and supplies. The losses suffered by the 319th GIR and the 320th GIR were higher than the losses of the associated 325th GIR mainly because the two battalions landed on a LZ that was not secure, with many casualties inflicted by enemy anti-aircraft and machine-gun fire.

The 3rd Battalion, 505th PIR, seized Sainte-Mère-Eglise, making it the first town liberated in France. Elements of the 508th, 507th and 505th PIRs captured and secured Cauquigny against a German attack by a combined infantry and tank force. Brigadier General Ridgway commented on May 1972 that taking Cauquigny on 9 June 1944 was 'the hottest single incident' he had experienced in all his combat service 'both in Europe and later in Korea'.[39] By early July, the 82nd Airborne Division had seen thirty-three days of severe combat and casualties had been heavy. Losses were 5,245 men killed, wounded/injured or missing. The three PIRs of the 82nd suffered a 55 per cent casualty rate, while casualties among the glider troops were even higher, at 58 per cent. Although in divisional reserve, the 325th GIR lost 280 men in Normandy. The casualty rate of the division was higher yet. Of the twelve battalion commanders who jumped in Normandy on D-Day, only one, Lieutenant Colonel Louis Mendez, emerged from the campaign unhurt.[40] Between 6 June and 14 August 1944, the German army had suffered 23,000 men killed in action, 67,240 wounded and 198,616 missing or taken prisoner.[41]

Southern France

The early days of June 1944 found the British 2nd IPB on the Italian mainland, fighting as part of the British Eighth Army. The brigade was at Salerno when it received orders to join the 1st Airborne Task Force (ATF), commanded by Brigadier General Robert T. Frederick, for airborne operations in the south of France. Four other units, all American, were also part of the force, which was formed on July 1944 and was also identified as 1st Provisional Airborne Division. These were the 509th PIR, the 517th RCT and two battalions, the 550th (glider) and the 551st (parachute). Two French parachute battalions were also to be attached to the 1st ATF but were withdrawn following disagreements between the Allied high command and General Charles De Gaulle.[42] The British and American airborne forces were to take part in Operation Dragoon, a general attack on Southern France launched with the objective of capturing the vital ports of Marseilles and Toulon and increasing the pressure on the German forces by opening another front. The paratroopers were tasked with preventing German reinforcements from moving to the coast and seeking to interfere with the build-up of the main invading force coming by sea. The airborne assault part in Dragoon was code-named Operation Rugby. The initial idea was for simultaneous landings to be performed in Normandy and in the south of France, but the plan eventually had to be revised due to a shortage of landing craft and transport planes. After some preliminary operations, including a brigade-size parachute drop behind enemy lines, the Allied troops would land on the beaches of the Côte d'Azur supported by an 880-vessel naval task force. Against them were the scattered forces of the German Army Group 'G'. The 1st ATF was to land by parachute or glider at some distance from the assault beaches and secure communication links, prevent German reinforcements from moving to the coast and open the way into Le Argens and the Nartuby river valley, near Le Muy, for the invading forces of the American Seventh Army. The airborne landings would concentrate in an area around Le Muy, halfway between Draguignan and the landing beaches at Fréjus – Saint-Raphaël (Operation Rugby). The village of Le Muy, not far from Saint Tropez, was strategically important, being a three-road junction, some 15 miles (24km) inland from Fréjus. The three battalions of the 2nd IPB were to be taken to Le Muy from airfields at Ciampino, near Rome and Galera, in the Umbria region in central Italy.[43]

On 14 August, twenty-four hours before the airborne landings, commando units, including the US-Canadian First Special Service Force (FSSF), made an amphibious assault on Hyères, a group of four islands in the Var region. Two days later, with Hyères captured and Operation Dragoon in progress, the FSSF was transferred to the French mainland and attached to the 1st ATF. The sea landings started on 15 August at 08.00 – a few hours after the airborne assault. It was 03.30 when the first British paratroopers reached the ground. Half the 4th Battalion, a company of the 5th (Scottish) Battalion and most of the 6th (Royal Welch) Battalion landed on their DZ. Most of the rest were scattered over an area of nine miles (14km) north-west of Le Muy, around Fayence, as a result of the cloudy weather. According to Saunders, only seventy-three planes out of 126 dropped the British paratroopers in the correct locations.[44] Other parachutists landed as far away as Cannes. The 5th Battalion went astray mostly because its men were to be dropped on a signal from the leading aircraft. Due to a technical problem, the pilot of the leading aircraft was unable to pick up the Rebecca Eureka beacon beamed from the DZ by the pathfinders. Unable to find the DZ, he started drifting over mountainous country. Three-quarters of the 5th Battalion were scattered over a wide area some 15 to 20 miles (24 to 32km) away from their destination and further inland. 'B' Company proved more fortunate as it landed on the DZ in relatively good order. In mixed parties 'A', 'C' and 'D' Companies, having determined their whereabouts, began the long march to Le Muy.

The American parachute drop started at 04.30. The 509th PIR was scattered more than the British. Only two companies of the regiment and two batteries of the 439th Parachute Field Artillery Battalion landed correctly. Of the American parachutists some landed eight miles (13km) to the east of Le Muy and others thirteen miles further. The 517th RCT fared even worse as none of its men landed on their assigned DZ. Once on the ground, the paratroopers regrouped. Most of the 1st and the 2nd Battalion of the 517th RCT reached their assembly areas shortly after dawn and the British troops who had landed near Callas arrived there late in the morning. Overall, less than 40 per cent of the troops in the pre-dawn drops landed in their DZs and by dawn at 06.00 only about 60 per cent of the men had assembled in the Le Muy area. Only seventy-three 'sticks' out of 126 landed on the right DZs.[45] The 4th and the 6th Battalions landed correctly, but two-thirds of the 5th Battalion were scattered over a wide area some 15–20 miles (24–32km) away from its destination and further inland. However, fog still blanketed the landing areas when the aircraft towing gliders arrived. Some pilots turned back without cutting their tows, finally returning at 18.00. The 551st Battalion dropped into the 517th's DZ at 18.10 as planned, while the 550th arrived in their gliders at 18.30, also on schedule. Support units that came in by gliders later in the day also landed according to schedule. By 19.00, 90 per cent of the troops and equipment brought in by the gliders was ready for action. Meanwhile, the scattered paratroopers of the 2nd IPB on their way to Le Muy were inflicting much damage to the enemy. In places, the Germans resisted stoutly and Lance-Corporal Warnock and Private Kadique of 'D' Company found themselves holding a farm for an hour and a half against a sizeable enemy force armed with machine guns.

Allied paratroopers interrupted the communication lines of the German LXII Corps at Draguignan and eventually trapped its headquarters in the city. The British, having secured the high ground along both sides of Le Argens River and the high ground to the north of the village, established roadblocks and launched aggressive patrols. At the same time, the 517th RCT occupied the hills overlooking the Toulon – Saint-Raphael corridor in the vicinity of Les Arcs, five miles (8km) west of Le Muy. The 509th PIR had already dug in on the high ground south of Le Muy with eleven 75mm guns in position overlooking the town. An attempt to capture Le Muy was mounted by the 550th (Glider) Battalion after dark, but the attack failed and the battalion had to withdraw. On the morning of 16 August, the 550th GIB attacked Le Muy again and by 15.30 it was in Allied hands. The German withdrawal from the Les Arcs area started during the night. The following day the counter-attacks launched by the Germans were largely defeated and Allied mobile forces were eventually linked up with the airborne troops in Le Muy.[46] At 23.00 on 16 August, men of the 551st (Parachute) Battalion stormed the German headquarters at Draguignan and General Ludwig Bieringer was captured at his desk.

With the seizure of this town the 1st ATF's work was complete – all of its objectives had been taken and were being secured. Hindered by total Allied air superiority and a large-scale uprising by the French Resistance, the weak German forces tried to establish a defence line at Dijon, central France and when that became impossible, they started to withdraw orderly from Southern France. With the Germans retreating, Allied forces captured Toulon on 26 August and Marseilles twenty-four hours later. Most of Southern France was liberated in a span of only four weeks, during which the Allied airborne and glider-borne units had suffered 450 killed, missing and wounded/injured. Following Operation Rugby, the 1st ATF moved north-east, covering the right flank of the Seventh Army and contributed to the liberation of Cannes and Nice. Nice was liberated by the 551th PIB on 29 August. The battalion was later deployed to the Alpes Maritime area in a static role. On 23 November, the 1st ATF was disbanded with most of the units being attached to the American XVIII Airborne Corps. The 2nd IPB had returned to Italy from the beginning of September. The brigade moved from Rome to Bari, where it started preparations for an airborne landing in Greece.

Chapter 7

Allied Airborne Operations in Europe (II)

After Normandy, the Allied airborne forces were withdrawn to England with the exception of the British 6th Airborne Division, which remained in northern France until early September. On 16 August 1944, the First Allied Airborne Army (FAAA) was created as a result of requests for better coordination of airborne operations. The 'First Triple A' was made up of the American XVIII Airborne Corps, commanded by Major General Matthew B. Ridgway, and the British I Airborne Corps, commanded by Lieutenant General Frederick 'Boy' Browning. The command of the FAAA was initially given to Lieutenant General Lewis H. Brereton, United States Army Air Force (USAAF). One of the first orders to come from Brereton was that all future airborne operations would be conducted in broad daylight.[1] This was made possible by the fact that the Allies had the control of the skies and could provide their airborne forces with the required umbrella of air cover on all future jumps. After sweeping through France and Belgium and following the pursuit of the German armies northwards and eastwards, Eisenhower intended to keep the retreating Germans under pressure. He believed that advance on a broad front would soon cause German forces to collapse. Field Marshal Bernard Montgomery, commanding the Anglo–Canadian 21st Army Group, wanted to liberate Holland as soon as possible in order to neutralize the V-2 rockets' launch sites which were bombarding London from Dutch soil.[2]

Arnhem

Montgomery, who had been appointed Colonel Commandant of the British Parachute Regiment after Normandy, suggested an airborne operation, which could enable the Allies to reach the North German Plain. The Allied forces were going, as Browning put it, to advance into Germany over a 'carpet' of airborne troops.[3] The plan, as outlined by Montgomery, required the seizure by airborne forces of several bridges on Highway 69 across the Maas (Meuse) River and two arms of the Rhine (the Waal and the Lower Rhine), as well as several smaller canals and tributaries. Crossing these bridges would allow British armoured units to outflank the Siegfried Line defences, advance into northern Germany and encircle the Ruhr, Germany's industrial heartland, thus ending the war. If successful, the plan would open the door to Germany and hopefully force an end to the war in Europe by the end of 1944.[4]

The initial proposal was for a British and Polish operation code-named Comet. It involved the British 1st Airborne Division, including the division's 1st Airlanding Brigade, and the Polish 1st Independent Parachute Brigade in a coup-de-main operation to secure bridges on the Rhine River. The plan was eventually expanded to include two subsidiary operations, an airborne assault by most of the FAAA (including two US airborne divisions) to seize key bridges and towns along the expected Allied axis of advance (Market) and a ground forces' attack (Garden). Market-Garden was to be the largest airborne operation up to that point in the Second World War. The airborne would drop along a 50-mile (80km) strip of highway running from Eindhoven to Arnhem, seizing control of bridges, strategic military positions and towns along the way. Monty had underestimated the problems of carrying out such a deep penetration on a narrow front. As Browning famously protested to Monty: 'Sir, I think we might be going a bridge too far!'[5]

Market would be the largest airborne operation in history, delivering over 34,600 men of the Allied airborne forces – 20,011 were to land by parachute and 14,589 by gliders. Gliders were also to bring in 1,736 vehicles and 263 artillery pieces. To deliver the thirty-six battalions of airborne infantry and their support troops to Holland 1,438 C-47 transport aircraft and 321 converted RAF bombers had to be used as well as 2,160 Waco, 916 Horsa and 64 Hamilcar gliders.[6] Only 60 per cent could be delivered in one lift, so it was decided the split of the troop-lift over successive days. The strategic goal of the operation was to encircle the Ruhr in a pincer movement.

The plan consisted of two operations. Airborne forces to seize bridges and other terrain operating under the tactical command of the Allied I Airborne Corps, commanded by Lieutenant General F. Browning, in Operation Market and ground forces of the British Second Army, commanded by Lieutenant General Brian Horrocks, to move north spearheaded by the XXX Corps in Operation Garden. Initially expecting an easy advance, the XXX Corps was to reach the airborne force at Arnhem within two to three days.[7] Market would employ three of the six divisions of the FAAA, led by the British 1st Airborne Division. Also assigned to the operation were two American airborne divisions, the 82nd and the 101st, and the Polish 1st Independent Parachute Brigade, commanded by Brigadier General Stanisław Sosabowski. The 504th PIR, now back at full strength, was reassigned to the 82nd Airborne Division, while the 507th PIR was assigned to the 17th Airborne Division. The latter was left out of the operation because it had only recently arrived from the United States and was considered to be unprepared and not trained in time for combat.[8] The division remained in England as a theatre reserve.

The operation depended on taking a total of nine bridges, the last being at the city of Arnhem over the Rhine River. The 101st Airborne Division, commanded by Major General Maxwell D. Taylor, was assigned the southernmost bridges at Eindhoven, Son, St. Oedenrode and Veghel. The division would drop in two locations north of XXX Corps to take the bridges north-west of Eindhoven at Son and Veghel. The 101st Airborne was to anchor the British Airborne Corps' southernmost flank and secure a 15-mile (24km) sector between Eindhoven and Veghel. The 82nd Airborne Division (82nd Airborne), under Brigadier General James M. Gavin, would drop north-east of them to take the bridges at Gave and Nijmegen. The British 1st Airborne Division, commanded by Major General Roy Urquhart, with the Polish 1st Independent Parachute Brigade attached, would drop at the extreme end of the route, tasked with capturing the road bridge at Arnhem and the rail bridge at Oosterbeek. The 52nd (Lowland) Infantry Division, a unit recently trained to become air-transported, would be flown to the captured Deelen Airfield on D+5.

Also assigned to Operation Market-Garden was the 1st Airborne Division's 1st Airlanding Brigade, which was part of the strategic reserve during the landings in Normandy. The plan of the operation called for the majority of the brigade to land on Day 1. The division's parachute brigades would head for Arnhem and capture the bridges over the Lower Rhine, while the 1st Airlanding Brigade would secure the drop zones for units arriving on the second and third day of the operation.[9] When all the division's units had arrived, the brigade would take up defensive positions at the west of Arnhem.[10] The Poles would land on 19 September on the south side of Neder Rijn (Lower Rhine) almost due south of the Arnhem Bridge and somewhat east of the town of Elden. Their mission was to reinforce the British 1st Airborne Division with clean-up operations and secure the bridge. The British and the Poles had been given the most hazardous and difficult objective of Operation Market-Garden. The bridge at Arnhem was, in effect, the gateway to Germany and every German in the area could be expected to lay down his life to keep it from falling into Allied hands. During the operation's planning stages the high command agreed to allow the division commanders to choose their own drop and landing zones. Taylor and Gavin were shocked when they saw the DZs and LZs chosen by the British. They were six to eight miles (10 to 13km) west and north-west of their objective, the Arnhem highway and bridge. Urquhart had paid attention to the RAF pilots complaining that Arnhem was too heavily defended by enemy anti-aircraft batteries and warnings of heavy losses among the airborne troops if they were forced to fly within range of them.

The commanders of the troops taking part in the operation were told to expect only limited resistance from second-rate German units. This was far from the truth. By 7 September, two German infantry divisions, the 719th and the 176th, were dispatched to Holland to stop the Allied advance. At this stage, the II SS-Panzer Corps was also deployed on Dutch soil. There were also seven regiments of the First Parachute Army, commanded by Major General Kurt Student.[11] At the time of Operation Market-Garden, two infantry divisions from the Fifteenth Army were deployed in Brabant to act as a reserve. Intelligence information about the location of the 9th and the 10th Panzer Divisions at Nijmegen and Arnhem were rejected by Montgomery who refused to alter the plans for the landings of the 1st Airborne Division.[12] On 16 September 1944, five Dutch-speaking troopers of the 5th Belgian Independent Parachute Company of the SAS were dropped into Holland to operate around Arnhem. Their mission, code-named Fabian, was to collect intelligence concerning enemy dispositions and the location of V-2 rocket sites.[13]

Market-Garden was initially successful. Several bridges between Eindhoven and Nijmegen were captured by the American 82nd and 101st Airborne Divisions. Then came the really difficult part of the whole operation: keeping open the highway along which the British Second Army had to pass to reach the British airborne forces which were fighting at the northern end of the 'corridor'. However, the demolition of the division's primary objective, a bridge over the Wilhelmina Canal at Son, a municipality near Eindhoven, delayed the capture of the main road bridge over the Maas until 20 September. Faced with the loss of the bridge at Son, the 101st Airborne unsuccessfully attempted to capture a similar bridge a few kilometres away at Best but found the approach blocked. Other units continued moving to the south and eventually reached the northern end of Eindhoven. At 06.00 on 18 September, the Irish Guards, part of the British Guards Division, resumed the advance while facing determined resistance from German infantry and tanks. At around noon, the 101st Airborne were met by the lead reconnaissance units from the British XXX Corps. At 16.00 a radio message alerted the main force that the Son bridge had been destroyed. By nightfall, the Guards Division had established itself in the Eindhoven area, but transport columns were jammed in the packed streets of the town and were subjected to German aerial bombardment during the night. XXX Corps engineers constructed a Bailey bridge within ten hours across the Wilhelmina Canal. The longest sector of the highway secured by the 101st Airborne later became known as 'Hell's Highway'.

The PIRs of the 101st Airborne were to jump on 17 September. The 327th GIR was to arrive on D+1 and the artillery units were scheduled for D+2, on the 19th. The PIRs had to take off from Membury, Aldermaston and Chilbolton airfields. The drop was made from an altitude of 1,500ft (452m).[14] The 506th PIR landed near Zon and the 502nd further north. The 501st jumped north of the 502nd, near the town of Veghel. The 1st Battalion, 501st PIR (1/501st PIR), was dropped some five miles (8km) east of the planned DZ. In spite of the paratroopers' scattering, the four bridges in Veghel were captured intact. Elements of the regiment also gained control of the rail and road bridges over the Wilhelm Canal and the Aa River. The 506th PIR captured the road bridges over the Dommel River at St. Oedenrode and guarded the DZs for later use by the glider-born force. The 2nd and 3rd Battalions, 506th PIR, methodically cleared Zon, while the 1st Battalion moved to the south to secure the bridge crossing the Wilhelmina Canal. When the battalions appeared advancing, the Germans blew the bridge. The 508th PIR, after the jump, established and held a vast area having German troops on three sides of their position. The regiment additionally seized and held the Berg en Dal hill from where they could control the Groesbeek-Nijmegen area. They also cut Highway K preventing the movement of enemy reserves. Some 933 gliders were used by the 101st Airborne to transport troops, guns and supplies. The 506th PIR managed to cross the river and the following day to liberate Eindhoven. With the exception of a bridge south of Best, the division had achieved all its Day 1 objectives. The next mission was to hold and keep open 'Hell's Highway' despite German counter-attacks. Near Best elements of the 502nd PIR and the 327th GIR managed to encircle a large German force which was forced to surrender. On 22 September, elements of the 506th PIR and the 327th GIR, plus the 1/401st GIR, defended Uden and Veghel, respectively, against German counter-attacks. On 25 September, elements of the 506th PIR stopped another German attack at Koevering, thus keeping the highway open.

Fighting off German counter-attacks, the 101st Airborne captured its objectives between Grave and Nijmegen. However, the failure of the British 1st Airborne Division to seize the Arnhem bridge allowed the Germans to move defenders to the

Nijmegen bridge, while the 82nd Airborne failed to capture Nijmegen bridge when the opportunity presented itself early in the battle. When the British XXX Corps arrived in Nijmegen six hours ahead of schedule, they found themselves having to fight to take a bridge that should have already been in Allied hands. In the afternoon of Wednesday, 20 September 1944, the 82nd Airborne conducted a successful assault on the river crossing of the Waal river, capturing the north end of the Nijmegen road bridge. The paratroopers attacked the bridge from the south with British tanks providing supporting fire. At the same time, the men downstream paddled their tiny craft from the opposite shore while the Germans fired upon them from the north shore with everything from rifles and machine-guns to mortars and artillery. Many men were killed in mid-stream by this fire, while others drowned after falling from capsized boats. The assault force finally made it across and charged across yards of open shoreline through withering fire. Many Germans were not given a chance to surrender.[15] By 19.15, both the railway and the main road bridges at Nijmegen were securely in Allied hands. The Americans lost 134 men (killed, wounded or missing) taking the Nijmegen bridge. The costly success of the Nijmegen bridge seizure was followed by the failure to take the main prize: the British 1st Airborne Division was lost at the Battle of Arnhem. Market-Garden turned into a defensive operation for several units. During the operation, 19-year-old Private John R. Towle, of the 504th PIR, was posthumously awarded the 82nd Airborne's second Medal of Honor. Between 27 and 30 September, the 325th GIR (including 2/401st GIR), which had landed in Holland on 23 September, was involved in the battle for Kiekberg Forest, an area full of steep hills and valleys. By 30 September, half of the forest had been cleared from enemy troops. The regiment held their ground against a German counter-attack. The 325th lost 217 men in Holland.

It was decided that the 1st Parachute Brigade and the 1st Airlanding Brigade of the British 1st Airborne Division would land on the first day of the operation. The division's 4th Parachute Brigade would arrive on the second day.[16] The DZs and the LZs would be secured by the 1st Airlanding Brigade. The division's mission was to capture intact the road, rail and pontoon bridges over the Lowe Rhine at Arnhem and hold them until relieved, which was expected to happen two or three days later. Twelve Stirlings carried the six officers and 180 other ranks of the 21st Independent Parachute Company. They were the British pathfinders under Major B.A. Wilson who landed near Arnhem.[17] Their duty was to lay out the various aids and indications on the DZ. The drop of the main force in Arnhem started thirty minutes after the pathfinders, at 13.30. The drop of the 1st Airborne Brigade and the landing of the gliders with the 1st Airlanding Brigade were more successful than anything which had so far been achieved by the airborne forces of either side in the war, even during an exercise. Nearly 100 per cent arrived at the right time and place. By 15.00, the units were ready to move.

On 17 September 1944, the 1st Parachute Brigade and the 1st Airlanding Brigade landed some distance from its objectives and was heading towards Arnhem. They were quickly hampered by unexpected resistance, including Panzer units. The airlanding brigade dug in to secure the landing grounds. There was a serious communication problem among the units because most of the radio equipment used by the British had an effective range of only up to 3 miles (5km). Of the Parachute Brigade only the 2nd Battalion, largely unopposed, made it to the bridge. The railway bridge was blown up as the British paratroopers approached it. Elements of the 2nd Battalion, led by Lieutenant Colonel John Frost, had taken the northern end of the Arnhem road bridge. Frost's plan was for 'A' Company to move straight to the main bridge, while 'C' Company, following in the rear, to seize the railway bridge. 'B' Company was allotted to capture the nearby pontoon bridge and the high ground controlling the entrance to Arnhem from the west at Den Brink. The force at the bridge under Frost's command eventually amounted to between 300 and 400 men. 'C' Company remained near the railway bridge under fire from an armoured car and from machine guns posted in Den Brink. Frost established his headquarters in a house just north-west of the northern end of the bridge. Meanwhile, XXX Corps was unable to advance north as quickly as anticipated. Their advance, led by tanks and infantry of the Irish Guards, started with the parachute drop, but, after crossing the Dutch border, they were attacked by German forces including tanks and elements from two *Fallschirmjäger* regiments. They could only advance as far as Valkenswaar. The operation was already starting to fall well behind schedule. By the end of the first 24 hours' fighting, a British force, including the 2nd Parachute Battalion, was holding the northern end of the Arnhem bridge and had successfully repelled the attacks. Their casualties, however, were increasing and they were in urgent need of reinforcements.

On the night of 17/18 September, the divisional commander, Major General R.E. Urquhart, was reported missing. The commander of the 1st Airlanding Brigade, Brigadier Philip Hicks, then assumed command of the division.[18] Urquhart was not a trained parachutist and so flew to Arnhem by glider. On landing, he had set out to visit units of the 1st Parachute Brigade. On reaching the 3rd Battalion, he met Brigadier Lathbury in the latter's HQs in Heelsum near Arnhem. The area was under attack by German forces. It was not until the morning on 19 September that he was able to leave the house he was hiding in at a German-controlled area and reach the divisional headquarters at Hartenstein. By the second day, the 9th SS-Panzer Division arrived in Arnhem deploying to the west of the city and cutting off access to the bridge. In the early hours of the following morning, the defenders of the bridge were reinforced by elements of the 'B' Company and a platoon of the 3rd Battalion. The fight was still well-sustained, but ominously the number of wounded grew steadily higher and higher.

By this time, the men were desperately short of water, food, sleep and, above all, ammunition. A 24-hour ration was all that a man carried and until the division was resupplied there would be no more. Day 2 of the operation found in the bridge only the 2nd Parachute Battalion as other divisional units had been halted by the German defences. The 1st Airlanding Brigade's 2nd South Staffordshire (Staffords) Regiment was then ordered to link up with the 1st Parachute Brigade in an attempt to reach their objectives. However, the 1st Staffords failed to break through the German defenders. At 15.00, several hours behind schedule, the 4th Parachute Brigade landed under fire from the enemy. The brigade's 11th Battalion was sent towards Arnhem to assist in the attempt to break through to the bridge linking up with the 1st and the 3rd Battalions of the 1st Parachute Brigade. The 10th and the 156th Battalions moved to take up their planned positions north-west of Arnhem. The men of the 4th Parachute Brigade parachuted with a four-hour delay because of the fog in the English airfields. They were shortly attacked by enemy forces with the fighting lasting until nightfall. Most of the units after landing headed towards the main bridge. Some of these units never made it as they fell on tanks and had to withdraw suffering heavy casualties. 1st Airlanding Brigade's 1st King's Own Scottish Borderers (KOSB) was attached to the 4th Parachute Brigade, guarding the landing ground for the arrival of the Polish airborne unit on day three. On day two, attempts by the 1st and the 3rd Parachute Battalions, 1st Parachute Brigade, to fight through to the Arnhem bridge were unsuccessful. At the bridge, the 2nd Parachute Battalion continued to hold out against German armoured and infantry attacks.[19] By the afternoon of Tuesday, all attempts to reach the bridge by the reinforcements, whether parachute or glider-borne, had failed and would continue to fail as the enemy was very strong and moreover possessed armour and heavy weapons. Meanwhile, the advancing XXX Corps was facing determined resistance from German infantry and tanks. By nightfall, elements of the corps managed to reach Eindhoven – being always behind schedule.

As Day 3 dawned, the 2nd Staffords and the 1st Parachute Battalion attacked at 04.00 – their objective being to link up with the 3rd Parachute Battalion that was trapped around St. Elizabeth's Hospital. The attack failed but allowed Major General Urquhart to rejoin the division from the position where he had been trapped by the Germans.[20] The 1st Airlanding Brigade then came under attack from the west and north-west. During the night, the KOSB had tried to take the high ground at Koepel but were stopped by heavy machine-gun fire and instead dug in. The remainder of the 4th Parachute Brigade, advancing north of the railway line, also encountered a strong German defence line and were unable to progress any further. All three battalions were ordered to withdraw south of the railway line towards Wolfheze.

In the morning of the third day, 19 September, the 1st, 3rd and 11th Battalions, as well as the 1st Airlanding Brigade's 2nd (Airborne) Battalion, Staffordshire Regiment, tried to fight through to the bridge. Trapped in the open, the 1st Battalion was decimated and the 3rd had to withdraw.[21] The 11th Battalion was now exposed by the withdrawal and overwhelmed. Unable to break through the German line, the remaining men retreated towards the main force, now at Oosterbeek. In the north, the 10th and the 156th Battalions were spotted as they attempted to seize the high ground of the woods north of Oosterbeek. Both battalions came under German fire and were unable to advance any further. Ordered to fall back on Wolfheze and Oosterbeek, they had to fight all the way with the Germans in close pursuit. In the continuous attacks by the Germans against the defensive pocket at Oosterbeek Lance Sergeant John Baskeyfield of the Staffords destroyed with anti-tank guns three enemy tanks before he was killed by a shell from a fourth tank. For his actions he received a posthumous Victoria Cross.[22] The KOSB had by now arrived at the perimeter being formed around Oosterbeek and took positions south of the railway line just north of the divisional headquarters. At 08.20, XXX Corps managed to get as far as Grave. In the afternoon of 19 September, supplies were parachuted to the British paratroopers, but some of them fell into German hands. On numerous occasions the DZs were under German control thus making the work of the pilots more dangerous. Meanwhile, at the Arnhem bridge, the 2nd Battalion still held out but being short of supplies, their position was becoming untenable. The Germans had started destroying with tank, artillery and mortar fire the buildings occupied by the battalion. At Oosterbeek, the divisional area was under continuous mortar and artillery attack.

The first Poles had landed in Holland by glider on 19 September, but due to bad weather (dense fog) over England the parachute section of the Polish 1st Independent Parachute Brigade was held up.[23] The thirty-five gliders, mainly carrying anti-tank guns and vehicles, were able to take off, but had the misfortune to arrive above the LZ as the British 4th Parachute Brigade was retreating across it. The gliders came under fire on landing from Germans pursuing the British. The remnants of the Poles eventually reinforced the British airborne force at Oosterbeek. Owing to bad weather and a shortage of transport planes, the drop of the Polish parachute infantry battalions east of the village of Driel, some 2.5 miles (4km) south-west of Arnhem, on the south bank of the Lower Rhine, was delayed by two days. The Poles were carried to Arnhem on 21 September. Nearly half of the 114 C-47s had to abort and come back to England because sometimes they flew into increasingly bad weather. When the Poles jumped at 05.00, they descended into an inferno, as their newly-assigned DZ was under the control of the Germans that had set up machine guns and mortars. Many Polish paratroopers were killed getting out of their harness and while retrieving their gear. The Poles sustained casualties, but managed to assemble in order. They dug in and relieved part of the pressure on the British airborne division, as some German forces were diverted to confront them. The Poles were without anti-tank capability as the brigade's light artillery battery had been left in England due to a shortage of gliders. They set up a defensive hedgehog position. As they couldn't cross the Lower Rhine to reinforce their British colleagues since no ferry could be found, the Poles spent the night ferrying men across the river on small boats – four and five at a time. Most of them made it across, but many were either wounded or killed by enemy fire. In total, 200 Polish paratroopers crossed the Lower Rhine in two days. They were able to cover the subsequent withdrawal of the survivors of the British 1st Airborne Division. On 26 September, the Poles were ordered to march towards Nijmegen. In Holland, the Polish airborne brigade lost 25 per cent of its fighting strength, amounting to 590 casualties.[24] Some 92 Poles were killed in action or died of their wounds, 111 were declared missing and 1,486 were safely withdrawn.

By Day 4, the battered division was too weak to make any attempt to reach the bridge. Of the nine infantry battalions, only the 1st Battalion, the Border Regiment, still existed as a unit; the others were just remnants and battalions in name only. On Day 5, Major Robert Henry Cain of the Staffords disabled a German tank with a PIAT and then although wounded by machine-gun fire positioned one of the artillery guns and destroyed it. This was the first of a number of actions by Cain that led to the award of a Victoria Cross.[25] This second medal for the Staffords meant it became the only British battalion to receive two Victoria Crosses in one battle during the Second World War. Meanwhile, the remnants of the 10th and 156th Battalions at Wolfheze began to fall back, but several elements were surrounded and captured.[26] Some 150 men of the 156th Battalion were pinned down just west of Oosterbeek. These men broke out in the late afternoon, with ninety of them making it into the perimeter. With the failure of the attempts to break through to Arnhem and the division left without any offensive capability, Urquhart made the painful, though unavoidable, decision to abandon Frost at the bridge and rally what men the division had left into the defensive pocket near Oosterbeek. On 21 September, another supply drop was attempted but only a few of the canisters fell upon the British positions. The last resupply drop was made two days later.

On Day 4, Lieutenant Colonel Frost was told on the radio that reinforcement was doubtful, as the XXX Corps was stopped to the south in front of Nijmegen Bridge.[27] Shortly afterwards, Frost was badly wounded in the leg by a mortar bomb and was carried to a basement. The command passed to Major Frederick H. Gough, who kept on referring to Frost for major decisions. Just after dark, with the building burning down over them, Frost gave the order to the wounded to surrender and to those still unwounded to make it to the division's defensive perimeter at Oosterbeek. Gough arranged a two-hour truce to evacuate the wounded. Frost, the 'mad colonel of Arnhem' as the Germans called him, was taken to hospital where his wounds were seen to by a German surgeon. When he recovered, he joined his men in captivity. At the bridge, some managed to hold out, while several others tried to break out towards Oosterbeek. The remaining paratroopers continued to fight – some even with knives. The last message broadcast from the Arnhem bridge was: 'Out of ammo. God Save the King.' By 05.00 on 21 September, all resistance at the bridge had ceased.[28] A group of survivors withdrawing towards Oosterbeek, led by Major Tony Hibbert, was captured by the Germans.

In Oosterbeek, the battle had settled into a routine of mortaring and small probing attacks supported by armoured vehicles and sniper fire. Food and water shortages took their toll on the men with foraging parties subjected to sniper fire. Due to the disastrous course of events, the 52nd (Lowland) Infantry Division was not deployed.[29] On the eighth day, Lieutenant General Brian Horrocks, whose XXX Corps stopped the advance only five miles (8km) south of Arnhem, decided not to reinforce the positions north of the Rhine. Although XXX Corps held Nijmegen and part of the road leading to Arnhem, the country between Waal River and Lower Rhine was still in German hands. For nine days the 1st Airborne Division fought unsupported against armoured units of the II SS-Panzer Corps. Suffering increasingly heavy casualties, the British airborne forces desperately held on to an ever-shrinking defensive perimeter until orders were received for the remnants of the division to withdraw across the Rhine on 25 September.[30] On the ninth day, German troops penetrated the British perimeter at Oosterbeek and threatened to cut off the division from the river. Then it was decided the evacuation of all survivors in a rescue operation code-named Berlin.

To prevent the Germans learning about the evacuation, the plan was kept secret until the afternoon and some men (mainly wounded) remained behind to give covering fire through the night. At 21.45 on 25 September, the withdrawal began and was covered by a massive artillery barrage on German positions by the British on the south shore of the Lower Rhine. There were not enough boats available, so the strong swimmers had to plunge into the flood and swim some 400 yards to safety. Some boats were so overloaded that they sank. Men either swam or drowned. Halfway through the evacuation the operation was discovered by the Germans, who started firing upon the evacuees with small arms, mortars and artillery. When a rainy dawn broke, some 1,700 of all ranks of the division and about 420 glider pilots had crossed the Lower Rhine. The survivors were taken first to Driel and then on to Nijmegen. Some 300 men, most of them wounded, had been left behind. A second attempt to evacuate them failed. A hundred men of the 1st Airborne Division were in the town of Elde where they remained until 15 October. Fifty more men were scattered in farms or in the countryside and another 100 were somewhat further away in the direction of Arnhem. All had been successful in evading capture and were being collected and looked after by members of the Dutch underground movement. Some 500 men were still in hiding north of the Rhine and over the coming months most of them were able to escape and reach the Allied lines. The Polish brigade was withdrawn to Nijmegen and helped to defend the corridor before returning to England in early October.

The British and the Poles had gone in Arnhem with a combined force of 10,005 troopers. Their losses at the time of the evacuation were, 7,528 killed, wounded and missing. Only 2,163 British and 60 Poles, as well as 75 downed airmen, returned. In Operation Market-Garden, the British 1st Airborne Division suffered 1,200 dead and 6,482 wounded. It means that in nine days of heavy fighting the division lost over three-quarters of its strength. It never saw combat again.[31] Of the 2,526 men of the 1st Airlanding Brigade there were 230 killed, 476 evacuated and 1,822 missing or taken prisoner.[32] On 20 September, Lieutenant Colonel Kenneth B. Smyth, commanding the 10th Battalion, was badly wounded and later died in German captivity. The following day Lieutenant Colonel Sir Richard de Voeux, commanding the 156th Battalion, was killed. The only awards of the Victoria Cross to the British Parachute Regiment in the war were for the Battle of Arnhem. The recipients who were posthumously honoured were Captain John Hollington-Grayburn, of the 2nd Battalion, and Captain Lionel Ernest Queripel, of the 10th Battalion. Major Robert H. Cain, of the 2nd Battalion, was the only VC recipient to survive the battle. Two American paratroopers were posthumously awarded the Medal of Honor. They were Private Joe E. Man and Private John T. Towle, of the 101st and the 82nd Airborne Divisions respectively. By way of comparison, the 101st Airborne, whose roster listed 14,266 men going in Holland, suffered 3,762 casualties and the 82nd Airborne reported 3,400 casualties. Official figures on German casualties have never been released.

The 1st Airborne Division, when it returned to England, was so weakened that the 4th Parachute Brigade had to be merged with the 1st. The division was disbanded on October 1945. It is believed that the main cause of failure in Arnhem were the three parachute drops. Matters went awry because there were not enough aircraft to put the 1st Airborne Division down as one unit all together. It meant the initial landing party would have to be divided, leaving units to stand guard on the field and stockpile there, while the rest had to march out at the double for the objective. The refusal to consider night drops, two lifts on Day 1 or a coup-de-main assault on Arnhem Bridge were regarded as fundamental errors by various commentators. Another reason was the choice of the DZs, which were situated too far away from the main objectives. The assaulting troops had to march at least five miles (8km) and in other cases eight miles (13km) to the Arnhem Bridge through close country infested with the enemy. Such a march could not be accomplished in less than four hours and this was ample time for the defence, consisting as it did of many trained troops, to organize resistance. Frost believed that the distance from DZs to the bridge and the long approach on foot was a 'glaring snag'.[33] He was highly critical of the 'unwillingness of the air forces to fly more than one sortie in the day [which] was one of the chief factors that mitigated against success'.[34] Urquhart, who made the decision on the DZs and the LZs (by accepting the airmens' proposals), although very qualified as a ground combat infantry commander, was inexperienced in airborne tactics, which dictate that airborne troops drop directly on or as close as possible to their target. The American generals Gavin and Taylor were 'shocked' when they saw the DZs and the LZs on the map but held off saying anything because they didn't want to offend the British who 'were more experienced in warfare'.[35] Gavin later commented that he would rather sustain 10 per cent casualties on an unsuitable DZ closer to his objective than land on a more suitable one eight miles' or five hours' march away.[36]

Before 17 September, Taylor, on examining the original plan, noted, also, that there was no provision for an alternate route from Eindhoven to Arnhem anywhere along the 50-mile (80km) corridor. If, for some reason, the road was made impassable, either by destroyed bridges or the enemy cutting the road anywhere along the line, there was no plan for bypassing the obstacle. That, in brief, is why the XXX Corps failed to get further than Nijmegen. According to Gavin, there was no failure at Arnhem. If an implication or failure is considered historically, it has to do with the failure of the ground forces to arrive on time to exploit the initial gains of the 1st Airborne Division.[37] Many military historians and commentators believe that the failure to secure Arnhem was not the fault of the airborne forces, as they had held out far longer than planned. The failure was of the operation as a whole. Frost noted that 'by far the worst mistake was the lack of priority given to the capture of Nijmegen Bridge'.[38] He was unable to understand why Gavin was ordered to secure the Groesbeek Heights before Nijmegen. The decision to drop the 82nd Airborne on the Groesbeek Heights, several kilometres from Nijmegen Bridge, has been questioned because it resulted in a long delay in its capture. Combined with the British 1st Airborne Division's delays in Arnhem, which left the (Arnhem) bridge open to traffic until 20.00, the enemy was given vital hours to create a defence on the Nijmegen bridge. On 4 October, the German forces mounted another offensive north of Nijmegen in a narrow strip of land between the Lower Rhine and the Waal Rivers, locally known as the 'Island'. The 101st Airborne was deployed in the area the following morning. The fighting in and around Opheusden was fierce and dozens of soldiers were killed on both sides. The 82nd Airborne was also deployed in the area. To clear the village the American paratroopers had to fight from house to house for three days. 'E' Company of the 327th GIR was engaged in hand-to-hand combat south of Opheusden. Before long, the fighting developed into a static war of aggressive patrolling and attrition. On a mortar attack, near Heteren, on 8 October, Lieutenant Colonel Howard R. Johnson, commander of the 501st PIR, was mortally wounded.

The Battle of the Bulge

Two airborne divisions, the American 82nd and 101st, played a pivotal role in the Battle of the Bulge, following the blitzkrieg-type German offensive through the densely-forested Ardennes region of Wallonia in eastern Belgium, which caught the Allies completely by surprise. Three more US Army airborne units participated in the fighting, the 17th Airborne Division, 507th PIR and the 193rd GIR, which had to be transferred from England. The British 6th Airborne Division was also in England, training for the Allied invasion of Germany. The 82nd and the 101st Airborne Divisions were kept as theatre reserves in France, when, on 16 December 1944, thirty German divisions with 2,000 artillery pieces and 1,000 tanks launched an attack through the thinly-held lines of the US First Army between Monchau and Wasserbillig.[39] Field Marshals Walter Model and Gerd von Rundstedt were put in charge of the ambitious operation. On 17 December, some 300 German paratroopers were dropped into the American rear tasked with securing and holding the crossroads at Belle Croix Jalhay until the arrival of the 12th SS-Panzer Division. The airborne mission, code-named Stösser, was a failure. Adolf Hitler's planned goal was to split the enemy forces in half, encircling large portions of Allied troops, to eventually capture their primary supply port at Antwerp in Belgium and thus prompt a political settlement. It took the high command almost 24 hours to realize that the fighting in the Ardennes was a major offensive by the enemy and not a local counter-attack. Eisenhower then decided to commit his theatre reserve to the Ardennes in an attempt to halt the German advance.

The 82nd and the 101st Airborne Divisions, which were stationed at the time at Sissones in France, were ordered to rush by road to contain the bulge of the Allied lines. When the Germans launched their offensive, the 101st commander was in the United States and the deputy commander in England, leaving the artillery commander, Brigadier Anthony McAuliffe, in command of the whole division. Trucks were arranged immediately because the weather was unsuitable for a parachute drop. While the 82nd and the 101st Airborne Divisions were able to immediately make their way to the Ardennes, bad weather prevented the American 17th Airborne Division from flying in from England for several days. The 82nd Airborne Division and the 101st Airborne Division were ordered to concentrate around the town of St. Vith. On 17 December, the 101st Airborne was assigned with holding Bastogne and the 82nd Airborne was deployed at La Gleize, Bastogne, located on a 1,463ft (446m) high plateau some 107 miles (172km) away from the 101st Airborne's camp in France, was the key to the German offensive and had to be held at all cost. The 82nd Airborne took up positions further north to block the critical advance of Kampfgruppe Peiper (KP) towards Wermont. Its assigned objective was to break through the American lines through Spa and take the bridges on the Meuse between Liège and Huy. They captured Stavelot and advanced as far as Cheneux where the advance stalled mainly through lack of fuel. German efforts to reinforce KP were unsuccessful. At Cheneux, US paratroopers from the 82nd Airborne engaged the Germans in fierce house-to-house fighting. The Germans were forced to withdraw. They abandoned their vehicles and retreated through snow-covered forests until reaching friendly lines thirty-six hours later. The 508th Parachute Infantry Regiment (508th PIR) played a major part in the Battle of the Bulge during which they screened some 20,000 troops from St. Vith and defended their positions against the German Panzer divisions. The regiment also participated in an assault that led to the capture of the strategically-significant Hill 400.

Between 17 and 23 December, the Germans were halted near St. Vith by the 82nd Airborne and Bastogne by a roadblock defended by the US 7th Armored Division and the 101st Airborne. To help reinforce the siege of Bastogne the entire 17th Airborne Division was finally committed to combat in the European Theatre of Operations. The 82nd Airborne, with an official strength of 8,520 men, was committed to the northern face of the bulge near Elsenborn Bridge. The 504th PIR started for Bastogne on tracks but along the way their destination was changed to Werbomont – a point more seriously threatened. The 504th conducted a night movement on foot for eight miles (13km) to take up defensive positions. On 19 December, the 504th PIR was ordered to link up with the 505th PIR at Trois Points. The 1st Battalion, 504th PIR (1/504th PIR), was ordered to take the towns of Brume, Rhier and Cheneux. On 20 December, the 82nd Airborne was assigned to take Cheneux, where they would force the SS-Panzer Division into a fighting retreat.

The fall of Cheneux, because of the enemy's fierce resistance, resulted in very heavy losses to the 504th PIR. It had also given the Germans their first defeat of the Battle of the Bulge. On 21–22 December, the 82nd Airborne faced counter-attacks from three powerful Waffen-SS divisions. The German efforts to relieve Kampfgruppe Peiper failed due to the stubborn defence of the 82nd Airborne.[40] On 23 December, the German divisions attacked from the south and overran the 325th GIR holding the Baraque-Fraiture crossroads on the 82nd Airborne's southern flank, thus endangering the entire division. The attack failed in its objective to outflank the 82nd Airborne and eventually reach the stranded, yet still powerful, Kampfgruppe. On 24 December, the 82nd Airborne was facing off against a vastly superior combined force of 43,000 men and over 1,200 armoured vehicles and artillery pieces. Due to the circumstances, the 82nd was forced to withdraw for the first time in its combat history.[41] The Germans pursued their retreat with two Panzer divisions. The 2nd SS-Panzer Division Das Reich engaged the 82nd Airborne until 28 December when it and what was left of the 1st SS-Panzer Division Leibstandarte Adolf Hitler was ordered to move south to meet Patton's forces attacking in the area of Bastogne. The 9th SS-Panzer Division tried to breakthrough by attacking the positions of the 508th PIR and the 504th PIR, but ultimately failed.[42] The failure of the 9th and the 2nd SS-Panzer Divisions to break through the 82nd Airborne's lines marked the end of the German offensive in the northern shoulder of the Bulge.

Meanwhile, the 101st Airborne was packed into trucks for an overnight rush to Bastogne, the hub of a major radial road net, to stem the oncoming Germans.[43] After a gruelling truck ride, the 501st PIR reached Bastogne at 22.30 on 19 December.

The regiment was ordered to move out on the eastern road through Longvilly and seize and hold a key road junction. 1/501st PIR stopped the enemy advance the following morning and held their positions until the rest of the division could arrive. On 19 December, by noon, the entire 101st Airborne had been deployed at Bastogne ready to defend the city. The 705th Tank Destroyer Battalion, US 10th Armoured Division, and three artillery battalion, each having twelve 155mm howitzers, had also been deployed in Bastogne. The 502nd PIR held positions on the north and north-west portion of the surrounded city. The 506th PIR was sent to the eastern sector of the siege. By 21 December, Bastogne was completely surrounded by German forces. During the siege, there were reports of problems with tying in the gap between the 501st and the 502nd PIRs. To stall the Germans, so that the defence could be set up, 1/506th PIR was sent out to attack and slow down the Germans in the towns of Noville and Foy. One-third (about 300 men) of 1/506th were lost, but in the process had taken out thirty enemy tanks and inflicted 500–1,000 casualties. At Bastogne, the 327th GIR, including the 401st GIR that was acting as the regiment's third battalion, held half the perimeter. Numerous intense fights erupted along the 327th GIR's sector, including two brutal actions at Marvie and more to the west in the 401st GIR's sector. The 1/401st GIR set up defensive positions in the area of Bastogne and beat back attack after attack. At Marvie, where the Germans lost six tanks, the 327th GIR was outnumbered by fifteen to one.

On 22 December, the cloud cover broke for a short time in the Bastogne area and allowed a supply drop by parachutes of food, ammo and medical supplies. The drop helped to some extent as the short-notice move had left the division short of food, ammunition, arms and winter clothing. When the German commander, Generalleutnant Heinrich Freiherr von Luttvitz, requested Bastogne's surrender, Brigadier McAuliffe wrote 'Nuts' on the paper delivered to him. Colonel Joseph Harper, commander of the division's 327th GIR, who passed the note over to the Germans, had some explaining to do: 'If you don't know what "nuts" means', he told them, 'in plain English, it is the same as "go to hell!" . . . '[44] During the night of 23 December, the enemy attacked in force with tanks. The glider men had fallen back 500 to 1,000 yards, but did not break. The all-out German assault, involving seven divisions, was launched on Christmas Day with numerous German tanks penetrating the American lines in the village of Hermulle or Hemvoulle. Simultaneously, further north, a strong infantry force infiltrated the town of Champs. Despite the initial success the assault was finally defeated. On 26 December, the US 4th Armored Division, the spearhead of Patton's Third Army, broke through the German lines, thus ending the seven-day siege. The 506th PIR of the 101st Airborne then spearheaded the entire offensive, liberating Foy and Noville in early January 1945. The 327th GIR cleared Champs from German troops and then attacked towards Bourcy, north-east of Bastogne. The 502nd PIR reinforced the 327th GIR and the two regiments captured Bourcy.

Meanwhile, on 23 December, the weather cleared and the 17th Airborne Division was finally flown to France by emergency night flights. They moved initially to an assembly area near Rheims and then by truck to southern Belgium.[45] On Christmas

Day, as part of Patton's Third Army, the division was assigned a 30-mile (48km) long defensive position that ran along the Meuse River near Charleville. The division was ordered to immediately close in at Mourmelon-le-Grand airfield. After taking over the defence of the Meuse River sector from Givet to Verdun on 2 December, the paratroopers moved to Neufchâteau in Belgium. Then they marched through the snow to Morchet, establishing a divisional command post. During the initial advance, the 17th Airborne engaged German forces, including armour, north-west of Bastogne. The division entered combat for the first time since it was activated as an airborne unit in April 1943. The battle lasted three days and the paratroopers suffered nearly 1,000 casualties. It was during this battle that the division earned its first Medal of Honor. Staff Sergeant Isadore S. Jachman, of the 513rd PIR, was killed by machine-gun fire after destroying two German tanks with a bazooka. Another Medal of Honor recipient from the regiment was Private First-Class Stuart Stryker. The paratroopers and the glider-men captured a number of key towns and villages to the west of Bastogne in order to prevent German forces from encircling the town. The 17th Airborne, spearheaded by the 194th GIR and the 513rd PIR, halted the German advance. Two more airborne units, the 193rd GIR and the 507th PIR, moved to support their flank.

Between 19 and 26 January, the division broke through the German lines and captured several towns. After it had captured the town of Espeler on 26 January, the 17th Airborne was transported by truck to Luxembourg.[46] In January 1945, the 513rd PIR was sent into the assault on Flamierge. Two regiments, the 513rd PIR on the right and the 194th GIR on the left, attacked the town of Flamierge, while the 193th GIR and the 507th PIR were held in reserve to counter an anticipated German counter-attack. On 11 January, the 193rd GIR drove on with American armoured units to seize the town of Houffalize. Five days later, the 17th Airborne was in pursuit of the 9th Panzer Division, the Panzer Lehr Division and the 26th Infantry Division which were retreating towards the Siegfried Line. After seizing the town of Compogne, the 193rd GIR along with the 507 PIR led an attack across Luxembourg to the Our River on the border of Germany. The German 5th Parachute Division made a vain attempt to maintain a bridgehead on the Our, but the 507th PIR managed to cross into Germany and probe the Siegfried Line. Private Joe Gandara, of the 507th PIR, earned the Medal of Honor for single-handedly attacking three German machine-gun emplacements.

By 26 December, the British 6th Airborne Division had been transported from England to Belgium by sea to cover the crossing of the Meuse. The division's 5th Brigade was then ordered to move toward Grupont. On 3 January, the 13th Parachute Battalion advanced against the village of Bure. Although they had to fight against tanks and infantry which caused them heavy losses, the British paratroopers cleared and held Bure. Meanwhile, the 7th Battalion was ordered to attack the village of Wavreille. By nightfall, they had overcome about 100 Germans supported by tanks and self-propelled guns. On 14 January, the 3/502nd PIR, 101st Airborne, was bombed accidentally by Allied planes, while advancing through a forest near Michap. The battalion's commander, Lieutenant Colonel John Stopka, and thirty of his men were killed. On 20 January, the now battered 101st Airborne was hurried to Alsace, where a German offensive was threatening a sector of the Seventh Army. The 502nd PIR, now to 60 per cent strength, took up defensive positions.

Earlier, on 3 January, the 82nd Airborne had mounted a counter-attack. After several days of fighting, the destruction of the 62nd Volksgrenadier Division and what had been left of the 9th SS-Panzer Division was complete. Meanwhile, on 26 December 1944, the 551st PIB reported to the 508th PIR near Basse-Bodeux with the task of attacking the German-held village of Noirefontaine. From 3 to 8 January, the 551st PIB assaulted the small hamlets of Mont-de-Fosse, St. Jacques and Dairomont. On 4 January, the battalion conducted a rare fixed-bayonet attack on enemy machine-gun nests. Fighting through cost the unit heavy casualties. When it arrived in Werbomont on 21 December 1944, the 551st PIB had a strength of 643 officers and other ranks. On 7 January 1945, when the battalion was down to 250 men, they were tasked with taking the Belgian village of Rochelinval along the Salm River over open ground and without artillery support. Lieutenant Colonel Wood Joers, the commanding officer of the 551st PIB, was killed during the assault. Although successful in capturing Rochelinval and eliminating the last German bridgehead for over 10 miles (16km) on the Salm River, the battalion was virtually wiped out, having suffered more than 85 per cent casualties.

The 17th Airborne was relieved by the 6th Armored Division and returned to camp at Châlons-sur-Marne in France on 11 February. In mid-February the 504th PIR was relieved and moved back to Grand Halleux where it spent several days before being trucked across the Belgian-German border. From Aachen, the first large German city to be taken by the Allies, it moved by train back to Laon in France. On 2 April, the 501st PIR, 101st Airborne, moved to the Ruhr pocket to help in mopping-up operations. Here the 502nd PIR went on the line facing the Rhine south of Dusseldorf. The 501st PIR paid the high price of 580 killed, wounded or missing. One casualty was Lieutenant Colonel Julian Ewel, who was badly wounded. The failure of Hitler's counter-offensive in the Ardennes exhausted Germany's strategic reserves, leaving it ill-prepared to resist the final Allied campaigns in Europe.

East of the Rhine

On 2 October 1944, during Operation Market-Garden, elements of the American 101st Airborne Division reached a wooden area outside Groesbeek, south of Nijmegen, and on their own initiative, briefly crossed the border into Germany.[47] According to the same source, men of the American 82nd Airborne Division, having been in the same area even before their 101st Airborne colleagues, were probably the first Allied soldiers to set foot (albeit briefly) on German soil. By March 1945, the Allied forces had advanced into Germany and eventually crossed the Rhine. This was the last major water obstacle for the Allies short of Berlin. On 7 March, US troops captured the last remaining intact bridge across the Rhine, the Lundendorff Bridge at Remagen. Within the next two days, six divisions had established a bridgehead on the eastern side of the river. The Allied forces were now some 300 miles (480km) from Berlin. On 22 March, the US Third Army crossed the Rhine and formed a second bridgehead. Four days later, the US Sixth Army Group crossed the Rhine and established a bridgehead at Worms, about 25 miles (40km) south of Mainz. A fourth Rhine crossing, involving ground and airborne troops, was planned. This was to be the largest airborne operation in history. Operation Market-Garden was a larger operation but the drop zones were split over three distinct areas and spread over several days. Operation Varsity, as the airborne part of the Anglo-American-Canadian assault to cross the northern Rhine was code-named, was to be conducted on a single day and in one location.

The paratroopers would land on the eastern bank of the Rhine behind the German lines to help the assault troops of the 21st Army Group, commanded by Field Marshal Bernard Montgomery, cross the river and secure a foothold. The initial plan called for the dropping of three airborne divisions but during the planning it became apparent that there were only enough planes available to transport two divisions effectively. The divisions assigned to the operation were the British 6th Airborne and the American 17th Airborne. The division that was left out was the American 13th Airborne. The 6th Airborne Division, commanded by Major General Eric Bols, was a veteran unit, having fought with distinction during the Normandy landings. The 17th Airborne Division, on the other hand, commanded by Major General William Milley, had yet to take part in a combat drop. The 6th Airborne Division had started preparations for an invasion into Germany as early as September 1944. The division had been put through a course of severe training during which street fighting had been practised in the ruined areas of Southampton, Birmingham and other cities.[48]

The plan for Varsity was based on the experience gained at Arnhem and elsewhere and therefore differed in a marked degree from previous operations of the same type. First, the decision was taken to transport all the airborne troops, both those who would land by parachute and those carried by gliders, in a single lift.[49] Secondly, the whole force was to land not near to but on top of the objective. There would be no approach march during which the enemy might get wind of their presence, as had happened at Arnhem, and have time to put themselves in a state of defence. Finally, the airborne troops were to land not before but after land operations on the largest scale had begun. The drop should be made some thirteen hours after the Allied ground forces' assault began. Having learned from the mistakes that led to the disaster at Arnhem, the operation planners decided that the airborne forces should be dropped only a relatively short distance behind enemy lines, thereby ensuring that reinforcements in the form of Allied ground forces would be able to link up with them within a short period.

The two airborne divisions would land around Wesel in order to aid the advance of the British-Canadian forces towards that particular key town. They were tasked with capturing Vessel across the Rhine in a combined paratrooper and glider operation conducted in daylight. The 6th Airborne Division had to capture the nearby village of Hamminkeln and seize certain bridges over the River Issel and a forested area overlooking the Rhine. The 3rd Parachute Brigade was tasked to clear the DZ and establish a defensive position at the end of the DZ and to seize the Schnappenburg feature astride the main road running north and south of it. The 1st Canadian Parachute Battalion (1st CaPaBa) was ordered to seize and hold the central area on the western edge of the woods, where there was a main road running north from Wesel to Emmerich and to a number of houses. It was believed that this area was held by German paratroopers. The 6th Airlanding Brigade was given several objectives. The 2nd Oxfordshire and Buckinghamshire Light Infantry (OBLI), after landing on the north, had to secure bridges over the river Issel. The 1st Royal Ulster Rifles (RUR) had the main road bridge over the river from Hamminkeln to Brunen as their objective and the 12th Devonshire Regiment were to capture the town of Hamminkeln.[50]

By the night of 23 March, the Allied had the equivalent of thirty divisions ready for the crossing of the Rhine, while the Germans fielded around ten divisions, all weakened by constant fighting and casualties. The best German formation defending the area of the Allied invasion was the 1st Parachute Army, made up of seven divisions. In the area there were also, according to Allied intelligence, seventy-five tanks and about twenty to thirty self-propelled guns. Operation Plunder, involving the ground forces, started on the evening of 23 March. Varsity, the airborne part of the operation, began in the first hours of the following day with the airborne and the glider-borne troops taking off from their bases in England and France. The airborne operation was preceded by two days of round-the-clock activity by Allied air forces. The Second Army's 1st Commando Brigade slipped across the river and waited within a mile of Wesel, while the town was bombed by the RAF.

At 07.00 on 24 March, the 122 C-47s transporting the 3rd Brigade took off from England in three waves. The first wave carried brigade HQs and the 8th Parachute Battalion and the second carried the 1st CaPaBa. The 9th Parachute Battalion came last. The gliders transporting the brigade's heavy equipment were scheduled to arrive forty minutes after the third wave. The planes began to rendezvous over Brussels before turning north-east for the Rhine DZs. There were 541 transport aircraft containing airborne troops and a further 1,050 towing 1,350 gliders.[51] The armada was protected by 2,153 fighter aircraft. At 10.00 British and American airborne troops, after a two-hour and thirty-seven minute flight, began landing on German soil. The 3rd Parachute Brigade arrived over the DZ in 122 aircraft and the 5th Parachute Brigade in 121 planes, mostly C-47s although a number of C-46 Commandos was also employed. As soon as the river Maas was passed, the paratroopers hooked up, for there were barely two minutes to go, and then started jumping from the planes at between 800 to 1,000ft (224 to 305m). They were therefore in the air for a longer time than usual. Hundreds of men landed on fields but also on fences and trees. The descending parachutists were met with heavy fire from the German defenders which caused several casualties. The 6th Airborne Division was to protect the northern part of the landing area. They had six DZs around the town of Hamminkeln. The first element of the British 6th Airborne Division to land was the 8th Parachute Battalion, part of the 3rd Parachute Brigade, commanded by Brigadier James Hill. The 3rd Parachute Brigade was made up of the 8th and 9th Battalions plus the 1st CaPaBa.

The brigade was actually dropped nine minutes earlier than scheduled. They successfully landed on DZ A while facing significant small-arms and 20mm anti-aircraft fire. The fire came from the woods surrounding the DZs and caused casualties, among them Lieutenant Colonel Jeff S. Nicklin, the commanding officer of the 1st CaPaBa, who was killed on landing. Following the death of Nicklin, Lieutenant Colonel G.F. Eadie took over as commander of the Canadian paratroopers. Major Kippin and Lieutenant A. Cox of the 8th Parachute Battalion also lost their lives on the DZ as did Lieutenant J. England, an intelligence officer, who was struck by a glider which came down through the smoke and haze. Despite the fact that some of their paratroopers were dropped some distance from their DZs, the 1st CaPaBa managed to secure its objectives quickly. The brigade suffered a number of casualties, but by 11.00 the DZ was clear of enemy forces and all battalions of the brigade had formed up. The DZ had been secured by the 8th Parachute Battalion and the opposition had been silenced. This was the battalion's initial objective. The 9th Parachute Battalion and the 1st CaPaBa then moved against the wooded feature called the Schappenberg.[52] In three hours, they secured all their objectives. The 9th Parachute Battalion were establishing themselves on the forest, while the Canadians took up positions close beside it.

The next airborne unit to land was the 5th Parachute Brigade, commanded by Brigadier Nigel Poett. They arrived in the second wave of aircraft. The parachute descent was made under fire and the DZ itself was also subjected to artillery and mortar fire. They would land on the northernmost DZ (B) and hold the area west of the Wesel railway line. Due to poor visibility, the brigade landed mostly around DZ B. The DZ was subjected to shellfire and mortaring by the enemy which inflicted casualties in the battalion rendezvous areas. After landing, the 13th Parachute Battalion troopers pulled off their steel helmets, put on their red berets and begun to rally to the cries of 'Tally-ho' and the hunting horns blown by their officers.[53] The 7th Parachute Battalion secured the DZ, while the 12th and the 13th Parachute Battalions headed for another brigade's objective, the road from the DZ to Hamminkeln. The 5th Parachute Brigade was then ordered to move due east and clear an area near Schneppenberg, as well as to engage German forces gathered to the west of the farmhouse. By 03.30, the brigade had secured all of its objectives and linked up with other British airborne units. By then, the brigade had suffered 700 casualties.[54] By 15.30, the 5th Parachute Brigade was digging in.

The third unit that formed part of the 6th Airborne Division was the 6th Airlanding Brigade, commanded by Brigadier Hugh Bellamy. As had happened in Normandy, the division's parachute brigades were already on the ground before the 6th Airlanding Brigade started landing at 10.30. The German defenders had been alerted and the gliders were met by a concentrated anti-aircraft barrage. This caused the air landing brigade around 40 per cent casualties in men and 50 per cent in equipment.[55] The brigade was tasked with landing in company-sized groups and capturing several objectives including the town of Hamminkeln. The gliders containing the airborne troops of the brigade landed in four LZs. The landing was made even more difficult due to the presence of a great deal of haze and smoke. However, the majority of the gliders landed correctly, allowing the battalions to secure intact the three bridges over the River Issel that they had been tasked with capturing, as well as the village of Hamminkeln with the aid of American paratroopers of the 513rd PIR, who had been dropped by mistake nearby. By 11.00, the 2nd OBLI and the 1st RUR had captured their objectives. The 12th Devons landed amongst a German armoured formation, but managed to gather enough men together to begin their attack on Hamminkeln at 11.35. They had secured the town by midday. The 6th Airlanding Brigade secured all of its objectives shortly after capturing Hamminkeln. Before the night, about 700 prisoners of war had been taken by the British.[56] At midnight, the 2nd OBLI were attacked by a force of tanks and infantry, but this had to retreat the following morning when most of the tanks were destroyed by Allied planes or by the brigade's anti-aircraft guns. The main road bridge, held by the 1st RUR, was attacked at 07.00 by infantry and two tanks were destroyed by the division's anti-tank guns. Later that day, elements of the 15th Scottish Infantry Division, supported by tanks, had advanced to the divisional area and took over the 6th Airlanding Brigade's position.

The 507th PIR, under the command of Lieutenant Colonel Edson Raff, was the lead assault formation and was consequently the first American airborne unit to land as part of Operation Varsity. The drop was not accurate. Raff and about 700 of his paratroopers landed north-west of the DZ, near the town of Diersfordt with the rest of the regiment landing correctly in the designated DZ W. He rallied his separated paratroopers and led them to DZ W. Raff engaged a battery of German artillery en route, killing or capturing the gun crews, before reuniting with the rest.[57] By 14.00, the 507th PIR had secured all of its objectives and cleared the area around Diersfordt, having engaged numerous German troops and also having destroyed a tank. The 513rd PIR was the second American airborne unit to land after the 507th PIR, under the command of Lieutenant Colonel Hames Coutts. En route to the DZ the transport aircraft carrying the 513rd PIR had the misfortune to pass through a belt of German anti-aircraft weapons, losing twenty-two of the C-47s and damaging a further thirty-eight. The 507th PIR and the 513rd PIR suffered from pilot error due to the ground haze and as a result the regiment actually were dropped on one of the LZs designated for the British 6th Airlanding Brigade. Despite this inaccuracy, the paratroopers swiftly rallied and aided the British glider-borne troops, who were landing at the same time, eliminating several artillery batteries that were covering the area. By 14.00, the 513rd PIR had secured all of their objectives, having knocked out two tanks and two complete regiments of artillery during their assault.

The third component of the 17th Airborne to take part in the operation was the 194th GIR, commanded by Lieutenant Colonel James Pierce. The 194th GIR was the third wave of the 17th Airborne's assault. Prior to the operation, the remnants of the 193rd GIR and the 550th PIB were attached to the 194th GIR as the regiment's third battalion. Troopers of the 194th GIR landed accurately on LZ S but their gliders and tow aircraft took heavy casualties. Twelve transport planes, C-47s and some C-46s, were lost due to anti-aircraft fire and a further 140 were damaged. The 193rd GIR landed in the midst of a number of German artillery batteries that were engaging Allied ground forces crossing the Rhine. However, these artillery batteries and their crews were defeated by the glider-borne troops and the regiment was soon able to report that its objectives had been secured, having destroyed forty-two artillery pieces, ten tanks, two self-propelled anti-aircraft vehicles and five self-propelled guns. All of the objectives that the airborne troops had been tasked with, had been met usually within a few hours of the operation beginning. The bridges over the Issel River had been successfully captured. The forested area (Diersfordter) had been cleared of enemy troops and the roads through which the Germans might have routed reinforcements against the Allied advance had been cut by airborne troops. Finally, Hamminkeln had been secured by air-lifted units. By 27 March, the Allies had fourteen divisions deployed on the eastern bank of the Rhine penetrating up to 10 miles (16km).

A Canadian medical orderly, Corporal Frederick George Topham, was awarded the Victoria Cross for his efforts to recover casualties and take them for treatment at great personal risk and despite his own wounds.[58] The casualties taken by both airborne formations were quite heavy although lighter than expected. Casualties for the 6th Airborne Division were 347 dead and 731 wounded. Most of them belonged to the 8th Parachute Battalion. By nightfall of 24 March, the 6th Airborne Division had suffered around 1,400 personnel killed, wounded or missing in action out of 7,220 who were landed in the operation. The 5th Parachute Brigade had lost about 200 men on the DZ. The division also claimed to have secured around 1,500 prisoners of war. The 3rd Parachute Brigade had 80 dead and 190 wounded that day.[59] The 17th Airborne suffered around 1,300 casualties out of 9,650 personnel who took part in the operation. They also claimed to have taken 2,000 prisoners of war. Fifty-six aircraft in total were lost on 24 March, while 21 out of the 144 aircraft transporting the 17th Airborne were shot down and further 59 were damaged by anti-aircraft fire. Of the 416 gliders of the 6th Airborne Division that had landed, only 88 remained undamaged by enemy fire. Between 20 to 30 per cent of the glider pilots were casualties. The 194th GIR had two-thirds of their gliders hit and suffered heavy casualties as they landed.

The German forces defending the area had been greatly surprised by the speed with which the two airborne divisions had landed their troops. Their sudden appearance had had a 'shattering effect' on the greatly outnumbered defenders. The outcome of operation was the defeat of the I Fallschirmkorps in a day and a half. General Eisenhower called Varsity 'the most successful operation carried out to date'.[60] G. G. Norton argued that Varsity benefited from the lessons learned from previous operations.[61] Brian Jewel agrees, stressing that the airborne forces gave the defenders little time to recover. Thus ended the last airborne operation of the war. In late March, the 506th PIR, 101st Airborne, was sent into the Ruhr in Germany to assist in the encirclement of the Ruhr Pocket, capture Berchtesgaden, the mountain home of Adolf Hitler, and aid the mopping-up of the remaining German forces. In Berchtesgaden, the 1/401st GIR would stay until the end of the world. On 4 April, the 502nd PIR, 101st Airborne, was also deployed in Berchtesgaden. Later in April, the 101st Airborne moved into Rhineland and eventually reached the Bavarian Alps. In April, too, the 513rd PIR went into action around Munster. Elements of 194th GIR arrested a senior Nazi official, Franz von Papen, at his estate near Essen. On 27 March, the 6th Airborne Division started to advance further into Germany. The 6th Airlanding Brigade also advanced with the 1st RUR and 2nd Devons leading. Ulze and Luneurg were captured by

Air Landing Division's units on 11 April. Four days later, the 1st CaPaBa encountered the Bergen-Belsen concentration camp.

Between 29 March and 2 May, the 6th Airborne Division was the spearhead of the Anglo-Canadian ground forces, the 21st Army Group, commanded by Field Marshal Bernard Montgomery, that marched more than 300 miles (482km) to Wismar, a large town on the shores of the Baltic Sea. Lübeck, Osnabrück and Minden were some of the towns that were taken by British paratroopers, who often had to overcome desperate resistance by enemy forces. They also seized key bridges intact and captured an airfield in the Wunsdorf area, following a brief battle against second-rate German troops. Lübeck was defended by two panzergrenadier companies. A hand-to-hand battle ensued lasting 18 hours, eventually drawing in all three battalions of the 3rd Parachute Brigade. The advance of the Anglo-Canadian forces developed into a race between the leading troops of the Soviet armies and the British 6th Airborne Division for Wismar.

On 30 April, the division's two parachute brigades crossed the river Elbe. That afternoon the leading troops of the 3rd Parachute Brigade reached Mecklenburg and made contact with leading elements of the Red Army, advancing from the east. The objective was now Wismar – to take the city and prevent the Soviet troops from advancing too far west. The 3rd Parachute Brigade won the race and led the division to Wismar arriving there on 2 May – only half an hour before the lead troops of the Red Army advancing from the east. While the rest of the brigade remained in Wismar, 'B' Company of the 13th Parachute Battalion was sent to Denmark to liberate Copenhagen. On 30 April, the Reichstag was captured in Berlin, signalling the military defeat of Nazi Germany and the end of hostilities in Europe. Meanwhile, the 1st Parachute Battalion that had fought at Arnhem was transported to Copenhagen to relieve the 13th Parachute Battalion. One of the units that were deployed in occupied Berlin was the American 82nd Airborne.

Chapter 8

Japanese, Indian, Gurkha and Chinese Paratroopers

The Japanese

In the Japanese armed forces parachutes were issued to pilots after the First World War, as had already happened in most major countries. A British officer, Major Thomas Orde-Lees, taught 'parachuting techniques' to Army and Naval Air Force personnel in Japan, after resigning his commission in the Royal Marines in 1919.[1] Two years earlier he had jumped from Tower Bridge in London into the River Thames River some 160ft (49m) below, to persuade his country's top brass of the usefulness of the parachute for pilots.[2] The Japanese Army started planning an airborne force in the mid-1930s, but the programme did not receive attention by the General Headquarters until the successes of similar units by the Germans in 1940.

The first paratroop units were organized in Japan on the very eve of the Second World War. It is believed that General Hideki Tojo, War Minister and Chief of the Army General Staff, was responsible for their raising. The Army and the Navy in Japan fielded their own airborne units during the Second World War. The first display jumps by Army parachutists were performed on 28 October 1940 on the island of Kyushu. In charge of the trial unit that was raised for this purpose at the Army's flight school at Hamamatsu airbase was Lieutenant Colonel Keigo Kawashima. A few days later, a 26-man trial unit, headed by Lieutenant Masao Samabe, was formed in the Navy. The trials were conducted at Yokosuka naval air station in Tokyo Bay with the first live jump being performed on 15 November. In the Army, live jumps started on 20 February 1941 – after experimenting with dummies, as their Navy counterparts had done earlier. It is believed by many outside Japan that German advisors were involved in the training of Japanese paratroops but in fact, Nazi Germany provided no assistance with parachute instruction or doctrinal development.[3] The Japanese developed their own training and operational techniques equipment, organization and doctrine, although much was certainly based on studies, published accounts and attaché reports of foreign experiences.

In less than two months about 1,500 combat-ready paratroopers had been trained in Japan.[4] All recruits were volunteers and had prior training in other military units. The Navy began training volunteers in June 1941 at Tateyama, Chiba, where Captain Toyoaki Horiuchi was in charge of parachute training. On 11 January 1942, he jumped from a height of 492ft (150m). His display drop was recorded on film for propaganda purposes. In the parachute school training, session 'A' was almost a week long with session 'B' lasting ten days. The daily programme of session 'A' included descents from a tower and landing techniques for one hour and parachute packing and maintenance for three hours. During session 'B' the prospective parachutists had to perform four jumps – the fourth with arms and equipment. As a confidence-builder, before his first jump, the trainee had to throw a dummy fitted with a parachute packed by himself from a plane.

The parachutes used by the Japanese military, although locally designed, looked similar to those issued at the time to German paratroopers. The padded leather helmet was later replaced by a steel one although evidence suggested that German helmets were actually issued to Japanese airborne units. The uniform of the Japanese paratroopers was also based on the German model. Its colour was dark green for the Navy paratroopers and khaki for the Army paratroopers. They all wore brown leather boots and gloves. Headgear was similar to the Army field cap but with a chinstrap and integral side and neck piece. Army paratroopers wore badges depicting a golden kite, similar to pilot's wings, as well as a roundel emblem depicting an open parachute and a star. Navy paratroopers wore a badge with an emblem of two crossed opened parachutes and an anchor, topped with a small flower. Although parachute training in the Army was different from that of the Navy, naval paratroopers were also, trained at the Army base on Kanto plain. These paratroopers were led by naval officers who had attended the Army Infantry School. Many weapons were the same with the ones the Army had, but some heavy weapons were provided from Navy stocks.

There were two airborne units initially authorized in the Navy. These were the Yokosuka 1st and 3rd *Tokubetsu Rikusentai* (Special Naval Landing Forces – SNLFs), which were activated in November 1941. They were under the operational control of the *Dai-Nippon Teikoku Kaigun Koku Hombu* (Imperial Japanese Navy Air Service). The Yokosuka 1st SNFL, commanded by Captain Toyoaki Horiuchi, was activated on 20 September 1941 at the Yokosuka district. The Yokosuka 3rd SNFL, commanded by Captain Kuichi Fucumi, was formed at the same district a few days later. Another unit, the Yokosuka 2nd SNLF, was activated on 20 November 1941. Captain Kyoshi Tomonari was the unit's commanding officer.[5] Each force had 850 men of whom 100 were not paratroopers, and were intended for seizing naval bases and spearheading amphibious assaults.

The Navy planned to use the paratroop force as a diversion, by coordinating the timing of a sea-borne assault and parachute drop to create maximum surprise at the point of contact. Naval paratroopers would jump inland from beaches where major assaults were to be mounted. It was intended that paratroopers would disable airfields, thus preventing enemy aircraft from interfering with amphibious landings. The Yokosuka 3rd SNLF was involved in the invasion of Dutch West Timor as airborne-inserted infantry, setting off from the captured air base at Kendari. The Yokosuka 2nd SNLF took no part in any airborne operation and eventually became a defensive island base unit. In June 1944, the Yokosuka 1st and 3rd SNLFs merged to form an 850-strong airborne unit.

The Japanese Army began training its own special shock troops, the *Teisin Shudan*, in a newly-established school at Hamamatsu Air Base on the south coast of Honshu

Island. In mid-February 1941, 250 trainees moved to Ichigaya airbase. In May 1941 the Army paratroopers were transferred to Baichengzu in Manchuria for reasons of secrecy. The officers and the other ranks of the airborne units were forbidden at the time to say even to their families what they were doing in the military. In August, these units returned to Japan to be stationed at Nyutabaru in Miyazaki prefecture on Kyushu. Nyutabaru remained the Army paratroopers' central training establishment throughout the war. On 1 December 1940, the 1st Raiding Regiment was raised having Lieutenant Colonel Takeo Takeda as commanding officer. The 2nd Raiding Regiment, commanded by Lieutenant Colonel Seiichi Cume, was formed a few weeks later. In 1944, the two regiments merged into the 1st Raiding Group and placed under the command of Major General Rikichi Tsukada. Two parachute brigades were organized into the Army at the main airborne base in Karasehara airfield, at Kyushu, as the first division-level raiding unit. They had an estimated 5,575 personnel. Although structured as a division, the 1st Raiding Group's capabilities were much lower as its six regiments had manpower equivalent to a standard infantry battalion and it lacked any form of artillery. They also had to rely on other units for logistical support.

By 1944, the 1st Airborne Raiding Group included glider troops with 75mm guns and a unit of Type 94 tankettes. The first glider tank troop was formed with four Type 95 Ha-Go light tanks in July 1943. This unit was eventually expanded to battalion size with a tank company of fourteen Type 2 Ke-To light tanks, an infantry company and a motorized transport company. However, the 1st Airborne Raiding Group never participated in conventional operations. Instead, some of the paratroops were used for two small-scale suicide missions against American-held airfields on 6 December 1944 in the Buraen-Dulag area at Leyte in the Philippines.[6] These paratroopers were wiped out by elements of the American 11th Airborne Division during a bitter five-day engagement. Army paratroopers were also employed in suicide assaults on American-held airfields on Okinawa. The Japanese paratroopers had no weapons heavier than 37mm anti-tank guns. Their lightly armed units were intended to assault coastal areas supporting amphibious landings or enemy-held airfields and other strategic objectives. They were not meant to become entangled in large-scale pitched battles. However, their operational use would prove to be contrary to this doctrine.

For most of the war the Japanese paratroopers were deployed as an elite infantry. In November 1944, the Japanese Army formed the *Giretsu Kuteitai* in order to reinforce home defence. They were an airlifted commando unit tasked with attacking and destroying island airfields used by the USAAF to bomb Tokyo and other Japanese cities. It was commanded by Lieutenant General Michio Sugahara. Initially, 126 men were selected among volunteers from the 1st Raiding Brigade. The *Giretsu* operations were effectively suicidal, as there was no provision for extraction of the strike force.

Japanese paratroopers were first involved in combat during the invasion of Borneo in December 1941. The campaign's main objectives were the oilfields at Miri in the Sarawak region and Seria in Brunei and an airfield close to the border with British Malaysia (Sarawak). The invasion started on 16 December. When they landed, the Japanese forces, including the 2nd SNLF, met little resistance from British troops. It did not take long the invaders to seize and secure Miri, Seria, and Luntong, as well as the oilfields and a strategically-important airfield. Smaller units, of company or even detachment size, were then deployed in parts of west Borneo. On 31 December, a seaborne paratroop force, commanded by Lieutenant Colonel Genzo Watanabe, moved northward to occupy Brunei, Labuan Island and Jesselton (now called Kinabalu). As a result of this campaign, Japan controlled not only Borneo, but also the Kingdom of Sarawak, north of the island, and the western part of Kalimantan, part of the Dutch East Indies.

The first combat jump in the history of the Japanese airborne forces was conducted in January 1942, when naval paratroopers of the Yokosuka 1st SNLF were ordered to support the landings against Dutch defenders at Manado in Indonesia. The Battle of Manado was fought on the northern part of the island of Celebes (now known as Sulawesi) from 11 to 13 January, following an attempt by Japanese forces to open a passage for a future invasion of Australia through the eastern part of the Dutch West Indies. The Yokosuka 1st SNLF would fly about 380 miles (610km) from the Philippines in three and a half hours and jump over Loangoan to capture a nearby airfield. The Dutch force at Manado was approximately 1,500 men strong. A mobile team, made up of forty-five men, had been tasked with responding to any airborne assault by enemy forces. For the defence of the entire island the Dutch could deploy mostly native and over-aged soldiers supported by a number of irregulars. This limited force had to defend the airfields at Loangoan and Mapanget, the naval base at Tasoeka and Manado. On 11 January, at 09.30, twenty-eight two-engined Mitsubishi G3M-L3YI transport planes appeared overhead, carrying 334 naval paratroopers. The DZ was close to the Dutch oil installations, 37 miles (60km) south of Manado. Captain Toyoaki Horiuchi, who led the paratroop force, jumped first. The drop was made from an altitude of 500ft (150m) and the men landed twenty-eight seconds after leaving the plane door. Some men, after landing, opened fire with pistols, while others ran for the parachuted containers to get heavier weapons.[7] The 1st and 2nd Companies of the Yokosuka 1st SNLF attacked Loangoan and the seaplane base at Cacas respectively. On 12 January, at about 09.00, Yokosuka 1st SNLF's 3rd Company were dropped on and around the Loangoan airfield, which was defended by Dutch troops, reinforced by an armoured car. By 11.30, the airfield was in Japanese hands. The remaining Dutch troops retreated inland and started a guerrilla war.

At 03.00, more Japanese troops, including three Type 94 tankettes, landed unopposed. Until the end of the day, the naval paratroopers had seized and secured the Loangoan airfield, the town of Cacas, the southern end of Lake Tondano and some of the surrounding area. In a battle that lasted almost five hours 140 Dutch and native defenders were killed and a further 48 were wounded. The Japanese had thirty-five paratroopers, including three officers, dead in shot-down planes. A further ninety were wounded. Enraged by their heavy losses, the Japanese killed thirty of the surrendered Dutch with swords, mostly officers. Although he did not order the slaughter, Captain Horiuchi was tried in 1947 as a war criminal, condemned to death and executed. The naval paratroopers stayed in Manado until 24 April. They were also used to seize other islands in the region. The Yokosuka 1st SNLF never made another combat jump after the assault on Manado.[8]

A few days later, a Japanese Navy force, including paratroopers, moved southward and captured Kendari airfield. On 19 February 1942, 242 Japanese planes took off from Kendari airfield and bombed Darwin in Australia. In November 1942, the Yokosuka 1st SNLF was sent to defend the island of Saipan. Almost two years later, in January 1944, 200 men of the unit were sent to protect Rabaul in New Britain. On the way, the force was diverted to Truck Atoll in the Caroline Islands, where they quietly sat out the remainder of the war. On the night of 16/17 June 1944, the unit was decimated when it launched an uncoordinated attack against US Marine invaders. By the end of the Saipan campaign, the unit had been virtually wiped out while fighting as conventional infantry.[9]

The first combat jump by Japanese Army paratroopers was made in February 1942 against the oilfields of Palembang, the capital of Sumatra, in the Dutch West Indies. The 1st Raiding Regiment (RR) was to have participated in assault on Palembang. They left Nyutabaru in Kyushu, bound for Indonesia on board the cargo ship *Meiko Maru*. On 3 January, while sailing in the south China Sea, their transport caught fire and eventually sank. The paratroopers were rescued by the Japanese cruiser *Kashii*, but their equipment was lost. After that, the 1st RR was sent to Hainan island for recuperation and the 2nd RR had to be brought in. The unit was in Cambodia at the time. The plan was for an airborne assault at dawn with the mission of seizing the airfields of the capital Palembang, 70 miles (113km) inland, and preventing the destruction of the oil installations of the region. The attacking airborne force included the 2nd RR and an air-transported regiment. The aircraft carrying the 425 paratroopers took off from southern Malaya. At 11.25 on 13 February, when the air attacks on and around the DZ were concluded, the massive parachute drop started. The paratroopers were divided into task forces 'A' and 'B'. A third task force, consisting of eighty-six men, parachuted west of the DZ to capture a smaller airfield. The paratroopers of task forces A and B were widely scattered. The main reason for that was the fact that the aircraft pilots, trying to avoid the anti-aircraft fire, made the drop from a higher altitude than planned. Task force 'A' advanced to Palembang. The oil facilities, including the most important oil refinery, were captured intact. Palembang, a town of 50,000 inhabitants, was secured by the evening. The Allied forces were forced to abandon the area, including the two airfields, and withdrew to the south-west of the island. The Japanese paratroopers had fulfilled their mission after fighting on their own behind enemy lines for over 40 hours. Of the 339 men dropped near Palembang, thirty-nine were killed, two died from parachute malfunctions and a further eleven paratroopers were wounded or injured on landing. The Army paratroopers saw no further action on Sumatra.

The 2nd RR returned to Pnomhpenh in Cambodia. In February 1942, naval paratroopers spearheaded the invasion of the Dutch West Timor by Japanese forces. At the time, Timor was defended by an ill-equipped 1,400-man force of Allied troops, predominantly from Australia, Great Britain and the Dutch East Indies. The paratroopers belonged to the Yokosuka 3rd SNLF. Captain Koichi Fucumi led 632 men in the airborne assault. Some 308 paratroopers landed on Penfoi airfield at 09.30 on 20 February and further 325 were dropped near Usua, 14 miles (22km) east of Kupang at 10.00 the following day. The seizure of the particular airfield by the Japanese would seal off a 1,600-mile (2,575km) air route between Java and Australia. The paratroopers who were dropped on 21 February were to support the landing of seaborne troops in Kupang and cut off the Allied retreat line towards Champlong. The operation couldn't have gone worse. Men were massively scattered up to 10 miles (16km) from the designated DZ. Casualties on 20 February were thirty-six dead and thirty-nine wounded/injured. In the Kupang sector the paratroopers suffered many casualties while fighting against elements of the Australian 2/40 Battalion, a commando-type unit. In Timor, although the Dutch East Indies had surrendered on 8 March, the Japanese campaign lasted until 10 February 1943, when the remainder of the Allied (mainly Australian commando) force was evacuated. As a result of the activity of Australian commandos, an entire Japanese division was tied up on Timor for over six months, preventing its deployment elsewhere. In Timor the Japanese naval paratroopers performed their last combat jump almost two and a half years before the end of the war. On 8 April 1943, an airborne assault against Lashio in Burma, involving the 1st RR, was called off because the ground forces had advanced so fast that there was no need for their support. Almost three weeks later, on 29 April, seventy aircraft with Army paratroopers aboard took off from Toungoan airfield, north of Rangoon, taking part in the Burma campaign. The operation had to be called off because the weather conditions at the DZ were unsuitable. Army paratroopers remained stationed in Rangoon until July 1943, when they returned to Kyushu in Japan.

In December 1944, a 750-man force, mainly from the 2nd RR, was ordered to attack US bases in Luzon and in the Buranen area of Leyte in the Philippines on the night of 6 December in what seemed from the start to be a large-scale suicide mission. The Army paratroopers were flown in Ki-57 transport aircraft, most of which were shot down before reaching the DZs. Only Buranen airfield tested the desperate courage of the Japanese attackers. One aircraft managed to crash-land inside the airfield and those who survived and could still fight got off to join their colleagues who had already landed by parachute. The paratroopers managed to destroy some planes and inflict numerous casualties to the base personnel before they were annihilated during a five-day engagement by elements of the American 11th Airborne Division.[10]

Almost three months before the end of the war in the Pacific, the Japanese Sixth Air Army ordered *Giretsu* commandos to neutralize American-held airfields on Okinawa's west coast. Twelve Mitsubishi Ki-21 heavy bombers, carrying fourteen commandos each, took off on 24 May 1945. Eight aircraft were assigned to attack Yontan airfield. Kadena airfield was the objective for the remainder. Of the aircraft involved in the operation, three were shot down and further four had to abort the mission because of engine problems. The remaining five Ki-21s managed to crash-land at Yontan, taking advantage of the confusion caused to the base a few minutes earlier by a Japanese air raid. About ten surviving raiders, armed with sub-machine guns and various explosives, then wreaked havoc on the supplies and nearby aircraft. The commandos, before being annihilated by the defenders, killed two US servicemen and wounded a further eighteen. They also destroyed or damaged thirty-eight parked aircraft. Only one member of the raiding party survived. He was able to make his way to the Japanese lines on 12 June.[11] Yontan airfield was out of action for 24 hours because of the debris on the runway. This was the only attempt by the Japanese to land airborne troops on Okinawa during the campaign.

The Indians and Gurkhas

On 29 October 1941, the 50th Parachute Brigade was formed by the British in Delhi in India. A parachute training facility was established and run by Ringway instructors at Willingdon airport until 1942 when it was relocated to Chaklala near Rawalpindi. The 50th Parachute Brigade's initial composition included the 151st British Parachute Battalion and the 152nd Indian Parachute Battalion. When the 151st was transferred to England and became part of the 1st Airborne Division as the 156th Parachute Battalion, they were replaced in India by the 154th Gurkha Parachute Battalion. Other components of the brigade included the 411th (Royal Bombay) Parachute Squadron, Indian Engineers and the 50th Medium Machine Gun Company. The 154th Gurkha Parachute Battalion was formed from the 3rd Battalion Gurkha Rifles in August 1943. It was re-designated the 3rd Parachute Battalion, Indian Parachute Regiment, in March 1945 and disbanded in October 1946. In March 1944 the Brigade saw extensive action at Sangshak and later on the Imphal Plains on the Burmese border against two reinforced Japanese divisions.[12]

The Gurkha battalion was not mobilized for the operation as the men had not completed air training. They stayed back to attain airborne status. Early in 1944, the brigade was expanded to form the 44th Indian Airborne Division. The 50th Parachute Brigade was split into two brigades, the 50th and the 77th. The 152nd Indian Parachute Battalion was in turn split to form the 1st and the 4th Indian Parachute Battalions. The 77th Indian Brigade consisted of the 3rd Gurkha Parachute Battalion and two British parachute battalions, the 15th and 16th. Both battalions were raised from Chindit survivors of the Burma campaigns and mustered at Rawalpindi in March 1945. The two ad hoc brigades which had been involved in Chindit operations in Burma were also included to the new formation. The 15th (King's) and 16th (South Stafford) Battalions moved to Bilapur two months later and were re-titled 15th and 16th Parachute Regiments. On 1 March 1945, the Indian Parachute Regiment was formed consisting of four battalions and an equal number of support companies. In November 1944, the 14th Airlanding Brigade was formed from the 2nd King's Own, the 2nd Black Watch and an Indian Battalion, the 4th Rajputana Rifles. In April 1945 the 2nd King's Own was relieved by the 6th Battalion of the 16th Punjab Regiment.

On 1 May, a reinforced Gurkha Parachute Battalion was dropped into Burma at Elephant Point in what was the division's first and only combat jump. Later on, parachute elements of the 44th Airborne Division jumped on minor operations in Malaya, Thailand, French Indochina and the Dutch West Indies. In September, the 50th Parachute Brigade carried out a seaborne landing at Morib beaches in Northern Malaya. The brigade moved on to Singapore before rejoining the 6th Airborne Division in Palestine in May 1946. In late 1945, the Indian Parachute Regiment was disbanded as part of restructuring of the post-war British Army in India. Towards the end of

1945, the 44th Indian Airborne Division was re-designated the 2nd Indian Airborne Division. The new formation moved from Bilapur to Karachi and finally to Qetta. After independence, the units of the 44th Airborne Division were divided between the armies of India and Pakistan.[13]

The Chinese

There were two types of Chinese paratroopers during the Second World War, those trained by the US Army to fight against the common enemy, Japan, and those trained by the Red Army. The latter were the officers and men who escaped to the Soviet Union in the spring of 1941 after the defeat of China's North-east Army by invading Japanese forces. Many of these Chinese volunteered for parachute training and consequently served in Red Army scout units deployed in what is now the border province of Heilongjiang. Their parachute training involved jumping from 2,000ft (610m) at least ten times.[14]

When the Soviet Union declared war on Japan on 8 August 1945 and before the latter's surrender, Red Army's Chinese paratroopers had a chance to fight against the common enemy, the Japanese, near Vladivostok. The majority of Chinese paratroopers during the Second World War had American instructors. They made up a parachute regiment that was formed in February 1944 as part of Chiang Kai-shek's Nationalist Army. In March 1945, forty uniformed Chinese, including two generals, arrived to the United States for jump training at Fort Benning, Georgia.[15]

China's first parachute regiment was not involved in any major airborne operations until the end of the war. Chinese paratroopers were only deployed in various parts of their country following the departure of the Japanese occupation forces. In January 1945, officers and men of the Chinese 1st Parachute Regiment were transferred to the commando units that were organized by the American Office of Strategic Services (OSS). These units were called Operational Groups (OGs) and were like the OSS's Special Operation (SO) teams that had been fighting already in German-occupied and Japanese-occupied parts of Europe and South-East Asia. The OGs, unlike the SOs, operated in military uniform. In China the OGs, having 200 men each, were trained in infantry tactics, guerrilla warfare, demolitions, intelligence-gathering and parachuting. In all, twenty such units were eventually organized. Between 1942 and 1944, the OSS had conducted operations mainly along the Arakan coast of Burma. Several Chinese commandos with their OG advisors conducted operations against the Japanese before the final surrender. In the early 1950s, some Chinese-Americans were trained at the Parachute School in Fort Benning for Central Intelligenc Agency (CIA) sponsored assignments. They would drop in Communist China so they 'could work their way into the population' and sent back reports.[16]

Chapter 9

Allied Airborne Operations in the Pacific

Until now, the majority of literature regarding airborne operations has focussed on the experience of US airborne forces in the European theatre of operations during the Second World War, thanks to the 'Germany First' policy of the Allies.[1] The literature of the war in the Pacific is not nearly as prolific.[2] From 1940 to 1945, there was a total of twelve airborne operations in the Pacific – seven conducted by the Allies (mostly Americans) and five by the Japanese.[3] Two American units, the 11th Airborne Division and the 503rd RCT, were the only Allied airborne forces that fought in the Pacific during the war – the former in a more traditional role and the latter being reserved for special missions.

Dutch New Guinea

The US 11th Airborne Division arrived in Dutch New Guinea (DNG), east of Papua, on 11 June 1944 following a 28-day voyage from San Francisco. The 503rd PIR landed in Cairns in Australia on 2 December 1943 after a voyage of forty-three days. The 503rd PIR was the first airborne unit to fight against the Japanese as an independent group. The regiment, commanded by Lieutenant Colonel Kenneth H. Kinsler, was expanded into an RCT with the assignment of the 462nd Parachute Artillery Battalion on 29 March 1944 and the 161st Parachute Engineer Company six months later. In its three years in the southern Pacific the 503rd RCT was involved in five major operations in DNG and the Philippines. The 187th and the 188th GIRs were deployed in DNG on 29 May 1944. The 11th Airborne, commanded by Major General Joseph M. Swing, was based at Dobodura airfield, where the division remained until their deployment to the Philippines five months later. The first airborne operation in the Pacific was the landing at Nadzab on the island of Noemfoor, off the coast of DNG. The operation was necessary for the capture of Lae, occupied by a 10,000-strong Japanese force. The 503rd RCT's major mission was to seize, secure, and prepare the Nadzab airfield for air-lifted units of the Australian 7th Division. Once in the possession of Lae, the Allies could dominate the western approach of the Witiaz Straits and establish bases for the attack on Cape Gloucester, thus contributing to the further isolation of Rabaul, the Japanese stronghold in New Britain.[4] The 503rd PIR's 1st Battalion would land directly onto the local airfield, while the 2nd and the 3rd Battalions would drop north and east of the airfield, respectively.

The ninety-six C-47 transport aircraft carrying the 503rd PIR's paratroopers, supplies and artillery took off from Port Moresby airfield in the morning of 5 September. On board were also thirty-four volunteers from an Australian artillery unit. After receiving intensive parachute training, the Australians jumped on Nadzab to man two light field guns in support of the 503rd RCT. The flight to Nadzab lasted two hours. A total of 146 US fighter planes were employed to protect the transports. As a result of the close air support, the Japanese did not intercept the drop of the American airborne force. Prior to the parachute drop, which was performed in daylight, six squadrons of B-25 medium bombers delivered a furious bombardment on the areas in the Markham Valley where the three battalions were to land. The Dakotas reached the DZs in three columns at a jump altitude of 400–500ft (123–152m). At 10.09 the transport planes started dropping the 1,700 paratroopers, while General MacArthur circled above in a B-17 observation plane. In the drop, that lasted one minute and ten seconds, the 503rd RCT suffered three fatalities due to parachute malfunctions and thirty-six jump injuries.[5] To avoid further casualties the drop of the 2nd Battalion was called off at the last moment. It was also decided that the battalion would be delivered amphibiously two days later. The landing was unopposed, but the seaborne paratroopers were later attacked by enemy bomber planes.

At 10.00 on 6 September the first C-47s landed at Nadzab, bringing in excavating equipment and flamethrowers.[6] By midday, the 7th Division's headquarters and the Australian 25th Brigade had been air-transported to Nadzab. By 10 September, the entire 7th Division, some 3,500 men, equipment and vehicles, had been deployed around the airfield. The same day, American paratroopers and units of the Australian 25th Brigade attacked down the Markham river road towards Lae, encountering moderate resistance. The Japanese troops were encircled and forced to evacuate their major military outpost at Lae, abandoning their equipment. When the Japanese defenders realized that their rear had infiltrated, their lines of communication severed and that their position was rapidly becoming untenable, they had no option but to withdraw to Kiari.[7] The 503rd RCT played a major role in the elimination of the Japanese garrison on the island.[8] Sergeant Ray E. Eubanks was posthumously awarded the Congressional Medal of Honor for his heroic actions in Noemfoor. The deployment of airborne troops in order to seize Nadzab's airfield was the essential component of the Allies' successful capture of Lae. The use of paratroopers in the Noemfoor battle 'unlocked Lae's back door and facilitated the rapid introduction of the entire 7th Division into the enemy rear'.[9] The airborne operations to seize the Nadzab airfield created operation shock, thus leading to the enemy's paralysis and ultimate defeat. The successful deployment of parachute troops in the Markham valley has been credited with saving the concept of vertical envelopment from being abandoned following several less-than-successful engagements in the European theatre of operations, particularly in Sicily. By October, Nadzab boast six different runways, one 6,000ft (1.8km) in length, surfaced with all-weather bitumen.[10] The construction works on the Noemfoor airfield facilitated the Allied plans for an invasion in the Philippines.

The Burma Campaign

The only land campaign by the Allies in the Pacific theatre of operations during the Second World War was mounted in Burma. The Japanese army had captured most of this British colony in South East Asia and were threatening India. After an unsuccessful counter-offensive by British and Indian forces in the Arakan, a mountainous coastal province in the north-west of the country, it was decided to deploy a long-range penetration unit led by Lieutenant Colonel Orde Wingate. When he arrived in Japanese-held Burma in March 1942, he was tasked with organizing guerrilla operations. Wingate's experimental force, also known as Chindits, later became the 77th Indian Infantry Brigade. The brigade was deployed to Burma in March 1944 in what is also known as the 2nd Chindit Expedition. The Chindits infiltrated through the Japanese front lines and marched deep into Burma, tasked with cutting the main north–south railway. Wingate's vision of the operation was that his columns, spread throughout northern Burma, would break and disrupt the Japanese Army's rail artery, raid bases and harass patrols.

The airborne invasion of Burma was conducted on the night of 5 March 1944. Three brigades of 12,000 men, 2,000 mules, anti-aircraft guns, equipment, stores and much other 'warlike paraphernalia' were transported behind enemy lines in gliders.[11] The first few gliders landed safely managing to avoid the crashed gliders and other obstacles, but many of them ditched and became immovable. Several other gliders crashed into stationary gliders before they had been unloaded. The total losses on the ground amounted to about thirty killed and twenty-one wounded, including British troops and American air crews. Sixty-six officers and men were missing. Of the fifty-four gliders that took off for the operation, thirty-four landed on the designated LZ and further six fell into Japanese-held territory. The remainder landed in British-held territory in Assam. The operation lasted three months, during which time the invaders conducted guerrilla warfare.

Some 3,000 men entered Burma in multiple columns. They damaged Japanese communications in northern Burma, cutting the railway for possibly two weeks. By early May, the Chindits had 818 casualties. The survivors were so debilitated by disease, wounds, and malnutrition that all but 600 had to be eventually discharged for medical reasons. The 2nd Chindit Expedition was somehow 'a failure that became a triumph'.[12] Mosaung and Myitkyina were the turning point in the Burma war.[13] Myitkyina fell in Allied hands on 3 August 1944. It could now be used as a base for aircraft supplying China. The capture of Myitkyina was the successful climax of the north Burma campaign. Meanwhile, the Independent 50th Indian Parachute Brigade, commanded by Lieutenant Colonel Maxwell Hope-Thompson, had taken part in the Battle of Sangshak that took place in Manipur in the forested and mountainous frontier area between India and Burma from 20 to 26 March 1944. The Japanese drove units of the Independent 50th Indian Parachute Brigade, fighting as infantry, from their positions with heavy casualties, but suffered serious losses themselves. The battle has been credited with delaying the Japanese forces moving up for the Battle of Imphal and allowing British and Indian reinforcements to reach Kohima.

The Battle of Imphal, together with the simultaneous Battle of Kohima, was the turning point of the Burma campaign. The Battle of Kohima was the largest Japanese defeat to that date in their history.[14] On 1 May 1945, the 154th Gurkha Parachute Battalion, part of the independent 50th Indian Parachute Brigade, was dropped on Elephant Point and cleared the mouth of the Yangon River in a large-scale operation, resulting the liberation of Rangoon, Burma's capital and principal seaport, five days later. Elephant Point had to be neutralized as the 26th Division was to carry out an amphibious landing not far from there.[15] The pathfinders, led by Major Hedley, a former Chindit, parachuted at 05.50 from two transport planes. The battalion (less one company) was carried by thirty-eight C-47s over a DZ situated five miles (8km) west of the point. The jump started at 06.00 and concluded by 07.15. The drop was unopposed and accomplished with only five minor casualties. While heading towards Elephant Point, the paratroopers were bombed mistakenly from the air by Allied Liberator aircraft, causing thirty-two casualties among the Gurkhas. At 16.00 leading elements of the paratroopers engaged the enemy at the Elephant Point. The fight was short and fierce. Of the thirty-seven Japanese defenders only one remained alive. The Gurkha casualties were one man killed and fifty-seven wounded.[16] Late afternoon saw the Gurkhas, after a trudge through the same torrential rain, on top of the Japanese gunners.[17] The point was taken and the 26th Division could come in off the increasingly rough seas and secure Rangoon.

The Invasion of the Philippines

The US 11th Airborne Division played a prominent role in the assault on the island of Leyte in the Philippines in late 1944. The division landed amphibiously at Bito beach on Leyte Gulf on 18 November. The 188th GIR was to secure the southern part of the sector. The 1st Battalion, 188th GIR engaged the enemy on the coast of Leyte. They had to protect the 511st PIR as it moved west. The 11th Airborne, pushing inland, cleared the Ormoc-Burauen trail, an important Japanese supply line. The division's general mission was to seize and secure within its zone all exits from the mountain into Leyte valley and, most importantly, to assist the attack of the 7th Division towards Ormoc. The 511th PIR performed this mission during harsh, monsoonal weather in steep and heavily forested terrain.

On 6 December, the Japanese conducted two unsuccessful raids, involving a number of Army paratroopers, around Burauen airfield, where the headquarters of the 11th Airborne was located.[18] It was a major attack during General Tomoyuki Yamashita's ambitious effort to recapture the airfields in the Burauen-Dulag area. The raiders, who had landed near San Pablo airstrip, were eliminated in a five-day engagement by an ad hoc combat group, made up of the division's artillerymen, engineers and support troops and led by the divisional commander, Major General J.M. Swing. When the enemy was repelled, the 1/187th GIR was ordered to clear the Buri strip. The 511st PIR was then reinforced by the 2/187th GIR.

On 17 December, the 511st PIR broke through the enemy lines and arrived at the western shoreline of Leyte, linking up with elements of the American 32nd

Infantry Division.[19] The fighting went on until 23 December, when Hacksaw Hill was captured by American paratroopers. Following the landing on Leyte, the 503rd RCT conducted a major amphibious operation on Mindoro island, south of Luzon, in the central Philippines, on 15 December 1944. Originally, it was intended for the unit to jump on Mindoro, but due to inadequate airstrip facilities on Leyte an airborne landing was not possible. The 503rd RCT, after landing, was subjected to intense air and naval actions, at one point being shelled for twenty-five minutes by a Japanese naval task force. One company of the 503rd RCT engaged in a fierce battle against a company-size Japanese force defending an enemy air-raid warning station on the north end of the island.

The success of the Mindoro operation enabled the USAAF to construct and operate airstrips and forward air bases on the island to support later landings in the Philippines at Lingayen Gulf in Luzon. The main goal for the Allies was now the envelopment of Manila, the Philippines' capital and a key logistical node. In the light of this goal an airborne operation to seize Tagaytay Ridge was also decided upon. In early January 1945, the Japanese forces stationed in the greater area of Manila were estimated at 152,000.[20] On 22 January, the 11th Airborne was ordered to open a second Allied front south of Manila.[21] The Allied plan called for one airborne and two amphibious operations conducted as part of the Allied advance on Manila from the south. The ambitious portion of the operation was assigned to the 187th GIR and the 188th GIR, while the 511th PIR, 11th Airborne, would perform an airborne assault onto Tagaytay Ridge. Once ashore at Mindoro, the division had two primary tasks: to seize Tagaytay Ridge and envelop Manila from the south.[22] The 187th GIR and the 188th GIR were to assault Nasughu Point, 60 miles (97km) south of Manila, on the west coast of the island of Luzon.[23] On the morning of 31 January, the 188th GIR led the assault and by 10.30 the regiment had pushed deep into southern Luzon, creating space for the 187th GIR to also come ashore. By 14.30, after the establishment of a beachhead, the 1/188th GIR advanced, reaching Palico River and securing a vital bridge intact. The glidermen then captured enemy positions on Mount Aiming, while a company of the 188th GIR withstood a Banzai-type suicide attack by Japanese soldiers. The two glider regiments went on advancing towards Tagaytay Ridge and stopped the enemy from setting up defensive positions. Allied intelligence estimated that approximately 7,000 Japanese troops held defensive positions guarding the mountainous approaches to Manila.[24] By midday, on 1 February, the 188th GIR launched an assault and managed to break through the Japanese positions. The two glider regiments kept advancing uphill towards Tagaytay Ridge. In this area, situated 32 miles (51km) south-south-west of Manila, the 511st PIR commanded by Lieutenant Colonel Orin D. Haugen, was to perform their first combat jump. With only forty-eight C-47s available, the operation would be conducted in three stages.[25] The regimental HQ, the 2/511th PIR and half of the 3/511th PIR would drop first. The rest of the regiment would arrive in the second lift and the 45th Parachute Field Artillery Battalion would drop in third. The 511th PIR was to be dropped on the highest ground between the 11th Airborne and Manila in a position just behind the location the regimental commander, Major General J. M. Swing, had correctly anticipated that the Japanese would choose to make their stand. At 07.30 on 2 February, the first aircraft, carrying the 2/511 PIR and half of the 3/511th PIR, took off from San Jose airfield at Mindoro, some 80 miles (120km) from Tagaytay, and in less than an hour had reached the DZ.[26]

The unopposed parachute drop started at 08.15. The first eighteen 'sticks' of the first drop, approximately 350 men, landed with perfect precision. Unfortunately, the next thirty aircraft dropped their paratroopers six miles (10km) east of the DZ, owing to jumpmaster miscalculation.[27] In General John R. Galvin's words: 'The jump was a small-scale repetition of such earlier jumps at North Africa and Sicily, where nothing seemed to go right except the accomplishment of the assigned mission and the defeat of the enemy.'[28] The second drop, involving the 1/511th PIR and the remainder of the 3/511th landed on the same DZ five hours later.[29] The third drop was conducted the following day, at 08.15, bringing in the 457th Parachute Field Artillery Battalion. Most of the paratroopers, with the exception of the artillery unit, landed on the wrong drop zone owing to jumpmaster miscalculation.[30]

On 2 February, it took the mis-dropped paratroopers some five hours to rendezvous with their colleagues at the previously-assigned rally points. By 15.00, the two glider regiments that had landed by sea, the 187th and the 188th, eventually reached 511 PIR's position at Tagaytay Ridge. They had marched 35 miles (56km) uphill from the beachhead at Nosughu. The third drop of paratroopers joined the airborne force at Tagaytay Ridge at 08.15 on 3 February. The airborne drops of 2 and 3 February facilitated the insertion of three fresh rifle battalions and one battalion of field artillery onto the high ground. By emplacing their 75mm guns on Tagaytay Ridge, the 11th Airborne was able to maximize indirect fire assets. After clearing Tagaytay Ridge of its remaining defenders, the 11th Airborne continued their attack north in order to envelop Manila.

The paratroopers encountered occasional enemy resistance on their way to the Parañaque River, the southern boundary of Manila, reached by nightfall of 4 February. The advance was resumed the following day, after the crossing of the river by the American airborne force. The enemy resistance, meanwhile, was becoming stiffer and stiffer. The city was protected by the Genko Line, a major Japanese defensive position that stretched from Nichols Field/Fort William McKinley to Laguna Bay along Manila's southern edge.[31] Some 17,000 troops, mostly marines, were deployed for the defence of the capital of the Philippines.[32] The 11th Airborne fought as infantry for the retaking of Manila. They also participated in the mopping-up operations in south Luzon and the kicking out of Japanese troops from north Luzon. The division was ordered to breach the Genko Line and drive into Manila. All three rifle regiments were committed to the assault. Spearheading the division's attack on 5 February, the 511th PIR overcame fierce resistance and broke into the Japanese position.

On 7 February, the 187th and the 188th GIRs stormed the area around Nichols Field. The 1/187th GIR attacked the airfield from the north-west, while the entire 188th GIR moved in from the south and the south-east. The airfield formed the centre of the Genko Line. At the same time, elements of the 511th PIR fought house-to-house and in the streets. The fighting was to the death with hand-to-hand combat using bayonets and knives. By nightfall, the 187th and the 188th GIRs cleared most of the field of enemy combatants. The enemy kept retreating to the east. The pincer movement succeeded in taking the airfield on 12 February and, despite a local counter-attack, by nightfall the position was secured.[33] The 511th PIR fought through the Japanese Genko Line, penetrating as far as Manda before turning east to join the attack on Fort William McKinley (Fort Bonifacio) on 7 February. The commander of the Japanese defenders on Luzon, Rear Admiral Sanjii Iwabuchi, who had his headquarters at the fort, ordered his troops to fight to the death. Fort William McKinley was recaptured by the 1/188th GIR on 8 February. From then on, the 11th Airborne's rapidity of advance was replaced by intensive sieges and urban warfare. On 15 February, the 1/187th GIR, alongside other American units, launched an attack on Mabato Point, a heavily fortified position. It would take six days of hard fighting, multiple airstrikes and the frequent use of napalm bombs and heavy artillery before the point was secured.[34] On 17 February, having taken heavy casualties on its approach to Fort William McKinley, the 11th Airborne assaulted the fort. The 511th PIR led the break-in and by the end of the following day the area had been cleared of its defenders.

America's Return to Corregidor

Although Manila was almost under Allied control, the harbour remained inaccessible due to the enemy's possession of the island of Corregidor. At 3.5 miles (6km) long and 1.25 miles (2km) wide, Corregidor's small size betrays its operational significance, as it controls access to one of the world's finest deep-water ports.[35] It was, at the time, one of the four island-fortresses in Manila Bay and in the South China Sea that provided interlocking fields of fire.[36] Corregidor seemed the key to converting Manila from a burned-out ruin into a functioning Allied base. An assault on Corregidor was therefore a top priority for the Allied high command in the Pacific theatre of operations. The island had been the bastion which withstood a fierce siege in 1942 and 1943, before falling in Japanese hands.

The five-month resistance of Corregidor interrupted the Japanese advance to Australia. The island was an ideal defensive structure in the narrow intersection of Manila Harbor, as its near-vertical cliffs rise to a height of 500ft (152m) on the north, west and southern sides.[37] It contained coastal artillery batteries, anti-aircraft guns and machine-gun nests. Corregidor's network of underground tunnels, constructed by the Americans before the war, provided bombproof living quarters, a communications centre, a hospital, food stores, ammunition dumps and a bulk petroleum storage. These facilities made Corregidor a resilient strongpoint. Taking into consideration the heavy price paid by the Japanese in their invasion three years earlier, MacArthur came up with a combination of a three battalion-size airborne assault and a battalion-size amphibious assault. It was also, decided that Bataan Peninsula should be captured by US Marine forces before 14 February in order to clear the entrance to Manila Harbor.

'Rock Force' was the name given to the force assigned to invade Corregidor from the air and sea. The force was made of Lieutenant Colonel George M. Jones' 503rd PIR, augmented with the 462nd Parachute Field Artillery Battalion and the 161st Parachute Engineer Company.[38] The amphibious portion of the Rock Force consisted of the 3/34th RCT, 24th Division. The 3/503rd PIR would drop onto DZs Alpha and Bravo to secure the Topside of the island and provide overwatch for the 3/34th RCT's amphibious landing to secure Malinta Hill. The operation would be followed by the 2/503rd PIR that was assigned to conduct a relief-in-place with the regiment's 3rd Battalion. The 1/503rd PIR, designated as the Rock Force reserve, was scheduled to jump later, after the second drop.[39] Prior to the airborne assault, the island was to be bombed by air forces for ten days and by naval forces for three days. The paratroopers left Mindoro for the 75-minute flight to Corregidor, while the 3/34th RCT, were heading to the island's Black Beach on twenty-five landing craft.

At 08.30 on 16 February, the furious air and naval bombardment ceased and the sky over the Corregidor was filled with the blossoming parachutes of the 3/503rd PIR. After landing, they secured the DZs on the Topside of the island and established overwatch positions covering Black Beach in preparation for the following on amphibious assault. Elements of the battalion neutralized the command centre, killing Captain Akira Itagaki, the commanding officer. At 10.28, leading elements of the 3/34th RCT landed successfully on Black Beach. The seaborne force quickly secured Malinta Hill and blocked the approach to Topside.[40] They also unloaded key equipment, including some M4 Sherman tanks and 75mm self-propelled guns. At 12.40, the 2/503rd PIR began to drop on the Topside DZs. The battalion encountered significant enemy resistance, in the form of small arms, mortar and anti-aircraft fire, compared to what the 3/503rd PIR had experienced earlier, because the element of surprise was gone, as the Japanese were by now very much aware of the paratroopers' presence. Braving intense fire, the paratroopers rushed forward and overcame the heavy blockhouse defences, dropping explosives into embrasures to kill hidden Japanese gunners. By 14.00, the 2/503rd PIR was assembled on the ground and had conducted the relief-in-place with the 3/503rd PIR. This action allowed the 3/503rd PIR to expand the Topside's clearing operation and attack Japanese troops, blocking the defenders' access to the road leading to Black Beach. On their way, the paratroopers encountered strong resistance. As darkness fell on the island, Lieutenant Colonel Jones directed his force to cease offensive operations and establish defence perimeters. In recognition of the high level of jump casualties (14.2 per cent), he cancelled the 1/503rd's drop.

By then, the airborne force was at its most vulnerable point, as they were divided and outnumbered three to one. The paratroopers on Topside could subsist only from airdrops. If the Japanese had been able to wage a coordinated counter-attack, they would have likely overwhelmed the Allied ground forces and retained possession of Corregidor. The Japanese attack, although fanatical, was uncoordinated and failed. The paratroopers on the Topside of the island and the infantry at Black Beach survived their first night on Corregidor. The fight went on the following day, 17 February. In the afternoon, a daring convoy led by Sherman tanks ran the Japanese gauntlet twice to the top to deliver water and ammunition. It was fortunate for the Allies that the Japanese were without anti-tank weaponry. At 16.35 pm on 17 February, the 1/503rd landed at Black Beach. On 18 February, US forces using napalm bombs, flamethrowers and grenades started clearing one-by-one the Japanese emplacements that were mostly inside caves or underground. On the morning of 19 February, the American forces had to endure suicidal Banzai-type attacks. At 06.00, approximately 600 Japanese marines launched an attack on Topside. Despite their fanatical fervour, they faced prepared defensive positions reinforced by 75mm artillery. By 08.00, the Japanese attack had been soundly defeated.[41]

From 19 February, the Allies on Corregidor worked to systematically clear the island, killing hundreds of Japanese. By 23 February, the western part of the island was declared secure. In response to the clearing action, the Japanese conducted a final counter-attack on 24 February.[42] The battle ended with the Japanese failing to accomplish their objective. On 26 February, the clearing operations went on. At 11.00 the Japanese set off a massive ammunition dump on Corregidor's eastern end. The explosion instantly killed 52 1/503rd PIR paratroopers, who were on a mopping-up mission in the area, and grievously wounded another 144.[43] The mopping-up operation went on until 2 March. During the course of the entire operation, the invading forces sustained 1,105 casualties (killed, wounded or missing) out of a total force of 6,000 men. Only twenty Japanese were taken prisoner. Japanese sources have estimated there were 6,550 Japanese on the island when the Allied forces landed. Of those only fifty survived. The 503rd PIR, however, lost 169 men killed and many more wounded or injured. Corregidor was the most vicious combat action in which the regiment engaged during its existence. For its successful capture of the island fortress, the 503rd PIR received its nickname 'The Rock Regiment'. Corregidor, after its recapture, became a symbol of victory for the Allies and a turning point in the Pacific War.

The Los Baños Raid

On 30 January 1945, a combined force of US Army Rangers, Alamo Scouts and Filipino guerrillas liberated 522 prisoners of war and civilian internees from a Japanese camp near Cabanatuan on the island of Luzon. Almost a month later, the 11th Airborne was tasked with organizing an operation for the rescue of 2,147 American and European nationals held by the Japanese in a college at Los Baños, 40 miles (64km) south-east of Manila. Some 250 Japanese soldiers were guarding the college-turned-concentration camp, which was situated some 20 miles (32km) behind enemy lines. At 07.00 on 23 February, 'B' Company of the 1/511th PIR, parachuted close to the concentration camp. The drop was made from ten C-47s at 500ft (150m). The guards outside the concentration camp had already been neutralized by members of a platoon of the regiment that had been deployed in the vicinity since 21 February and was acting in cooperation with local guerrillas. The parachuted company then stormed the camp and by 07.30 the remainder of the guards had been dealt with. By 11.30, the internees had been transported across Laguna lake to safety. In the meantime, the 188th GIR, supported by tanks and artillery, had launched a diversion attack across the San Juan river. They, also, cut off the road between Los Baños and the 10,000-strong Japanese force that was stationed in the area. Two 188th GIR troopers and two Filipino guerrillas were killed in what is considered as the most successful rescue operation in contemporary military history. In 2003, in the United States General Colin L. Powell, the Chairman of the Joint Chiefs of Staff, stated: 'I doubt that any airborne unit in the world will ever be able to rival the Los Baños Prison raid. It is the text book airborne operation for all ages and all armies.'[44]

The Last Combat Jump in the Pacific

Meanwhile, in Manila the 11th Airborne launched an attack with the men being engaged in a ferocious street fighting. The Japanese had destroyed large parts of the city, having converted several houses into machine-gun nests. There were 800,000 inhabitants in the city at the time. Over 100,000 of them perished during the battle in the Pacific Theatre's Stalingrad, as Manila was characterized. The capital of the Philippines was liberated on 21 February, but sporadic fighting in the city continued until 3 March, when all organized Japanese resistance ended.[45] On the day the Los Baños internees were freed, the 11th Airborne was ordered to advance south of Manila and contribute to the destruction of the remaining Japanese in southern Luzon. It would take until the end of April for the American forces to subdue these troops. After returning to Mindoro from Corregidor, the 503rd RCT was called upon to bolster the US 40th Division, which was bogged down on the island of Negros in the central Philippines. On 7 April, the 503rd RCT was inserted into Negros by landing craft, although it had been alerted for another combat jump. The objectives of the proposed jump, a strategic bridge and a large lumber mill, were destroyed by Japanese forces, thereby eliminated the first objectives of the 503rd RCT. The American paratroopers engaged in fierce battles against frantic enemy resistance in the mountainous areas of Negros for more than five months. The 40th Division was then ordered to move to Mindanao, leaving the 503rd RCT to battle the Japanese on their own.

The paratroopers would spend the remainder of the war conducting mopping-up operations on the island often against fanatical enemy resistance. After Japan's surrender in August 1945, some 6,150 Japanese soldiers surrendered to the 503rd RCT, although some continued to hold out until October.[46] In Luzon, all enemy resistance in southern Luzon had ended by 1 May. Then the 11th Airborne established a base at an airstrip near Lipa and started preparations for Operation Downfall, the planned invasion of Japan. On 23 June, a battalion-size combat team was to perform the last operational jump in the Pacific, being dropped on Camalanugan Airfield, 10 miles (16km) south of Aparri. The unopposed jump of the 187th GIR on Japanese soil on 30 August 1945 was performed after the surrender and was just for show. The combat team was made up of the 1/511st PIR, two companies of the 2/511th PIR and detachments of artillery, engineers, signal and medical airborne units. They were to be transported by fifty-four C-47s and thirteen Douglas C-46 Commando aircraft, as well as by six Waco CG-4A gliders, which would carry jeeps and supplies for the task force.[47] Gliders were to be used for the first time in an operation involving American troops in the Pacific. The airborne force was tasked with cutting off the retreat of the Japanese commander, General Yamashita.

The jump started at 21.00. Strong winds and uneven ground around the airfield caused two fatalities and seventy injuries during the drop. After landing, the paratroopers advanced southwards. The Japanese resistance was stiff, but still inadequate to restrain the advancing enemy. Three days later, the American airborne force encountered lead elements of the 37th Infantry Division advancing from the south. The 511st PIR remained in the Lipa-Batangas area, preparing for the invasion of Japan, until the atomic bombings of Hiroshima and Nagasaki. The total battle casualties for the 11th Airborne were 2,431 men, of whom 497 were killed in action and further 120 died of wounds or injuries, 1,926 were wounded and 11 were missing.[48] In one month, during the Luzon campaign, the 1/188th GIR, lost 40 men and a further 103 wounded in action. US War Department estimated to 10,000 the Japanese killed by the 503rd RCT during combat operations in the southern Pacific. The 11th Airborne spent 105 days in combat from the landing at Nasaghu to the end of the Luzon Campaign.

The division was sent to Australia where the 187th and the 188th GIRs were upgraded to three-battalion glider-parachute regiments on 20 July. The 11th Airborne was chosen by General MacArthur to lead the Allied forces into Japan after the surrender. The 511th PIR went to Tokyo and then, on 16 September, to northern Honshu. Paratroopers were deployed in Okinawa on 12 August and then to the main Japanese island of Honshu. On 30 August, the 188th GIR landed at Atsugi airfield, near Yokohama, with 1,096 men to occupy the city and guard the docks of the harbour. The 187th GIR quickly followed with 1,257 men and the 511th PIR with 1,165 men.[49] The 187th GIR was the only Allied unit parachuted onto Japanese soil.[50] By early November, all paratroopers with lengthy service had been rotated back to the United States, while those who had served in the combat team for a shorter time had been reassigned to the 11th Airborne and deployed as occupation troops around Japan. The division was mainly based to northern Japan along the coast of Honshu and on the island of Hokkaido.[51] On February 1946, the 511th PIR returned to the United States. American paratroopers remained in Japan until May 1949, when the 11th Airborne Division was relieved and recalled to the United States.[52]

A fully-equipped American paratrooper climbing into a transport plane hours before the Normandy landings on 6 June 1944. (Center of Military History, US Army)

As early as 1934, the USSR had twenty-nine paratroop and glider battalions. On 30 November 1939, during the Red Army's invasion of Finland, Soviet paratroopers made the first combat jump in history. (www.quora.com/were-there-any-Soviet-paratroopers-during-ww2-)

Italian Air Force General Alessandro Guidoni. He was fatally injured on 27 April 1928 at Montecelio airfield, near Rome, at the age of 48, while testing a new parachute for the *Regia Aeronautica*. (Italian Air Force)

Major General William C. Lee. (1895–1948). As a junior officer, he formed US Army's first paratroop platoon and then commanded the Jump School at Fort Benning, Georgia. In August 1942, he assumed command of the 101st Airborne Division. Lee is often referred to as the 'Father of the US Airborne'. (General William C. Lee Museum, Dunn, North Carolina)

A German paratrooper ready to exit from a Junkers Ju 52 for an operational jump in the early stages of the Second World War. Arms and ammunition were available to the *Fallschirmjäger* at the time inside canisters that were also parachuted in the drop zone. (Bundesarchiv, Bild 101I584-2154-06A)

German paratroopers on the attack after landing in the drop zone. (https: // mxdoc.com / queue / osprey-combat-oo1-british-paratrooper-vs-fallschirm-jager-medhtml)

Some 10,000 German paratroopers and 750 glider-borne troops landed on the Greek island of Crete on 20 May 1941 in what was the first mainly airborne invasion in military history. (Arthur Conry / Wiki-Ed / Wikimedia Commons / CC BY-SA 3.0)

Friedrich August Freiherr von der Heydte (1907–94) commanded German paratrooper units during the Battle of Crete in 1941 and the Ardennes Offensive in 1944. After the war, he was reinstated in the West German armed forces, achieving the rank of general and taught International Law at the University of Würzburg. (Bundesarchiv, Bild 183-H 26044)

On 22 June 1940, British Army's No. 2 Commando was turned over to parachute duties. Five months later, the unit had reached battalion size, reinforced with a glider wing. (https://arnhemjim.blogspot.com/2012/ii/earlybritish-paratroop-training.html: 30 November 2012)

British paratroopers at the central training establishment in Ringway near Manchester in January 1941. The converted A.W. 38 Whitley, seen in the background, was the type of medium bomber that had been selected a year earlier as the standard paratroop transport. (Imperial War Museum)

British airborne troops inside an Airspeed Horsa glider ready to take off from RAF Brize Norton, Oxfordshire, during the Second World War. (Public Domain)

Major (later Major General) John D. Frost (1912–93) was one of the first officers of the British Army to join the newly-formed Parachute Regiment in 1941. He led his men in many wartime operations in France, North Africa, Sicily, on the Italian mainland and subsequently in the Battle of Arnhem in Holland. In the photograph, taken on 27 February 1942, Frost wears the uniform of his former regiment, the Cameronians. (Scottish Rifles). (Public Domain)

American paratroopers before jumping over Normandy on 6 June 1944.
(US Army Signal Corps)

Chinese paratroopers, members of the uniformed Operational Groups
(OGs), and their US Office of Strategic Services (OSS) instructors prior
to a tactical jump performed in 1945 in China on the eve of the Japanese
surrender. (http: // www.soc.mil / oss / operational-groups.html)

SAS recruits being trained in parachute jumping at Qabrit in Egypt during the Second World War (www.dailymail.co.uk/news/article-2076967/ www2-sas-raid-deep-Rommel-territory-convinced-brass-help-win-war. html)

The founder of the SAS and its first commander, Lieutenant Colonel David Stirling, in 1942 in North Africa, standing next to one of the Regiment's jeep-mounted parties that were employed for raids or aggressive patrolling in the desert. (Imperial War Museums: E 21338)

Luftwaffe Major Erich Rudorffer (1917–2016) was shot down sixteen times during the Second World War, in nine of which he parachuted to safety! He flew over 1,000 missions, engaging in combat on 3,012 occasions, and scored a total of 334 victories. (Bundesarchiv, Bild 183-2007-1218-501/CC-BY-SA 3.0)

Captain (later Lieutenant Colonel) Klavdia Y. Fomicheva. (1917–58) was one of the Soviet female pilots who parachuted to safety during the Second World War. She was forced to bail out on 23 June 1944, when her Petlyakov Pe-2 bomber was hit and set on fire by an enemy flak, during a combat mission. At the time, she was the commander of the Soviet Air Force's 125th Guards Dive Bomber Regiment. (en.wikipedia.org)

RAF Group Captain Douglas Bader (1910–82), who flew combat missions with artificial legs during the Second World War, was forced to bail out over France on 9 August 1941, when his fighter plane was shot down probably by friendly fire. He was captured by the Germans and held at Colditz until the end of the war. This photo was taken at Duxford airfield in September 1940. (Public Domain)

Aleksander K. Gabszewicz (1911–83) was a Polish pilot who had to bail out when his fighter plane was shot down in the first day of the German invasion of Poland in 1 September 1939. He later made it to England, where he served in the RAF, commanding Polish fighter squadrons. In December 1943, Gabszevicz was appointed commander of the 131st Wing, RAF. (Public Domain)

Canadian Flying Officer Vernon C. Woodward (1916–2000), of the Royal Air Force, dons his parachute before taking off in a Hawker Hurricane Mark I at Fuka airfield in Egypt in 1941. (Public Domain)

USAAF Second Lieutenant. (later Major) Owen J. Baggett (1920–2006). He is referred to as the only person ever to shoot down an enemy fighter with a pistol. It occurred on 31 March 1943 near Pyinmana, in Burma, when Baggett's B-24 bomber was crippled by a Japanese Ki-43 fighter, which then attacked the American pilot as he was descending in his parachute. (RallyPoint.com, 29 January 2018)

The US 187th Airborne Regimental Combat Team was dropped on 20 October 1950 25 miles (40km) north of Pyongyang, the North Korean capital, with the objective of cutting off retreating enemy forces during the battle of Yongju. (Public Domain)

Over 100 C-119 Flying Boxcar transport aircraft drop the US 187th Airborne Regimental Combat Team at Munsan-ni, close the Demilitarized Zone, on 23 March 1951, in a combined operation designed to trap large numbers of Chinese and North Korean troops between the Han and Imjin rivers, north of Seoul. (Public Domain)

The paratrooper commanders at Dien Bien Phu. (From left to right): Lieutenant Colonel Pierre Langlais, Major Marcel Bigeard, Captain André Botella and the partially hidden Major Maurice Guiraud. (ECPAD)

Captured French soldiers from Dien Bien Phu, most of them paratroopers, walk to a prisoner-of-war camp guarded by Viet Minh troops. (Public Domain)

American soldiers are dropped off by US Army UH-1 Huey helicopters in South Vietnam in 1965. (Horst Faas/Associated Press)

US Army helicopters flying over combat patrols in South Vietnam in 1968. (Overseas Weekly Collection/Hoover Institution Library and Archives)

One of the British SAS units that was deployed during the Falklands War. (Newsrep.com/57879/sas-sbs-war-operation-corporate-part-4: 27 July 2016)

For many years after the Second World War the Red Army had the largest airborne force in the world. (https://Maximietteita.blogspot.com/2017/02/history-of-soviet-airborne-forces-ww2.html?m=1)

Elements of the US Army's 82nd Airborne Division in a mass paratroop drop near Andrews Air Force Base in Maryland on 20 May 2006. (Public Domain)

Chapter 10

Second World War Special Operations Units

A number of special operations units emerged and fought remarkably during the Second World War on both the Allied and the Axis sides. A common characteristic of these units was the fact that their officers and other ranks were qualified paratroopers.

The SAS

The British Special Air Service, better known by their initials SAS, was and remains to this day the world's 'most famous and deadly elite military unit'.[1] General Miles Dempsey, who fought as an SAS officer in Sicily and Italy, has outlined the six reasons for the unit's success: good training, fair discipline, physical fitness, the men's confidence in their abilities, careful operational planning and the right spirit.[2] The SAS was found by Lieutenant Colonel David Stirling, who became the unit's first commander. A lieutenant in the Scots Guards, in 1940 Stirling volunteered for the Army's No. 8 Commando, which was deployed at the time in North Africa. While in hospital following a parachuting accident, he formulated his plans for establishing a 200-man raiding unit. His idea was for teams of parachute-trained soldiers to operate behind enemy lines, hitting strategic targets and gathering intelligence. Stirling believed that small teams of men stood a better chance of achieving surprise and that their chances would be increased still further if they were trained to reach the target by land, sea or air. He succeeded in bringing his ideas to the attention of General Sir Claude Auchinleck, Commander-in-Chief Middle East. He was persuaded that the unit was to be used to attack targets which would aid the overall grand plan and not as combat troops operating ahead of the front line.[3] The plan was endorsed by the British army high command and permission was given for the raising of the unit. It was named 'L' Detachment, Special Air Service Brigade, although its strength, when it was formed in July 1941, was five officers and sixty other ranks. By doing so, the British high command wanted to deceive German intelligence into thinking that a whole new airborne brigade had been established.[4] Stirling, promoted to major, became commanding officer. He was personally involved in training and recruiting matters. One of Stirling's great attributes, which was essential to the success of the SAS, was his ability to spot and enlist men of talent into the unit. Such men were 'Paddy' Mayne, 'Jock' Lewes, Johnny Cooper and Reg Seekings. The flaming sword of Excalibur, the legendary weapon of King Arthur and symbol of truth and justice, was chosen for the insignia and the winged dagger badge of the unit. The colours of the wings were red and blue. The parachute wings were worn on the sleeve with the exception of the men who had made three parachute drops behind enemy lines, who were permitted to wear the wings over the left breast pocket. White was initially the colour chosen for the men's headgear. The white beret was soon replaced by a khaki forage cap until a final decision was made for the famous ever since beige SAS beret. The unit's motto, 'Who Dares Wins', was reportedly Stirling's idea.

'L' Detachment was based at Qabrit, by the river Nile, on Egypt's Suez Canal, until it was moved to Jalo, some 149 miles (240km) from Benghazi, in Libya's Cyrenaica province. In October 1941, 'L' Detachment was officially renamed the Special Air Service (SAS). The unit's first combat mission, a parachute drop in support of an Allied offensive in North Africa, was conducted a month later. The unit was to be dropped behind the German lines in the Libyan desert, attack airfields in Gazala and Tmimi, gather intelligence and harass the enemy wherever possible. Hours before the attack, on the night of 16/17 November, a powerful storm smothered the designated DZ with strong winds. The high command offered Stirling the option to have the airborne assault cancelled but he decided to proceed with the mission, because he believed that cancelling it would be the end of the SAS experiment. Due to Axis resistance and adverse weather conditions the airborne assault was a complete disaster.[5] The paratroopers were scattered and never reached their targets. One-third of the force was killed or captured.[6] Out of the sixty-six men on the mission, only twenty-two returned to base. This debacle convinced Stirling that parachute insertion was too risky for SAS-type missions.[7]

The next missions were more successful. Moving by land, SAS parties attacked several airfields around the Gulf of Sirte, destroying at least sixty Axis aircraft on the ground.[8] Airfields were hit at Agheil, Tamit, Agedabia and Nofilia. Thirty-seven aircraft were destroyed at Agedabia, near Benghazi, on the night of 21 to 22 December and further twenty-seven at Tamit two nights later.[9] On 26 December, a party led by Lieutenant 'Jock' Lewes raided an airfield at Nofilia, destroying two parked aircraft. On their way back to base, the SAS men were attacked by an Italian fighter plane and Lewes was fatally wounded. By the end of the year, the number of Axis aircraft destroyed on the ground by Stirling's raiders rose to ninety-seven.[10] The raids went on the new year with the port of Benghazi being hit by the SAS three times – in March, June and September. Tobruk was also raided along with airfields, shipping facilities and supply dumps. On the night of 23 January 1942, a jeep-mounted fifteen-man detachment, led by Stirling, attacked the port of Buerat near Benghazi.[11] The raiders, split up into small groups, blew up oil tanks, warehouses and the harbour communications station before retreating without loss.[12] Until June, SAS parties raided Axis airfields in Barce, Medina and Berka (Main), destroying several enemy aircraft.[13] By that time, Stirling was referred to by the Germans as the 'Phantom Major'.[14] Under his command was also the SBS, a canoeist raiding unit that was formed on the Suez Canal in the spring of 1941 mainly for beach and harbour reconnaissance. By the end of 1941, 'Z' Section, another seaborne raiding unit, was absorbed to into the SAS.

On the night of 13 June 1942, a team of Free French SAS volunteers, who were disguised as Germans, attacked an Axis airfield at Martuba. All but two of them, following betrayal, were killed or captured.[15] French volunteers had already taken part in the SAS raids on the Greek islands of Crete and Rhodes. On the night of 7 June, three SBS parties had landed in Crete from the sea to destroy German aircraft in the Castelli, Tymbaki and Maleme airfields. Of these raids only the Tymbaki attack was successful – with seven aircraft being destroyed on the ground by the SBS troopers.[16] Six days later, an SAS/SBS party, made up of four SAS and two SBS men, landed from the sea to attack the Heraklion airfield. Twenty-one aircraft were destroyed on the ground, but the reaction of the German guards, who had been warned about the raid, was fast and decisive. Of the SAS men, who were Free French volunteers, one was killed in the exchange of fire and the rest, including their leader, Commandant Georges Berge, were captured. The SBS men, being Captain George Jellicoe and a Greek-born trooper, managed to escape and return to North Africa.[17] At the same time, two airfields on the island of Rhodes were attacked by another SAS party. Three Italian aircraft and a fuel dump were destroyed but the cost for the invaders was high as only two of them were not killed or captured.[18] A month later, in North Africa, a jeep-mounted SAS party, led by Stirling, carried out raids at Fuka and Mersa Matruh airfields. Thirty enemy aircraft were destroyed on the ground.[19] On the night of 26 July, an SAS detachment mounted on fourteen jeeps raided Sidi Haneish airfield, destroying forty enemy aircraft. The raiding party had one man killed.[20]

In September 1942, the SAS was officially placed on the roll of regiments in the British Army, listed as 1st Special Air Service (1 SAS). Stirling, promoted to lieutenant colonel, had under his command eight squadrons – four British, two French, one Belgian and one Greek – plus the SBS and the Special Interrogation Group (SIG). The SIG was a special unit made up of twelve Jewish refugees who were fluent in German and carried out intelligence-related assignments wearing German uniforms. At about the same time, 'M' Detachment was formed to carry out SAS-type missions in Iraq and Persia. It was made up of 150 volunteers who were trained in parachuting and infiltration techniques before being deployed to the Lebanon. They were led by Captain Fitzroy Maclean who had been wounded in May 1942 during an unsuccessful SAS raid on Benghazi harbour. On the night of 23 December 1942, large numbers of Italian troops surrounded a regional base of the SAS at El Fascia, west of Tamit. A number of men, including Major Vivian Street, were captured. During their transfer to Italy in a submarine, Street and six other captives managed to escape and were later rescued from the sea by a Royal Navy ship.[21] By January 1943, 1 SAS had an establishment of 47 officers and 532 other ranks. On 22 January, a jeep-mounted party led by Stirling was heading to attack Sousse, a Tunisian port used by the Germans to bring in supplies. On their way through Gabes Gab the SAS men were surrounded by a special anti-SAS unit set in ambush by the Germans and had to surrender.[22] Stirling remained in prisoner of war camps in Italy and later in Germany until the end of the war despite his numerous attempts to escape. He was replaced in the command of 1 SAS by Lieutenant Colonel 'Paddy' Mayne.[23] Three months later, the Greek squadron returned to the Greek army-in-exile, fighting in North Africa against Axis forces as part of the Allied war effort. At the same time, Major George Jellicoe was given command of the waterborne element of the SAS, which became the SBS and was based at Athlit in Palestine. In April 1943, 1 SAS was reorganized into 1st Special Raiding Squadron (SRS) under Mayne.[24] A month later, 2 SAS was formed in Algeria with Lieutenant Colonel William Stirling, David's brother, becoming its commanding officer. The SRS and 2 SAS were involved in Operation Husky, the invasion of Sicily. On 10 July, the SRS conducted an amphibious assault, capturing an enemy gun battery on the top of Capo Murro di Porco in Sicily. Two days later, the unit successfully carried out an attack on the harbour of Augusta. On 12 July, two 2 SAS parties were inserted by parachute into northern Sicily to disrupt enemy communications.[25]

The first operation on the Italian mainland was the SRS raid from the sea on the port of Bagnara on 3 September 1943. The town was captured but the invaders soon came under enemy mortar and machine-gun fire from the surrounding hills. The operation cost the squadron five killed and seventeen wounded. On 3 October, a 207-strong seaborne SRS force, along with two British Army commando units, captured Termoli, a port on the Adriatic coast. Two days later, the Germans mounted an unsuccessful counter-attack to retake the port. The action at Termoli was the SRS's last operation in Italy. Once on the Italian mainland, 2 SAS was mostly employed in advance of the main Allied forces. The unit assisted in the capture of Taranto, undertook numerous operations along Italy's Adriatic coast and supported the landings at Anzio. Between 2 and 6 October 1943, sixty troopers from 2 SAS were tasked with rescuing British prisoners of war who had escaped from camps when their Italian guards abandoned their posts following Italy's surrender in September. Small SAS teams were either landed from the sea between Ancona and Pescara or parachuted in farther inland between 2 and 6 October. Contact was made with hundreds of former POWs but due to bad planning only fifty were evacuated.[26]

On 7 September, two seven-man parties from 2 SAS were dropped into the Spezia/Genoa area of north-east Italy. They operated behind enemy lines for fifty-four days, mostly derailing trains. One of the men was captured by the German and shot.[27] On the night of 27 October 1943, a 2 SAS detachment, led by Major Roy Farran, landed from the sea between Ancona and Pescara and spent six days behind enemy lines. They blew up a railway line in several places and mined the main coast road before being extracted by motor torpedo boat minus two troopers who had been captured. On 30 January 1944, a 2 SAS party landed on the coast and successfully destroyed a vital bridge between Pescara and Fano. Meanwhile, the 1st SRS, after being renamed 1 SAS, had moved to Scotland to prepare for the 1944 invasion of France. A month later, in January 1944, the 2,500-strong SAS Brigade was raised as part of the British I Airborne Corps. It was commanded by Brigadier Roderick McLeod and consisted of 1 SAS, 2 SAS, 3 SAS (3rd Free French Parachute Battalion), 4 SAS (4th Free French Parachute Battalion), 5 SAS (5th Belgian Independent Parachute Company) and 'F' Squadron. The 'F' Squadron men operated with SAS parties to gather intelligence and lay it back to headquarters by wireless. The men were ordered to swap their beige berets with the maroon ones of the British paratroop units. The SAS brigade then started a period of training for their participation in the Normandy invasion with the exception of 2 SAS that was still involved in Italy.

On 7 January 1944, four four-man SAS parties were parachuted north of Rome and cut rail communications between the Italian capital and the coast. Their mission was accomplished but all the men were captured by the Germans. Four other SAS parties that were dropped the same day to severe railway lines around Terni and Orvieto never turned up at a beach evacuation rendezvous. It has been surmised that they either drowned or were captured and executed by the Germans.[28] On the night of 12 January, a five-man party, led by Major Tony Widdrington, were dropped in central Italy and destroyed with explosives seven parked German planes on a heavily-guarded airfield at San Egidio. Widdrington was killed and a trooper was injured when a bomb exploded prematurely. The injured man was taken to a German hospital from where he managed to escape and make it to friendly lines by mid-March. On 27 December, thirty-four men of 2 SAS were parachuted into the area between Genoa and La Spezia in northern Italy to support the forthcoming offensive by the US Fifth Army. The party, in cooperation with local partisans, inflicted 150 casualties on German forces.[29] On 17 February 1945, a 2 SAS party was dropped by parachute north of Verona in northern Italy in an ill-fated mission to sabotage a railway line leading to the Brenner Pass. The men were scattered on landing due to adverse weather conditions. Their leader, Captain Littlejohn, and a member of the thirteen-strong party were captured and subsequently executed by the Germans under Hitler's Commando Order.[30] On 4 March 1945, a party of 2 SAS, led by Major Roy Farran, was parachuted in the area between La Spezia and Bologna. They carried out a raid on a German corps headquarters at Albinea.[31] The Italian campaign proved that the SAS could operate in any theatre and not just in the sandy wastes of North Africa.

In Normandy, the SAS Brigade's main task was to prevent reinforcements reaching the vulnerable beachhead by being parachuted behind the lines to assist the French resistance.[32] SAS units also had to provide small-scale tactical support for Montgomery's 21st Army Group by cutting enemy lines of communication and providing intelligence on the German forces' movements and dispositions. SAS parties were to be inserted by air deep behind enemy lines to establish a base, link up with local Maquis forces and disrupt enemy logistics. These parties sometime operated for periods of up to three months. Almost half the SAS force landed in Normandy on D-Day. The rest was delayed in England because of shortage of air transport. Reconnaissance operations were carried out some 50 miles (80km) ahead of Allied forces in Normandy.[33] Troopers from the French and the Belgian units of the SAS Brigade were tasked with several missions as they had the advantage of better communications with the local Maquis force and the population in general. These missions are highlighted in Chapter 5 in which the French and the Belgian paratroopers are covered. A number of missions were carried out in Normandy by the SAS's British squadrons. Between 6 and 21 June 1944, a total of 144 men from 1 SAS, nine jeeps and two 6-pounder anti-tank guns were dropped by parachute near Dijon and established a base in the wooded hills to the west of the city. The SAS force, led by Major William Fraser, severed enemy communications and repeatedly cut the railway lines around Dijon. On 3 August, a German attack on the raiders' base was beaten off. Between 6 June and 6 September, 220 enemy personnel were killed or wounded by the raiders.[34] Six trains were derailed, twenty-two lines were cut and seventy vehicles were destroyed. On 11 June, fifty-five men from 1 SAS were parachuted into the Vienne area in southern France to prevent reinforcements reaching the Normandy area after the D-Day landings. They carried out a number of sabotage and intelligence-gathering missions in cooperation with the local French resistance. Six days later, four jeeps and their drivers were dropped by parachute. On 3 July, the SAS 'base' at Verriere was attacked by large numbers of German troops. Only sixteen troopers managed to get away. Six were killed and a further thirty-three were captured. The latter were later executed by the Germans.[35]

In mid-June, a 'camp' was set up in the forest of Fontainebleau by SAS men who were parachuted in the area and began sabotage activity in cooperation with French resistance forces. On 6 August, the camp was attacked by large numbers of German troops, following information received by an informer in the ranks of the Maquis. A few SAS men, including their leader, Major Ian Fenwick, were killed in the firefight and those captured were later executed by the Germans. Those who got away continued operating until mid-August. On 8 July, seven men from 1 SAS were dropped near Le Mans, in north-west France, to collect intelligence on German troop movements and dispositions. On 23 July, an aircraft carrying a 2 SAS detachment to be parachuted near Reims in eastern France crashed, killing all aboard.[36] Two days later, a five-man 2 SAS party, led by Captain William Lee, was parachuted south-west of Paris. On 12 August, they attacked a German army headquarters in the town of Mantes-la-Jolie, killing twelve enemy soldiers.

Between 27 July and 1 September, fifty-five men and twelve jeeps from 2 SAS, led by Captain Grant Hibbert, were parachuted into eastern France to collect information concerning German activities and conduct offensive actions against the enemy. On 3 August, fifty-nine men of 2 SAS were dropped into eastern Brittany, north-west France, to observe enemy movements in the Rennes/Laval area. The best accomplishment of this mission was the rescue of 200 downed Allied airmen.[37] On 12 August, ninety-one men of 2 SAS, led by Lieutenant Colonel Brian Franks, were dropped by parachute near Vosges in eastern France. Heavily outnumbered by enemy forces, they operated in the area until 9 October, attacking military installations and gathering intelligence. Two SAS men were killed in action and thirty-one were captured and executed by the Germans. On 17 August, 102 men from 1 SAS, 2 SAS and the 5th Belgian Independent Parachute Company (5 SAS) were parachuted into twelve DZs north-west of Paris to harass the retreating Germans. Between 13 August and 26 September, 107 men of 1 SAS were deployed near Auxerre in central France. They began aggressive patrolling until 23 August when they came up against large numbers of German troops in the village of Les Ormes and had to withdraw. Elements of the SAS raiding force linked up with the French First Army which was advancing from the south. On 19 August, a sixty-man force from 2 SAS and a number of jeeps landed by parachute at Rennes. Eleven days later, the SAS men attacked a German headquarters in the town of Chatillon.

The SAS played only a minor part in the defeat of the German offensive in the Ardennes in December 1944–January 1945. The only units involved in missions were the brigade's Belgian battalion and one of the two French battalions. They were mainly engaged in ground reconnaissance operations in the region to support

Allied – mostly American – units. In March 1945, a former Chindit commander, Brigadier Mike Calvert, took over command of the SAS Brigade. When the Allied forces crossed the Rhine and started advancing on German soil, detachments form 1 SAS and 2 SAS and the 5th Belgian Independent Parachute Company (5 SAS) carried out a number of reconnaissance missions. The high mobility of the jeep-mounted SAS force, which had reached Kiel by 3 May, made a significant contribution to the rapid advance of the 21st Army Group. Between 6 April and 6 May 1945, elements of 1 SAS, mounted on forty jeeps, spearheaded the Canadian 4th Armoured Division's advance towards Oldenburg in north-west Germany. The SAS force, led by 'Paddy' Mayne, advanced 31 miles (50km) in three days. On 15 April SAS men discovered the notorious concentration camp of Bergen-Belsen.

William Stirling was continuously at loggerheads with his superiors concerning the proper use of his men. He believed that they should have been employing in attacking strategic targets and not merely in a support role. Despite the SAS successes in North Africa and later in Italy, the high command still insisted on using the unit just ahead of the front line. William Stirling's anger finally erupted on the eve of Operation Overlord, the Allied invasion of Europe. Supreme Headquarters Allied Expeditionary Force (SHAEF) wanted to use the SAS just behind the beaches, between the enemy infantry and the German armoured reserves. Stirling resigned, seeing this task as near suicidal and a complete waste of his unit. William Stirling deserves to be remembered as for his efforts to impress upon the higher echelons of the British Army that the SAS was (and still is) a deep-penetration unit which, given proper support, can achieve results out of all proportion to its size.[38] Closely tied to regular formations while fighting on German soil, the SAS columns were subjected to several ambushes and losses were disproportionately high.[39] By the time the war ended, the SAS Brigade had suffered 330 casualties.[40] Twenty-two SAS men who were captured by the Germans were shot despite the fact that they operated in uniform at all times.[41] The successes of the SAS in North Africa had provoked Hitler in October 1942 to issue an order (*Kommandodobefehl* or Commando Order) according to which any Special Forces men that were captured should be shot and not afforded the protection of the Geneva Convention. In the final days of the war, one of the main tasks of the SAS was to hunt down the men who had committed these atrocities along with SS and Gestapo thugs.[42] By any measure, SAS operations in France, Belgium, Holland and Germany were very successful. Around 2,000 Germans were killed and a further 4,784 were captured. They also destroyed seven trains, derailed a further thirty-three and destroyed 700 vehicles. They also cut railway lines on 164 separate occasions and reported a host of bombing targets to the RAF. This list omits the wealth of valuable intelligence which was continually relayed back to England.

In May 1945, 1 SAS and 2 SAS were deployed in Norway to disarm the 300,000-strong German garrison. The 845-strong SAS force was based at Bergen to administer the operation. The Germans gave no trouble, although there were clashes with Norwegian collaborators.[43] The Belgian (5 Squadron) unit were sent to Denmark and Germany in counter-intelligence operations. The SAS Brigade was broken up soon afterwards. In September, 5 SAS were handled over to the reformed Belgian Army.

On 1 October, the 3 and 4 SAS Squadrons were handed over to the French Army. On 8 October 1945, the British 1 and 2 SAS regiments were disbanded. After the war, a new SAS regiment was raised as part of the Territorial Army. On 1 January 1947, the new 22nd SAS Regiment came into existence. Five years later, the SAS was reorganized into the 22nd SAS Regiment and the 21st SAS Regiment (Artists' Rifles) – the latter on reserve role. Ever since, SAS troopers have been assigned missions in various parts of the world (Korea, Malaya, Aden, Brunei, Borneo, Oman, Yemen, Gambia, Northern Ireland, Gibraltar, Iraq and Afghanistan).

The 'Devil's Brigade'

In early 1942, Geoffrey Pyke, an English journalist working for the British Combined Operations Command, suggested the formation of an elite force that could land by sea or air in enemy-occupied countries like Norway or Romania on sabotage missions against strategic targets such as hydroelectric plants and oilfields.[44] The US Army eventually acted on Pyke's proposal (code-named Project Plough) by forming the First Special Service Force (FSSF), made up of American and Canadian volunteers.[45] All of them had already been serving in paratroop and other elite units of their countries. The unit, also known as the 'Devil's Brigade' or the 'Black Devils', fought with distinction during the Italian campaign and in southern France. Although they were all trained in airborne assault missions, the men of the FSSF were employed in an elite infantry role throughout the war.

The brigade was activated on 9 July 1942 as a joint US-Canadian force consisting of three small regiments and a service battalion. Lieutenant Colonel Robert T. Frederick, a legendary figure in the history of the US Special Forces, was SFFS's commanding officer, with his deputy being the Canadian Lieutenant Colonel Don Williamson. Winston Churchill declared later that 'if we had a dozen more like him, we would have smashed Hitler in 1942'.[46] Frederick replaced Lieutenant Colonel Howard R. Johnson, the first commander, who left the US-Canadian force pretty soon to command the newly-formed 501st Parachute Infantry Regiment of the 101st Airborne Division. The 1,400-strong FSSF was stationed at Fort William Henry Harrison, at Helena in Montana, where emphasis was given to parachute training as well as in skiing and mountaineering. The formation patch was a red spearhead with the words 'USA' written horizontally and 'CANADA' written vertically. The men wore red, white, and blue piping on their garrison cap and on their breast behind their parachutist wings. Their uniform was olive-coloured and their boots were initially the same as those issued to parachute regiments, although during the Italian campaign, the FSSF men had to wear infantry combat boots.[47]

On 10 July 1943, the Americans regained control of the Aleutian Islands, off Alaska. The operation was unopposed as the Japanese occupation forces had already withdrawn. The Special Force brigade was among the troops that landed on one of them, named Kiska.[48] In November, the brigade arrived to Casablanca in French Morocco and from there was deployed to the Italian mainland. A month later, the FSSF successfully conducted a series of operations in mountainous areas such as

Monte la Difensa, Monte la Renetanea, Monte Sammucro and Monte Vischiatro.[49] The capture of La Remetanea seemed too formidable a task, as the main fortification was atop a cliff that jutted steeply upwards for 1,000ft (300m).[50] In order to reach the fortification, the FSSF men had to climb up with ropes during the night under a storm of fire. After three days and nights of attacks, La Remetanea was captured on 9 December. The brigade's casualties during the whole operation were 91 dead, 313 wounded or injured and 9 missing.[51]

On 1 February 1944, the Special Force brigade was deployed at the beachhead established by Allied forces at Anzio, south of Rome. They held the right flank of the beachhead and conducted nighttime aggressive patrols into Axis territory. There were cases that FSSF patrols went as deep as 500 yards (460m) behind enemy lines.[52] It was at Anzio, where the FSSF fought for ninety-nine days without relief, that the Germans dubbed the US-Canadian unit the 'Devil's Brigade'. The men of the unit were also referred to as 'Black Devils' because they used to patrol and fight during the night having their faces coloured with black boot polish. On 2 February, Frederick was promoted to full colonel. On 27 May, elements of the brigade captured intact the seven bridges of the strategically important municipality of Rocca Massima, 25 miles (40km) south-east of Rome. On the night of 4 June, FSSF men were among the first Allied troops to entered the Italian capital. On 23 July, an American officer already serving in the FSSF, Lieutenant Colonel Edwin A. Walker, was promoted to full colonel and succeeded Frederick, thus becoming the unit's second and last commander.[53] Frederick left on promotion to command the 1st Airborne Task Force (1ATF).[54] At the age of 37, Frederick along James M. Gavin, commander of the 82nd Airborne, who was eight days younger than him, were US Army's youngest divisional commanders during the war.[55] Frederick's 1st AFT, a short-lived division-size formation, was created to spearhead the Allied invasion of southern France,[56] consisting of one British and five US airborne units. On the eve of the invasion, the FSSF carried out an amphibious landing on Hyères, off the coast of the French Riviera, and captured all five forts on the island after defeating a reinforced German garrison. After seizing Hyères and the nearby islands, the invading force moved to the French mainland. On 22 August, seven days after the landing of the 1st ATF by parachute or glider in southern France, the FSSF was ordered to replace the British 2nd Independent Parachute Brigade. On 7 September, the US-Canadian Special Force moved to defensive positions on the Franco-Italian border. The 'Devil's Brigade' was disbanded four months later and its men became replacements in paratroop or commando units of the US or Canadian Army.[57]

SOE and OSS

Military personnel, as well as civilians, were recruited and trained by the Allies to carry out spy and clandestine missions in Axis-held parts of Europe and the Pacific during the Second World War. Almost all of them were qualified parachutists. They were members of the British Special Operation Executive (SOE), the American Office of Strategic Services (OSS) and the multinational Jedburgh teams. The SOE was established by the British on 22 July 1940 to carry out espionage, sabotage and reconnaissance missions in Axis-occupied areas of Europe and South East Asia. The organization, whose first director was Sir Frank Nelson, directly employed some 13,000 agents, including 3,200 women.[58] The majority of the recruits were civilians and most of the organization's military personnel were officers and non-commissioned officers from various Allied countries. The organization's headquarters was in London (64 Baker Street), but subsidiary headquarters, stations or branch offices were set up in Cairo, India, Algiers, Brindisi and Naples.[59] SOE recruits underwent commando training at Arisaig in Scotland and parachute training at Atrincham in Cheshire. Nearly 300 of them had come from Czechoslovakia, following the occupation of their country by the Germans. The Cairo recruits used the parachute training facility at Ramadan David near Haifa.[60] Some 400 agents were sent into France where SOE operated between 1941 and 1944. SOE agents operated also in other Axis-occupied countries such as Belgium, the Netherlands, Norway, Denmark, Poland, Czechoslovakia, Hungary, Romania, Yugoslavia, Albania and Greece. Missions were also carried out in West Africa and South East Asia. The most high profile of SOE's missions was the assassination in May 1942 in Prague of Reinhard Heydrich. Heinrich Himmler's protégé and a leading figure in the SS, Heydrich was killed by a bomb thrown by two SOE agents, members of the Czechoslovak army-in-exile, Josef Gabčik and Jan Kubiš, who had been dropped into their German-occupied country by parachute. SOE was dissolved on 15 January 1946.

The OSS, the forerunner of the post-war CIA, was established on 13 June 1942 to collect strategic information and conduct special operations not assigned to military units.[61] Most of the personnel, estimated to 13,000, belonged to the US Armed Forces. Civilians, including women, from the United States and other countries were also recruited as agents. The agency, headed by Colonel (later Major General) William J. Donovan, was initially developed with British assistance as the first agents were trained by SOE instructors at Oshawa in Canada.[62] The training included parachuting, sabotage, self-defence and weapons/explosives training. Training camps were established by the organization during the war in the United States, Great Britain, French Algeria, Egypt and later, as the Allied troops advanced, in southern Italy. In the Far East, OSS recruits were trained in India, Ceylon and China. In many Axis-held countries the organization cooperated with local partisans. OSS espionage activity developed in neutral countries like Spain, Switzerland, Sweden and Turkey. The most highly-decorated OSS agent was US Marine Colonel Peter Ortiz.

The Jedburgh Teams

In June 1944, SOE and OSS successfully pooled their personnel and resources to mount Operation Jedburgh, providing large-scale support to the French Resistance after the Allied air and sea landings in Normandy. The Free French *Bureau Central de Renseignements et d'Action* (BCRA) also joined in. Eighty-three American, ninety British, 103 Free French, five Belgian, five Dutch and two Canadian officers and other ranks were initially trained for the missions. The recruits, who were all qualified parachutists, received special training in the Scottish Highlands and were later stationed in England at Milton Hall, near Peterborough, or in London.[63] Three hundred teams were eventually formed. Such teams were activated also in the Pacific and carried out missions in Burma, French Indochina and China. They were called 'Jedburghs' after the codename of their first mission in France. Team sizes varied from two to four men. A Jedburgh team normally consisted of three men – the commander, the executive officer and the non-commissioned wireless operator.[64] One of the officers would be British or American and the other would originate from or speak the language of the country to which the team deployed. The Jedburghs' assignments, in contrast to SOE's and OSS's basic role, did not normally include espionage. The men were to act as liaison between the Allied forces and resistance fighters. They also conducted sabotage and guerrilla warfare and led the local resistance in actions against the enemy.[65] In addition, they organized parachute drops of arms and equipment to Resistance fighters. In contrast with the SOE and the OSS agents, who were dropped into enemy-held territories in plain clothes carrying a gun and false papers, the Jedburgh personnel wore their military uniforms and were equipped with a variety of arms and personal equipment.[66] In the event of their capture, however, the Jedburghs could expect similar treatment to spies.[67] The first team parachuted into Central France, near Châteauroux, the night before D-Day. In total, ninety-three Jedburgh teams operated in fifty-four areas of France between June and December 1944. From September 1945 to April 1945, eight teams were active in the Netherlands. A Jedburgh team parachuted into Arnhem to liaise between the British 6th Airborne Division and the Dutch Resistance. The American commander, Lieutenant Harvey Todd, was captured and was later executed by the Germans. His compatriot, Sergeant Carl Scott, the wireless operator, and the Dutch executive officer, Captain Jacobus Groenewould, managed to avoid capture and reach friendly forces. Groenewould was killed later near the Arnhem Bridge, after linking up with the British 1st Parachute Brigade. Scott was killed on 2 November 1944 near Wageningen, north of the Rhine, while on patrol with elements of the American 101st Airborne Division. About 100 missions were carried out by Jedburgh teams in Europe during the Second World War and a further thirty in the Far East. Many of the tactics and techniques employed by these teams were later adopted for training early Special Forces in the 1950s.

The Brandenburger Division

The German Brandenburgers came into being as an elite company in October 1939 to conduct surveillance and sabotage operations behind enemy lines on behalf of the Abwehr, Germany's military intelligence service.[68] The unit grew during the war to eventually become an infantry division. After recruitment, the men were sent to Brandenburg (hence the name), a Prussian province, for training. A number of the men also had to go through courses in skiing and parachuting. Most of the personnel were fluent in languages spoken in East European countries, the Soviet Union and the Middle East. From that time on, pro-Nazi nationals from these countries were recruited for service in the Brandenburgers. In April 1940, an airborne platoon of the unit participated in the German invasions of Denmark and Norway.[69] Between June 1942 and February 1943 elements of the unit carried out clandestine operations behind enemy lines in Egypt, Libya and Tunisia.[70]

On 26 December 1942, a parachute company of the Bradenburgers, which was a regiment-size unit at that time, was transported by gliders on a mission in North Africa. Some of the gliders were shot down while flying over enemy lines. Most of the men were killed during the mission.[71] In September 1943, a Brandenburger unit and a Luftwaffe parachute battalion were involved in an airborne assault on Kos contributing to the recapture of this Dodecanese island.[72] The Dodecanese Islands were at the time under the control of British and pro-Allied Italian forces. In February 1943, the Brandenburgers, being a regiment at the time, were enlarged to become an infantry division. The formation was deployed to the Eastern Front with the exception of 1,800 officers and other ranks who were qualified paratroopers. They were transferred to a newly-established SS special operations unit, Otto Skorzeny's 502nd Battalion. On 25 May 1944, Brandenburger elements, attached to the SS-*Fallschirmjägerbataillon* 500, participated in the unsuccessful airborne operation to capture Yugoslav partisan leader Jozip Broz Tito.[73]

The SS Special Operations Unit

In early 1942, a special operations unit was formed by the Waffen-SS to be inserted to Ireland by parachute in case of an American invasion of the southern part of the country, as US troops had already been deployed in Belfast. The unit, consisted of about 100 experienced volunteers from various SS units, was named SS-*Sonderlehrgang Oranienburg*. An officer, the reportedly Dutch-born SS-Captain Pieter van Vessem, was put in command. The unit's proposed deployment to Ireland never transpired because the feared American invasion did not occur. In early 1943, five members of the unit were parachuted into Iran to assist guerrilla opposition to the Allied occupation of the country. In May 1943, SS-*Sonderlehrgang Oranienburg* was designated SS-*Sonderlehrgang zbV Friedenthal* (SS-SzbVF) and was placed under the command of SS-Major Otto Skorzeny. In September 1943, sixteen members of the unit took part in the Gran Sasso raid, the rescue of the deposed Italian dictator Benito Mussolini. Five months later, a third company was formed, made up of volunteers of Flemish and Dutch origin. In February 1944, 'A' and 'B' Companies were deployed to the Eastern Front for a month. On 20 July, 'A' Company was sent in Berlin to protect the Reichstag and a month later fifty members of the unit carried out an airborne mission in Romania, destroying road and railway bridges in order to delay the Soviet advance. In September 1944, the unit was dissolved and its personnel absorbed into a new battalion named SS-Jagdverband Mitte.

The SS Parachute Battalions

An abortive attempt to form an SS airborne unit was made in Nazi Germany between May and July 1937 at a parachute school at Stendal. The second attempt was made six years later, during the Second World War, when the SS 500th Parachute Battalion (SS-*Fallschirmjägerbataillon* 500) was established to carry out daring operations behind enemy lines. Fifty per cent of the recruits were volunteers from various Waffen-SS units. The remainder were disgraced SS officers and other ranks who had broken military law and were in prison. These men were given the opportunity to redeem themselves from minor sentences on the battlefield as elements of the new battalion. Established in October 1943 under the command of SS-Major Herbert Gilhofer, the SS 500th Parachute Battalion was initially trained in the Mataruška Banja area, near Kraljevo in Serbia, and later in various parts of Hungary. In April 1944, the unit was deployed in Yugoslavia in anti-partisan sweeps. The same month, SS-Captain Kurt Rybka took over command and was ordered to lead the battalion in its first and only combat parachute drop and glider assault performed during the war. The Communist partisan leader Josip Broz Tito's headquarters, situated in a well-defended cave in a mountainous area of Bosnia near the town of Drvar, was the target of the airborne assault. On 25 May, two companies (314 men) were dropped by parachute in two waves and further two (340 men) were landed by glider. The second wave of paratroopers missed the target altogether as they landed a few miles away. Of those dropped with the first wave many were killed by the Yugoslav partisans who also delayed with their fire the invaders' approach to the cave, giving their leader time to escape. Some 800 of the troops participating in the operation by air and land were killed, wounded or injured. Among the wounded was Rybka, the commander of the unit.

The battalion, after the unsuccessful attempt to kill or capture Tito, was sent to Petrovac for a subsequent anti-partisan operation. In early June 1944, the fit elements of the battalion moved to Ljubljana for recuperation and reorganization. On 26 June, SS-Captain Siegfried Milius took command of the battalion. By 30 June, of the 1,000 battle-ready men only 15 officers, 81 non-commissioned officers and 196 enlisted men remained. They were then deployed to Kaunas in Lithuania, participating in the defence of the Baltic Sea area. The battalion's personnel, mounted on tanks, struggled to stem the tide of the Soviet armoured thrust on Vilnius to the south-east. By 20 August, the SS 500th Parachute Battalion was down to ninety men.[74] From Lithuania the unit made an orderly withdrawal to Zichenau in East Prussia and from there to Ostmark in Austria, where it was incorporated with SS-*Fallschirjägerbataillon* 600. The SS 2nd Paratroop Battalion was formed in November 1944. In December 1944, two companies of the new airborne unit were incorporated to Otto Skorzeny's 150th Panzer Brigade (*Panzerbrigade* 150) and took part in Hitler's ill-fated Ardennes offensive. Then, the SS 600th Parachute Battalion was rushed to the Oder front to dig in on the eastern bank of the river against the flow of Soviet troops. The battalion stayed on the eastern bank until 1 April 1945, when it was forced into an orderly retreat. It was eventually isolated in a pocket near the town of Hagenow, in northern Germany. In early May, the SS 2nd Parachute Battalion surrendered to US forces.

Chapter 11

Parachutes and Pilots in
the Second World War

Tens of thousands of Allied and Axis airmen who had to bail out when their planes went down during combat missions in the Second World War owed their lives to their parachutes. The same had happened to numerous German pilots in the final year of the First World War. Hundreds of pilots, as well as aircrews in general, German, Italian, British and American mostly, parachuted to safety during the Second World War, a practice not so common among the Japanese. In Japan, although parachutes were issued to airmen, bailing out was considered an act of cowardice. The short list of Japanese pilots who bailed out during the Second World War is headed by Colonel Yasuhiro Kuroe, who used his parachute three times.[1]

The first Japanese pilot to bail out and land safely by parachute was Lieutenant Johiro Ofusa. It happened in Burma on 24 November 1943, when Ofusa's plane was damaged over Meikuterra by the gunner of a USAAF B-24 Liberator.[2] Another Japanese pilot, Lieutenant Akira Yamamoto, had also bailed out, but he was killed because his parachute didn't open. On the other hand, there were a small number of Axis and Allied pilots who didn't bail out because they simply didn't trust their parachutes. Johannes Steinhoff, a Luftwaffe fighter ace between 1939 and 1945 and a general of the West German Air Force after the war, was one of them. He was shot down twelve times and is recorded as having admitted: 'I never trusted the parachutes. I landed my damaged planes hoping not to get bounced on the way down when I lost power.'[3]

Among the pilots who bailed out during the Second World War were some leading fighter aces like the Luftwaffe's Erich Hartman (352 aerial victories), Günther Rall (275), Adolf Galland (104), Werner Molders (101) and others, the RAF's Australian Pat Pattle (40) and others, Canadian Flying Officer George F. Beurling (32), Canadian Lieutenant Irving F. Kennedy (10) and others, South African Albert G. Lewish (18) and others, US Navy Commander Alexander Vraciu (19), the USAAF's Major Walter C. Beckam (18), Lieutenant Colonel Thomas J. Lynch (16), Captain Pierce W. McKennon (12) and others, the Red Army Air Force's pilots Alexander I. Pokryshkin (65), Dmitriy Glinka (50) and others, and the *Regia Aeronautica*'s Captain Franco Lucchini (21 or 22) among others. The Royal Air Force's Flight Lieutenant Peter Townsend was forced to bail out on 31 August 1940 over Tonbridge in Kent.[4] A mass bail-out was recorded on 17 August 1943, when 194 USAAF B-17 Flying Fortresses bombed factories in Germany. Thirty-six bombers were shot down that night and a total of 150 airmen were forced to bail out.

Deadly Bail-outs

There were several pilots who bailed out unsuccessfully during the Second World War. The Luftwaffe's Captain Hans-Joachim Marseille was one of them. His fighter suffered engine failure on 30 September 1942 near El Alamein and he had to abandon it. He struck the rudder and was either killed instantly or incapacitated and was unable to open his parachute.[5] The USAAF's Major Don M. Beerbower's P-51 Mustang fighter was hit over Saint-Thierry in north-eastern France on 9 August 1944. It stalled and dove straight down to the ground. Beerbower managed to get out of the aircraft but hit the tail. He never opened his parachute. The plane crashed and the pilot was killed.

An Italian Macchi C.205 fighter was hit on 5 July 1943 near Catania in Sicily during a dogfight with Allied aircraft. The pilot, Lieutenant Leonardo Ferrulli, who had twenty-one victories since the beginning of the war, was forced to bail out. He was killed because his parachute didn't open. Flying Officer George N. Keith was a Canadian pilot flying with the RAF during the Second World War. On 4 August 1943, his Spitfire Mk V was struck by anti-aircraft fire near Sicily and Keith was forced to bail out at 2,000ft (667m). The tail of the plane struck him and broke both his legs. His parachute did not open until 300ft (100m) from the sea where he landed. He was picked up by air-sea rescue but soon died of his wounds. Luftwaffe's Major Kurt Ubben bailed out on 27 April 1944 near Fère-en-Tardenois in northern France, but his parachute failed to open.[6]

Another German pilot, Sergeant-Pilot Albert Brunner, died on 7 May 1943 near Petsamo in Finland, when his parachute also failed to open. The RAF's Australian Squadron Leader Russel G. Foskett was killed on 31 October 1944. His aircraft developed engine trouble and he was forced to bail out over the Aegean Sea between the islands of Skiathos and Skopelos. His parachute failed to open.[7] The Luftwaffe's Lieutenant Colonel Hans Philipp was credited with 206 enemy aircraft shot down in 500 combat missions before being forced to bail out on 1 October 1943 between Hardenburg and Itterbeck in north-eastern Germany.[8] His parachute failed to open and the jump from an altitude of 160ft (50m) caused him fatal injuries.

The Luftwaffe's Lieutenant Gerhard Loos was hanging in his parachute from a high-voltage power line on 6 March 1944 near Reinsehlen in north-eastern Germany after bailing out from his downed fighter. He fell to his death after releasing his parachute that had stuck 60ft (20m) from the ground.[9] On 10 October 1940, two RAF Spitfires collided near Brighton while attacking a Luftwaffe Dornier Do 17. Flying Officer Fraser J. Drummond, one of the pilots, bailed out but was too low for his parachute to open effectively. He was still alive after hitting the ground. He died later in the arms of a priest.[10] The second Spitfire crashed not far away with the pilot already dead in the cockpit.

On 5 March 1944, the USAAF's Colonel Neel E. Kearby was shot down near Dagua airfield in Papua New Guinea by a Japanese Ki-43 Hayabusa fighter. His P-47 Thunderbolt crashed in the jungle, while he, after bailing out, became tangled with his parachute in a tree. He died there of bullet wounds suffered in the dogfight. Two German airmen, the pilot, Captain August Geiner and his radio operator, had to abandon a Messerschmitt Bf 110 shot down over the Zuiderzee in north-western Holland by a RAF Bristol Beaufighter. They both drowned.[11] The Luftwaffe's Captain Joachim Kirschner was forced to bail out on 17 December 1943, when his Messerschmitt Bf 109 was shot down over Croatia by a USAAF P-47 Thunderbolt. He landed safely near a village (Donje Hrasno) but was captured by Communist guerrillas and was eventually executed. The Luftwaffe's Sergeant-Pilot Karl-Heinz Meltzer was shot down over enemy territory near Kharkov in Ukraine on 19 August 1943. He was seen to land with his parachute, but was never heard from again, as happened to hundreds of Axis and Allied bailed out pilots during the Second World War. The Luftwaffe's Lieutenant Hans-Joachim Kroschinski, during an attack on Soviet Petlyakov Pe-2 bombers over Fravenburg in northern Poland on 21 December 1944, was wounded by return fire and had to abandon his Fw 190 A-9 fighter. He landed safely but as a result of his wounds he lost both his eyes and his right leg. The Luftwaffe's Captain Emil Bitsch was killed in action against a number of USAAF P-47 fighters over Schijden in southern Holland on 15 March 1944. He had claimed 108 aerial victories, one of which was the shooting down and subsequent death of the Soviet female ace Yekaterina Budanova on 19 July 1943 in Novokrasnovka, in eastern Ukraine.[12] Budanova's shooting down had also been claimed by another Luftwaffe ace, Captain (later General) Georg Schwientek.

Bailed-out Airmen and Airwomen

Nearly a hundred female Soviet pilots were assigned combat missions by the Red Army Air Force during the Second World War. They flew a combined total of 30,000 combat sorties in Yak-1 or Ilyushin Il-2 fighters or in Polikarpov Po-2 or Petlyakov Pe-2 bombers. Two of these pilots were forced to bail out. Lieutenant Anna A. Timofeyeva-Yegorova bailed out near Magnuszew, in east-central Poland, when her Ilyushin Il-2 was hit by anti-aircraft fire on 22 August 1944. She was seriously injured on landing because her parachute had only partially opened. After receiving medical treatment from the Germans, Timofeyeva-Yegorova was transferred to a prisoner-of-war camp at Küstrin in western Poland. She was freed when the Red Army overran the area on 31 January 1945. Lieutenant Colonel Klaviya Y. Fomichyova had to bail out on 23 June 1944 during a bombing mission, when her Petlyakov Pe-2 was hit by enemy flak.[13] She and her navigator, Galina I. Dahunkovskaya, landed safely, although Fomichyova left the plane at an altitude of 492ft (150m) from the ground. On 22 March 1943, a Bf 109 9/JG3 bomber was shot down by the Soviet ace Lydia Litvyak near Kharkov in Ukraine. Two members of the crew, Franz Muller and Karl Otto Harloff, bailed out and survived. There were thousands of Axis and Allied airmen who survived their plane crash during the Second World War having successfully bailed out.

The Luftwaffe's Major Paul A. Zorner had fifty-nine aerial victories claimed in 272 missions, including 110 night sorties. On 24 July 1943, his plane, a Messerschmitt Bf 110 G-4, developed an engine problem and he had to abandon it. While bailing out, the parachute snagged and Zorner had to clamber back into the cockpit to unhook it before parachuting to safety.[14] The Luftwaffe's Lieutenant Peter Düttmann, flying a Messerschmitt Bf 109, was shot down or crash-landed seventeen times during operational missions, mostly on the Russian front. On 13 November 1944, his plane was hit by an Ilyushin Il-2 rear gunner. He bailed out at 1,000ft (300m) and landed behind enemy lines. Düttmann, who claimed 152 aerial victories in 398 missions during the Second World War, eventually managed to reach friendly forces. The Luftwaffe's Major Erich Rudorffer was shot down by flak or enemy fire sixteen times and had to take to his parachute nine times.[15] He is number 34 on the list of his country's Second World War fighter aces with 222 victories claimed. The Luftwaffe's Captain Helmut Lipfert was shot down fifteen times without being injured.[16] It is still unclear the number of bail-outs and the number of forced landings he made. A German colonel, Herbert Ihlefeld, survived being shot down eight times. He ended the war credited with 130 enemy aircraft shot down in over 1,000 combat missions.[17] The Luftwaffe's Captain Rudolf Trenkel was forced to bail out five times within ten days.[18] He was credited with the destruction of 138 enemy aircraft during the war. The Luftwaffe's Sergeant-Pilot Willi Reschke was shot down eight times, bailing out in five of them.[19] The Italian pilot Luigi Gorrini had five parachute jumps, while Luftwaffe's Captain Walter Grislawski made four. On 18 January 1943, he was shot down by Soviet Ilyushin Il-16 fighters. On 24 January 1944, Grislawski was forced to bail out over Baske in Croatia, when his plane was hit by a USAAF P-51 Mustang. He had to use his parachute again on 27 July and on 26 September 1944, following attacks by RAF Spitfires.

   A Luftwaffe pilot of Russian origins, Squadron Leader (Staffelkapitän) and later Air Force General Walter Krupinski, who ended the war credited with the destruction of 197 enemy planes in 1,100 operational sorties, also bailed out four times. The USAAF's Major Kenneth H. Dahlberg bailed out three times during the Second World War. The first was in August 1944, when he landed near Paris and was sheltered by the French Resistance before reaching Allied lines and the second was in Belgium, during the Battle of the Bulge on 19 December 1944, when he was rescued by five US infantrymen.[20] On 14 February 1945, Dahlberg bailed out near Bitburg in westernmost Germany. On landing he was captured and spent the remaining three months of the war in a prisoner-of-war camp. The RAF's Squadron Leader Neville F. Duke was shot down three times during the Second World War – on 30 November 1941, on 5 December 1941 and on 7 June 1944. In his third bail-out, Duke fell into Lake Bracciano, north-west of Rome and almost drowned, as he had difficulty releasing his parachute harness. He sheltered with local partisans until the arrival of Allied troops in the area. The Luftwaffe's Captain Heinze Knoke bailed out two times. On 4 October 1943, he fell into the bitterly cold North Sea after his plane was shot down by an Allied B-17. He was rescued later and before long he was back in action. On 25 August 1944, he landed with his parachute in northern France after having to bail out again. He managed to reach friendly lines, after keeping off with his pistol a number of French Maquis.

   Wing Commander John Milne Checketts, a New Zealander serving with the RAF during the Second World War, was shot down twice by German Fw 190s – the first over the English Channel and the second over Serqeux in Seine-Maritime in northern France. When he landed in the sea, the Royal Navy came to his rescue. Over France his plane was set on fire. Checketts, who was burned and wounded, struggled to bail out. He was sheltered by the French Resistance and in October 1943 he was able to make it to England on a fishing boat along with eleven other downed pilots. On 12 August 1940, Flying Officer and later Air Commodore Alan C. Deere, a New Zealander flying with the RAF, was trapped in an unequal dogfight over the English Channel with Luftwaffe Bf 109s. He survived although he was only able to open his parachute at low altitude. He was shot down again a few days later, on 28 August, but managed to parachute safely again.[21] The third time Deere was forced to bail out was five months later, in January 1941, when he collided in mid-air with a replacement pilot during training.[22] Podporucznik (Lieutenant) Adolf Pietrasiak, of the RAF's Polish 303rd Squadron, was shot down on 19 August 1940 over France and landed by parachute. Although wounded in the leg, he managed to return to England via Spain and Gibraltar.[23] In July 1942, a RAF Wellington was downed during a bombing mission against the port of Hamburg. Greek-Cypriot-born Sergeant Glafcos Clerides, the aircraft navigator-radio operator, was among the crew members who survived after bailing out. He spent the rest of the war in Stalag VIIIB prisoner-of-war camp in Germany. Fifty-one years later, Clerides was elected President of Cyprus.

On 2 September 1944, US Navy Lieutenant George H.W. Bush Sr, who later became President of the United States, had to use his parachute after a bombing mission in Ogasewara Archipelago in the Pacific because his Grumman TBM Avenger had been hit by flak. He spent four hours in the sea before being rescued by a submarine, USS *Finback*. A US Navy pilot, Commander James J. Southerland, was shot down in a dogfight with Japanese A6M2 Zero fighters earlier, on 7 August 1942, during the Battle of Guadalcanal in the Pacific. He had taken off from the aircraft carrier USS *Saratoga* in a Grumman F4F Wildcat fighter. Southerland bailed out but his pistol got caught and remained in the cockpit. He fell with his parachute into the sea – well behind enemy lines and unarmed. He also had eleven wounds. Southerland swam to an island where he was sheltered by some natives. He was evacuated from the island on the first US patrol boat which landed there on 20 August 1942. Sergeant George Booth, a navigator with the RAF's 107th Squadron, was the first British POW of the Second World War. He was captured when his Bristol Blenheim was shot down over the German coast on 4 September 1939.[24] On 3 June 1940, seven Junker Ju 88 bombers were intercepted by French fighters as they bombed Etampes aerodrome. One of the Ju 88s was shot down. Its crew bailed out and were captured. One of them was Captain (later General) Josef Kammhuber, who was later to become, after being released from his brief French captivity, head of the German night fighter force.[25] USAAF navigator/bombardier Raymond F. Halloran was forced to bail out from 24,000ft (7,315m), when his B-29 Superfortress bomber was shot down over Tokyo. He was beaten up by civilians and policemen after landing with his parachute. In March 1945, Halloran was exhibited in a cage at Tokyo's Ueno zoo. Civilians, mostly schoolchildren, were encouraged to go and see him. He was later transferred to a prisoner-of-war camp at Omori, south-west of Japan's capital. He remained there until he and other Allied POWs were liberated by US troops on 29 August.

There have been some extraordinary cases of bailing out during the Second World War, such as the survival of James Doolittle's bombers of Tokyo, for example, or the bail-out by a RAF fighter ace flying combat missions although he had had his legs amputated. Eighteen airmen, the crews of two B-25B Mitchell medium bombers, had to bail out over the Chinese coast, after the first bombing of Tokyo and other Japanese cities by the USAAF on 18 April 1942. One of them, Lieutenant Robert M. Gray, was killed during his attempt. Fifteen of the planes that participated in the daring air raid had run out of fuel after flying thirteen hours since their launch from the aircraft carrier USS *Hornet*.[26] They crashed or belly-landed on Chinese soil or ditched off the coast. The sixteenth plane managed to land at Vladivostok in the Soviet Union. The Tokyo raid, during which other Japanese cities were bombed as well, was planned and led by Lieutenant Colonel (later Brigadier General) James Doolittle, who was one of those who parachuted to safety. Eight of the airmen were eventually captured by the Japanese Army in China and three of them were later executed. Of Doolittle's raiders, two were drowned when their bomber crashed into the sea. The survivors, including Doolittle himself, were helped by Chinese soldiers and civilians before re-joining US forces.[27]

The RAF's Group Captain Douglas Bader, when his Spitfire VB was hit over the French coast on 9 August 1940, had a problem in bailing out. His right prosthetic leg became trapped inside the cockpit (Bader was at the time the only disabled person in the world flying combat missions).[28] He escaped only when the leg's retaining straps snapped after he pulled the ripcord of his parachute.[29] The Luftwaffe notified the British of the pilot's damaged leg and on 19 August permission was given by Berlin for a RAF plane to fly over German-occupied northern France and deliver a replacement by parachute.

Two more pilots, one Soviet and one Japanese, were later assigned combat missions during the Second World War after having their legs amputated. Soviet fighter ace Alexey Maresyev was badly injured on 4 April 1942 when his Polikarpov I-16 was shot down near Staraya Russa in Veliky Novgorod and he had to bail out. Both of his legs had to be amputated below the knee. By June 1943, Maresyev had returned to flying and was credited with a total of eleven aerial victories in eighty-six combat missions during the Second World War. Japanese Army Air Force Colonel Yohei Hinoki was wounded on 27 November 1943 over Insei near Rangoon in Burma, during a dogfight with a USAAF Mustang P-51A fighter. His Nakajima Ki-43 fighter was damaged, but he managed to fly back to base. His leg was amputated soon after landing. Outfitted with an artificial leg, Hinoki continued to fly combat missions. It is estimated that during the war, he shot down more than twelve enemy aircraft.

Bail-outs in Suicidal Mid-Air Attacks

Allied pilots who bailed out after waging suicidal attacks against enemy aircraft in mid-air deserve to be mentioned as special cases. Four years before the activation of the first Kamikaze unit in Japan, voluntary suicidal attacks had been performed in the European theatre of operations by Allied fighter pilots. On 15 September 1940,

RAF Sergeant-Pilot Raymond T. Holmes in his Hawker Hurricane over London was chasing a German Dornier Do 17 bomber heading towards Buckingham Palace. When he discovered that his machine guns had failed, he decided to ram the enemy plane.[30] Holmes flew his fighter into the bomber, cutting off the rear tail section with his wing. Holmes had to bail out because his Hurricane went into an uncontrollable dive. He landed near Victoria Station.[31] The German pilot, identified as Feldwebel R. Zehbe, also bailed out, but died later of wounds suffered during the attack. His bomber crashed near the grounds of Buckingham Palace. In June 1941, Holmes, who was feted by the Press as a war hero, was promoted to Flying Officer and a year later, rose to the rank of Flight Lieutenant.[32]

Two months after Holmes' attack on the German bomber, a Greek pilot did exactly the same to an Italian bomber over northern Greece. On 2 November 1940, the Royal Hellenic Air Force's Captain Marinos Mitralexis attacked a *Regia Aeronautica* Cant Z 1007 bomber heading towards Thessaloniki with his PZL P.24 fighter. When he discovered that his machine guns couldn't fire any more, he brought down the enemy aircraft by ramming its tail with the nose of his plane.[33] As a result of the smashing of its rudder, the Italian bomber went out of control and crashed in the Langadas area, killing the pilot and another member of the crew. Mitralexis, having a serious problem with his fighter's propeller, made an emergency landing near the crashed enemy bomber and took the four Italian airmen who had managed to bail out and land with their parachutes prisoner at pistol-point. One of them, Lieutenant Brussolo Garibaldo, on his way to a prisoner-of-war camp, confirmed the unorthodox way his plane was attacked by the Greek pilot.[34] The rest of the bailed-out airmen were identified as D. Peteruzo, M. Capelani and B. Trezolani.

Holmes' and Mitralexis' practices were later copied by the Germans with the formation of a 'special' Luftwaffe squadron, consisting of volunteer pilots, 18 to 20 years of age. Manning lightened and unarmoured Bf 109 fighters, they were trained to down enemy bombers by ramming the tail or control surfaces with the propeller of their plane and then bail out if possible. They were involved in combat only once, on 7 April 1945, when 120 airmen took off for a mission and only fifteen came back.[35] It is believed that behind this ill-fated scheme was the Luftwaffe's Colonel Hajo Herrmann. Earlier, in April 1943, another Luftwaffe officer, Captain Günther Josten, had asked pilots of Luftwaffe's VI Group, who were stationed at the time at Schmoldow, near Meckleburg-Vorpomnem in Germany, to volunteer for suicide attacks against Soviet targets. None of the pilots did.[36] The establishment of a suicide-attack air unit was formally discussed in Nazi Germany in late 1943. The idea, proposed by Otto Skorzeny and Colonel Hajo Herrmann, was the deployment of a manned version of the V-1 flying bomb for attacks in which the pilot was likely to be killed or at the best to parachute down at the target area.[37] Test flights were carried out in the autumn of 1943 by Heinz Kensch and Hanna Reitsch.[38] On 5 November, during a test, something went wrong and Kensch had to parachute to safety.[39] On 15 March 1945, Adolf Hitler was persuaded by his officials that suicide missions were not part of the German warrior tradition and the whole project was called off.

Owen Baggett

It was called a rare story for the ages! During the Second World War, an American pilot, while parachuting to the ground from his destroyed bomber, shot down a Japanese fighter plane with his sidearm! On 31 March 1943, USAAF's Second Lieutenant Owen John Baggett had to bail out, when his plane, a B-24 Liberator, was hit by enemy fire over Burma.[40] The USAAF bomber, among other B-24s on their way to destroy a railway bridge at Pyinmana, had been intercepted by thirteen enemy Nakajima Ki-23 fighters.[41] During the intense air-battle Baggett's plane was fatally damaged and a few members of the crew managed to escape just seconds before it exploded. Five out of the nine aboard the downed USAAF bomber were killed either in the plane or by being strafed by enemy fighters as they were descending in their parachutes. The Japanese pilots killed two bailed-out airmen and wounded Baggett in the arm. The latter decided to play dead, hanging limp in his parachute's harness, in the hopes that he'd be left along long enough to at least make it to the ground. Suddenly, a Japanese plane approached within feet of Baggett's parachute, cruising at near-stall speed, and the pilot opened his canopy. He wanted to get a better look at his victim.[42] Then the Texas-born Baggett pulled out his M1911 from his holster, aimed at the pilot and squeezed the trigger four times. He watched the plane stall and spiral towards the ground.[43] At least one credible report said the Japanese plane was found crashed and the pilot dead with a single bullet in the head.[44] A Japanese officer said to an American prisoner of war, USAAF Colonel Harry Melton, that they had found one of their pilots near the wreckage of his plane with a bullet wound to his head.[45] This account is not consistent with Japanese wartime records discussed in the book *B-24 Liberators vs Ki-43 Oscars China and Burma 1943*, Osprey Publishing, 2010 by Edward M. Young on page 57. The circumstantial evidence retrieved from US records suggest though that Baggett had pulled the trigger during the historical duel between a fighter pilot and a parachuting airman that took place at 4,000 to 5,000ft from the ground. Lieutenant Lloyd K. Jensen, the first pilot, and one of the B-24's turret gunners (Sergeant Crostic) landed with their parachutes near Baggett. All three were captured by the Japanese and spent two and a half years in a prisoner-of-war camp near Singapore. They were liberated prior to the Japanese surrender by a team of OSS agents. Baggett became legendary as the only person ever to down a warplane with a .45 calibre M1911 pistol, while parachuting.[46] After the war, Baggett remained silent about the event. He chose to remain in the military, transferring to the newly-formed USAF in 1948 and later fought in Korea. He rose to rank of full colonel in the USAF before retiring. He died on 27 July 2006 in San Antonio, Texas.

Shooting at Bailed-out Airmen

In 1940, many air force pilots on both sides performed remarkable escapes particularly during the Dunkirk evacuation. Several pilots, with their aircraft disabled, took to their parachutes only to be killed by small-arms fire as they drifted down, for the troops on the beaches often blazed away indiscriminately at friend and foe alike.[47] In the Pacific the Japanese gained a bad reputation for shooting enemy airmen dangling in their parachutes. It had to do with the fact that the Japanese viewed surrender as dishonourable and to them bailed-out airmen, particularly pilots, were considered to have surrendered. For this reason, the treatment of prisoners of war in Japanese camps was much harsher in comparison to the POW camps ran by Germans or Italians. There were countless attacks against Chinese, Russian, Dutch, British and American airmen, like the one USAAF Lieutenant Baggett had experienced. On 5 May 1945, a USAAF B-29 bomber was shot down by Japanese fighters over Japan's island of Fukuoka. Of the nine crew members who managed to bail out, one was killed in mid-air by a Japanese pilot. Of the eight who landed by parachute, one shot himself with his sidearm and another was stabbed by a civilian. The rest were sent to a prisoner-of-war camp. The only one who survived was the pilot, Captain Marvin S. Watkins. The rest died at the University of Kyushu where they were used by the Japanese in 'scientific experiments'.

The question of shooting at bailed-out airmen aroused a debate as early as June 1918, when parachutes were issued for the first time to German and Austro–Hungarian pilots. Until the beginning of the Second World War, the dominant idea in Western Europe and the United States was for the descending pilot to be left to land with his parachute as an act of chivalry on the part of the person who caused the downing of the enemy aircraft. This idea had been formally adopted in 1923 by the Hague Rules of Air Warfare (HRAW). 'When an aircraft has been disabled', according to Article 20 of the HRAW, 'the occupants when endeavouring to escape by means of parachute must not be attacked in the course of their descent.' Despite that, there was no legal prohibition to targeting parachuting enemy airmen as the HRAW never came into force.[48] On 1 and 2 September 1939, during the German invasion of Poland, two Polish pilots who were forced to bail out in dogfights were attacked while hanging in their parachutes by Luftwaffe pilots. They both survived. One of them, Lieutenant Aleksander Gabszewicz, eventually made it to England and served in the RAF. During the Normandy landings in June 1944, Gabszewicz commanded 131st Wing.

In 21 December 1940, during the battle for Greece, a RAF pilot, Squadron Leader William Hickley, had to bail out. He was subsequently killed in his parachute by the Germans. His squadron (the 80th) was stationed at the time near Trikala in central Greece. On the other hand, there are verified accounts of German fighter pilots ceasing their attacks to allow Allied airmen to parachute from fatally-damaged stricken bombers. A Luftwaffe fighter ace, Adolf Galland, is mentioned as having publicly rejected the idea of shooting enemy pilots in their parachutes, even if they were over their own territory, characterizing the practice as 'equal to murder'.

The question of shooting a pilot parachuting over his own territory arose in 1940, during the Battle of Britain. It was viewed by some at the time, mostly in Nazi Germany, that RAF pilots could be shot at while descending by parachute over British soil, whereas the Luftwaffe ones could be spared. The reason behind this view was that German pilots shot down over England would become prisoners of war after landing, whereas the RAF pilots were still potential combatants – capable of using new planes and be assigned new missions. During the Battle of Britain, Polish and Czech pilots serving in the RAF reportedly shot Luftwaffe pilots in parachutes over England.[49] An Australian pilot, Group Captain Clive Caldwell, had stated that he never shot any parachuting pilot who landed where he could be taken prisoner.[50] Caldwell's nickname was 'killer'. A reason for this was that he had shot at enemy airmen after bailing out from their plane. 'It's your life or theirs,' he commented once. 'This is war!' On 4 July 1941, Caldwell saw a German pilot shoot and kill a close friend, Pilot Officer Donald Munro, who was descending to the ground in a parachute.[51] On 31 August 1940, Winston Churchill condemned this practice by saying that shooting a parachuting pilot was like 'drowning a sailor'.[52]

On 2 October 1942, a *Regia Aeronautica* Macchi C.202 fighter was hit during a dogfight with five Spitfires in North Africa and Captain Livio Cessoti, had to bail out. On his way down by parachute, the Italian pilot was reportedly strafed and killed by RAF fighters.[53] The Luftwaffe's Captain Josef Zwernemann was reported killed in his parachute on 8 April 1944 over Altmark, northern Saxony, in Germany.[54] He was forced to bail out, when his plane, a Fw 190, was hit by USAAF P-51 Mustang fighters. The Luftwaffe's captain Emil Omert is reported to have been shot and killed by marauding US fighter aircraft, while hanging in his parachute.[55] It happened on 24 April 1944 during an attack on enemy bombers over the Finta Mare area in southern Romania. Some of the USAAF pilots who carried out air raids over German-occupied Europe during the Second World War claimed they had received unwritten orders from their officers to shoot Axis airmen parachuting over their territory so they could not fly again to kill more Americans. German sources claim that US pilots frequently practised shooting at enemy parachutes – especially closer to the end of the war when Germany had more planes than pilots.[56]

The majority of USAAF pilots insisted that they were trying to destroy aircraft rather than kill pilots during dogfights with the enemy. US General Dwight D. Eisenhower formally forbade the practice. The Supreme Allied Commander of the Allied Forces in Europe, in a directive issued to the USAAF and RAF top brass before D-Day in June 1944, clarified that enemy airmen compelled to escape by parachute were not legitimate military targets and must not being deliberately attacked.[57] In 1949, as a result of the widespread abuses committed during the Second World War, the newly updated version of the Geneva Conventions came into force did not include an explicit prohibition in the shooting of parachuting enemy combatants. It was done in 1977 when the practice codified in Protocol 1 to the Geneva Conventions. According to Article 42, 'no person parachuting from an aircraft in distress shall be made the object of attack during his descent. Upon reaching the ground in territory controlled by an adverse Party, a person who has parachuted from an aircraft in distress shall be given an opportunity to surrender before being made the object of attack, unless it is apparent that he is engaged in a hostile act.' It must be emphasized that airborne troops are not protected even by the modified edition of the Geneva Conventions.[58]

Chapter 12

Other Paratroopers

The airborne forces of ten countries from Europe, Asia and South America have been included in this chapter. These countries have been selected, in addition to the ones that have already been presented, as their airborne forces have also been involved in combat, either between 1939 and 1945 or in the post-war period. Israel, the major Arab countries and Iran will be the subject of a separate chapter covering the Middle Eastern wars.

The Bulgarians

In Bulgaria the first parachute jumps were performed in 1927 by four military officers at Bozhurischte airfield in the country's capital, Sofia. They were the 2nd Lieutenants Boris Stoev, Hristo Hristov, Vasil Velkov and Boris Tsvetanov. The beginning of military parachuting in this Balkan country dates from the autumn of 1940, when the formation of a parachute company in Bulgaria's (then Royal) Air Force was formally approved. In December 1942, 300 men were selected out of 5,000 applicants by a committee including German military officers. Those admitted were sent to Germany, Bulgaria's ally at the time, for six months training at the Luftwaffe's *Fallschirmschule* 3 (3rd Parachute School) at Broitzem airport in south-western Braunschweig. After the fourth parachute jump, during which a trainee (Private Georgi Shterionov) was fatally injured on landing, the training course was abruptly halted and the Bulgarians returned home. On 18 March 1943, 243 of the German-trained Bulgarian parachutists formed a parachute *Druzhina*, a battalion-size unit, based at Vrazhdebna airfield, near Sofia and commanded by Captain Lyubomir Noev. On 28 January 1944, the unit, now numbering 429 officers and other ranks, was relocated to Pleven. When Bulgaria joined the Allies, after a communist coup on 9 September, the country's paratroopers entered combat against the German Army. They attacked German forces in Kumanovo in southern Yugoslavia, during the Battle of Stratsin.[1] After seizing a fortified position with an airdrop, the Bulgarians fought for a month and a half, blocking the withdrawl from Greece of German Army Group 'E'. On February 1951, the battalion was transferred from the Air Force to the Intelligence Department of the General Staff. On 1 October 1975, the 68th Independent Parachute Reconnaissance Regiment 'Spetsnaz' (68th IPRRS) was created and the parachute reconnaissance companies, which were assigned to each of Bulgaria's three armies, were expanded into battalions. On 30 July 1993, the 68th IPRRS was restructured into a brigade. Seven years later, the 68th Special Operations Forces Brigade was formed. It was renamed the 68th Brigade of Special Forces in 2012. On 1 February 2017, the brigade was taken out of the structure of the land forces and represents ever since the unconventional warfare branch of the Bulgarian armed forces. It is directly subordinated to the Chief of Defence. It is also one of the two special operations units, the other being the navy's far smaller Special Reconnaissance Detachment.

The Romanians

In Romania the first paratrooper unit was formed on 10 June 1941, although a parachute training establishment had started operating at Pantelimon, near Bucharest, as early as 1937. The first initiative to form a paratrooper unit in this Balkan country came from the Air and Navy Ministry, where discussions started in September 1940. General Alexandru Ioanitiu, the Chief of the General Staff, was among the officials in favour of the creation of an airborne unit. On 10 June 1941, the first Romanian parachute company was formed. All the recruits were volunteers. In mid-June 1942, shortly after Romania's entry into the Second World War on the side of the Germans, the unit was incorporated into the *Aeronautica Regala Romana* (ARR), the country's air force at the time, as the 8th Parachute Company. It was followed a year later, by another company, the 9th. The 10th Parachute Company, created in 1943, was a heavy weapons unit. The three companies merged into Romania's 4th Parachute Battalion. Most of the equipment, including the jump helmets, had been 'imported' from Germany, but their parachutes were American, made in Romania under licence from the Irving Chute Ltd. The men were transported by German-built Junkers Ju 52 transport planes and the equipment (mortars and anti-tank guns) by gliders towed by Romanian IAR 80 fighters. The 4th Parachute Battalion was declared operational in August 1944 with its men not having fought yet against the Soviets. In September 1944, after a coup led by King Michael I, Romania sided with the Allies.[2]

The paratroopers were then deployed in and around Bucharest, mainly in the Baneasa Forest, against their former allies, the Germans. Fighting alongside the Red Army, they wiped out a 400-man German force that parachuted onto Otopeni airfield, north of Bucharest.[3] Despite its potential, the 4th Parachute Battalion didn't make a significant impact on the Romanian armed forces during the Second World War.[4] By the end of 1944, most of the paratroopers had been transferred to infantry units and the battalion was disbanded in March 1945, as the Soviets were eager to get rid of the elite formations of the Romanian armed forces. The battalion was re-activated five years later. On 1 November 1950, the Armed Forces Minister, General Emil Bodnăras, ordered the establishment of a paratrooper battalion in Teruci, at the aviation training centre.[5] Bodnăras had deserted from the Romanian armed forces in 1931, taking refuge in the Soviet Union, where he attended a Secret Police (NKVD) school. In 1944, he landed on Romanian soil by parachute and was imposed by the Soviets high up in the Romanian Communist Party's hierarchy.[6] During communist rule, Romania had several Special Forces units (mountain, marine and naval), including six airborne battalions. Most of these units were disbanded with the remainder eventually merging into a new formation called 1st Special Operations Regiment. It was replaced, in October 2006, by the 620th Special Operations Regiment. In October 2011, the 6th Special Operations Brigade 'Mihai Viteazul' was established, being Romania's special operations formation, by the expansion of the former 620th Special Operations Regiment and the incorporation of three more (610th, 630th and 640th).

The Finns

The training of the first military paratroopers in Finland began in 1941. The sixteen volunteers who completed the Finnish-organized course were mostly Estonian refugees. A total of 110 Finnish officers and NCOs underwent parachute training until mid-1944. They belonged to the Army's reconnaissance patrols and they never formed an airborne unit. They were only assigned missions behind enemy lines and they always operated in small teams. In the night of 30/31 August 1942, thirteen Finnish-trained Estonians parachuted behind the Soviet lines from a Junkers Ju 52.[7] The mission was ill-fated as the paratroopers were either killed or captured by the Red Army.[8] It was almost two years until the next combat mission. On the night of 20/21 July 1944, a Finnish Army officer was dropped behind enemy lines from a Heinkel He 115 seaplane.[9] Three more Finns parachuted into the same region the following night to patrol behind enemy lines. Only the latter were able to return to friendly lines after the completion of their assignment. The last combat mission was carried out on 31 August, when three paratroopers were dropped from an He 115 to gather intelligence. Only one eventually returned.

The first parachute course was run at the Luonetjärvi airfield in central Finland in April 1941, where the participants were trained in landing techniques and parachute packing, before performing two jumps from a Douglas DC-2 plane. The forty-two volunteers who underwent parachute training in March 1942 at Naarajärvi airfield in eastern Finland qualified with one jump from a Junkers F 13 plane. The parachute school then moved to Utti airfield in south-eastern Finland, where a total of eighty-seven volunteers trained between April and May 1944. They qualified with two jumps from Junkers Ju 52 MS (minesweeper) planes with the exception of the last nineteen-man group of trainees that performed five drops from Heinkel He 59 biplanes.[10] The Ju-52s were also provided by the Luftwaffe. However, there is still no information about the presence of any German instructors at Utti, although the Finnish army was fighting against the Red Army at the time along the Wehrmacht.[11] The summer of 1944 found the Finnish Army having 120 jump-trained patrolmen. In fact, they were not qualified paratroopers by Axis or Allied standards. They were simply trained to jump if necessary. When the Winter War started in November 1939, following the Soviet invasion, there were four patrol groups comprised of fourteen troopers each. As the war progressed the patrol's ranks increased to forty or fifty men. They were tasked with gathering intelligence, destroying enemy personnel and material assets, and disrupt supply and communication lines. The jump-trained patrolmen, re-organized in companies, became part of the *Erillinen Patalijoona* 4 (Detached Battalion 4) that was formed on 1 July 1943. After the war, these units were demobilized until 1 February 1962, when Special Forces training began in Finland with the establishment of the *Laskuvarjöjääkärikulou* (Parachute Jaeger School) at Utti. On 1 January 1979, the Utti Jaeger Regiment was formed by merging the Parachute Jaeger School, the Military Police School and a Helicopter Wing. The Parachute Jaeger School was later reformed into the Special Jaeger Battalion and the Helicopter Wing reinforced into a Helicopter Battalion.[12] The *Jääkäriprikaati* (Jaeger Brigade), established in 1979, is based in Sodankylä and Rovaniemi in Finnish Lapland. It is the northernmost brigade-level unit of Finland's defence forces and specializes in Arctic training and air assault. The brigade employees 400 officers and NCOs, almost all qualified parachutists, as well as approximately 2,200 conscripts who carry out their national service in the unit annually.

The Portuguese

The first Portuguese paratroopers were twelve Timorese soldiers who were trained by the Australians in 1942. Some of them were dropped and fought against Japanese forces occupying Portuguese Timor. In Portugal, the first airborne unit was formed as part of the air force in 1956. It was a battalion which six years later was enlarged to become a regiment. Some 160 green–beret Portuguese paratroopers were killed in the early 1970s fighting against guerrillas in Portugal's African colonies, such as Angola and Mozambique. In 1975, the *Corpo de Tropas Paraquedistas* (Parachute Troops Corps) was formed in the air force. In 1993, the airborne corps was transferred to the Army as *Brigada Aerotransportada Independente* (Independent Airborne Brigade). The formation is being restructured to become Portugal's *Brigada de Reacção Rápida* (Rapid Reaction Brigade). It includes mostly airborne and helicopter–borne units trained in special operations.

The Spaniards

Spain has had paratroopers since the late 1930s. Some of them were trained by German instructors and others by Soviets during the Civil War, but none were used in airborne operations. This elite force remained inactive during the Second World War because of Spain's neutrality. In 1953, an airborne battalion was raised in the Spanish army and seven years later elements of the unit performed a combat jump during a Moroccan Moujahidin insurgency in the Spanish West Sahara. On 25 November 1957, sixty paratroopers were dropped from five CASA 352 transport aircraft onto a Spanish outpost in Tiluin struggling to hold off a force of several hundred Moroccans. By 1965, the airborne battalion had developed into a fully-fledged brigade. *Brigada 'Almogáraves VI' de Paradaista* is comprised of two parachute infantry regiments, the 4th and the 5th, and an air-cavalry regiment, the 8th, based in two cities, Madrid and Murcia. The black-bereted Spanish paratroopers spearhead their country's Rapid Reaction Force along with the 19th Special Operations Group 'Maderal Oleaga', which is stationed in the port city of Alicante in southern Spain. Until 2002, this airborne unit was an elite component of Spain's Foreign Legion. Formed in 1920, it is the Spanish equivalent of the French Foreign Legion.

The Serbians

In Serbia, formerly part of Yugoslavia, the first parachute jump was performed in 1926. On 2 September, Second Lieutenant Dragutin Dolanski was dropped onto Vojvodina's Novi Sad airfield from an altitude of 2,100ft (650m). Twelve years later, ten civilians, including a female parachutist, carried out a display drop at the Zemun airfield near Belgrade, the Yugoslav capital.[13] In 1939, a parachute training school was established by the Yugoslav Army in Pančevo. In mid-1944, during their country's occupation by the Germans, Yugoslav volunteers were taken to Bari to become paratroopers. Nearly 200 Yugoslavs went through training at Gravina, Puglia, in southern Italy. At the same time, volunteers had been taken for airborne training to the Soviet Union as well. In Italy, an airborne unit was made up of Allied-trained Yugoslavs. It was commanded by Lieutenant Čedimir Vranič. The 1st Yugoslavian Airborne Battalion, as the unit was named, was shipped to Dubrovnik in December. The battalion had no combat experience whatsoever, particularly in airborne warfare. In mid-July 1945, Yugoslavia's first parachute unit was disbanded. The following year, a parachute training course was run and supervised by the Air Force and an airborne unit, the 46th Parachute Battalion, was created at Bela Crkva in Vojvodina. On 5 February 1953, the 63rd Parachute Brigade was formed at Šabac to be reactivated six years later. It was replaced by three independent parachute battalions, the 159th, the 127th and the 148th, which were stationed at Skopje, Batajnica and Cerklje.[14] A parachute school was established in Niš. In 1967, the 63rd Parachute Brigade was formed again after the merging of the 148th Parachute Battalion and the Parachute School Battalion. In 1992, after the dissolution of Yugoslavia, Serbia, one of the independent states that emerged, created the 72nd Reconnaissance-Commando Battalion that is stationed in Pančevo. It became part of Serbia's Special Brigade that was established in September 2006 consisting of airborne, diving and counter-terrorism units.

The Turks

Turkey is one of several countries which adopted military parachuting after the Second World War.[15] In 1952, a Special Forces unit was formed in the Turkish Army.[16] It was trained to carry out covert operations behind enemy lines and its men were qualified parachutists. Elements of this unit acquired combat experience during the Korean War as part of their country's expeditionary force. Turkey's *1' Inci Komando Tugay Komutanliği* (1st Commando Brigade) was established in 1965.[17] It contained, airborne units, as well as Special Forces teams of the Hakkâri Mountain and Commando battalion and the *Jandarma Özel Harekat* (JÖH), the Special Operations units of the Gendarmerie.[18] The 1st Commando Brigade, which is still located at Kayseri in central Anatolia, was nicknamed *Bordo Bereliler* (Maroon Berets) in 1992. A year later, the *Özel kuvvetler Komutanliği* (OKK – Special Forces Command) was established to run special operations and spearhead the fight against terrorism. The Special Forces of Turkey's army and navy have been placed under this command, which receives orders directly from the General Staff. All personnel are parachute-trained. OKK's naval

Special Forces include the *Sualti Savunma* (SAS – Underwater Defence) and *Su Alti Taarruz* (SAT – Underwater Offense), both based at Foça Naval Base near Izmir.

Parachute troops were involved in the Turkish invasion of Cyprus in 1974. At 06.00 on 20 July, 120 Turkish paratroopers were dropped over Mia Millia, near Nicosia, the island nation's capital. They were assigned with capturing Nicosia airport. The following day, twelve commandos, who had landed by parachute, ambushed a Greek-Cypriot military convoy on the Mirtou-Asomatou road near Kyrenia in north Cyprus. On 22 July, an unspecified number of Turkish paratroopers was dropped near the Boghazi-Argypta pass near Famagusta in eastern Cyprus. Turkey's company-sized parachute and commando forces would later engaged Kurdish separatists in operations within and across the country's borders with Iraq and Syria.

The Peruvians

Peru has a prominent place in the history of military parachuting, being the first country in the western hemisphere to use paratroopers in combat. This occurred on 27 July 1941, during the war against Ecuador, when Peruvian paratroopers seized an Ecuadorian port. In Peru, it had all started thirteen years earlier, when an air force officer became the country's first military parachutist.[19] On 10 May 1928, Second Lieutenant César Alvarez Guerra performed a display jump onto Las Palmas airfield, near Lima, Peru's capital, from a plane cruising at 3,000ft (914m). The jumps went on at Las Palmas, when Commander Fernando Melgar Conde and Sergeant José Pineda Castro parachuted on 16 May. Six days later, a junior naval officer, Ensign Pedro Griva, also performed a display drop. On 23 September, a large-scale parachute drop, the first of its kind in the Americas, took place involving Captain Davide Roca, Ensign José Quiñones, and the 'sub officers' Luis Alferano, Oscar Alamo, Antonio Braudaríz, Ricardo Colmenares, Nestor Madalegoitia and Carlos Raffo. The paratroopers were dropped from Italian-built Caproni Ca.III bombers. The first parachute training facility was established eleven years later at Chiclayo Air Base and Guerra, now an air force colonel, was put in command. A paratrooper company was formed and started training in airborne warfare. In a large-scale jump, on 14 November 1940, a non-commissioned officer, Sergeant Lázaro Orrego, fell to his death when his parachute didn't open.[20]

In July 1941, when tension escalated on the Peruvian-Ecuadorian border, the Peruvian Air Force's paratrooper company was mobilized. The war began on 5 July and four days before the ceasefire, Peruvian paratroopers, dropped from Caproni Ca.III bombers, seized the Ecuadorian port city of Pueblo Bolívar. Although the conflict between the two nations coincided with the Second World War, it had nothing to do with it as neither Peru or Ecuador were affiliated with or supported by the Axis or the Allies. They had their own differences in what has been one of the longest-lasting territorial disputes in the western hemisphere. On 4 November 1959, an army parachute school was established, commanded by Captain Walter Mackelburg and staffed by officers and NCOs who had gone through parachute training in Brazil and Argentina. In 1970, the Peruvian Navy started training personnel in parachuting. Four officers were the first to qualify for airborne operations, Lieutenants Jorge Marzano Patrón, Luis Polar, Juan Ramírez, Alberto Gambetta, and Ensign Percy Navarro. In early 1974, Special Forces (SF) came into being and until June 1975 a total of 400 men had joined the country's elite unit. Women volunteers were admitted to the SF and those who became qualified parachutists eventually formed an all-female company. On 13 November 1979, Peru's Special Forces Group (GRUFFE), commanded by Colonel Jorge Valdez, was formally activated.

The Argentinians

The first parachute unit in Argentina was formed in June 1944 in Cordoba, a city located some 435 miles (700km) north-west of the country's capital, Buenos Aires. Their jump helmets were similar to the ones issued to British paratroopers at the time, whereas their equipment was based on that of the Germans. In Argentina, the first large-scale display drop, involving some thirty military parachutists, was performed in November 1944. A Special Forces capability was set up with American assistance in the early 1960s with the formation of a commando brigade that was modelled along US Ranger lines. The Catamarca airborne school was established and in 1964 the 4th Parachute Brigade was formed. It consists of three parachute battalions, an air-cavalry squadron and various supporting (artillery, engineer, signals, etc) units. The 601st and the 602nd Commando Companies, which were created in January and May 1982 respectively, are based in Campo de Mayo, a military base located 19 miles (30km) north-west of Buenos Aires. The 601st Commando Company was deployed to the Falkland Islands in April 1982 during the Argentinian invasion and fought running battles with the British SAS. In January 2003, the 601st Commando Company was transformed into an air-assault regiment and two years later into a Special Operations Forces Group. In Argentina, there is also the *Buzos Tacticos*, the Navy's 100-strong combat diver unit, elements of which were also involved in action during the Falklands War. Qualified paratroopers serve in the *Comandos Anfibios*, the Argentine Marines' Special Forces. The 4th Airborne Brigade, the 601st Special Operations Forces Group, as well as an army mechanized brigade comprise Argentina's Rapid Deployment Force, headquartered at Campo de Mayo. Qualified paratroopers also serve in the *Brigada Especial Operativa Halcon* (Falcon Special Operations Brigade), a national police unit created in 1986 to combat terrorism.

The Brazilians

Civil parachuting was introduced to Brazil in 1943 at the former Alfonsos Field of Aeronautics, near Rio de Janeiro, by an air force gymnastics instructor named Achile Garcia Charles Astor, who also found and ran the first parachute training course in this Latin American country. Three years later, the Brazilian Army established a parachute school, now named the General Penha Brazil Parachutists' Instruction Center. A year earlier, in 1945, an airborne unit was formed as part of the country's land forces. In 1956, Major Gilberto Antonio Azevedo e Silva went to the United States and underwent training in airborne warfare and special operations at Fort Benning, Georgia and Fort Bragg, North Carolina, respectively.[21] He later created and supervised Brazilian Army's Special Operations Qualification course. In 1961, a group of Brazilian paratroopers travelled to the United States to be introduced into Army Rangers' and Special Forces' tactics. Two years later, an Airborne Rescue (Para-SAR) unit was formed in the Brazilian Air Force (BAF). Elements of the unit in 1973 became instructors at the BAF's Parachute School. Brigada de Infantaria Paraquedista, headquartered in Rio de Janeiro, is Brazil's airborne brigade. It is comprised of five parachute infantry battalions, two parachute companies, an air-cavalry squadron and various supporting (artillery, engineer, signals, etc) units. In the Air Force, paratroopers consist the Para-SAR (Air-Rescue) Squadron, *Esquadrão Aeroterrestre de Salvamento* in Portuguese, which is based in the city of Campo Grande in centre-west Brazil. There is also the Combat Divers Group of the Navy and the Marines' Special Operations Battalion, whose personnel are qualified paratroopers. Both units are headquartered in Rio de Janeiro. In June 2002, *Brigada de Operações Especiais*, a special operations brigade, was established in Rio de Janeiro. Airborne and helicopter-borne units of Brazil's armed forces are assigned to the country's Strategic Rapid Reaction Force.

Chapter 13

Post-1945 Operations (I)

Airborne operations were also conducted in the post-war period. The outbreak of wars in Indonesia, Malaya, Korea, Indochina and Algeria, the Suez Crisis and the 1961 Tunisian incident required the deployment of parachute troops. The main characteristic of post-war airborne operations was in most cases their small size. Large-scale operations involving paratroop and glider forces, like the ones conducted in Crete by the Germans or in Holland by the Allies, were the exception. In July 1945, the British 5th Parachute Brigade was sent to India as 6th Airborne Division's advance formation, but the war ended before it could commence operations. Instead, the brigade took part in disarming the Japanese forces in Dutch East Indies, Malaya and Singapore.

Indonesia (1946–1949)

In December 1945, the British 5th Parachute Brigade, commanded by Brigadier Kenneth Darling, was deployed to the Dutch East Indies (DEI), as Indonesia was known before gaining independence. The brigade's mission was to disarm the remaining Japanese forces and restore order.[1] On arrival in Batavia, now Jakarta, the paratroopers were attacked by Indonesian nationalists, to whom the Japanese had previously handed over their weapons.[2] Despite the attacks, the brigade seized the docks and the airport, and eventually managed to clear Batavia of all dissident elements. In January 1946, British paratroopers were deployed to Semarang in central Java. On 26 April, the 5th Parachute Brigade was relieved in the DEI by a Dutch force and moved to Singapore. A number of British-trained Dutch paratroopers were involved later in the war that led to the independence of Indonesia. In the DEI, *Korps Insulid* was formed by the Dutch army on 22 March 1942 to conduct guerrilla warfare in Sumatra against the Japanese invaders. This unit was the precursor of Holland's Special Forces. In mid-September 1945, two weeks after the Japan's formal surrender, eight British-trained Dutch commandos, led by the Royal Netherlands Navy's Lieutenant Commander C.A.M. Brondgeest, parachuted into north Sumatra. They were tasked with locating and rescuing Dutch military personnel and civilians who had been detained by the Japanese. These men had fought during the Second World War as part of No. 10 (Inter-Allied) Commando – an elite British Army unit made up of volunteers from various countries.

One of them was Sergeant Raymond 'Turk' Westerling, who had been dropped into the German-occupied Netherlands in October 1944 to organize a resistance movement. Raymond Westerling was nicknamed 'Turk' because of his birthplace being

Istanbul. His father was of Dutch and his mother of Greek origin. In June 1945, Westerling received a commission as a reserve lieutenant in the Royal Netherlands Colonial Army and was deployed to the DEI. He was promoted to captain before assuming command of the 570-strong *Depot Speciale Troepen* (DST – Special Forces Depot). This unit was made up of personnel from the disbanded *Korps Insulide* and former members of British No. 10 Commando's Dutch Troop. The DST's training was primarily based on Westerling's experience with the British (Army) commandos. The unit's 570 commandos wore the green beret with the 250 men of the DST parachute company being red-bereted. In December 1945, the unit were accused of pacifying southern Sulawesi using arbitrary terror techniques in an effort, led by Westerling, to eradicate anti-colonial resistance in the area. As many as 3,000 Republican militia and their supporters were killed in a few weeks.[3] In September 1946, the DST numbered about 130 soldiers. Most of them were combat-experienced Dutch volunteers, but among them could be found also other Indo–European soldiers, as well as natives – particularly Moluccans. On 20 July 1947, the Dutch launched a major military offensive with the intent of recapturing the areas controlled by the nationalist rebels. The first airborne operation of the Indonesian war of independence took place on 7 October 1947, when fourteen Indonesian paratroopers were dropped near Kotawaringing in Kalimantan on an infiltration mission. The counter-insurgency operations, during which combat jumps were also conducted, started in December 1946 and lasted until February 1947. On 9 December 1947, Dutch troops killed many civilians in the village of Rawagede (now Balongsari) in Karawang, west Java.

In January 1948, *Korps Speciale Troepen* (KST) was formed headquartered in Batavia with DST being used as a core. In late 1948, negotiations for a settlement between the Dutch government and the nationalist rebels broke down. On 19 December, the Dutch launched a military offensive. By the end of December, all major rebel-controlled cities in Java and Sumatra were in Dutch hands.[4] Although the Dutch forces conquered the towns and cities in the rebels' heartland in Java and Sumatra, they could not subdue the villages and the countryside.[5] Combat jumps were performed by Dutch paratroopers on two occasions during the Indonesian war – the first during the attack on Yogyakarta on 19/20 December 1948 and the second, during the assault on the oil-rich Jambi area in Sumatra between 29 December 1948 and 23 January 1949. Dutch paratroopers captured the airport of Yogyakarta as an prelude to the capture of the city of the same name, which was the rebels' temporary capital. Meanwhile, green-bereted and red-bereted commandos, led by Westerling, conducted nighttime raids to kill or capture nationalist or communist rebels opposing the restoration of Dutch rule. On several occasions, they impaled the victims' heads on stakes as a warning to others. Westerling's men also provided protection to Dutch, European, Chinese and to pro-Dutch Indonesians from nationalist zealots. Even though some Dutch commanders disagreed with his methods, they seemed to acknowledge Westerling's success in suppressing the resistance. By now, his elite force was 800 strong. In January 1949, Westerling was forced to resign his commission, when his activities were revealed by the press not only in Holland but also in other countries, including the United States.

In late 1949, it was decided in The Hague to withdraw from the country's former colony, ending a five-year war during which more than 5,000 Dutch soldiers had been killed. Estimates of Indonesian deaths for the same period range from 45,000 to 100,000.[6] On 27 December, sovereignty was formally transferred to a republican administration headed by Sukarno. Indonesia was proclaimed a unitary state on 17 August 1950 Meanwhile, in April 1949, the Stormschool relocated itself from Bloemendaal, a municipality in north Holland, to Roosendaal, a city in the south of the country. In this school, which was established in 1945, volunteers were trained in commando warfare mostly by former No. 2 Troop personnel. In early 1950, elements of the KST, which was still based in Indonesia and acted without the consent of their superior officers, were involved in an attempted coup against Sukarno's regime on 22/23 January 1950.[7] The coup was led by ex-Captain Westerling, who failed to seize Jakarta. The Dutch government condemned the coup. Indonesian independence was secured through a blend of both diplomacy and force. Following its return to Holland, on 1 July, KST was renamed *Regiment Speciale Troepen* (RST). It merged with Stormschool to form the present *Korps Commandotroepen* (KCT), which is modelled after the British SBS. Its headquarters and main garrison are located in Roosendaal. In 1995, the KCT switched from a part-conscript–part-professional force to a fully professional unit. Elements of the unit have been deployed in a peacekeeping or on international security assistance role in various countries, including Iraq, Afghanistan, Bosnia-Herzegovina, Ivory Coast and Kurdistan. Paratroopers can be found also in Netherland's Maritime Special Operations Force (MARSOF) that was established on 22 February 1973. MARSOF's 'C' Squadron can be deployed by submarine, underwater transport, parachute and snowmobile.

Albania (1947–1952)

In 1947, twelve agents were parachuted into Albania in a covert paramilitary operation to subvert the Balkan country's communist regime. They were anti-communist Albanian émigrés, who had been recruited in Italy, Greece and Turkey by the British Secret Intelligence Service (SIS) and trained in Libya in the use of weapons, sabotage techniques, intelligence-gathering and in parachuting. The idea was that if Britain could parachute in enough agents, they could organize a popular revolt, which the Allies would support by airdrops. The Americans were shortly persuaded to join in, as Britain wanted the United States to finance the project and provide bases in Italy and Greece. In case of success, the British had a replacement for the Albanian strongman Enver Xoxha, the country's first and only monarch Zog I, who had been deposed by the Italians in 1939 and was in exile at the time in Alexandria. The agents were dropped throughout 1947 onto the mountains of Mati in central Albania. The local population, a tough clannish community of Roman Catholics, were not impressed by the agents. The operation, code-named Valuable, dragged on for a couple of years. There were sabotage attempts on the Kucova oilfields and the copper mines in Rubik in north-central Albania, but no real success by the agents in raising a revolt. The idea for a counter-revolution in Albania was adopted by NATO on 6 September 1949 in

Washington. NATO wanted the overthrow of the Moscow-dominated (at the time) Xoxha. They were already concerned that the USSR was building a submarine base on Albania's Karaburun Peninsula, near the port of Vlora. Meanwhile, thirty more Albanian émigrés had been recruited by the SIS. After a two-week training session in Malta, nine of them were selected for subverting action in Albania. On 3 October at about 21.00, they disembarked from a Greek fishing boat on the Karaburun Peninsula.[8] A few weeks later, another eleven-man party infiltrated Albania the same way. The two landings were not successful. The agents failed to inspire any anti-regime movement among the local population and had to flee south to Greece. Until early 1952, a small number of American agents infiltrated Albania by air, sea or on foot to gather intelligence.

The last infiltration occurred in April 1952, when four Albanian émigré SIS agents were captured at Shen Gjerj (Saint George), near the town of Elbasan, after landing by parachute. Some time after his defection to Moscow, Harold Adrian 'Kim' Philby, the notorious Soviet spy, admitted being the source of information on SIS activity in Albania, which Moscow passed on to Hoxha.[9] The four captured Albanian agents were summarily executed. Several civilians directly or indirectly connected with Operation Valuable were arrested, tried and either condemned to death or to long prison sentences. The subversive activity by SIS and CIA agents in this small Balkan country between 1947 and 1952 cost the lives of at least 300 Albanians.

Malaya (1948–1960)

In 1946, the British 5th Parachute Brigade became involved in disarming Japanese forces in Malaya. Four airborne units were among the British and Commonwealth forces deployed to South-East Asia's British-dominated Malay peninsula in 1948, when Communist guerrillas attempted to seize power by force of arms. These elite units were the Malayan Scouts and three SAS squadrons – British, Rhodesian and New Zealand. Elements of the British Parachute Regiment also saw action in Malaya; the Parachute Regiment was at that time part of the newly-formed 16th Independent Parachute Brigade.

'Z' Squadron of 21st SAS (Artists') Regiment were deployed to Malaya in early 1951, although they were about to be sent to Korea. In Malaya, the SAS squadron was placed under the command of a British veteran of the Chindit campaigns in Burma during the Second World War, Lieutenant Colonel Mike 'Mad Mike' Calvert, who was already there. He had formed the Malayan Scouts, made up of British, other Commonwealth and Far Eastern war veterans, mostly ex-SAS and ex-Chindits, who volunteered to fight against the Communist guerrillas. A squadron was formed from local volunteers, who had seen service during the war with SOE or Force 136. In Calvert's elite force, the 100-strong Malayan Scouts and the 21st SAS became 'A' and 'B' Squadrons. 'C' Squadron was made up of a hundred SAS-trained Rhodesian volunteers. 'A' Squadron was based at Ipoh, north of Kuala Lumpur, with 'B' and 'C' Squadrons being deployed to the south of the Malaya peninsula, at Johore, where an intelligence cell, headed by Major John Woodhouse, was also established. By 1956, the force had been enlarged, when British Parachute Regiment elements were added to it as 'D' Squadron.[10]

The need for the deployment of a deep-penetration unit became apparent in Malaya several months after the beginning of the conflict, when the guerrillas were forced by the Commonwealth forces to retreat deep into the jungle.[11] This unit could remain in the jungle for longer than the three-week period which was the maximum possible for conventional troops. One of the SAS patrols spent 103 consecutive days in the jungle. Calvert's force was tasked to seek, find and destroy guerrilla groups and prevent their infiltration into protected areas. Their main tactic was long patrols, as well as to ambush terrorists and track their bases.[12] They were also trained to direct RAF air strikes. By November 1950, the Malayan Scouts were operating in the jungle with three-man or four-man patrols, laying ambushes and tracking guerrilla bases. In November 1951, Calvert was replaced by Lieutenant-Colonel John 'Tod' Sloane. The 8,000 guerrillas were supported by about 60,000 sympathizers providing food and intelligence. In early 1952, the 22nd SAS was formed in Ipoh from the Malayan Scouts. On 9 February 1952, fifty-four men of 'B' Squadron, 21st SAS, were dropped onto the Belum Valley to block a road leading to the Thai border. On 27 January 1953, an SAS detachment was parachuted north of Johore to establish an advance base and four months later, on 24 May, another detachment was dropped south of Johore on a similar assignment. Using a parachute technique pioneered by their regiment during the campaign in Malaya, the SAS men landed on the jungle canopy and then descended to the ground by rope. In Belum Valley the paratroopers took part in a combined operation, involving Gurkhas, Royal Marines, Malay security forces and SAS foot patrols. 'Tree-Jumping', as it became known, was used again by the SAS in several small-scale operations.[13]

On 8 July, 200 men of 'A', 'B' and 'C' Squadrons were dropped close to guerrilla hideouts.[14] In this operation, code-named Termite, probably the largest conducted by the British in Malay, the 1/6th Gurkhas, the Royal Scot Fusiliers and elements of the West Yorkshire Regiment and the Singapore Royal Artillery also participated. In 1954 also, elements of 'A' Squadron, led by Captain Johnny Cooper, killed Ah Poy, a local communist official, during a sweep carried out south of Ipoh. At the beginning of 1955, Lieutenant Colonel Oliver Brooke, who had replaced Sloan, was injured and was replaced by Lieutenant Colonel George Lea.[15] On 26 March 1955, the 76-strong Independent Parachute Squadron (IPS), a sub-unit of the British Parachute Regiment, joined the SAS for operations in Malaya. The Paras, led by Major Dudley Coventry, were involved in aggressive patrolling in swamps of southern Malaya for several months. The patrols penetrated deep into the jungle on foot, by parachute drop or helicopter insertion. The second year of the Paras' deployment in Malaya was spent mostly in a mountainous area between Ipoh and the Cameron Highlands.

On 2 April 1955, 'A' Squadron, 22nd SAS, landed by parachute to seize territory in an area called Ulu Langat, in south-east Malaya. During a month-long sweeping operation near Fort Chubai, elements of the 22nd SAS and the New Zealand SAS Squadron were dropped in June 1956. The New Zealanders had replaced the Rhodesian SAS Squadron, when the latter returned home. By 1956, the 22nd SAS numbered 560 men divided between five squadrons, including the New Zealand and the Parachute Regiment ones. By 1957, the number of guerrillas in Malaya had fallen to 2,000.[16]

In 1957, because of military cuts decided in London, 'B' Squadron was disbanded and its men were absorbed by the understrength 'A' and 'D' Squadrons. The last major operation was conducted by 'D' Squadron in the swamp near Telok Anson, south of Kedah, in the spring of 1958. After ten days of searching, the SAS troopers tracked and encircled an enemy camp. Ah Hoi, a notorious guerrilla leader, and ten of his men were eventually forced to surrender to an SAS force. By the end of 1958, 6,400 guerrillas had been killed with further 3,000 captured or surrendered. On 31 July 1960, the war ended with a parade of the victorious Malayan and Commonwealth forces in Kuala Lumpur.

Korea (1950–1953)

On 8 May 1948, in a record-breaking exercise, nearly 2,200 American paratroopers flew some 500 miles to make a mass jump at Fort Campbell, Kentucky.[17] Two years later, however, a US airborne force had to be deployed a great deal further, when the Korean conflict broke out. The war started on 25 June 1950, following the surprise invasion of the Republic of Korea by its northern neighbour, the communist People's Republic of Korea. A total of twenty-one United Nations (UN) member states contributed forces to prevent the South Koreans from collapsing.[18] General Douglas MacArthur, the American supreme commander of UN forces in Korea, had 'specifically' requested the deployment of the British SAS.[19] But the 21-man detachment of 'B' Squadron, 21st SAS, which was earmarked for service in Korea, was sent to Singapore and then to Malaya instead. The American 187th Airborne Infantry Regiment, two parachute-trained companies of the US Army Rangers and a detachment of the 60th Indian Parachute Field Ambulance were the only airborne units that fought in Korea as part of the UN Expeditionary Forces. The regiment selected for deployment was the only Allied unit to parachute on Japanese soil in August 1945 before resuming occupation duties. On 1 August 1950, the 187th Airborne Infantry Regiment, now assigned to the 11th Airborne Division, became the 187th Airborne Regimental Combat Team (ARCT), when supporting units were added. Brigadier General Thomas J.H. Trapnell, who had previously commanded the 82nd Airborne Division's 505th PIR, was appointed commander of the 187th ARCT. The formation arrived in Japan on 23 September and at South Korea's Kimpo airfield three days later. The 187th ARCT consisted of the 187th Airborne Infantry Regiment, two airborne artillery battalions (one field artillery and one anti-aircraft) and an engineer battalion. By late August, more units had been added to the formation, including pathfinders from the 11th Airborne Division.

The 2nd and the 4th Ranger companies were deployed to Korea in December 1950. The 2nd Ranger Infantry Company was a segregated unit as all of its personnel, including officers, were African-Americans. They became the only all-black Ranger unit in the US history. The 2nd and the 4th were two of the eight companies, which went through airborne training at Fort Benning, Georgia, between August 1950 and January 1951. Each Ranger airborne assault company numbered 125 men.[20] Among the first to be recruited were qualified paratroopers, who were already serving in the

82nd Airborne Division's 505th PIR and the 80th Anti-aircraft Artillery Company. In Korea, the Ranger airborne assault companies were used in a reconnaissance and scouting role, probing North Korean or (later) Chinese positions for artillery and air attacks. Only a few of them had a chance to make a combat jump later on as only one Ranger operation throughout the Korea conflict required an airborne landing.[21]

On 20 October, a day after the fall of Pyongyang to American forces, the 187th ARCT conducted its first combat jump some 25 miles (40km) north of the North Korean capital as part of a UN offensive towards the Yalu River.[22] The paratroopers were to drop onto the Sukchon and Sunchon areas ahead of the advancing 27th British/Commonwealth Brigade. Their main objective was to cut off the North Korean forces that were withdrawing up the west coast of the Korean Peninsula.[23] They also had to cut the road going to China and, thus, preventing North Korean leaders from escaping from Pyongyang and American POWs being moved northward.[24]

United States Air Force Combat Cargo Command dropped by parachute approximately 4,000 men, led by Colonel (later Major General) Frank S. Bowen, and more than 600 tons of equipment and supplies, including twelve 105mm howitzers, four 90mm anti-aircraft guns and thirty-nine jeeps. The operation began at 14.00 on 20 October, when 1,470 men from Lieutenant Colonel Harry Wilson's 1st Battalion, 187th Regiment were flown by Fairchild C-119 Flying Boxcar and Douglas C-47 Skytrain (Dakota) transports that had taken off from Kimpo airfield. The force was parachuted south-east of Sukchon, where the men encountered only limited resistance on landing. Casualties included twenty-five men injured in the jump, while one group, which landed 1.5 miles (2.4km) east of the drop zone, lost a man killed in his parachute by the North Koreans.[25] After landing, Wilson dispatched patrols towards Naeman-ni.[26] The 3/187th, commanded by Lieutenant Colonel Delbert Munson, jumped next on another drop zone. After landing, the 3/187th adopted a defensive position on the low hills, 1.9 miles (3km) south of Sukchon. They also established roadblocks across the highway and railway. After seizing their objectives by 17.00, the 3/187th killed five North Koreans and captured forty-two others without loss. The 2/187th, commanded by Lieutenant Colonel William J. Boyle, was parachuted at 14.20 some 1.9 miles (3km) south-west of Sunchon. Although the 2/187th suffered twenty men injured in the drop, the battalion secured its objectives by nightfall, almost unopposed.[27] Two companies established roadblocks to the south and west of the town, while a third company linked up with elements of the South Korean 6th Division at Sukchon.

The following morning, the 1/187th captured the high ground of Sukchon and established a blocking position on the main highway running north. At 09.00, the 3/187th began to advance south to clear the Sukchon to Yongju road towards Pyongyang. 'I' Company was moving along the railway line and 'K' Company along the highway. At 13.00, 'I' Company reached Opa-ri, where it encountered a strong North Korean force, estimated as a battalion, which was equipped with 120mm mortars. After a battle lasting two-and-a-half hours, the company was forced to withdraw to Hill 281, having ninety men missing. Despite their success, the North Koreans withdrew to their own defensive position in the high ground around Opa-ri. Amid the fighting, a US medic attached to 'I' Company, Private First-Class Richard Wilson, was killed while attempting to rescue a wounded soldier. He was posthumously awarded the Medal of Honor, the US military's highest decoration.

Meanwhile, heavy fighting took place north of Yongju. It forced the paratroopers to request assistance from the 27th British/Commonwealth Brigade.[28] It came soon enough in the form of the British 1st Battalion, Argyll and Sutherland Highlander. Meanwhile, the 2/187th had remained out of contact at Sunchon, as the South Korean 6th Division completed the clearance of the town. The North Koreans were then found themselves caught between the US paratroopers and advancing Australian troops.[29] On 22 October, elements of the 3rd Battalion, Royal Australian Regiment, supported by eighteen US M4 Sherman tanks, attacked with the bayonet from the rear. At 11.00, elements of the 27th British/Commonwealth Brigade linked up with the American paratroopers, leaving the North Korean 239th Regiment 'practically destroyed'.[30] The total North Korean losses in the entire Battle of Yongju were 200 killed and 500 captured. Meanwhile, the 3/187th reported killing 805 North Koreans and capturing 681 around Yongju. Altogether, US casualties were forty-eight killed in action and eighty wounded – a further one killed in the jump and fifty-six injured. The airborne assault itself was successful, as it encountered almost no opposition, but most of the enemy forces had succeeded in withdrawing north. They had crossed the Chongchon River, while the government and other officials had moved to Kanggye in the mountains 20 miles (32km), south-east of Manpojin. Also, no US and South Korean POWs could be rescued as they had been moved toward the Manchurian border.[31] Before returning to Pyongyang, elements of the 2/187th found the bodies of sixty-six POWs who had been executed and seven more who were found to have died of disease or malnutrition.[32]

On 20 October 1950, after the first combat jump in the Korean War, thirty-five paratroopers were evacuated by Sikorsky H-5 helicopters, the first use of helicopters in support of an airborne operation.[33] H-5s also evacuated seven American POWs from the area. Earlier, on 25 September, a whole battalion of the 187th ARCT was moved by helicopter to guard American X Corps' northern flank as it moved out from Inchon. The first H-5s had been deployed to Taegu on 23 July. Helicopters were also used in Korea for search and rescue (SAR) operations. On 4 September 1950, a bailed-out pilot, USAF Captain Robert E. Wayne, who had landed behind enemy lines near Hanggandong, was picked up by a helicopter. On 10 November, a USAF Boeing B-29 Superfortress heavy bomber was shot down near the Yalu River. The twelve members of the crew parachuted to safety but were all captured by the North Koreans. On 7 December, eight C-119s dropped bridge spans to US troops, so that they could cross a 1,500ft (457m)-deep gorge. It was the first airdropped bridge in the history of warfare. On 3 March 1951, the 2nd and 4th Airborne Assault Companies of the US Army Rangers were attached to the 187th ARCT. They were to join the 187th ARCT, along with a detachment from the 60th Indian Parachute Field Ambulance, in the second-largest combined operation of the war, code-named Courageous. The operation involved an airborne assault near Munsan-ni in South Korea, code-named Tomahawk. The 60th Indian Parachute Field Ambulance Platoon was to provide medical care for the operation, dropping a surgical team of seven officers and five other ranks.

According to the plan, troops were to be inserted by parachute in an area 9 miles (14.5km) north of the then UN front lines, thus trapping large numbers of Chinese and North Korean forces between the Han and Imjin Rivers, north of Seoul, the South Korean capital.[34] General Matthew B. Ridgway, commander of the US Eighth Army in Korea, had made his final decision on the airborne operation on 22 March, after being assured that the weather could be satisfactory on the next day. Ridgway had commanded the 82nd Airborne Division during the Second World War. The 120 transport planes started to take off from Taegu airfield at 07.00 on 23 March. At 09.00, the C-119 and the Douglas C-46 Commando aircraft, escorted by sixteen F-51 Mustang fighters, dropped 3,437 men, led by Colonel Frank S. Bowen, and 220 tons of equipment and supplies. There were two drop zones – the 'north' north-east of Munsan-ni and the 'south' south-east of the town. The 3/187th Regiment and the 4th Ranger Company landed correctly on the north zone with the 2/187th Regiment and the 2nd Ranger Company landing, also correctly, on the south zone. The 1/187th landed incorrectly on the south zone. The airborne assault force landed almost unopposed. Eighty-four paratroopers, including two Rangers, were injured in the jump and were later evacuated by helicopter. By mid-day, the paratroopers and the Rangers had started aggressive patrolling in the greater area and on 24 March the Chinese-defended Hill 228 was captured. Combat casualties among the airborne troops were light, totalling nineteen men, including three dead. The Chinese casualties were 136 dead and a further 149 captured. The North Koreans had withdrawn behind the Imjin River well before the airborne landing. The 187th was relieved by elements of the South Korean I Corps and returned to Taegu. The Ranger companies remained, mostly patrolling, in the Imjin River area throughout April.

On 11 May, the 3rd Airborne Assault Company of the US Army Rangers was assigned division reserve duties. In August, the Ranger airborne assault companies were deactivated. Officers and other ranks of the 2nd and 4th Companies were folded into the 187th ARCT.[35] Besides evacuating wounded personnel from front-line areas in Korea, helicopters were repeatedly called upon to rescue UN pilots who were forced to bail-out behind enemy lines. On 3 April 1951, a US Sikorsky H-19 helicopter picked up a bailed-out Mustang pilot south-east of Pyongyang. On 24 April, a Sikorski H-5 helicopter rescued first the pilot and then the navigator of a downed B-26 near Chorwon, 15 miles (24km) north of the 38th Parallel. On 5 May and on 19 May, H-5 helicopters rescued bailed-out F-51 pilots north of Seoul and south-west of Chorwon, respectively. On 1 June, a C-47 dropped fifteen American-trained South Koreans into enemy territory to retrieve parts of a crashed North Korean MiG-15 but they were all captured by the enemy. On 26 June 1951, the 187th ARCT was withdrawn to Japan, where it became a strategic reserve. In November, the 187th ARCT made a 'simulated combat drop', landing 3,000 troops and 100,000lbs of equipment in South Korea, a demonstration of wartime airlift capability.[36] On 10 September 1951, south of Pyongyang an H-5 helicopter rescued a Lockheed F-80 Shooting Star pilot, Captain Ward Millar. He had suffered two broken ankles following his ejection from the jet but escaped after two months as a POW and then evaded recapture for three weeks. On 23 October, two helicopters rescued the twelve-man crew of a downed B-29, the highest number rescued on any day in the war. On 28 April and 4 June of the same year, H-19 helicopters picked up two bailed-out pilots, Dutch and British, respectively. On 24 May, the 187th ARCT was employed in suppressing the rebellion of 80,000 Chinese and North Koreans at the UN-administered Koje-do Island POW camp. Some forty prisoners were killed during the uprising.[37] After this, the 187th ARCT returned to Japan on 18 October 1952 and made its final return to Korea on 22 June 1953. On 22 June 1953, twenty-seven C-46s and sixty-one C-119s transported the 187th ARCT to Korea to reinforce the US Eighth Army reserves. Some 3,252 paratroopers and 1,771 tons of cargo were transferred in two days.

From late 1952 to late 1953, the 187th was commanded by Brigadier General William C. Westmoreland. At the age of 38, Westmoreland was one of the youngest US Army generals in the post-Second World War era.[38] On 12 April 1953, USAF Captain Joseph C. McConnel, after he had ejected from his battle-damaged North American F-86 Sabre, was picked up from the Yellow Sea by an H-19 helicopter. Three months earlier, on 13 January 1953, a B-29 on a psychological warfare leaflet-drop mission was shot down over North Korea.[39] The crew, including Colonel John K. Arnold, commander of the 581st ARCT, bailed out and were captured. They were tried and condemned as spies but the thirteen airmen were released by the North Koreans on 4 August 1955. Shortly after the Korean War, the 187th ARCT was considered for use in an airborne drop to relieve the surrounded garrison of Dien Bien Phu in Indochina, but the United States government decided not to send troops into the combat zone. After returning from Korea, the 187th Airborne Infantry Regiment was assigned to the reactivated 101st Airborne Division and subsequently inactivated in 1956 with the exception of two battalions. The regiment's 1st and 3rd Battalions of the 187th have ever since been with the 101st as air-assault units.

French Indochina (1946–1954)

Nearly 100 combat jumps were performed in Vietnam by French paratroopers, mostly during the war against the Viêt Minh (VM), the communist rebels – a war that led to France's withdrawal from South East Asia as a whole. Eight airborne battalions were committed in operations between 1946 and 1954 in Indochina as part of the *Korps Exppéditionnaire Française en Extrême-Orient* (French Expeditionary Corps in the Far East). Paratroopers were used in a total of approximately 150 missions. Five of these operations were large scale and fifty-two were commando actions. Sixty-three missions were conducted to reinforce or assist in the disengagement of French outposts and the rest (about thirty) were part of search and destroy operations. Of the airborne battalions three belonged to the French Foreign Legion (FFL). The parachute units involved in what is also known as the First Indochina War (1946–54) were the 2e *Demi-Brigade Coloniale de Commandos Parachutistes* (2ᵉ DBCCP – 2nd Colonial Parachute Half-Brigade), the 1er *Régiment de Chasseurs Parachutistes* (1er RCP –1st Parachute Chasseur Regiment), and the FFL's 1er–3e *Bataillons Ètrànger de Parachutistes* (1er–3e

BEP – 1st–3rd Foreign Parachute Battalions) and 1re *Compagnie Ètrangère Parachutiste de Mortiers Lourds* (1er CEPML – 1st Foreign Parachute Heavy Mortar Company). The 1er CEPML, when it was parachuted into Dien Bien Phu in November 1953, became the first heavy (120mm) mortar unit ever to be dropped in an airborne operation. This company had been formed in Hanoi in 1953 as a support unit to the 1er BEP.[40] The 6e *Bataillon Coloniale de Commandos Parachutistes* (6e BCCP – 6th Colonial Parachute Battalion) was attached to the 1er RCP 1st on 31 December 1953. Over half of the 'Colonial' airborne unit were French volunteers with the other half being of Vietnamese origin.

The 1er BEP was formed as regiment in 1948 in North Africa from the parachute unit of the FFL's 3e *Régiment Ètrànger d'Infanterie* (3e REI – 3rd Foreign Infantry Regiment). It became a battalion three years later. The 2e BEP was raised in North Africa in 1948, as well. The 1e BEP arrived in Saigon in February 1949 and saw combat in Cambodia and Vietnam. The 3e BEP was formed in North Africa in 1949 and was deployed to Indochina as late as 25 May 1954 – days after the disastrous Battle of Dien Bien Phu. The 2e DBCCP was created in Indochina in 1948 from Second World War Special Forces veterans, mostly French who had fought against the Axis with the British SAS. The 1er RCP, which was formed in 1943 in North Africa, had its three battalions deployed in Indochina since the summer of 1947.

In South East Asia seven French-trained and officered parachute battalions made up of Vietnamese, Cambodian and Laotian volunteers also fought, the 1er–7e *Bataillons de Parachutistes Vietnamiens* (1er–7e BPVN – 1st–7th Vietnamese Parachute Battalions). The 1er BPVN was formed in 1951 in Saigon with the 3e BPVN coming into being in Hanoi a year later. The 5th and 7th Vietnamese Parachute Battalions were raised in 1953 in Hanoi. Another Vietnamese battalion, the 6th (Parachute) was formed in Saigon in 1954. The French also created two more parachute battalions in Indochina, one Cambodian and one Laotian. The 1er *Bataillon de Parachutistes Khmers* (1er BPK – 1st Cambodian Parachute Regiment) was formed from Cambodian recruits in 1952. The 1er *Bataillon de Parachutistes Laotiens* (1er BPL – 1st Laotian Parachute Battalion) was raised in Ventiane and by mid-1952 had a strength of 853 men. The number of qualified parachutists in Indochina rose from a few hundred in 1946 to 10,639 in 1951 as parachute artillery, engineers, signals and medical units were added.

It had all started in September 1945, when Hô Chi Minh, leader of the pro-Soviet Vietnamese nationalists, declared his country independent from France. In December 1946, VM forces attacked Hanoi, the largest city in northern Vietnam. On 30 July 1947, the 1er RCP's three battalions were deployed to Indochina. They fought successively in and around the Tonkin delta in northern Vietnam. In a single raid on 7 October 1947 1,100 French paratroopers were dropped to capture the VM leadership at Bac Can, north of Hanoi.[41] At the same time, infantry units had been attacking VM Commander General Vô Nguyên Giáp's forces between Lang Son and Cao Bang. These units had to come to the rescue of the paratroopers, who having failed in their objective, as Hô Chi Minh and other communist officials had escaped, found themselves surrounded by numerically superior enemy forces.[42] During the combined operation, about 6,000 French and 9,000 VM were killed or wounded.[43]

On 12 November 1948, the 1er BEP, commanded by Commandant Pierre Seg-rétain, disembarked in Indochina and was engaged primarily in combat operations in the Tonkin area. Two combat jumps were conducted by French airborne forces in September 1950, during the Battle of Dông Khê, fought mostly in north-western Tonkin. By now, the VM military strength had grown in size, numbering 100,000 combatants. On 17 September, elements of the 1er BEP were dropped south of Dông Khê, at the centre of a highway (Route Coloniale 4 or RC4) used to supply a major French military base at Cao Bang. The FFL paratroopers failed to recapture a French outpost that had been seized by VM troops. Twenty-one officers, 46 non-commissioned officers and 420 Legionnaire were killed near Cox Xa over the course of the battle, including Commandant Segrétain. Of the airborne landing force, 130 men, led by Captain (later Lieutenant Colonel) Pierre Jeanpierre, managed to escape to French lines.

On 7 October, two companies of the 6e BCCP, led by Major (later General) Marcel Bigeard, and a 120-strong company of the 1e BEP were dropped onto That Khê to provide support to retreating land forces. The battalion resisted an enemy force four times larger for an entire night. Following a five-hour close-quarters battle, the paratroopers endured the loss of fifty-one men with further ninety-seven being wounded. Nearly half of the 600-strong 6e BCCP were able to make their way back to French lines, including twenty-three survivors of the attached company of the 1er BEP. Following the VM victory in Dông Khê, vast border areas were secured by their forces and there were no more obstacles to the passage of men and arms from China.[44]

In March 1951, the 1er BEP was reformed from the survivors of the battalion attached temporarily to the 2e BEP and reinforcements coming from Algeria and Morocco. The reconstituted battalion was assigned to combat operations at Chon Ben, on the Black River, and Annam. Meanwhile, the 6th Vietnamese Parachute Battalion was among the French forces that repelled a massive communist attack against Mao Khê, a town situated 20 miles (32km) from the strategically important port of Hai Phòng. The VM were forced to retreat on 27 March, after a bloody hand-to-hand confrontation, suffering heavy casualties – 3,000 dead, wounded or captured by French estimations. When Giáp mounted a conventional-type campaign on 30 May 1951 in an effort to control the Red River Delta in the Gulf of Tonkin, the French mobilized two parachute battalions and three RCTs for the defence of the area. The VM were forced to retreat on 18 June, leaving behind 1,600 dead, wounded or captured. The French losses in the Battle of Day River, as this particular campaign went down in history, were 585 men. Three months later, the French mobilized eight airborne and ten infantry battalions to mount a large-scale offensive against Hòa Bình, situated 39 miles (62km) from Hanoi. On 10 November, two companies of the 2e BEP stormed the VM defences east and west of their commanding post. At the same time, the 1er BCCP and the 7th Vietnamese Parachute Battalion attacked Cho Bén, forcing the communists to retreat from the area.[45] During a communist counter-attack that was launched on 10 December, a company of the 5th Vietnamese Parachute Battalion was ambushed, suffering heavy casualties. On 30 January 1952, the Viet Minh battled with a company of the 8th Vietnamese Parachute Regiment. By 25 February, the French were forced by the enemy to withdrawn from Hòa Bìn. At the height of the battle, General Giáp had forty battalions fighting at different locations throughout the province. Although they suffered heavier casualties than the French in this battle, the VM forces emerged victorious once again.[46] The French evacuation of Hòa Bình enabled communication between the VM and the area of north Amman 'liberated' by their troops. On 29 October, the 6th BCCP, led by Major Bigeard, was parachuted onto Tu Le, participating in Operation Lorraine.[47] Being encircled by an entire division and outnumbered ten to one, the French paratroopers managed an orderly retreat through the jungle carrying all their wounded. After days of marching, they finally reached a French fort.[48]

On 9 November, a French offensive in northern Vietnam included another parachute drop. The 1er BEP and the 6e BCCP were parachuted into combat near Phu Doan, capturing a VM-held area. The French high command wanted to draw the enemy into a set-piece battle, but the VM ignored the challenge. Five days later, after losing 314 men (killed, wounded or missing) and a tank in the fierce fighting, General Raul Salan, the commander of the French forces in Indochina, called the operation off and ordered the withdrawal of his troops from Phu Doan.[49] Between 15 and 24 November, 576 men of the 1st Laotian Parachute Battalion were dropped into Sam Neua in the north-east of Vietnam to reinforce its garrison. Three parachute battalions, the 1st and the 2nd Foreign and the 3rd Vietnamese, spearheading a 15,000-strong combined force, were air-transported to Ná San from Hanoi on 24 November 1952 to defend an outpost and a nearby airstrip in the middle of a valley in north-west Vietnam. General Giáp's strategic aim was to capture and secure the T' Ai region. On 4 December, after nearly two weeks of fierce fighting, the attacking VM were forced to withdraw, leaving behind 1,544 dead and 1,932 wounded or captured.[50] The French casualties and losses in general in the Battle of Ná San were around 500 men. In May, July, August and September 1953, and in June 1954, the 3rd Vietnamese Parachute Battalion was assigned operations in various parts of Indochina. In May 1953, General Salan was replaced by General Henri Navarre, who planned right away one of the largest combined operations of the First Indochina War. The 2nd Battalion of the 1er RCP and the 3rd Vietnamese Parachute Battalion spearheaded the 10,000-strong French task force, also involving marine commando units, that was mobilized for this operation. Navarre's aim was to control and secure Route Coloniale 1 or RC1, a critical north-south artery along the coast of Vietnam. At 06.00 on 27 July, French marine commandos landed to the coast of central Annam to engage the VM 95th Regiment deployed in the area. A parachute drop was conducted (well behind schedule) at 16.50, near Phu An, as a back-up to the advance of ground forces. In the operation the French had seventeen dead and about 100 wounded.[51] The VM casualties were 200 killed and 1,350 wounded or captured. Although the operation was successful for them, the French didn't have enough troops to secure RC1, particularly after the withdrawal of the airborne and marine commando forces from Annam.[52] The VM 95th Regiment survived the operation and by 10 August elements of the unit resumed ambushing French convoys on RC1.[53]

On 18 July, elements of the 6e BCCP participated in a raid against a VM supply depot near Lang Son. The paratroopers were dropped near Loc Bin to capture, repair and hold a river crossing until the arrival of the ground force that raided the depot.[54] They then formed the rearguard of the force and kept retreating until they all were extracted by sea the following day. In mid-August, four parachute battalions spearheaded a combined operation involving eighteen battalions in the southern reaches of the Red River Delta near Tonkin. The airborne units participating in the operation were the 1er and the 2e BEP and two Vietnamese parachute battalions, the 1st and the 3rd. By 11 October, when they were ordered to withdraw, the French had lost ninety-six men in the fighting against only ten confirmed VM dead.[55] Meanwhile, on 3 October, a French paratroop platoon descended onto a VM supply centre at Lao Kay near the Chinese border and destroyed it in a mission also involving a French-led guerrilla force composed of local tribesmen.

The 1er RCP participated, a few days later, on 15 October, in a combined operation against the VM 320th Division in the area of Phu Nho Quan, south of the Red River Delta.[56] Elements of the regiment were parachuted on a distant drop zone to mislead General Giáp about the real target of the operation. The 24,000-strong French force, including paratrooper and tank units, captured a crossroad at Lai Cac and held off Giáp's counter-attack. The VM lost 1,000 killed, 2,500 wounded and 182 captured. French casualties amounted to 113 dead, including seven officers, 505 wounded and 151 missing in action.[57] Although instructed by political authorities in Paris to ensure the safety of the Far East Expeditionary Corps, General Navarre proceeded offensively by sending six months later airborne troops to land at Dien Bien Phu, in north-west Vietnam. Navarre's aim was to draw the VM forces into a pitched battle advantageous for the French Army, as he thought.[58] Paris learned of Castor, as the operation was code-named, six hours after it started. Dien Bien Phu was to become the last major battle between French and VM forces in Indochina. The operation began at 10.35 on 20 November 1953. Over three days, about 9,000 troops, including 800 paratroopers, were flown in or dropped by parachute. The 6e BCCP, led by Major Bigeard, the 1er BEP, led by Major Giraud, and the 1er CEPML, led by Lieutenant Molinier, jumped into the valley at 15.00 on 21 November. Within 60 minutes the 100-man company reported itself ready to open fire with its twelve 110mm mortars which had been parachuted in containers. Air-transported regular French, FFL and Colonial (Vietnamese and North African) infantry units, equipped with artillery pieces and ten American-made M24 Chaffee light tanks, had already been committed to the garrison.[59] Clashes started, while the French deployment was in progress, with a hundred VM being killed. Between 8 and 20 December, the Dien Bien Phu garrison was reinforced with forces, including the 5th Vietnamese Parachute Battalion, led by Captain André Botella. Between 21 and 28 December, paratroopers conducted reconnaissance missions between the garrison and the Laotian border.

Now called Muong Thah, Dien Bien Phu was a large heart-shaped valley 12.5 miles (20km) long and 3.5 miles (6km) wide, surrounded by heavily-wooded hills. General Navarre wanted to transform the area into a forward base for operations close to the Laotian border. His aim was to cut off the supply lines of the Laotian communist guerrillas, whose country had been declared independent only a month earlier. Meanwhile, General Giáp ordered the massive deployment of troops around Dien

Bien Phu, which had been transformed into a fortress by the defenders. The parachute battalions left to defend the fortress, along with infantry forces, were the 1st Foreign (1r BEP) and the 1st Vietnamese. The other participants in the jump of 21 November 1953 had been withdrawn. On 12 January 1954, the clashes between the belligerents became heavier. By mid-February, VM artillery had started shelling French positions. On 12 March, Lieutenant Molinier was wounded during a recon operation. Lieutenant Paul Turcy, his successor as commanding officer of the 1er CEPML, was killed two days later, while defending Béatrice outpost. The Battle of Dien Bien Phu started in the afternoon of 13 March with a VM attack against the northernmost outpost, Gabriel. It was captured two days later. On 16 March, Anne Marie outpost fell into communist hands. The same day, the 6e BCCP, led by Major Bigeard, were dropped over Dien Bien Phu.[60] On 19 March, Lieutenant Colonel Maurice Lemeunier parachuted voluntarily onto the fortress and assumed command of the 13e *Demi-Brigade de Légion Étrangèr* (DBLE). Dien Bien Phu Commander was General Christian de Castries, a cavalry officer, but there were rumours at the time about a 'parachute mafia' overseeing combat operations.

Historian Bernard Fall asserts that by mid-March Majors Bigeard and Langlais, who led the 6th 'Colonial' and the 1st Foreign Parachute Battalions respectively, took de facto command of the fortress.[61] During the Battle of Dien Bien Phu, French aircraft delivered 3,879 personnel to the fortress (mostly by parachute) and evacuated 168 (all wounded). They also delivered tons of supplies (mostly by parachute). As of 27 March, air-supply deliveries were made from 6,600ft (2,000m) or higher, due to heavy losses from enemy fire near the landing strip. Dien Bien Phu's two airstrips, the main and the auxiliary, had already been rendered unusable because of the enemy's artillery and mortar fire. Thirty-six aircraft were shot down by the enemy during the battle and further 150 were damaged with a loss of seventy personnel killed or wounded.[62] By 30 March, the fortress was encircled by four enemy divisions, equipped with heavy artillery and anti-aircraft guns of Soviet origin. The Chinese had provided twenty-four of the American 105mm howitzers captured in Korea, as well as tons of ammunition for them.[63] These artillery pieces kept firing day and night. About 7,000 French troops were trapped in the fortress by at least 45,000 VM forces, who had occupied the hills and the high ground around the valley. Giáp was turning Dien Bien Phu into a virtual island, one that could be reached only by air.

On 1 April, the 2nd Battalion of the 1er RCCP, led by Major Bréchignac, jumped over Dien Bien Phu. A night jump was conducted on 9/10 April, when the 2e BEP, led by Major Liesenfelt, were dropped in two waves. Twelve men were killed during the jump, including Captain Delafond, and another fourteen were injured or wounded by enemy fire. On 18 April, Huguette VI outpost was evacuated by its defenders because of lack of water. Seventeen men of the 1er BEF were killed and further seventy-eight were wounded in an unsuccessful effort to reinforce the Huguette VI outpost. Three days later, Huguette I was captured by the Viet Minh, when the outpost defenders, eighty Foreign Legion paratroopers led by Captain Chevallier, fought to the last man. On 23 April, two more outposts, Huguette VII and Huguette VI, were lost. Lieutenant Jean Gurin, a platoon leader of the 2e BEP, was wounded on the airstrip and decided to kill himself. The following day, Opéra outpost was evacuated by its defenders. Between 24 and 30 April, tens of volunteers were dropped by parachute to reinforce the Dien Bien Phu defenders. The volunteers, most of whom did not have pass any parachute training, belonged to various Foreign Legion units. On 1 May, the VM mounted a new massive offensive. Two companies of the 1er BEP, while defending the Eliane I outpost, were annihilated. The following day, two more outposts, Dominique III and Huguette V, were seized. Lieutenant Colonel Charles Pirot, commander of the artillery units in Dien Bien Phu, committed suicide.

The last reinforcement jump was conducted on the night of 5/6 May, when 400 men from the 1er RCP led by Captain Tréhiou were dropped into Dien Bien Phu. Most of them were sent to reinforce the Eliane outpost. During the night of 6/7 May, the remaining defence positions were shelled with Soviet-made Katyusha rockets. Hours later, seven more outposts, Eliane II, Claudine V, Eliane III, Eliane IV, Eliane X, Eliane XI and Eliane XII, were seized by the communists. By 16.30, with four outposts still held by the French, a ceasefire was arranged.[64] At 17.30, the last of the defenders laid down their arms after fifty-six days of fighting. Meanwhile, the 1st Laotian Parachute Battalion were on their way to reinforce the Dien Bien Phu defenders. They were ordered back when the surrender of the French garrison became known. An isolated outpost (Isabelle), located 3.5 miles (6km) from the Dien Bien Phu HQ, did not surrender. The survivors tried to slip through the jungle towards Laos, but only a few eventually made it. Two-thirds of the retreating group were killed or captured by VM troops. In the Battle of Dien Bien Phu, General Giáp's dead numbered 14,000, according to the VM, and 20,000, according to French sources. The French casualties were 1,500 dead and 11,720 missed in action, captured or surrendered. More than 5,000 of those captured or surrendered were wounded. Those who could walk were forced to march for sixty days to prisoner-of-war camps located 500 miles (800km) away. Only 3,290 of them survived and were later liberated. Four airborne units were overrun by the VM in Dien Bien Phu – the 1er and the 2e BEP and two battalions, the 1st and the 3rd, of the 13e DBLE. The 1er BEP counted 575 killed or missing in action. On 19 May, the battalion was recreated from reserves and new recruits. For the reconstitution of the 2e BEP officers and men had to be transferred on 1 June from another unit, the 3e BEP, which was deployed to Vietnam six days earlier. The 1er BBCCP was transformed into the 1er *Régiment de Parachutistes d' Infanterie de Marine* (1er P.R.I.Ma – 1st Marine Infantry Parachute Regiment). Of the airborne units that fought in Dien Bien Phu the 1re CEMPL and the 1re CMML were never recreated. Back in Indochina, men of the 1st Laotian Parachute Battalion were parachuted at Phanop in Khammaouane Province in central Laos, on 3 August 1954.[65] It was the last battle of a war that ended France's colonial rule in Indochina.

Algeria (1954–1962)

After the French left Vietnam in 1954, all airborne units were upgraded to regiments over the next two years. Only the air force's *Commandos de l'Air* were excluded. Two years later, the French army grouped all of its airborne units within two parachute divisions, the 10e and 25e *Divisions Parachutiste* (10e and 25e DP – 10th and 25th Parachute Divisions). The 10e DP came under the command of General Jacques E. Massu with General Henri Sauvagnac taking over the 25e DP. Both divisions were employed as the main strike reserves in Algeria during the war that led to the independence of this North African country. The same war featured the first large-scale use of helicopters in combat operations.[66] Eight parachute and commando regiments were deployed to Algeria by late 1950. These units became also the vanguard of the French army's mobile forces. One of the parachute units was the 19th Battalion (Algerian). French-officered, it was formed in 1950 and disbanded in 1956.

The French paratroopers played a leading part in Algeria not only militarily, as they eventually revolted twice against the French government's decision to grant independence to the former colony. The Algerian conflict can be split into three phases with the first covering the period between late 1954 and late 1955. The second phase is extended between early 1956 and late 1958. The period between December 1958 and July 1961 is identified as the Algerian conflict's third phase. The revolution started on 1 November 1954, when members of the *Front de Libération Nationale* (FLN – National Liberation Front) attacked military and civil targets throughout Algeria. France, at the time, was reeling from nine years of disastrous colonial war in South East Asia. The French army, disgusted with what had happened in Indochina, was determined to 'get it right' in Algeria.[67] Pierre Mendès-France's government sent paratroopers to show the government's determination to keep Algeria French. The paratroopers right away won applause from European-descended (mostly French) Algerians, known as *Pied-noirs*, estimated to over one million. They proved fearless, committed to victory and, most importantly, familiar with the guerrilla tactics the Algerian revolutionaries were learning from Vietnamese communists. FLN fighters could be categorized into three types: the paid volunteers (*moudjahidin*), the unpaid auxiliaries (*mousseblines*) and those belonging to the terrorist cells (*fidayin*).[68] By early 1956, the total of FLN fighters had grown to 20,000 from the few handfuls that launched the revolution two years earlier, but they were always short of weapons and supplies. At peak strength, the FLN fielded an estimated 40,000 personnel in Algeria. Of the 58,000 French soldiers stationed in Algeria at the war's outbreak only about 14,000 were deployable to combat at short notice.[69]

In mid-1956, the army's presence swelled to nearly 500,000, both conscripts and reservists. As the number and effectiveness of the French units rose, the FLN shifted from targeting government-connected people and facilities to strictly civilian targets. Adopting the strategy espoused by the Brazilian guerrilla leader Carlos Marighel, the FLN technique of 'blind terrorism' was intended to provoke further repression by the French in a spiral of violence that could only incite all Algerians.[70] Naval and air force units were also deployed in Algeria, including helicopters. In addition to using them as flying ambulances and cargo carriers, the French forces utilized helicopters for the first time in a ground-attack role to pursue and destroy fleeing FLN guerrilla units. This idea had been discussed by the French high command in mid-1953. The French commanders were concerned about the deployment of troops not trained for air-assault missions. This is why they decided to employ mostly parachute troops and legionnaires, who were trained in airborne warfare, as the first wave of any air assault. The first operation of this kind was conducted on 4 May 1955, when helicopter-borne elements of the French Foreign Legion attacked an FLN mountain outpost.[71] Combat jumps began a year later.

On 27 March 1956, a parachute drop was conducted by elements of the 11e *Régiment Parachutiste de Shoc* (11th Shock Parachute Regiment) near the mountain hideout of a local FLN chieftain, who was later found dead as a result of a bomb explosion. On 6 April, 243 men of 1er REP were parachuted near Djeuf, spearheading a counter-attack against FLN fighters. On 18 May, 245 men of 1er REP carried out a combat jump in Chellala, in north-west Algeria, as part of a combined raid. A 280-man airborne force, also belonging to the 1er REP, was dropped onto Stah Guentis, in north-east Algeria on 9 June as reinforcements. Two days later, 267 men of the 2e REP were parachuted onto Tamentout, north-east Algeria, to participate in a raid along with ground forces. On 22 June, 380 men of the 2e REP were dropped near Duar, in Tamza, north-east Algeria, as reinforcements. On 4 July, 112 men of the 6th RPC were dropped onto Moroccan soil, at Foul El Hassan, to destroy FLN bases. A total of seven combat jumps were conducted during 1956. Meanwhile, on 18 March, fifteen French soldiers were killed and further three were wounded by FLN fighters in an ambush near the village of Djerrah, some 50 miles (80km) south-east of the Algerian capital, Algiers. Following the discovery of the mutilated bodies of French soldiers, forty-four Algerians were summarily executed by French paratroopers, who had been helicoptered into the area.[72] The village of Djerrah was also destroyed as a reprisal. French forces managed to regain control, but only through brutal measures, and the ferocity of the fighting sapped the political will of the French to continue the conflict. On 7 January 1957, when unrest was peaking in Algiers, the French government gave General Massu full authority for the maintenance of order in Algiers.

The cession of civil authority to the military would not be reversed until the end of the war. Each regiment was assigned to a designated sector of the city. The Casbah, the native quarter of Algiers, was assigned to the famous Colonel Marcel Bigeard, a hero of Dien Bien Phu now commanding the 3e *Régiment Parachutistes Coloniaux* (3e RPC – 3rd Colonial Parachute Regiment). There were 80,000 Arabs living in the Casbah, making it the most densely populated slum in the world at the time.[73] Massu and Bigeard essentially applied a stranglehold without regard for civil liberties. The paratroopers rounded up and incarcerated several thousand Algerians. Over 5,000 people were imprisoned and over 3,000 disappeared during the so-called 'Battle of Algiers'.[74] In searching for suspects, the military was uprooting people from their homes, shops or fields and putting them in camps. Out of fear of the French military, thousands of Algerians fled to the countryside and then to neighbouring Tunisia and Morocco. In a secret war, according to Massu, the paratroopers responded with secret methods. The commander of the 10e DP claimed that 'one cannot confront the revolutionary and subversive war conducted by international communism and its agents merely with classical combat techniques, but also with clandestine and counter-revolutionary method of action . . .'.[75] Massu's ideas were openly supported by the chaplain of the 10e DP, identified as P.R. Delarue. He was saying to the soldiers that the 'bandits' were to blame for the fact that paratroopers had to do 'this policemen's job'.[76] Swift and brutal raids crippled the FLN leadership. Helicopters were employed innovatively to deliver paratroopers to the rooftops above suspected FLN hideouts. Within a week, Massu's and Bigeard's paratroopers had restored order in Algiers, although their successes hinged on extra-judicial arrests and the extensive use of torture. Meanwhile, on 22 March, combat jumps were resumed. This time, the 20th Parachute Artillery Group landed on Boghari, in north-central Algeria, to participate in an offensive against FLN forces. On 18 June, an airborne raid involving 210 men of the 9e *Régiment de Chasseur Parachutistes* (9e RCP – 9th Parachute Chasseur Regiment) was carried out in Bou el-Hamama, some 150 miles (256km) east of Algiers. Three combat jumps were conducted by the 3e RCP in the area of Timimuin on 21 November, 3 December and 7 December.

In Algiers, thanks to Massu's paratroopers, order was restored and the FLN seemed soundly defeated, but in the countryside the situation remained out of the control of the French. The rebels employed hit-and-run tactics, specializing in ambushes and night raids. It also became apparent that they were avoiding contact with superior French firepower. Most of their attacks were aimed at military targets, but a significant amount of effort was invested in a terror campaign against those Algerians who deemed to support or encourage French rule. At the same time, counter-insurgency tactics were employed by the French army, during which the 5th Bureau of the 10e DP had a vital role to play. The 5th Bureau, led by Captain Paul-Alain Leger, a psychological warfare expert, played the principal role in covert operations against the FLN. By now, paratroop units bore the brunt of an offensive counter-insurgency campaign. Before long, the French regained the initiative on the battlefield because, instead of French outposts throughout Algeria being surprised by the FLN forces, the FLN forces were surprised by air-assaulting French paratroopers or legionnaires.[77] The arrival of more and more units allowed the French army to pursue a new course of action. In late 1957, the *quadrillage* (grid) system replaced the mobile column as the basis for operations. General Raul Salan, commanding the French forces in Algeria, instituted a system of surveillance, after dividing Algeria into sectors. Each sector was permanently garrisoned by troops responsible for suppressing rebel operations in their assigned territory. He also constructed a heavily patrolled system of border barriers to limit infiltration from Tunisia and Morocco. More than 80,000 soldiers were stationed along the border with Tunisia, determined to stem the flow of personnel and supplies to the insurgents in Algeria. The French managed to seal the borders with Tunisia and Morocco, while launching the mobile forces against any identified or suspected FLN base area within Algeria. Helicopter-borne troops moved to reinforce elements that had come under attack to pursue FLN groups that attempted to cross the borders of Tunisia and Morocco. At the time, 180,000 soldiers were involved in *quadrillage*, 80,000 were manning the barriers, 20,000 constituted the mobile reserves and the remainder were headquarters and support staff. The FLN continued military operations, however, with their leaders having fled to Tunisia since late 1947.

There were still terrorist incidents, but the vast majority of Muslims in Algeria seemed to be waiting for a resolution – simply tired of five years of horror. In 1957 and 1958, the French mounted at least five large-scale search-and-destroy operations throughout the country, based on acquired intelligence, pinpointing likely enemy command posts. Two operations were conducted in 1957 (April and July) and three in 1958 (two in August and one in September). In Operation Atlas, in April 1957, the entire 3e RPC formed the spearhead. On 31 March 1958, three helicoptered task force groups, including elements of the 9e RPC, simultaneously air-assaulted Djebels Ergou, in north-east Algeria, el Aloui and Djebels el-Azega, on the mountain of Guelma, to entrap enemy forces. Sixty-seven FLN fighters were killed and a further eight were captured during the operation, in which the French casualties were four killed and two wounded.

In 1958, only one combat jump was recorded. On 30 April, 132 men of the 1er REP were parachuted close to Guelma mountain, participating in a combined assault against FLN forces. From then on, until the end of the Algerian War, the French stopped using vertical envelopment techniques, as enemy movements larger than platoon size were easily spotted by air reconnaissance. At the end of 1958, the French Army shifted its tactics to the use of mobile forces deployed on massive search-and-destroy missions against FLN strongholds. General Maurice Challe, the new military commander in Algeria, supplemented the *quadrillage* with a light, mobile force to take the fight deep into the bled. Featuring Muslim trackers, the *Commandos de Chasse* not only attacked any size of insurgent group, but pursued it until all its members were killed or captured. General Challe appeared to have suppressed major rebel resistance and the FLN 'looked defeated'.[78] Their strength had fallen to 12,000 fighters. Political developments, however, were to overtake French military successes.

On the night of 13 May 1958, a French military junta seized power in Algiers. They demanded the formation of a government of national unity in Paris to prevent the 'abandonment of Algeria'. They even sent paratroopers to Corsica, who in a bloodless action seized power from the French civil authorities. Preparations were made in Algeria for the seizure of Paris and the removal of the central government. The operation was called off by the junta when their demands were met. At the time, there were over 200 infantry battalions in Algeria and the French army was the closest it would be to victory. Ten of these battalions were airborne – divided between the Army's two parachute divisions. Each parachute battalion numbered 1,271 officers and other ranks. It was comprised of four rifle companies, one motorized reconnaissance company (with thirty-three jeeps), a motorized support company and eight separate platoons. There were one anti-tank, three mortar and four Type 107 platoons in a battalion/regiment. A Type 107 platoon was specially trained to be helicoptered for air-assaults. In 1958, the French conducted only one parachute drop. On 22 July, Marine paratroopers were dropped at L'Akfedu to block retreating enemy forces. The war's last parachute drop was executed on 8 January 1960 at Bou Farik, near Algiers, where 340 Marine paratroopers carried out a search-and-destroy operation. Meanwhile and after this drop, paratroopers were inserted by helicopter close to the assigned objective. Fielding helicopters in Algeria, the French could conduct air-assaults of up to two battalions.

Pressure was building in France to grant independence to Algeria as the Algerian nationalists had managed to win over national and international public opinion.[79] Even politicians like John F. Kennedy, a US Senator at the time, became vocal advocates for Algerian determination. On 24 January in Algiers, large numbers of French-Algerians, convinced that de Gaulle was about to betray them, staged an insurrection, which went down in history as *le semaine de barricades* ('The week of barricades'). The order for the insurrection was given by Colonel Jean Garde, of 10e DP's 5th Bureau. As the Army, police and supporters stood by, civilians threw up barricades in the streets and seized government buildings. General Challe then declared Algiers under siege, but forbade the troops to fire on the insurgents. On 29 January, in a televised address from Paris De Gaulle called on the Army to remain loyal and rallied popular support for his Algerian policy. Most of the Army heeded the call and the siege of Algiers ended on 1 February. In January too, in Francoist Spain retired officers of the French Army formed the right-wing dissident, paramilitary *Organisation Armée Secrète* (OAS – Secret Armed Organization). This organization carried out terrorist attacks in France and in Algeria, including bombings and assassinations, in response to De Gaulle's policy on Algeria. Between April 1961 and its dissolution in April 1962, OAS claimed responsibility for 2,000 deaths in Algeria and Metropolitan France. On 21 April 1961 in Algiers, the paratrooper units supported the *Putsch des Généraux* ('Generals' Putsch') with which military leaders reacted to the secret negotiations the French government had started with the FLN. The three generals, Maurice Challe, André Zeller and Paul Salan, and the (Algerian-born) Air Force General Edmond Jouhaudwere, who led the coup, were hoping to seize control of Algiers, Oran and Constantine. They also had in mind even to drop paratroopers, led by Colonel Antoine Argoud, onto strategic airfields in France. On 22 April, all flights and landings at airfields in the greater area of Paris were forbidden. An order was also given to the armed forces to resist the coup by all means. The four generals only took control of Algiers.

During the night of 21 April, a thousand paratroopers, headed by Colonel Hélie de Saint Marc, held and secured all strategic points in Algiers. In the rest of the country nothing happened, particularly in Oran and Constantine, whose military commanders refused to join the coup. The heads of the putsch were forced to give themselves up on 26 April. Meanwhile, on 18 March, in Évian-les-Baines a treaty was signed between the French government and an FLN delegation, ending the 1954–62 Algerian war. A formal ceasefire was proclaimed for 19 March. In a referendum held on 8 April, the French electorate approved the Évian accords with almost 91 per cent in favour. Algeria was pronounced an independent country on 3 July. French military authorities listed their losses during the Algerian War at nearly 18,000 killed and 65,000 wounded. Algerian casualties, including FLN fighters and civilians, were estimated to be around 700,000.[80] The failed military putsch in Algiers resulted in the disbandment of the two parachute divisions. The ten regiments merged into a *Division Légère d'Intervention* (Light Intervention Division), which became the 11th Parachute Division in 1971 and the 11th Parachute Brigade in 1999.

Cyprus (1955–1960)

The 16th Independent Parachute Brigade (16th IPB) was one of the British units mobilized in 1955, when Greek-Cypriot nationalists revolted in Cyprus, seeking the

Freepost Plus RTKE-RGRJ-KTTX
Pen & Sword Books Ltd
47 Church Street
BARNSLEY
S70 2AS

DISCOVER MORE ABOUT PEN & SWORD BOOKS

Pen & Sword Books have over 4000 books currently available, our imprints include; Aviation, Naval, Military, Archaeology, Transport, Frontline, Seaforth and the Battleground series, and we cover all periods of history on land, sea and air.

Can we stay in touch? From time to time we'd like to send you our latest catalogues, promotions and special offers by post. If you would prefer not to receive these, please tick this box. ☐

We also think you'd enjoy some of the latest products and offers by post from our trusted partners: companies operating in the clothing, collectables, food & wine, gardening, gadgets & entertainment, health & beauty, household goods, and home interiors categories. If you would like to receive these by post, please tick this box. ☐

We respect your privacy. We use personal information you provide us with to send you information about our products, maintain records and for marketing purposes. For more information explaining how we use your information please see our privacy policy at www.pen-and-sword.co.uk/privacy. You can opt out of our mailing list at any time via our website or by calling 01226 734222.

Mr/Mrs/Ms ....

Address...

Postcode.......................... Email address...

Website: www.pen-and-sword.co.uk Email: enquiries@pen-and-sword.co.uk
Telephone: 01226 734555 Fax: 01226 734438

Stay in touch: facebook.com/penandswordbooks or follow us on Twitter @penswordbooks

end of colonial rule. All three battalions of the brigade's Parachute Regiment, along with other elements of Great Britain's military, were involved in operations at various times in this south-east Mediterranean island, which had been under the dominion of the British Empire since 1878. The 16th IPB was first deployed to Cyprus in June 1951 and before long it was sent to reinforce the Suez Canal Zone as a response to nationalists threatening the British bases there.[81] On 1 April 1955, in Cyprus the EOKA underground organization declared an armed struggle against the British. A state of emergency was then declared on the island by the governor-general, Field Marshal Lord Harding of Petherton.[82] The insurgency began on 1 April with a series of night attacks against British targets in Nicosia and other parts of Cyprus, with EOKA struggling not only for independence, but also for *Enosis*, the island's unification with Greece. Bombs were thrown at the houses of British personnel, police stations and British Army installations. The paratroopers carried on operations against EOKA enclaves right across the island although most of the time they were on assignment up in the Kyrenian and Troodos mountains and the Paphos Forest. Besides the urban guerrillas, who were often continuing their civilian jobs or schooling, EOKA had organized also mountain guerrillas, living in hidden camps in forested areas.[83] Some 241 attacks were mounted by April 1956, including an unsuccessful attempt to assassinate the governor-general. A time bomb, put under Harding's bed on 21 March, failed to go off.

The British response was search operations which rarely resulted in arrests or the discovery of arms. The British paratroopers, who had returned to Cyprus on January 1956, were assigned more specialized 'counter-terrorist' operations.[84] On 30 September, elements of the 16th IPB, along with the No. 1 (Guards) Independent Parachute Company, the brigade's Pathfinder unit, began a massive sweep through the hills near Kyrenia. During the operation, code-named Sparrowhawk, twenty EOKA fighters were killed. On 25 October, the brigade was ordered to withdraw from operations against EOKA across the Morphou hillsides and the Paphos forest. They had to prepare for deployment to Egypt. On 3 November, a British aircraft carrier with the 16th IPB on board left Limassol harbour, heading to Egypt. EOKA took advantage of the absence of the 16th IPB in particular and launched a total of 416 attacks, killing thirty-nine people. When the Suez Canal crisis ended, the strength of the British forces on Cyprus increased to 20,000 men, as a number of combat-tested units came back from Egypt.[85] 16th IPB's 3rd Parachute Battalion (3 Para) returned to Cyprus in December and the 2nd Parachute Battalion (2 Para) a month later.

By February 1957, the EOKA insurgents in the mountains came under increasing pressure from British forces. 16th IPB's 1 Para returned to Cyprus in April and stayed there until March 1959. On 3 March 1957, British forces, including paratroopers, surrounded EOKA's second-in-command, Grigoris Afxentiou, in a cave not far from Mahaeras monastery, near Nicosia. After an eight-hour firefight that resulted in four dead and forty-six wounded among the British, the surrounding troops burned him alive.[86] Between 1955 and 1958, the British Army lost 274 officers and other ranks in Cyprus to whom the casualties of the Royal Navy and the Royal Air Force, being twenty-eight and sixty-five men respectively, should be added. When it was realized that armed confrontation led nowhere, all parties involved signed the Zurich agreement in 1959 with Cyprus being proclaimed an independent republic in 1960. Four years later, 1 Para was back to Cyprus wearing light blue berets instead of red ones, as they were deployed this time as part of the United Nations force (UNFICYP) assigned to keep Greek Cypriot and Turkish Cypriot factions apart.

The Suez Crisis (1956)

British, French and Israeli paratroopers took part in the invasion of Egypt with which London, Paris and Tel Aviv reacted in late 1956 to the nationalization of the Suez Canal, an important conduit for oil, by Egyptian President Gamal Abdel Nasser. The French were also concerned that Nasser was supporting the increasingly violent independence movement in Algeria. Israeli forces, spearheaded by airborne units, stormed Egypt's Sinai Peninsula on 29 October, having as additional objective the opening of the Straits of Tiran. Eight days later, British and French paratroopers landed along the Suez Canal. The possibility of a British intervention in the region was discussed in London in July 1956 with Prime Minister Anthony Eden proposing the mobilization for this purpose of the 16th IPB.[87] The brigade had been flown into the Suez Canal Zone as early as October 1951 to be ready to intervene should it be required.[88] Egypt had just pulled out of the Anglo-Egyptian Treaty of 1936, the terms of which granted Britain a lease on the Suez Base for a further twenty years. Britain refused to withdraw from Suez and this resulted in a steady increase in acts of violence by Egyptian nationalists against British military personnel stationed in Egypt. By 19 October, paratroopers were among the British troops that, mostly unopposed, seized key points along the Canal Zone. Egyptian forces advanced towards the Canal Zone on 1 January 1956, but stopped five miles away. The 16th IPB's three battalions were then largely engaged on internal security duties particularly around the docks, while the brigade's artillery unit, the 33rd Parachute Light Artillery Regiment, guarded the British ordnance depot at Geneifa. At the same time, the Brigade's 1 Para was standby should the lives of British civilians in Cairo be threatened.

In early 1956, the 16th IPB was deployed to Cyprus, where the Office of the Commander-in-Chief, Middle East, had been transferred from Egypt two years earlier.[89] The British forces stationed in Cyprus, including the paratroopers, became heavily involved in counter-insurgency operations against EOKA, the Greek-Cypriot nationalist organization. The 16th IPB's role had deprived its personnel of airborne training for months. This is why the brigade's three battalions, one at a time, were recalled to England for a 10-day training exercise. Reservists had been also recalled to the airborne units for the first time since the Second World War. The French airborne units picked for the intervention were the 10e *Division Parachutiste*, including elements of the 2e *Régiment de Parachutistes Coloniaux* (2e RPC) and the FFL's *1er Régiment Ètranger de Parachutistes* (1er REP). The 11e *Régiment Parachutiste Choc* (11th RPC) was at that time heavily involved in the Algerian War. The role allocated to the British paratroopers was to lead the assault on Port Said in conjunction with a Royal Marine landing. On 29 October, when the Israeli invasion of the Sinai Peninsula began, a paratroop battalion was dropped east of the Suez Canal, near the Mitla Pass, while the 202nd Paratroop Brigade was advancing inland to reinforce infantry and tank forces. The British and the French provided 50,000 and 30,000 troops respectively for the operation, code-named Musketeer. Other forces for land operations, besides the airborne units, were three divisions and one brigade. The major units deployed to Egypt during the Suez crisis for land operations were the British 3rd Infantry and 10th Armoured Divisions, the French 7e *Division Mecanique Rapide* (7th Rapid Mechanized Division) and the British 3rd Commando Brigade, Royal Marines (RM).[90] The Egyptian Army fielded a 75,000-strong infantry force and about 300 tanks, half of which were Soviet-made T-34s and T-34/85s.

In early August 1956, the British aircraft carrier HMS *Theseus* left Portsmouth transporting elements of the 16th IPB to Cyprus which had been in England for training. They joined the rest of the brigade when *Theseus* stopped over at Limassol. At the Cypriot port, ships carrying the French troops that had also been assigned to the operation had also arrived. On 27 September, Britain and France issued a 12-hour ultimatum calling upon both the Egyptian and Israeli forces to withdraw from the Canal Zone. Israel agreed. When Egypt refused, British and French aircraft bombed military targets in and around Cairo and the Canal Zone with the Egyptian air force in the meantime having been virtually wiped out. A shortage of transport planes meant dropping the entire 16th IBP was not possible. The Royal Air Force could carry 668 men, six jeeps, four trailers, six 106mm anti-tank guns and around 170 supply containers. Two of the brigade's three battalions had to conduct a sea landing. At 08.20 on 5 November, 600 men of the British 3 Para, led by Brigadier M.A.H. Butler, were dropped near Gamil airfield, west of Port Said. Nine paratroopers were hit in the air by enemy fire, while a few more landed in the sea. The Egyptian troops deployed in the area were equipped with 120mm artillery pieces and mobile Soviet-made multi-barrelled rocket launchers. Although the defenders tried to make a stand, the airfield was captured by the paratroopers within half an hour. Having taken the airfield with a dozen casualties, 3 Para cleared and secured the area around the airfield. Soon after dawn, at 05.15, a second drop of 100 men of 3 Para with vehicles, heavy equipment and resupply was made at Gamil airfield. The battalion then moved up towards Port Said and at 13.00 they dug in to hold until the beach assault. 3 Para were up against stiff resistance. It was clear that Port Said could not be captured and cleared by the airborne units alone and that the seaborne force, including Royal Marine Commandos as well as British and French paratroopers, would have to make an opposed landing the following morning.

The first paratroopers assaulted in two echelons – firstly, on the southern exits from Port Said and secondly, on the southern end of Port Fuad. A few minutes after the British combat jump, 500 men of the 2e RPC, led by Lieutenant Colonel Pierre Chateau-Jobert, were dropped near the waterworks to the south of Port Said. Although nine of the transport planes were hit by enemy fire, there were no casualties and all returned to their base in Cyprus. Meanwhile, further 500 men of the French 2e RPC had been dropped on the southern outskirts of Port Fuad, along with a detachment of the British No. 1 (Guards) Independent Parachute Company. A port town on the Asian side of the Suez Canal, Fuad is considered a suburb of Port Said. After landing, the paratroopers secured the western bridge of the town at a cost of two dead. Some sixty Egyptian soldiers were killed by nightfall, when the capture of the area by the French was completed. The paratroopers seized Port Said's waterworks before attacking Port Fuad. During the fighting, French paratroopers executed a number of surrendered Egyptian soldiers. At 04.50 on 6 October, the leading waves of 40 and 42 Royal Marine Commandos came ashore and across the beaches, using landing craft. At the same time, a French assault force consisting of Foreign Legion's 1er *Regiment Etranger Parachutiste* and French marine commandos was making an unopposed landing on the beaches of Port Fuad. The objectives of 42 Commando, supported by tanks, was to get through Port Said as quickly as possible to seal off the southern exits of the town, while 40 Commando, supported by tanks, was to clear the vicinity of the harbour in order to enable craft to enter without coming under fire. The 16th IPB's 1 Para and 2 Para landed by ship in a fishing harbour, as Port Said's inner harbour had been destroyed by the Egyptians. At the same time, elements of Royal Marines' No. 45 Commando were helicoptered to the beach and directly into a combat zone.[91] In British Army General Charles Keightley's words 'this was the first occasion on which such an operation was carried out'.[92] General Keightley was the Commander-in-Chief of the Anglo-French forces during the Suez crisis. The Commandos landed using twenty-two helicopters from HMS *Ocean* and *Theseus* and 90 minutes later 400 men and 23 tons of stores were ashore without incident. After a day of street fighting, the Royal Marines linked up with 3 Para.[93] Meanwhile, 1 Para began its advance through Port Said, facing mostly sniper fire. 2 Para moved west along the coast and dug in, when they had to fight off an Egyptian counterattack. In Port Said, streets had to be cleared house by house and sometimes room by room. On the night of 6 November, 2 Para made a slow advance down to al-Quantarah, supported by Centurion tanks. Meanwhile, 3 Para, because of Egyptian sniper attacks, had slowed down its attempt to link up with the Royal Marine commandos. At 17.00 orders were received that a ceasefire was to take effect one minute before midnight. The Egyptian forces were defeated, but they were able to block the Suez Canal to all shipping.

Although the operation was a military success, the invading troops had to withdraw from Egypt, due to political pressure from the United States. Even Commonwealth countries like Canada openly opposed the intervention.[94] On the other hand, the Soviet Union threatened to intervene on the Egyptian side and launch missile attacks on Britain, France and Israel.[95] Anti-war protests were organized in Britain, where an opinion poll found on 11 November that 53 per cent of those questioned were supporting the war with 32 per cent being against.[96] By the time the ceasefire came into effect, 3 Para had reached and taken control of al-Cap, a small village near al-Quantarah. British paratroopers were holding Gamil airfield and French paratroopers were holding the water works of Port Said. During Operation Musketeer, British casualties were sixteen dead and ninety-six wounded, while the French had ten killed and thirty-three wounded.[97] The Egyptian casualties during the Anglo-French part of the invasion were estimated at 650 dead and 900 wounded.[98] The Suez debacle officially ended on 6 November 1956.

U-2 Bail-outs (1960)

In May 1960, a United States U-2 spy plane was shot down while flying a high-altitude reconnaissance mission deep into Soviet territory. The plane pilot, a retired United States Air Force captain, bailed out and was later captured, tried and imprisoned by the Soviets. In the same incident, one of the most emblematic of the Cold War period, a Soviet air force pilot was also forced to eject when his fighter plane was hit by friendly fire. It all started three years earlier with the operational employment of the Lockheed U-2 single-jet-engine ultra-high-altitude reconnaissance aircraft by the USAF. The plane, nicknamed Dragon Lady, could provide day and night all-weather intelligence gathering. In fact, the U-2 was developed to monitor the nuclear threat from the Soviet Union. On 1 May 1961, a U-2 took off from Pershawar in northern Pakistan. Francis Gary Powers was the pilot of the plane that was scheduled to land in Bøde in northern Norway, after crossing Soviet air space at altitudes of up to 70,000ft (21,336m).[99] Kentucky-born Powers, a Korean War veteran, had been discharged from the USAF with the rank of captain in 1956. He then joined a joint USAF/CIA programme involving aerial reconnaissance missions around the world.

Powers already had twenty-seven missions on U-2s before his latest assignment: to fly for the first time over the USSR. The Soviets began tracking Powers' U-2 fifteen minutes from the border – four and a half hours into the flight. When the plane was detected, MiG-19 fighters were ordered to take off and intercept the intruder. Meanwhile, the spy plane had come into the range of the Soviet surface-to-air missile (SAM) batteries, as it had lost altitude because of an engine problem. The U-2 was still out of range to the MiG-19s. A total of four S-75 Dvina missiles were launched. One of the missiles shot down the American aircraft over Kosulino, in Ural region, and another accidently hit one of the Soviet fighters operating in the area.[100] Powers bailed out close to Aramil in Sverdlovsk Oblast. He had to get off the falling fuselage, before using his parachute.[101] On his way down, Powers saw a parachute descending in the distance.[102] It was Lieutenant Sergei Safronov, whose MiG-19 had been hit by friendly fire. He managed to eject, but he later died of his injuries.[103] Safronov's participation in the incident was formally announced later in Moscow without any reference to the fact that he had been killed. His death was revealed thirty years later.

Powers landed safely and tried to hide, but his capture was a matter of time.[104] Moscow announced that a United States spy plane had been shot down in Soviet territory without revealing that its pilot was alive. Washington claimed that the downed aircraft was a weather plane, whose pilot strayed off course, having difficulties with his oxygen equipment. On 7 May, Nikita Khrushchev announced that Powers was alive and had confessed to spying on the USSR. The Soviet premier demanded an apology from the United States, which President Dwight D. Eisenhower refused.[105] As a result of the spy incident and the attempted cover-up by the Americans, a four-power summit, held in Paris in mid-May, ended early. The U-2 incident marked a deterioration in Soviet-American relations, already strained by the ongoing Cold War. Meanwhile, in Moscow Powers was interrogated for months by the KGB before making a confession and a public apology for his part in espionage. His trial began on 17 August before the military division of the Supreme Court of the USSR. The American pilot pleaded guilty and two days later was convicted of espionage. He was sentenced to three years' imprisonment and seven years' hard labour. Powers was transferred to Vladimir Central Prison, 150 miles (240km) east of Moscow. He served one year and nine months of his sentence before being exchanged for Rudolf Abel, a convicted Soviet agent, on 10 February 1962.

The wreckage of the U-2 was examined by Soviet aviation specialists, who were able to identify much of the plane's equipment. The debris of the downed U-2 was used by the Soviets to design a copy, the Beriev S-13. A large part of the wreck, as well as items from Powers' survival kit, are on display at the Central Armed Forces Museum in Moscow. A small piece of the plane was returned to the United States and is on display at the National Cryptologic Museum in Maryland. Pieces of the spy plane and Powers' uniform are on display at the Monino airbase museum near Moscow. CIA investigators found Powers had done well during interrogation in USSR. He was criticized by some for not using a CIA-issued 'suicide kit' to kill himself before being captured. After being released by the Soviets, Powers tried to be reinstated in USAF, but his application was rejected – apparently for having stated that the U-2 programme was civilian.[106] In 1998, newly unclassified information revealed that Powers' mission had been a USAF/CIA joint operation. Powers was killed in a helicopter crash in Santa Barbara county on 1 August 1977 at the age of 47. On 15 June 2012, Powers was posthumously awarded the Silver Star. In 1962, another U-2 was shot down over Cuba by a Soviet-supplied SA-75 missile. Major Rudolf Anderson, the pilot, lost his life in the mid-air explosion. He was the only American killed by enemy fire during the Cuban missile crisis.

Tunisia (1961)

France had to send paratroopers in Tunisia in the summer of 1961, although she was heavily preoccupied with the Algerian situation. Four years after gaining independence from France, Tunisia wanted the French out of an air and naval base they were still using at Bizerte. Charles de Gaulle, France's President, declared that France would not negotiate under pressure.[107] In early July, the personnel on the base numbered about 6,000 men, mostly technicians. When the Tunisian government realized that the French were upgrading the runway of their last holding in the country instead of evacuating it, they sent troops to surround the base and forbade unauthorized flights of foreign aircraft over Bizerte. Paris reacted after Tunisians fired warning shots at a French helicopter approaching Bizerte on 17 July. The crisis thus culminated in a brief and bloody battle. Three cruisers were positioned close to the harbour of Bizerte on 19 July and Noratlas transport aircraft reached the area, carrying the 800-strong 2e *Régiment de Parachutistes d'Infanterie de Marine* (2e RPRIMa – 2nd Marine Parachute Regiment). As a show of force, 414 men of the regiment were dropped by parachute over the base and descended under heavy enemy fire. The rest landed in their transport aircraft. Meanwhile, French A-7 Corsair fighter-bombers had blasted enemy anti-aircraft and artillery positions in and around the base with rockets. French planes transporting heavy equipment then landed on the runway. Before long, armoured vehicles, among them a few tanks, were rolling on Tunisian soil. The enemy roadblocks were destroyed by tank and 105mm howitzer fire. The following morning, the French mounted an attack on the town of Bizerte. A joint armoured and paratroop force penetrated into the town from the south, while marine units stormed the harbour using landing craft. Elements of the French Foreign Legion's 3e *Régiment Ètranger d'Infanterie* (3e REI), who had been flown in the base at the beginning of the crisis, were fighting alongside the paratroopers. Tunisian soldiers, paramilitaries and hastily organized civilian volunteers engaged the invaders in heavy street fighting, but were forced back by vastly superior forces.

On 23 July, when a United Nations' sponsored ceasefire was declared and hostilities ended, most of the town was occupied by the paratroopers. They also secured the Tunis-Bizerte road and railway. Paratroopers and legionnaires were later accused of 'executing prisoners' during the battle and in some cases 'deliberately mutilating' the bodies of soldiers or civilians.[108] Leon Carl Brown believes that these atrocities were caused by the 'brutally efficient organization of shock troops' and were not the result of 'calculated terror'.[109] The casualties for the invaders were 24 soldiers killed and nearly 100 more wounded. The Tunisian casualties during the so-called Bizerte crisis were estimated to 630 killed and 1,555 wounded. Following international condemnation, expressed in UN Resolution No. 164 on 22 July 1961, the French agreed to negotiate the handover of the Bizerte base. A withdrawal agreement was signed on 29 September 1961 by delegates of the belligerents in Tunisia. The French finally handed Bizerte on 15 October 1963 – well after the conclusion of the Algerian War.

Cuba (1961)

A paramilitary force, including parachutists, was sponsored by the US CIA to overthrow Fidel Castro's regime in Cuba. The force, consisting mostly of anti-communist Cubans who had fled their country after the communist victory in 1959, was christened Brigade 2506. The 1,400-strong unit was divided into six battalions, one of which was made up of qualified (émigré Cuban) parachutists. The training of Brigade 2506 was carried out in Florida and outside the United States, namely in Guatemala and in Panama. They were scheduled to participate in what became known as the Bay of Pigs invasion. On the night of 16/17 April, the main force landed from the sea in a southern coast of Cuba.[110] The 177 parachutists were dropped early in the morning in three locations in southern Cuba – on a road linking Palpite with Playa Larga (in Bahia de Cochinos or the Bay of Pigs) and at Hoquitas. For the jump, conducted at 07.30, five Curtiss C-46 Commando and one Douglas C-54 Skymaster transport aircraft were used. Some of the equipment was lost in swamps. In the initial stages of the invasion, Brigade 2506 did well, having to fight against poorly-organized and ill-trained militiamen and gendarmes. At the time, the militia could field 200,000 men and the gendarmerie was 9,000 strong. When Castro's army and air force became involved in the battle, the situation changed dramatically.

The Cuban army, 25,000 strong at the time, was equipped with Soviet-made T-34 medium tanks and IS-2 heavy tanks, as well as with warplanes, including Hawker

Sea Fury fighters and Lockheed T-33 jets, which were sent against the counter-revolutionary invaders. The failure of the parachutists to secure the Palpite-Play Larga road enabled the Cuban forces to reach the southern coast and prevent Brigade 2506 from gaining the interior of the island. Meanwhile, Castro's air force had rallied to strafe the landing site and the supply ships moored in the bay. One of the ships used for the invasion was sunk and the remaining three made it out to sea. Without resupply or air support the invaders were able to hold for two days before they were forced to surrender. Of Brigade 2506 114 or 118 were killed or drowned, 360 were wounded or injured and 1,183 were captured. Only thirty were rescued by US Navy ships. The Cuban army suffered 176 killed and over 500 wounded in the battle. The militia casualties were estimated to nearly 2,000 killed and wounded. Of the captured counter-revolutionaries, five were tried, convicted and executed with the rest being sentenced to thirty years in prison. On 14 April, sixty wounded or sick were freed and transported to the United States. Several others were freed later as part of an economic deal between Castro and the US authorities.

The Bay of Pigs veterans felt a sense of betrayal on the part of the US administration for not providing air support during the invasion. On the other hand, the failed operation embarrassed President John F. Kennedy, who decided not to send troops in Cuba being aware of the fact that only 3 per cent of Americans were in favour of a military intervention in 1961. After their return in the United States, members of Brigade 2506 were commissioned in the US Army. José Alfredo Pérez San Román, who had led the counter-revolutionaries in the invasion of Cuba, served as a lieutenant in the 82nd Airborne Division and eventually (in 1992) rose to the rank of Major General. Six other veterans of the 1961 invasion became colonels in the US Army, nineteen others rose to the rank of lieutenant colonel, nine became majors and further twenty-nine rose to the rank of captain.[111]

Chapter 14

The Arab-Israeli and Indo-Pakistan Wars

Airborne units were also assigned missions in the wars fought in the Middle East and the Indian subcontinent during the post-1945 period. In these wars, paratroopers were helicoptered to their targets or were used as elite infantry. The rarity of the (even medium-sized) combat jumps conducted by the belligerents is one of the characteristics of the Arab-Israeli and the Indo-Pakistani wars.

The Middle East Wars

During the four Arab-Israeli Wars that were fought in 1948, 1956, 1968 and 1973, only one combat jump was conducted. It is also one of the few combat jumps in the history of the airborne forces of Israel.[1] In October 1956, the invasion of the Sinai Peninsula by Israeli forces began when a paratrooper battalion was airdropped east of the Suez Canal, near the Mitla Pass. A motorized column of paratroopers, who belonged to the same brigade, then raced to reinforce their parachuted colleagues, thus spearheading the Israeli invasion of the Sinai Peninsula. General Moshe Dayan's plan wanted commandos parachuted deep into Sinai. His aim was to make the Egyptians believe that the invaders were going to seize the Canal, which was 31 miles (50km) west of Mitla Pass. The Israelis also wanted to provide the trigger for the military intervention of Britain and France in what went down in history as the Suez Crisis. The sixteen Douglas DC-3 transport planes carrying 395 men of the 890th Paratrooper Battalion took off from Tel Nof airbase, some 12 miles (20km) south of Tel Aviv, in the early evening of 28 October. The DZ had to be shifted by three miles (4.8km), because a reconnaissance flight had detected an Egyptian military presence in the pass. The paratroopers, led by Lieutenant Colonel Rafael 'Raful' Eitan, landed on the newly-designated DZ in the early hours of 29 October. In the meantime, the rest of the 202nd Paratrooper Brigade, mounted on four tanks and several trucks, crossed the frontier at Kuntilla and rushed across Sinai towards the Mitla Pass. At the head of the column was Colonel Ariel Sharon, the commander of the brigade. At the pass Eitan marched his men towards the intended objective, identified as Parker's Memorial, where they were ordered to dig in and wait. Supplies of weapons were later parachuted to them from French aircraft.[2]

As they were racing across the desert, Sharon's men were able to storm the town of Themed. On the morning of 30 April, they rolled into the perimeter near Nakla, where Eitan's men had dug in. Meanwhile, two Israeli infantry divisions, the 9th and the 4th, had advanced into the Sinai desert and had captured Rasal Naqb and al-Qusaymag respectively. As Dayan had no immediate plans for his men, Sharon decided to clear the nearby Mitla Pass of Egyptian troops. Some 1,575ft (480m) high the winding pass is a natural ambush site. Sharon was not aware that the Egyptians were there with a force twice the size of his. They were hidden among the rocky slopes that rose on either side of the 20-mile (32km) road through the pass. Sharon sent his lightly-armed men in against dug-in enemies who were equipped with machine guns and light artillery. In the afternoon of 31 October, two companies, led by Major Mordechai Gur, were sent into the pass without air or artillery support. They were about 400 men – almost one-third of Sharon's brigade. It took five hours of fierce fighting for Gur's paratroop force to overcome the Egyptian defences at the cost of thirty-eight killed and 150 wounded.[3] The Egyptians lost a total of 250 men. Sharon was later accused of capturing the Mitla Pass without authorization. He was also blamed for needlessly expending lives for an objective that was immediately abandoned, as his troops had to rush south in order to conquer the southern tip of Sinai. By 3 November, Israeli forces had taken the Gaza Strip, Arish and the Mitla Pass. Only Sharm el-Sheikh, one of the most strongly-fortified positions in the Sinai Peninsula, remained as their last objective. Israeli warplanes and naval vessels provided support to the 9th Infantry Division that was spearheaded in the attack by Sharon's paratroopers. On 5 November, following a barrage of artillery, bombing and napalm strikes, the Egyptian troops were forced to surrender. In the Sharm el-Sheikh battle the Israelis lost 10 killed and 32 wounded, while the Egyptian army had about 100 killed and 31 wounded. Another 864 Egyptians were taken prisoner.[4]

The 1967 War

The Six Day War broke out in June 1967, following Egyptian President Gamal Abdel Nasser's decision to close the Gulf of Aqaba to Israeli shipping and thus blockade the port city of Elat in southern Israel. The Israeli forces reacted aggressively on three fronts against their Arab neighbours, subsequently capturing the West Bank, including East Jerusalem, from Jordan and the Golan Heights from Syria. On 5 June, two Israeli brigades, the 7th Armoured and the 60th Infantry, invaded the Sinai Peninsula and advanced against Khan Yunis from the north and the south. On the Sinai front, Israel had deployed nine brigades and 700 tanks against the seven divisions and 900–950 tanks of the Egyptian army.[5] By nightfall, Bir Ranfan, in the southern Gaza strip, was captured by Israeli paratroopers, fighting as elite infantry. The 202nd Paratrooper Brigade, commanded by Colonel Rafael Eitan, was also tasked with silencing Egyptian artillery positions at Um-Katef, a heavily-fortified area near Abu Ageila, defended by the Egyptian 2nd Infantry Division. After being helicoptered deep into the enemy's rear and marching several miles over the dunes, the paratroopers, led by Colonel Danny Matt, surprised the Egyptian gunners and neutralized their batteries.[6] Fourteen Israelis were killed in the battle and a further forty-one wounded. The Egyptian casualties in Um-Katef were 300 killed and a further 100 taken prisoner. Within three days, the Israelis had captured the Gaza Strip and all of the Sinai Peninsula up to the east bank of the Suez Canal. On the morning of 8 June, Israeli troops entered el-Arish in north Sinai, the largest city of the peninsula. The plan was for the 55th Paratrooper Brigade to be dropped in the area, but the jump was called off as el-Arish was taken ahead of schedule by ground forces. A day earlier, Sharm el-Sheikh was captured by Israeli troops, including paratroopers in a ground role. During the Israeli offensive, six divers from the *Shayetet-13* naval commando unit managed to infiltrate Alexandria harbour and sink an Egyptian minesweeper before being captured. As the war progressed on the Sinai front, Colonel Mordechai Gur's 55th Paratrooper Brigade was brought back to Jerusalem to reinforce the Israeli forces in the West Bank. Five Israeli brigades were already deployed there.[7] The Jordanian Army had fielded there twenty artillery battalions, a paratroop battalion and a newly-raised battalion of mechanized infantry there.[8] Two infantry battalions were deployed by the Israelis in (Israeli) West Jerusalem. Hostilities on the Jordanian front had begun an hour and a half after the invasion of the Sinai Peninsula. On 6 August, Israeli paratroopers took the Jordanian outpost of Ammunition Hill in north Jerusalem after some of the fiercest hand-to-hand fighting of the war.[9] Leaving Ammunition Hill, the 55th Paratrooper Brigade moved deeper into (Jordanian) East Jerusalem. On 7 June, two paratrooper battalions attacked the high ground of Augusta-Victoria Hill, overlooking the Jordanian-controlled Old City of Jerusalem from the east. Elements of the 66th Paratrooper Battalion mounted attacks from Mount Scopus and from the valley between the mountain and the Old City. Paratroopers then linked up with elements of the 10th Infantry Brigade to block Jordanian reinforcements coming from the Dead Sea. Another paratrooper battalion, led by Colonel Gur, broke into the Old City, where they met minor resistance from snipers and stone-throwing civilians. The fighting that led to the occupation of East Jerusalem was conducted solely by the paratroopers. The Israeli high command did not employ armour, artillery or the air force during the operation for fear of inflicting severe damage on the Old City. A hundred and eighty-two paratroopers were killed in the battle for the capture of the holiest site in Judaism.

Meanwhile, in western Sinai Israeli ground and paratroop forces continued to push the retreating Egyptians towards the mountain passes. Israel completed the capture of Sinai as infantry units reached Ras-Sudar on the western coast of the peninsula. On 9 June, after delaying an offensive against Syria until it could free up troops from the Egyptian frontier, Israel moved against the Syrian army in heavily-entrenched positions on the Golan Heights. Paratroopers captured a series of posts overlooking the Hula valley in the southern sector of the Heights, enabling the passage of tanks deep into Syrian territory. On 10 June, Israeli units trapped Syrian forces on the Golan plateau. The balance of power shifted in Israel's favour and the Syrians were forced to flee. By the evening, an armistice was agreed, leaving Israel in control of the Golan Heights, including parts of Mount Hermon.[10]

On 7 June, the United Nations Security Council called for a ceasefire that was immediately accepted by Israel and Jordan. The ceasefire was accepted by Egypt the following day and by Syria on 10 June. Between 776 and 983 Israelis were killed and 4,517 were wounded during the Six Day War. The Egyptian casualties were 9,800 killed or missing in action.[11] According to Israeli sources, 15,000 Egyptian soldiers were killed and further 4,338 were captured.[12] Jordanian losses are estimated to be 700 killed and another 2,500 wounded.[13] The Syrians were estimated to have sustained between 1,000 and 2,500 killed and between 367 and 591 captured.[14]

The War of Attrition

After the Six Day War, Egypt and Israel became locked in a series of localized engagements along the Suez Canal in the so-called 'War of Attrition'.[15] On 21 March 1968, the Israeli 35th Paratrooper Brigade, led by Colonel Danny Matt, assaulted a Palestine guerrilla base on Jordanian soil and destroyed it, killing 150 guerrillas and capturing a further 128. Jordanian forces who attempted to intervene suffered 61 killed, 108 wounded and four taken prisoner. The Israeli Army sustained twenty-eight killed (eight of whom were paratroopers). On 31 October 1968, a helicopter-borne detachment from *Sayeret Tzanhanim* destroyed Egyptian electrical infrastructure in response to cross-border artillery barrages that had killed a number of Israeli soldiers. In the evening of 28 December 1968, helicopter-borne Israeli commandos raided Beirut International Airport, destroying fourteen Arab passenger planes and damaging airport facilities without causing or suffering any casualties. They also destroyed fuel dumps. The commandos, who belonged to the Israeli Army's elite *Sayeret Matkal*, were extracted later also by helicopter. The operation, which lasted 45 minutes, was in response to the attack on an Israeli airliner (EL AL Flight 253) two days earlier by militants of the Lebanon-based Popular Front for the Liberation of Palestine (PFLP). The Israeli raiders were unopposed except for some sporadic shots fired at them by airport police. The damage caused to the airport by the raid was estimated at US$100 million.[16] Beirut airport, one of the busiest in the Middle East at the time, is located 100 miles (160km) from the Israeli border.

In December 1969, elements of the 50th Paratrooper Battalion and a detachment of Sayeret Tzanhanim paratroopers captured and removed to Israel a newly-installed Egyptian P-12 radar system at Ras Gharib. On the night of 9/10 April 1973, elements of the Israeli Special Forces attacked Palestinian Liberation Organization (PLO) targets in Beirut and Sidon, Lebanon, in retaliation for the massacre of Israeli athletes by Palestinian terrorists during the 1972 Olympics in Munich.[17] In the operation, involving three separate teams, three PLO leaders were surprised at home and killed. Lebanese security personnel and civilian neighbours were also killed as were two Israeli soldiers. One of the executed Palestinians was Muhammad Yussef al-Najjar, an operational commander of Black September, the group responsible for the Munich massacre.

The Israeli commandos were elements of the *Sayeret Matkal* (the Special Reconnaissance Unit of the General Staff). They arrived off Beirut in Israeli navy torpedo boats and went ashore in Zodiacs. At the same time, fourteen Israeli *Sayeret Tzanhanim* paratroopers raided a multi-storey building that housed PFLF militants. Although it was guarded by nearly 100 men, the building was destroyed with explosives. The Israeli commandos were extracted by helicopter. At the same time, a force of *Shayetet-13* naval commandos landed north of Beirut and destroyed a small Al Fatah explosive workshop, while another paratroop unit raided and destroyed the PLO's main garage located south of Sidon.

The 1973 War

In October 1973, Egypt and Syria launched a multi-front surprise attack on Israel, triggering what went down in history as the Yom Kippur War. Shortly before 14.00 on 6 October, Syrian and Egyptian forces simultaneously launched artillery and air strikes across the 1967 ceasefire lines. On the Syrian front, these were accompanied by infantry attacks between the Israeli strongpoints into the Israeli-occupied Golan Heights. Syrian troops penetrated in the central sector of the ceasefire line as deep as 15 miles (25km). Syria's main target was the Israeli strongpoint on the slopes of Mount Hermon, called Position 102, which had been used for visual observation ever since the 1967 War. At around 17.00 on 6 October, the Syrian 82nd Para-Commando Battalion took the position, killing between twenty-five and fifty Israeli troops.[18] Two hundred commandos had advanced on foot from Mount Hermon at 14.45 to the southern slope, where the Israeli Army's advanced surveillance equipment was positioned. At the same time, elements of the 82nd Para-Commando Battalion were landed by four helicopters on the access road south of the position.[19]

On 8 October, elements of Israel's Golani Brigade tried to recapture the positions seized by the Syrians but failed, losing fifty killed in the attempt. The Israelis lost 147–170 men in these operations – 6 per cent of the fatalities suffered by them in the entire war. The Syrians were gradually pushed back and by 10 October, the Israelis had restored virtually all the pre-war border. On 11 October, Israeli forces advanced toward Damascus along the Quneitra-Damascus road until they met stiff resistance three days later. Even from where they stopped, the Israelis were able to shell the outskirts of the Syrian capital with M107 heavy artillery. The following day, *Sayeret Tzanhanim* paratroopers infiltrated deep into Syria. They destroyed a bridge in the tri-border area of Syria, Iraq and Jordan in an effort to disrupt the movement of troops and weapons to Syria. Iraq had already sent an expeditionary force to Syria, consisting of two armoured divisions – 30,000 men and 250–500 tanks. Meanwhile, east of the Suez Canal bridgeheads had been established by the Egyptians, on 7 October. Israel attacked the Egyptians on 15 October, as priority was given to the Syrian front, where the Syrians had pushed harder and deeper than the Egyptians into Israeli territory. Their attacks were also close to Israeli population centres. The Israeli command, therefore, decided to give priority to defeating the Syrians. The Syrians' attack initially involved three infantry divisions and one armoured division. The Israeli offensive started at 10.00 on 11 October with three armoured brigades moving across the 1967 ceasefire line. On 13 October, a hill (Tall as Shams) was captured in a night assault by two battalions of Israeli paratroopers.[20] The hill was protected by a Syrian battalion and a number of tanks. By early 14 October, the Israelis had captured virtually all the territory that was to be theirs and ten days later Syria was forced to accept a ceasefire.

After neutralizing the Syrian threat, the Israelis turned their attention southwards to deal with the Egyptians, who had dug in in defensive positions on the east bank of the Suez Canal. On 13 October, in a key engagement, the Egyptians used helicopters to land commandos behind Israeli lines. Between fourteen to twenty helicopters were shot down by the Israelis and the commandos who landed were killed. An Israeli tank brigade then crossed the Canal and turned north to push the Egyptians back from it. An airborne brigade followed to occupy the crossing site and establish the first bridgehead on the western side. Colonel Dan Matt's 27th Paratrooper Brigade crossed the Canal in rubber boats at 01.00 on 16 October.[21] They played a critical role in the operation which resulted in the encirclement and subsequent defeat of the Egyptian army. The Egyptians reacted with air force and commando assaults, but failed to eliminate the bridgehead. Of the nine divisions and the two brigades deployed by the Egyptians (a force of 80,000 to 100,000 men) only one brigade was located in the Israeli crossing area. On 18 October, an Egyptian paratrooper brigade was pushed back by Israeli forces advancing towards Ismailia. Six days later, Israeli armoured and paratroop units failed to capture Suez City. By 24 October, 20,000 Israeli troops and 500 tanks had crossed the Canal into the Sinai Peninsula. Israel had the tactical advantage at that point, as its forces had destroyed or neutralized most of the Egyptian air-defence system on the west side of the Canal. The Israeli Air Force was thereby free to attack the Egyptian armies in earnest. Matt also led his paratroopers in a daring deep penetration raid into the heart of Egypt's Nile Valley. On the night of 31 October/1 November, Matt's paratroopers, transported in three-engined Aérospatiale SA-321 Super Frelon helicopters over 186 miles (300km) of Egyptian airspace, attacked and destroyed two bridges over the Nile, as well as an electrical transformer, near the town of Hammadi.[22] The Israelis suffered no casualties, but the damage to Egypt's war effort was immense.

During the Yom Kippur War, *Shayetet-13* naval commandos infiltrated Egyptian ports numerous times, sinking five Egyptian naval vessels and heavily damaging a sixth. Two Israeli commandos went missing during these raids. By the end of the war, the Israelis had advanced to positions some 62 miles (100km) from Cairo and occupied 994 miles (1,600km) of territory west of the Suez Canal. They had also encircled the bulk of Egypt's Third Army.[23] Israeli casualties during the Yom Kippur War were 2,656 killed, 7,250 wounded and 293 captured. The Egyptian losses were about 5,000 killed and 8.372 captured. Syrian casualties were about 3,000 killed or missing in action and thirteen captured. The Jordanian casualties were twenty-three killed and seventy-seven wounded.

The Raid against Karameh

In March 1968, Israeli paratrooper forces were assigned their most dangerous military mission since the Six Day War: to spearhead a combined attack against Karameh in Jordan, considered to be the headquarters of the Palestinian resistance. A small refugee town located three miles (5km) east of the River Jordan and east of the Allenby Bridge, Karameh is a major crossing point between Jordan and Israel. The assault began at 05.30 on 21 March with an air attack on the target area. When the paratroopers were landing near Karameh, Israeli armoured and mechanized forces had crossed the 1967 ceasefire line and reached the river's eastern bank, using the three local bridges. Jordanian forces had advance knowledge of the attack and were able to inflict heavy losses in equipment and personnel on the invaders.[24] The operation, code-named Inferno, failed since, thanks to the early warning, the Palestinian officials were able to flee. Twenty-eight Israeli soldiers, mostly paratroopers, were killed or missing in action during the raid and further 172 were wounded or injured.[25] To the Israeli losses should be added a number of armoured vehicles destroyed and three Mystère fighters shot down.

Israeli Paratroopers

In June 1948, during the first Arab-Israeli War, the newly-formed Israeli Defense Forces (IDF) sent fifty volunteers to Czechoslovakia for parachute training.[26] The first Israeli paratroopers took advantage of their return flight to carry out a display jump onto the air base of Tel Nof. In August 1953, IDF created Unit 101 to deal with Arab infiltration and the terror of the *fedayeen*. In late 1954, Egyptian President Gamal Abdel Nasser began a policy of sponsoring raids into Israel carried out by desert tribesmen who always attacked civilians.[27] Numbering forty men and commanded by Ariel Sharon, Unit 101 carried out the vast majority of reprisal operations, more than seventy in all, from late 1953 until the Sinai campaign in 1956. A dramatic attack by Israeli Unit 101 in retaliation for *fedayeen* raids into Israel gave the Egyptian Army a bloody nose.[28] In January 1954, Unit 101 was merged with the newly-raised 890th Paratrooper Battalion, which was also at the forefront of Israel's counter-insurgency and retaliatory operations conducted throughout the 1950s.[29] A parachute training establishment was created at Tel Nof, near Rehovot, 20km south of Tel Aviv, where it remains to this day.

In February 1955, 155 paratroopers, led by Captain Danny Matt, carried out a night raid against an Egyptian military encampment, killing thirty-seven soldiers.[30] The raid was in retaliation for the murder of an Israeli teenager.[31] Also in 1955, the 890th Paratrooper Battalion successfully raided Egyptian military positions in the Khan Yunis area. The operation resulted in the destruction of military installations at the Tegart fort and the deaths of seventy-two Egyptian soldiers. There was one Israeli fatality during the raid. A mechanized force, led by Major Mordechai (Mota) Gur, attacked the fort, while another force, led by Major Rafael 'Raful' Eitan, secured the nearby 'Position 132'. The operation was conducted in response to the Egyptian sponsorship of *fedayeen* terrorist activity against Israeli targets. The 35th Paratrooper Brigade (*Hativat Ha T'zanhanim* in Hebrew) was created in the mid-1950s, when the commando Unit 101 merged with the 890th Paratrooper Battalion. Its personnel wear maroon berets and reddish-brown boots. They also wear their belt over the shirt. The IDF has four reservist paratrooper brigades: the 55th, the 226th, the 551st and the 646th. The 35th Paratrooper Brigade consists of three regular units, bearing the names of venomous snakes. These battalion-size units are the 101st (Elapidae), the 202nd (Viper) and the 890th (Echis). There is also the 5135th Reconnaissance Battalion. The Brigade's force also includes four companies – a special reconnaissance (the 5173rd), an anti-tank (the 5174th), an engineer (the 5105th) and a signals company. The 35th Paratrooper Brigade is part of the 98th Paratrooper Division, which also includes the 89th Commando Brigade, a regular formation established in 2015.[32] It consists of Unit 212 (Reconnaissance), Unit 217 (Counter-terrorism) and Unit 621 (guerrilla and urban warfare). All personnel are qualified paratroopers. Unit 217, specializing also in covert operations, is commonly known as *Durdevan* ('Cherry' in Hebrew).

Subordinate to the 98th Paratrooper Division is the 55th Paratrooper Brigade, also known as the 'Tip of the Spear' Brigade, which became a legend after capturing the Old City of Jerusalem and being the first Israeli unit to cross the Suez Canal in 1973.[33] The formation was re-designated as the 247th Paratrooper Brigade between 1969 and 2006. Qualified paratroopers are also the officers and men of Unit 269 and *Shayetet-13*. Unit 269, commonly known as *Sayeret Matkal* (meaning in Hebrew Special Reconnaissance Unit of the General Staff), was raised in 1957 to deal with hostage rescue and counter-terrorism. It is a 200-man strong unit modelled on the British SAS. Unit 669, which is assigned combat search and rescue (CSAR) missions, is based at Tel Nof air base. *Shayetet-13* (Flotilla-13 in Hebrew) is a special operations unit of the Israeli Navy, modelled on the US Navy SEALs and Britain's SBS. The 300-strong unit, which was raised in 1949, consists of three companies – one for raids, one for underwater missions and one for above-water missions. *Shayetet-13* is headquartered and garrisoned in Atlit naval base on Israel's northern Mediterranean coast. In February 1973, elements of the *Shayetet-13* (Unit 707) and *Sayeret Tzanhanim* commandos raided guerrilla bases in Nahr al-Bared and Beddawi in northern Lebanon. During the operation, about forty Palestinian militants were killed, sixty wounded and a Turkish military instructor was taken prisoner.

Egyptian Paratroopers

In 1954, the Egyptian Armed Forces founded the paratrooper training establishment, from which emerged the first airborne forces in the Arab region and the Middle East.[34] A delegation had been sent to England in 1951 to train in airborne techniques. Colonel Saad Mohamed el-Husseiny el-Shazly was the founder of Egypt's paratrooper training establishment and the commander (1954–9) of the army's first paratrooper battalion.[35] The 75th Paratrooper Battalion was made up of 350 Egyptian and 150 Syrian volunteers, who could speak either English or French, as their countries at the time had politically merged forming the United Arab Republic (UAR). Shazly commanded the Battalion, during the Suez crisis. He was also the commander of a UAR force in a United Nations mission to the Congo between 1960–1. The Egyptian/Syrian peacekeeping force was deployed in Léopoldville (to be renamed Kinshasa in 1966) in the north-west of the central African country.

In September 1962, Egyptian paratroopers from the 18th Brigade arrived in northern Yemen in Antonov An-12 transport planes (provided by the Soviet Air Force) to establish an airfield and secure roads for Egyptian troop movements.[36] President G.A. Nasser had sided with the country's revolutionary government and dispatched men and arms to its aid. Egypt's involvement in the Yemeni civil war grew steadily and it peaked at 70,000 troops and over 200 combat planes, in what became known in the West as 'Egypt's Vietnam'.[37] On 8 November, the rest of the brigade followed to reinforce the Egyptian presence in Sa'dah.[38] Four months later, paratroopers jumped from three transport planes over Sirwah, near Ma'rib, located 75 miles (120km) east of Yemen's modern capital, Sana'a.[39] The massive drop turned into a massacre for the paratroopers with many of them being shot at in mid-air by Yemeni loyalist tribesmen.[40] According to one source, 195 Egyptian paratroopers were killed.[41] El-Shazly commanded Egyptian army's Special Forces (commandos and paratroopers) from 1967 to 1969. At the time, there were three paratrooper brigades, the 150th, the 160th and the 182nd. Each brigade was comprised of three battalions and each battalion of three companies. The 182nd Paratrooper Brigade was assigned to the 2nd Army with the other two, the 150th and the 160th placed in general headquarters' reserve. In the 1973 War there were two regular brigades with the third (the 160th) being in reserve. The paratroopers fought in the Yom Kippur war of 1973 without conducting combat jumps. The 182nd Brigade under Colonel Ismail Azmy fought well, defending the area south of Ismailia. In the Battle of Ismailia, a combined force of paratroopers and commandos (Sai'qu) held their positions during a major Israeli offensive.[42] Egyptian paratroopers and commandos were also assigned missions on numerous occasions as heliborne forces. Egypt's three airborne brigades were eventually reduced to one, identified as the 414th. The brigade comprises three battalions (the 224th, the 225th and the 226th), a parachute reconnaissance company and the necessary supporting units.

Jordanian Paratroopers

The first Jordanian airborne unit was raised on 15 April 1963. It is garrisoned in Amman and its officers and other ranks wear red berets. The initial volunteers were trained in Jordan by US Army personnel. The Jordanian Special Forces evolved in the early 1980s from that multi-task company-size unit. In 1963, airborne and Ranger courses were run in the country under American supervision and in 1979 a Special Forces school was also established. Four years later, four training 'wings' were in operation, identified as 'Ranger', 'Airborne', 'Specialization' and 'Field'. In 1995, a training establishment for free-fall parachuting came into being. In January 1996, Jordanian army's airborne units acquired a new name, Special Operation Forces (SOF) and in 2001 their training establishment was christened 'Prince Hashem bin al-Hussein School for Special Operations'. With the beginning of the twenty-first century and the emergence of new threats to national security, Jordan established a paramilitary force – the Gendarmes. The new force is tasked with countering homeland security threats, thus allowing the army to focus on external defence threats. The Special Forces' Brigade consists of a Special Forces Group, a counter-terrorism battalion and a combat search-and-rescue (CSAR) battalion. The Rangers' Brigade is more geared towards fighting conventional threats with good capabilities to support internal security operations. In the summer of 2017, a three-brigade Joint Special Operations Command (JSOC) was established. At the heart of the new group are the 101st and the 71st Special Forces Battalions and the 81st and the 91st Para-Commando Battalions. The 101st and the 71st Special Forces Battalions were converted into Special Unit I/Special Operations and Special Unit II/Counter-terrorism. Special Unit II was established in 1973 and its personnel wear an entirely black uniform. In June 2014, the unit was dispatched for some time on the Jordanian-Iraqi border as a response to the capture of the Iraqi city of Ar Rutba by ISIS forces. In 2018, the Directorate of Special Operations and Rapid Intervention Forces was formed in Jordan, including the 'King Abdullah II Special Forces Group' and a Rapid Intervention/High Readiness Brigade. The 7,000-strong Special Operations' Forces of Jordan are equipped and trained to be able to operate behind enemy lines for a long period of time without logistical support.[43] Their primary role includes reconnaissance, counter-terrorism, combat search and evacuation, intelligence gathering and the protection of key sites.

Syrian Para-Commandos

The first Syrian paratroopers were trained in Egypt in 1954. They had British-trained Egyptian instructors and were later admitted to an Egyptian army airborne battalion – an indication of the cooperation between Cairo and Damascus as it was shaped after the 1956 Arab-Israeli War and expressed by the creation of a short-lived political union, the United Arab Republic (UAR). On 28 September 1961, a 120-strong force of Egyptian paratroopers landed on Latakia airfield, on the northern coast of Syria. It was Egyptian President and UAR leader Gamal Abdel Nasser's response to a coup by Syrian Ba'athist officers who demanded an equal footing with Egypt for their country. One of the coup leaders was Syrian Air Force captain Hafez al-Assad who, nine years later, in November 1970, would rise to become Syria's strongman.

Once Nasser was informed that his allies in Syria had been defeated, he ordered the withdrawal of the Egyptian paratroopers from Latakia.[44] This is why it was no possible for any Syrian having served in the Egyptian 75th Paratrooper Battalion to find a place in his country's army. As a matter of fact, there is no evidence of involvement of Syrian airborne troops in the 1948, the 1956 and the 1967 Arab-Israeli Wars.[45] The Six Day War of 1967, in particular, pointed to the weak airborne capability of the Syrian military. From 1968 onwards, Syrian officers were sent for special operations training, involving airborne operations, in the Soviet Union. As a result of this, during the 1973 Arab-Israeli War, Syrian commandos are mentioned for the first time as taking part in combat operations. They belonged to the 82nd Para-Commando Regiment, which captured an Israeli observation site on Mount Hermon, overlooking the approached to the Golan Heights, on 6 October 1973.[46]

Syrian Special Forces had come of age and their usefulness was further confirmed during the Israeli invasion of Lebanon nine years later, when a Syrian commando battalion ambushed an Israeli armoured unit at Sultan Yakoub, inflicting heavy casualties in both men and tanks. In the mid-1970s, more Syrians were trained by Soviet experts in special and airborne operations. From then on, Syrian Special Forces units started participating in exercises with the Soviet Army. The Syrian Army, since it came into being in August 1945, never considered raising conventional parachute units. Instead, it relied upon Special Forces units, whose members were qualified paratroopers. In 1981, the Syrians had four Special Forces regiments, two of which were trained for heliborne operations. From the mid-1970s the Syrian Army's Special Forces were organized and commanded by Major General Ali Haydar, who was a close confidante of President Hafez al-Assad. The Special Forces (SFs) enjoy a prominent place in the Syrian Army because they represent both a regime protection force and a critical component of Syria's national defence.[47] They were expanded in size to 25,000 men, becoming a key part of the Syrian government security apparatus. Traditionally, in the SFs all of the officers and most of the other ranks come from the Alawite sect to ensure loyalty to the government.[48]

The SFs are rivalled in Syria only by the Defence Companies (DCs) that were raised and controlled by Hafez's brother Rifaat. As such, the 14th Special Forces Division became a strong counterweight to the DCs as both formations are largely airborne divisions. The DCs were formed in 1971 and were organizationally and operationally independent from the regular armed forces. Their task was also to defend the Assad government and Damascus from internal and external threats. Most DC soldiers, including tank crewmen and artillery personnel, traditionally receive commando and parachute training. They were initially trained by Soviet Spetsnaz and Red Army airborne (VDV) forces. Most of the repression was carried out by the DCs and the SFs who have been accused of the killing and capturing of suspected government opponents. In the spring of 1982, elements of the SCs were deployed in Hama, in west-central Syria, to quell an Islamic uprising. The Special Forces and two armoured divisions are still the key elements of the security structure that protects Assad's government. Following a power struggle between Rifaat al-Assad and his rivals in the armed forces in early 1984, the DCs were renamed Unit 569 and reorganized as a standard armoured division with four armoured and three mechanized brigades. Afterwards, the SFs and the Republican Guard absorbed any soldiers and officers from the disbanded DCs, making it the third regime protection force that owes its lineage in part to those DCs along with the 4th Armored and the Republican Guard Divisions.[49]

By 1984, the DFs were 55,000 strong. In the mid-1990s, Hafez al-Assad split up the SFs command by standing up the 14th and 15th SF Divisions, each of which was made up of three regiments.[50] Hafez reduced to six the number of regiments under direct control of the SF Command. The 15th SF Division fell under the 1st Corps, garrisoned in the south, while the 14th SF Division was assigned to the 2nd Corps, oriented at the time along the Lebanese border. The 15th SF Division and its three regiments were located in the high ground of Jebal Druze, near the Jordanian border.[51] In 2006, the International Institute for Strategic Studies listed ten independent SF regiments.[52] The SF Command, along with at least three of its regiments, is garrisoned in the al-Dreij military complex, in the mountains between Damascus and the Lebanese border, behind the Presidential Palace.[53] The SF Command controls a large number of units. These are the 14th SF Division, comprising of the 35th, the 46th, the 54th and the 55th Regiments. In a more traditional role are five SF regiments, the 441st, the 44th, the 53rd, the 82nd and the 804th. These are commando-trained with a number of them being stationed for long periods in Lebanon. Each regiment has 1,500 soldiers divided into three battalions with 300 soldiers each. *As-Sa'iqa*, an independent commando force, also merged into the SFs. The main ground unit of the Syrian military is often called a brigade or regiment and is about 500–1,000 strong. It is considerably smaller than a corresponding Western formation of that designation. In 2015, the Republican Guard had an airborne brigade (the 104th), a SF brigade (the 124th) and two commando regiments (the 102nd and the 103rd). The SF Command had six independent regiments (the 41st, the 45th, the 46th, the 47th, the 53rd and the 54th). The 14th SF Division was made up of three regiments (the 36th, 554th and 556th), as many as those (the 35th, the 127th and the 403rd) of the 15th SF Division.[54] Syria's 14th SF Division specializes in air-assault operations but should be regarded as an elite force only in relation to the conventional armoured and mechanized formations of the former Soviet Army.

The Indo-Pakistani Wars

In October 1947, before even gaining independence from Britain, the dominions of India and Pakistan were already at war with one another. Airborne operations, including combat jumps, were carried out during the first three wars between Indian and Pakistani forces in 1947–8, in 1965 and in 1971. Two more Indo–Pakistani wars were to follow; the two countries fought over the disputed Siachen Glacier region in Kashmir from 13 April 1984 to 25 November 2003. In the meantime, between May and July 1999, India and Pakistan clashed in what became known as the Kargil Conflict. Before 1947, the forces of India and Pakistan were part of the British Indian Army (BIA). The 44th Airborne Division was divided, after the dissolution of the BIA, between the two new dominions. The 50th and the 77th Parachute Brigades went to India with the 14th Parachute Brigade becoming a formation of the Pakistani army. With a few notable exceptions, officers and other ranks picked sides in accordance with their religious beliefs. The Hindu personnel remained in or moved to units of the Indian army and the Muslim personnel to those of the Pakistani army. The 1st Indo–Pakistani War, also known as the Kashmir War, broke out in October 1947, when Pakistan invaded Jammu and Kashmir in northern India on the grounds that the majority of the population in this princely state were Muslims. Two companies of the 1st Battalion, The Sikh Regiment, led by Lieutenant Colonel Dewan Ranjit Rai, were airlifted in thirty Douglas C-47 Dakota transports to Srinagar, the largest city of the Jammu and Kashmir state. The Indian air-transported troops captured and held the Baramulla–Srinagar highway near the Beri Pattan bridge against numerically superior enemy forces. They also protected the Srinagar airfield thus enabling the arrival of reinforcements. On 27 October, Rai was fatally wounded near Pattan during an enemy counter-attack, thus becoming the first Indian officer killed in action in the country's history. During the 1st Indo–Pakistani War, the three battalions of the 50th Parachute Brigade participated in the battles of Nawshera, Jhangar and Poonch with the brigade commander, Brigadier Mohammad Usman, being killed in action on 3 July 1948.[55] In 1947, Usman commanded the 77th Parachute Brigade. He was then appointed commander of the 50th Parachute Brigade before the formation's deployment to Jhangar. The city had fallen into Pakistani hands on 25 December and had to be recaptured due to its strategic importance, as it was located at the junction of roads coming from Mirpur and Kotil. By late December, the enemy had been driven off and Jhangar had been recaptured by Indian forces. In early 1948, Indian paratroopers, led by Usman, repulsed fierce Pakistani attacks on Nowshera, another highly strategic location in Jammu and Kashmir. During the defence of Nowshera, Indian forces inflicted about 1,000 killed and 1,000 wounded on the enemy troops with themselves suffering 33 dead and 102 wounded.[56] In May 1948, the Pakistani forces tried to recapture Jhangar. During the defence of the city, Usman was killed by an enemy artillery shell. He became India's highest-ranking military commander to lose his life on the battlefield since the country's independence. Meanwhile, the Indian 77th Parachute Brigade, acting in an infantry role, under the command of Brigadier Kanhaiya Lal Atal, had failed to capture Zoji La, a high mountain pass, after the Pakistani invasion of Jammu and Kashmir. It should be mentioned that the 77th Indian Regiment was assigned to the Chindits during the Second World War and had fought against the Japanese in Burma. When the war started, the Pakistani 14th Parachute Brigade was undergoing training at Malir, near Karachi. In January 1948 the formation was concentrated at Rahwali, near Gujranwala.

The 2nd Indo-Pakistani War was a culmination of skirmishes between Pakistan and India that took place from April to September 1965. On the night of 7 September, commandos of the Pakistani Army's Special Service Group (SSG) were parachuted into three Indian territories in a highly ambitious clandestine operation to sabotage Indian airfields at Halvara, Pathankot and Adampur in Punjab, northern India.[57] According to Pakistani sources, the invading force, belonging to the country's newly-established airborne unit, was 200 strong with Indian sources raising the number of the parachuted enemies to between 800 and 900. Those who jumped near Pathankot and Halwara airfields were scattered by strong winds. They were later able to launch only a few disorganized attacks, failing to destroy any Indian planes.[58] Of those who landed close to Adampur airfield, the majority were eventually captured by the Punjab police. Given that the objectives were deep inside India, the operation was a failure with only twenty-two SSG men making it back alive. Twenty commandos were killed in encounters with the army and the police or with civilians, as the Indian authorities had responded to the operation by offering rewards for captured Pakistani spies or paratroopers.[59] Of the remaining commandos, ninety-three (136, according to Indian sources) were captured by 11 September, including the commander of the operation, Major Khalid Butt. The reason for the failure of the operation is attributed to inadequate planning and preparation. Two days later, elements of the Pakistani Army's 14th Parachute Brigade occupied Zafarwal (which was undefended). This was the brigade's contribution to a mostly tank battle fought in the area between Charwa and Chawinda from 8 to 21 September 1965. The 14th Parachute Brigade was commanded during the Battle of Chawinda by Brigadier Amir Abdullah Khan Niazi.

On 26 November 1971, Indian troops and Bengali nationalist forces attacked the then eastern part of Pakistan on twenty fronts. During the war that led to the independence of Bangladesh, the Indian paratroopers fought in numerous actions in both the eastern and western theatres of operations. In East Pakistan the only elite unit stationed at the time of the Indian invasion was the 3rd Commando Battalion of the Special Service Group, commanded by Lieutenant Colonel (later Brigadier) Tariq Mehmood Shaheed.[60] On 11 December, India airdropped the 2nd Battalion (also known as 2 Para), led by Lieutenant Colonel (later Major General) Kulwant Singh Pannu, in what is famous as the Tangail airdrop. Seven hundred paratroopers were involved in the operation.[61] The fifty transport planes took off at 14.30 from Dum Dum and Kalaikonda airfields, in India's West Bengal state. The aircraft were Soviet-made Antonov An-12s and US-made Fairchild C-119 Flying Boxcars and Douglas C-47 Dakotas. The paratroopers were reinforced by an airborne artillery battery and other supporting detachments from the 50th Parachute Brigade. The jump was planned for nighttime, but the Indian Air Force persuaded the planners to have it rescheduled for 16.30. The drop, at Tangail, in East Pakistan, was conducted in this order: 1. Pathfinders, 2. Light supplies, 3. Heavy supplies and 4. Paratroopers. There was no enemy interference at the time of the drop. On one occasion, near Dacca, Pakistani soldiers came out of their bunkers to cheer the paratroopers, as they mistook them for Chinese. Peking had promised to intervene in case of an Indian invasion of Pakistan, but it never kept its promise.

The drop was dispersed over a wide area and Pannu had to move from one location to another, mostly under enemy fire, to assemble his force's platoons. Of the guns of the 49th Parachute Field Regiment, three landed in water with the fourth falling on top of a house. There was no Pakistani interference at the time of the drop. One planeload landed 15 miles (24km) north of the dropping zone. These men were fired upon as they descended and later had to fight their way out, joining the rest of the force the following day. The main objective of the operation was the capture of the Poongli Bridge on the Jamuna River, thus cutting off the Pakistani 93rd Brigade, which was heading to defend Dacca, East Pakistan's capital and largest city. The paratroop unit was also tasked with linking up with the advancing 1st Maratha Light Infantry Regiment before they both advanced towards Dacca. By 19.00, the paratroopers had captured the vital bridge, cutting off the Pakistani 93rd Brigade that was retreating from the north at the time. That very evening, elements of the 1st Maratha Light Regiment broke through at Tangail road, reaching the bridgehead. The Pakistanis launched numerous counter-attacks, but failed to capture the Poongli bridge. Three hundred and seventy Pakistani soldiers were killed during the Indian airborne assault at Tangail. Over a hundred more were wounded with the number of those captured exceeding 600.[62] The Indian 2 Para had three killed and fifteen wounded or injured. The Tangail airdrop and the subsequent capture of the Poogli Bridge gave the advancing Indian Army the manoeuvrability to sidestep the strongly-held Tongi–Dacca road and then take the undefended Manikganj–Dacca road right up to Mirpur Bridge at the gates of Dacca. The result of the battle was a decisive Indian victory. Over 90,000 Pakistani troops found themselves completely surrounded and on 16 December they were forced to surrender, with Dacca falling to the Indian forces the same day.[63] 2 Para was subsequently the first Indian unit to enter East Pakistan's capital. When asked later as to the reason for the surrender, the commander of the Pakistani forces deployed in the eastern part of the country, Lieutenant General Amir Abdullah Khan Niazi, pointed to a copy of the *Times* of London carrying the title 'Tangail Para-Drop'.[64] Niazi, as brigadier, had commanded the 14th Parachute Brigade during the

1965 War. It is generally believed that the Indian airborne assault at Tangail caught the Pakistani leadership on the wrong foot and restricted the duration of the 1971 war to thirteen days.[65] By the time Dacca fell to Indian and Bengali forces, other battalions of the 50th Parachute Brigade had carried out lightning raids into Chachro and Sindh in south-east Pakistan, as well as into Mandhol in the Jammu and Kashmir state in northern India. In the greater Chachro area, a six-man commando team sabotaged an airfield and destroyed an artillery battery. The 50th Parachute Brigade became the only formation to see action on both the eastern and western fronts. The other parachute brigade, the 51st, fought in Sri Canganar, Rajastan in a ground role. East Pakistan was thus made independent from Pakistan and became the People's Republic of Bangladesh.

The Indian Army's Airborne Forces

In 1945, the British 44th (Indian) Airborne Division was renamed the 2nd Indian Airborne Division. Its three brigades were later divided between the two dominions emerging in the Indian subcontinent after the British withdrawal from the area. Two of these brigades became part of the Indian army with the third, the 14th Parachute Brigade, going to Pakistan. The Indians retained the maroon berets as the headgear for their paratroopers. Of the airborne brigades turning Indian, only the 50th remained. The 77th Parachute Brigade was disbanded, following the formation of Indian Army's Parachute Regiment on 1 March 1945. The Parachute Regiment units are rotated as the main force of the 50th Parachute Brigade. Initially, these units were the 1st Battalion, Punjab Regiment (Para), the 3rd Battalion, Maratha Light Infantry Regiment (Para) and the 1st Battalion, Kumaon Regiment (Para). On 15 April, the Parachute Regiment was re-formed by absorbing the three existing battalions of the 50th Parachute Brigade. The 1st Battalion, Punjab Regiment (Para), then became 1st Battalion, Parachute Regiment (Punjab), the 3rd Battalion, Maratha Light Infantry Regiment (Para), became 2nd Battalion, Parachute Regiment (Maratha) and the 1st Battalion Kumaon Regiment (Para) became 3rd Battalion, Parachute Regiment (Kumaon).

The raising of four more units followed. These were the 4th, 6th, 7th and 8th Parachute Battalions, which came into being in 1961, 1962, 1963 and 1964 respectively. In 1996, the 21st Battalion, Maratha Light Infantry Regiment, was transferred to the Parachute Regiment and was re-designated as the 21st Battalion, Parachute Regiment (Special Forces). Three years later, the 2nd Battalion, Parachute Regiment, was converted to a Special Forces role. The same applied to the Parachute Regiment's 3rd and 4th Battalions in 2002 and 2003, respectively. In 2010, another battalion, the 11th, was raised in Agra to augment the strength of the existing units. The Indian Army's Parachute Regiment Depot had been established on 15 April 1952 at Agra 128 miles (206km) south of New Delhi. During the 1965 Indo-Pakistani War, an irregular force made up of volunteers from various regiments, led by Major (later Lieutenant Colonel) Megh Singh of the Guards Brigade, successfully carried out a number of unconventional operations. Most of these fighters later joined two newly-created commando units, which were added to the 50th Parachute Brigade as the 9th and 10th Battalions. A second parachute brigade, the 51st, was later raised, but in 1976 it reverted to an infantry role. Of the original units of the 50th Parachute Brigade only the 411th Parachute Field Company of the Bombay Sappers and the 50th Parachute Brigade Signal Company remain active. The original medical unit, the 80th Parachute Field Ambulance, was disbanded and only one field ambulance was retained in the airborne role. The 50th Parachute Brigade's standard force includes two airborne battalions, one Special Forces battalion, one parachute field artillery regiment and one parachute air defence battery. In India, the President's Bodyguards are qualified paratroopers and comprise a combat unit within the Indian Army's special operations forces. Besides guarding or carrying out various ceremonial duties, the President's Bodyguards have also been trained to participate in airborne operations in a pathfinder role. India's airborne forces have been deployed abroad, whenever a military intervention was decided by the Indian government. On 12 October 1987, seventeen men of the 10th Battalion (Commando) were helicoptered into Jaffna, spearheading the Indian force that averted the seizure of northern Sri Lanka by Tamil secessionist rebels. The operation ended disastrously, failing to capture the objectives due to intelligence and planning failures. Two of the Indian para-commandos were killed in the firefight. A year later, 1,600 Indian paratroopers were deployed to the Maldives, following a coup d'état against the country's legitimate administration that was openly supported by the Tamil underground organization. The maroon-bereted elite soldiers air-landed on the island of Hulhule on 3 November 1988 and within hours had restored order in the Maldives, located south-west of Sri Lanka in the Arabian Sea.

The Pakistani Army's Airborne Forces

In the early 1950s, Pakistan had one of the three parachute divisions, the 14th, from the wartime British Indian Army. There was also a parachute training establishment in operation since 1964. It was then, when Lieutenant Colonel (later Major General) Aboobaker Osman Mitha was selected to raise a special operations unit. He was assisted in this task by a team of US Army experts headed by Lieutenant Colonel Dean F. Bundy. On 23 March 1956, Pakistani Army's Special Service Group (SSG) was established as a battalion with Mitha becoming its first commander.[66] The SSG is garrisoned in Cherat, a hill station near Peshawar in north-western Pakistan. Meanwhile, the 14th Parachute Brigade was converted to standard infantry unit before becoming a component of the 8th Infantry Division. This was decided because there were not enough aircraft for the operational employment of an airborne division. The SSG and the Presidential Guards are ever since the only airborne forces of the Pakistani Army. Initially, the SSG wore green berets. They later adopted the Baluch Regiment's maroon headwear.

In 1967, a deep diving team was raised with US assistance in Karachi. Since 1981, the Navy SSG has trained regularly with Britain's SAS. In 1970, the Musa Company was established in the Pakistani Army, specializing in anti-terrorist operations. Its members are also parachute-trained. The SSG was restricted to brigade level until 2013, when it was enlarged to a division. Each battalion has companies, specializing in desert, mountain, long-distance ranger and deep diving warfare.[67] Pakistan's special operations force is tasked with foreign integral defence, reconnaissance, direct actions, counter-terrorism and unconventional warfare.

Chapter 15

Post-1945 Airborne Operations (II)

A company of the 2nd Battalion (2 Para) of the Parachute Regiment and I (Bull's Troop) close support Parachute Battery of the 7th Parachute Regiment, Royal Horse Artillery (7 Para, RHA) were among the British forces deployed to Kuwait in 1961 to forestall a threatened invasion of the newly-independent emirate by its neighbour Iraq. On 30 June, Emir Abdullah III Al-Salim Al-Sabah of Kuwait asked Britain for help and within days 6,000 troops with strong naval and air support were moved to the Gulf. The force included one aircraft carrier, four destroyers, six frigates and an amphibious landing ship, as well as a squadron of RAF transonic Hawker Hunter fighter-bombers. A troop of 42 Commando, Royal Marines, was helicoptered from HMS *Bulwark*. 'A' Company of 2 Para landed from a Royal Navy assault craft, after having participated in exercises in southern Kuwait. The remaining units of 2 Para had moved to Bahrain and were garrisoned at Muharraq airfield. The British deployment continued until 7 July. Although Iraq was deterred, British troops remained in Kuwait until 19 October. Nevertheless, the political situation in Baghdad continued to be unstable, and there was always a fear that 'Iraq could have flown paratroopers to the south undetected'.[1]

In the aftermath, it was decided that the Arab League would deploy a peacekeeping force in the region. The countries contributing to this force were Saudi Arabia, Egypt, Syria, Sudan, Tunisia and Jordan. In late 1962, the withdrawal of the Arab League peacekeepers was decided on the grounds that no Iraqi military action against Kuwait had been detected. 2 Para remained in Bahrain until October 1961, when they were relieved by their 1st Battalion (1 Para). This was the start of one-year tours in South East Asia, rotating between the Parachute Regiment's three battalions which lasted until 1967.

Western New Guinea (1961–1963)

Airborne units spearheaded the Indonesian attacks against Dutch forces in Western New Guinea (WNG) between 1960 and 1963. It all started in the early 1960s, because of The Hague's policy towards the former Dutch East Indies (DEI). Although the rest of the DEI achieved independence, including Indonesia, the Dutch remained in WNG on the grounds of preparing the former colony for full independence. Indonesia, already possessing eastern New Guinea, was claiming the western part of it as well. The Indonesians believed that The Hague was planning independent status for WNG under Dutch guidance. Although his country had gained independence only ten years earlier, Indonesian President Sukarno turned aggressive in his effort to speed up the Dutch withdrawal from WNG.

In 1961, after acquiring weapons from the Soviet Union, Sukarno ordered attacks against Dutch military installations. In these raids Indonesia's newly-established airborne forces played a prominent role. The first parachute jump in Indonesia was performed in April 1946 at the Maguwo airfield by three PPP (airfield defence troops) men, who jumped from a converted former Japanese transport plane. Their names were Hamzah, Iswahyudi and Pungut. The first airborne operation was conducted on 17 October 1947, when twelve PPP men were dropped onto Sambi, in Central Kalimantan, on the island of Borneo. Six days later, the paratroopers were ambushed by the Dutch army and three of them were killed. The remainder were later captured, tried and imprisoned.

By 1950, paratroopers had been included in the central PPP unit in Jakarta. In 1950, Indonesia's parachute training establishment was transferred to Andir airfield, near Bandoeng in west Java. In February 1952, the PPP paratroopers made up what developed later into the *Kompi-Kompi Pasukan Geraton Tjerak* (PGT), the Indonesian Air Force's orange-bereted airborne forces. Two months later, on 16 April, the red-bereted *Resimen Para-Kommando Angkatan Darat* (RPKAD), a para-commando regiment, was raised in the Indonesian army. They were later re-named *Kopassus* or members of the *Kommando Pasukan Khusus* (Special Forces Command).

Between 26 April and 14 August 1962, air force and army paratroopers conducted fifteen combat jumps over areas of Dutch-controlled WNG such as Fakfak, Kaimana, Sorong, Tenimabuan and Merauke. The jumps were usually unopposed and most of the casualties related to them were caused by parachute malfunctions or unsuccessful landings. After a brief deployment in WNG areas to boost the morale of pro-Indonesian guerrillas and make an impression on the local population, the Indonesian paratroopers crossed the 620-mile (800km) common border with WNG to return to Indonesian soil. The Dutch seemed unable to cope with the situation in WNG. They couldn't count on their Second World War allies for support, as they already had problems of their own in their protectorates or colonies in South East Asia and North Africa. When the United States supported an Indonesian scheme for peace and stability in WNG, the Dutch realized that it was time for them to start packing. On 1 October 1962, the Dutch handed over their territory in New Guinea to the United Nations Temporary Executive Authority. Indonesia took control of WNG on 1 May 1963.

Borneo (1963–1966)

British forces, including airborne units, were involved in the conflict in Borneo caused between 1963 and 1966 by the so-called Brunei Revolt and the consecutive Indonesia-Malaysia Confrontation. In Brunei, a British protectorate in South East Asia between 1888 and 1984, located on the north coast of the island of Borneo, an insurrection against the monarch erupted in 1962. The insurgents were members of the North Kalimantan National Army (NKNA), a militia supported by Indonesia and linked to the left-wing Brunei's People's Party (BPP). At the head of the rebellion was a young sheikh named Azahari, who wanted to be the leader of a country encompassing Brunei, Sarawak and Sabah. Approximately, a thousand rebels fled to jungle and were joined in the fighting by the Clandestine Communist Organization (CCO), a pro-Chinese terrorist group.[2] Indonesia's leader Sukarno supported the CCO with arms and had allowed its members to maintain bases on Indonesian soil. The revolt started mainly with attacks against oil installations near the town of Seria and government facilities across the protectorate. It was suppressed with British assistance with troops rushing in from Singapore. Two Royal Marine Commandos, 40 and 42, were among the units deployed. The revolt began to break down, having failed to achieve key objectives such as the capture of Brunei's capital and the arrest of Omar Ali Saifuddien I, the 28th Sultan of Brunei. It was crushed in eight days.

Border surveillance and patrols mounted by elements of the British 22nd SAS Regiment placed major constraints upon the CCO's ambitions to threaten the status quo in the sultanate again.[3] The Brunei Revolt is considered as part of the subsequent Indonesia-Malaysia Confrontation in which British forces, including SAS squadrons and a battalion of the Parachute Regiment, became heavily involved as Britain was determined to guard her protectorates against Indonesian expansionism and communist revolution.[4] It was a protracted undeclared war between Indonesia and British-led British Commonwealth forces in Borneo, an island located north of Java and east of Sumatra, as a result of Indonesian opposition to the creation of a Malaysian federal state. Indonesia's armed forces, although equipped with Soviet weapons, could hardly afford a direct confrontation with the British war machine. Instead, Jakarta decided to support subversive movements already existing in Borneo, which were eventually supported in combat by Indonesian regular troops. A military infiltration of the third-largest island in the world was ordered by Indonesia's President Sukarno.[5]

On one occasion, Indonesian paratroopers conducted an airborne assault against British and Malaysian forces. 'D' Squadron of 22 SAS was one of the first British units to be deployed to Borneo, when the Indonesian incursion began in April 1963. It had arrived in South East Asia in the aftermath of the Brunei Revolt to gather information on the border about Indonesian infiltration.[6] The squadron, composed of seventy troopers, was led by 22 SAS Regiment's commander, Lieutenant Colonel John Woodhouse.[7] The SAS's tactical headquarters was established in the capital town of Brunei – in a building located next to the Palace of the Sultan.[8] Woodhouse also commanded a detachment of the SBS, a unit that had been part of the SAS during the Second World War, which successfully carried out a number of amphibious missions during the British campaign in Borneo.

By the end of 1963, Indonesian army regulars posing as guerrillas were crossing the border from Kalimantan to attack security or British Commonwealth units before quickly returning to Indonesian territory. Major General Walter Walker, commander of the British Commonwealth forces in Borneo, wanted the SAS squadron to act as a mobile reserve, dropping by parachute onto the jungle canopy and recapture areas controlled by the enemy. Believing that this tactic would result in heavy casualties and would waste his men's talents, Woodhouse suggested a 'shoot and scoot' policy.[9] Walker was convinced that SAS troops would be better suited to operating in small covert groups along the border, where they could provide early warning of any communist guerrilla or Indonesian military incursions.[10] The proposal was accepted by the high command and eventually became the model of action even for regular infantry units involved in these operations.

By using a combination of deterrence and small or medium-sized operations, the British succeeded in containing the insurgency to a low-level conflict. Combat was usually conducted by company or platoon-sized units on either side of the Indonesia-Malaysia border. Elements of the SAS carried out effectively a great deal of this task throughout the war. Between February 1965 and November 1966 Australian and New Zealand SAS units were assigned such missions in Borneo. Some local paramilitaries, who became known as Border Scouts, were armed and trained by the SAS. They proved particularly successful in intelligence-gathering missions. In the summer of 1964, the Cross-Border Scouts, made up of SAS-trained natives, were assigned raids into Kalimantan province. The period up to the end of 1963 saw 'D' Squadron undertaking the reconnaissance of a previously unexplored area, known as 'The Gap', in southern Sabah. The task facing General Walker was a formidable one, as his troops were required to defend 994 miles (1,600km) of jungle-covered border against an enemy who could readily retreat to safety. In addition, the British Commonwealth troops had to protect military facilities, installations of strategic importance and population centres in general from the activity, particularly in Sarawak province, of the CCO, whose recruits were mainly Chinese settlers.[11]

In April 1964, the British decided on more aggressive action. Detachments could cross the Malaysian-Indonesian border to obtain information or to pursue escaping infiltrators.[12] The objective of the cross-border operations, code-named Claret, was to wrest the initiative from the enemy. Initially, border penetration by General Walker's elite troops was limited to 3,000 yards (2,700m).[13] The first mission carried out by SAS troopers on Indonesian soil was a successful raid against a military camp at Nantakor, in Kalimantan, the Indonesian part of Borneo.[14] From then on, troopers of 'A' and 'B' Squadrons, operating in groups of four, regularly patrolled the territory immediately across the border. When a patrol spotted guerrillas or Indonesian regulars heading towards Malaysia, it would arrange for them to be ambushed after crossing the border.

On 3 September 1964, eighty-eight Indonesian paratroopers jumped from two C-130 Hercules over the Malay Peninsula. Fifty-two of them were dropped near Kesang River on the Johore-Malacca border with the remnant being parachuted near Pontian, south-west of Johore (now Johor). Due to a thunderstorm, the paratroopers were widely dispersed. It took a month for the British Commonwealth forces to hunt down the airdropped enemy soldiers and capture or kill them, for the loss of two men killed in action.[15] A number of paratroopers surrendered without firing a single shot. The units mobilized in the Malay Peninsula after the Indonesian parachute drop were the 1st Royal New Zealand Infantry Regiment, the 1st Battalion of the 10th Gurkha Rifles Regiment (1/10th Gurkhas) and units of the Malaysian army. On 3 September, another C-130, probably carrying Indonesian paratroopers, was reported to have crashed into the Malacca Straits, while trying to evade interception by an RAF Gloster Javelin fighter. A few days later, on 23 September, a detachment of Indonesian Army para-commandos unsuccessfully attacked a British Commonwealth artillery position at Long Bawan in north Kalimantan.

In January 1965, the 2nd Battalion of the British Parachute Regiment (2 Para) was flown to Singapore for jungle training and then to Borneo. They found a few of the pathfinder platoon of the Independent (Guards) Parachute Company already deployed there. 2 Para established a base close to the Indonesian–Malayan border. By then, fourteen British battalions totalling 60,000 men were involved in the Indonesian–Malaysian Confrontation. On 1 February, Australian and New Zealand SAS units arrived in Borneo. They were two Sabres (Squadrons) of the Australian SAS, which were deployed to Brunei (1st Sabre) and to the Malaysian province of Sarawak.[16] There were also forty troopers from the 1st Ranger Squadron, New Zealand SAS Regiment. Similarly-sized detachments from this regiment were rotated to Borneo until November 1966.

During the winter of 1964–5, SAS operations were aimed at preventing any Indonesian occupation of the Sarawak and Sabah provinces.[17] 'B' Squadron focused its activity in the Pueh range of hills in western Sarawak, a favourite route for communist guerrillas heading to Lundu, where communist cells were located. Captain Robin Letts was awarded the Military Cross for his role in leading a reconnaissance patrol which successfully ambushed an enemy force near Babang in Kalimantan province in April. The cross-border raids continued, especially along the Koemba River near Poeri, by British SAS troopers in co-ordination with New Zealand SAS and Gurkha patrols with varying levels of success. The last attempt by Indonesian forces to launch a raid into Malayan territory resulted with one of Indonesia-Malaysia Confrontation's major battles. Sukarno was desperate for a decisive victory as the fruitlessness of the conflict was having a damaging effect on his country and his regime.[18]

In the early morning of 27 April, a crack Javanese-Indonesian unit, numbering 150 to 400 men, supported by artillery and rocket fire, stormed a hilltop base of 2 Para at Plaman Mapu on the Indonesian-Malaysian border. Only thirty-six men were at the garrison at the time of the ferocious attack, as most of the company were out on various missions. The defenders, although outnumbered by at least five to one, managed to repel the Indonesian assault after an intense two-hour firefight. On one occasion, British paratroopers engaged in vicious hand-to-hand combat with enemy soldiers.[19] When British reinforcements were helicoptered in the area, the Indonesian troops were forced to withdraw. The attackers suffered fifty casualties at a cost of three paratroopers killed and seven wounded. Among the wounded was Sergeant-Major John Williams, who was decorated later with the Distinguished Conduct Medal.[20]

The Battle of Plaman Mapu was a propaganda disaster for President Sukarno. Six months later, a group of leftist military officers attempted to seize power in Jakarta. The coup was crushed by troops loyal to Major General Suharto. Indonesian paratroopers participated in widespread killings during Suharto's regime. Red-bereted soldiers of the *Resimen Para-Kommando Angata Darat* (Army Para-Commando Regiment) were involved in wiping out entire villages.[21] Suharto's rise to power coincided with a major transformation in Indonesian politics. Sukarno became a puppet president with the real power exercised by the army leadership embodied by Suharto. The new regime, concerned with suppressing communism in Indonesia, abandoned Sukarno's ambitious schemes, including the Indonesia-Malaysia Confrontation. After the coup that brought Suharto to power, military activity in Borneo's Malaysian territories by Indonesian regulars gradually died down.

In early 1966, 'G' Squadron was formed in the 22nd SAS Regiment from Guardsmen who had been undertaking SAS-type patrols along the central Sarawak border with their unit, the Independent (Guards) Parachute Company. They were also augmented by adding the Gurkha Independent Parachute Company to their strength.[22] In late May, SAS's 'D' Squadron was replaced in Borneo by 'A' Squadron, commanded by Major (later General) Peter de la Billière.[23] British and Commonwealth casualties in Borneo during the Indonesia-Malaysia Confrontation were 114 killed and a further 181 injured. A significant number of British casualties occurred during helicopter crashes. A Bristol Type 192 Belvedere crashed killing a number of SAS officers. On another occasion, on 12 April 1965, two Wessex 1s, returning from a troop lift, collided and both helicopters plunged into a river. The 2 Para men who were on board were killed. Indonesian casualties were estimated at 590 killed, 222 wounded and 771 captured. The SAS operations in Borneo were publicly disclosed by Britain in 1974 and by Australia in 1996.[24]

Aden (1964–1967)

In December 1963, the pro-British sheikhdoms of south Yemen, facing a serious threat by insurgent groups in the Radfan region and in Aden itself, called on Britain for military aid. The Marxist (North) Yemen Arab Republic was making territorial claims on the south of the Arabian Peninsula, where the sheikhdoms had merged with Aden, a British colony since 1937, forming the Federation of South Arabia (FSA) in 1959. In April 1964, 'B' Company of the Parachute Regiment's 3rd Battalion (3 Para) arrived in Aden as part of a force, code-named Radforce, that was deployed to the former colony. The force also included the Royal Marines' 45 Commando, as well as infantry, artillery and other supporting units. A detachment from 'A' Squadron, 22 SAS was secretly added to the force. The families of the seventy-five officers, NCOs and troopers of 22 SAS sent to Aden were under the assumption that their men were exercising on Salisbury Plain.[25] Radforce's task was to re-establish British authority over south Yemen and stop the flow of weapons to the rebel tribesmen. In fact, the British came to the rescue of the hard-pressed 15,000-strong Federal (South Arabian) Army, which had been trained for nine months in 1963 by British and French officers.

Pro-British tribes in south Yemen were supplied with weapons in nine airdrops carried out by Israeli planes.[26] The main insurgent groups in South Arabia were the North Yemeni-backed (Marxist) National Liberation Front (NLF) and the Egyptian-backed Front for the Liberation of Occupied South Yemen (FLOSY). The SAS detachment was garrisoned at Thumier, 62 miles (100km) north of Aden, near the Habilayn airstrip. It was led by Lieutenant Colonel Johnny Cooper, who had supervised the training of Yemeni tribesmen a year earlier and organized information-gathering on the Egyptian involvement in the country. A combat jump was decided on a few days after the deployment of Radforce, onto a location christened Gap Badge by the British. The plan called for 120 men from 'B' Company, 3 Para, to be parachuted from two Beverley transport planes in the night of 30 April/1 May. Instead of employing the paratroopers' pathfinder company, the operation planners ordered an SAS patrol to reach the designated DZ on foot and guide the Beverleys in.[27] The operation also included 3 Para (minus the airborne 'B' Company) and 45 Commando, Royal Marines (RM). They were assigned to capture the Dhanaba Basin, a Rafdan tribal stronghold, and clear a 'fortification' and village buildings at El Naquil. The SAS patrol was made up of men from 'A' Squadron's 3 Troop. Led by Captain Robin Edwards, the patrol failed to reach the designated DZ, as its ten members encountered vast numbers of hostile Radfani tribesmen by the time they entered Gap Badge. They were forced to withdraw and while retreating Captain Edwards and his signaller, Trooper Nick Warburton, were killed. After an orderly 24-hour retreat, the rest of the patrol were able to make it back to British lines. The rebel tribesmen took a grisly revenge.[28] The heads of the two SAS men were chopped off by the guerrillas and were later displayed in north Yemen.[29]

The intensity of fire in the area showed that the paratroopers would be facing numerically superior enemy forces immediately after landing. From an estimated 30,000 Rafdanis a 'band' of 7,000 fighters could be mobilized.[30] The planned drop was therefore cancelled and the operation went on without it.[31] Elements of 3 Para and 45 Commando crossed part of the mountainous Rafdan region on the night of 30 April/1 May. On their way, on a number of occasions they had to use ropes to either go up or down the cliffs. In the fight against local tribesmen the following day the British were covered by RAF Hawker Hunter fighter-bombers striking enemy positions with rockets. Later in the afternoon, RM Commandos drove the Rafdani snipers off the overhanging heights. When the area was eventually secured, the paratroopers and marines were relieved by an infantry battalion and were withdrawn to Aden. On 11 May, reconnaissance was stepped up with 'A' Squadron SAS mounting a number of successful intelligence-gathering missions in and around the Wadi Taym area.

In mid-May, a paratrooper/RM Commando force, led by a 3 Para officer, Lieutenant Colonel Anthony Farrar-Hockley, was assigned to clear and secure in a concerted operation the Bakri (Bakari) Ridge, housing significant rebel chieftains. On the night of 16/17 May, 'C' Company, 3 Para, led by Major Anthony Ward-Booth, advanced towards the highest point of Qudeishi, supported by elements of 1st Parachute Battery Royal Horse Artillery. RAF Hawker Hunters were also attacking enemy positions, using 3in high-explosive rockets as well as their 30mm cannon. The rebel fortification was eventually captured by the paratroopers. On 18 May, the combined force advanced as far as Wadi Dhubsan, an area never before penetrated by federal forces. This operation was intended to be a 'demonstration of force', during which grain stocks were to be destroyed. When the battalion began to expand their positions in the area, the Radfani resistance hardened.

On the night of 24/25 May, the paratroopers had to use 30ft ropes to abseil down the rock face. Having descended in the darkness, they surprised the guerrillas stationed in the village of Wadi Dhubsan. By 06.00 the village had been cleared without a shot being fired. By now, 'X' Company of 45 Commando was advancing on the right side of Wadi Dhubsan. Meanwhile, 'A' Company, 3 Para, was pushing along towards the heights to the left. The Bakri tribesmen were shooting accurately at 800yds (732m) range. In the afternoon 'C' Company, 3 Para, were able to overcome the tribesmen's well-concealed defences by marching round from Jebel Haqla. They did it so rapidly that the Radfani fighters covering the left flank of their forces were taken completely by surprise, but they stayed fighting until their positions were bombed by RAF Hunters. The Radfani fighters were forced to withdraw, leaving six dead behind. For the next 48 hours, villages in the area of Wadi Dhubsan were searched by paratroopers and marines. Several rebel tribesmen were killed.

On 28 May, the British began the long climb out of the wadi. On the heights, Wessex helicopters, operating from HMS *Centaur*, landed to lift RM commandos and paratroopers back to Aden. Future missions, involving 'A', 'B' and 'D' Squadrons, 22 SAS, on rotation from Borneo, were mainly concerned with establishing covert observation posts to keep track of enemy movements.[32] This role became particularly important as enemy activity intensified. The SAS were also assigned counter-insurgency missions against rebels and their supporters in the Radfan region. Small teams were inserted into enemy territory at night to establish concealed observation posts high on the rocky slopes, from where they directed air and artillery strikes against guerrillas moving through the passes.[33]

The SAS was also assigned missions in the port of Aden, where troopers in twos and threes, disguised as Arabs and carrying only a shotgun under their *futah* (robe), infiltrated the Crater and Sheikh Othman districts. Operating from the Khormaksar district, near Aden airport, between 1966 and 1967, a 20-strong SAS team, including Arab-looking Fijian members of the Regiment, was after NLF men assigned to kill British soldiers or their informers. In one of the last actions of the war a patrol from 1 Troop, 'A' Squadron SAS, operating near the Yemeni border at Dhi Hirran, called in an air strike against guerrillas trying to infiltrate the Federation of South Arabia.[34] The only tangible value of the conflict in Aden for the SAS was the acquisition of valuable experience in urban counter-terrorist warfare. Terrorist incidents in South Arabia had increased from thirty-five in 1964 to nearly 3,000 in 1967.[35] Between 1963 and 1967, the British military lost fifty-seven killed and suffered another 651 casualties in South Arabia.[36] The Egyptian and North Yemeni casualties in the same period were estimated at about 50,000.[37] No estimates are available for the Federal casualties.

The British forces adopted a policy of gradual withdrawal in their former colony. The date of leaving was set for November 1967. Less than a month earlier, the federal government collapsed. Belated arrangements for the transfer of power to the NLF were made in Geneva in mid-November. On 29 November, the last British soldiers were transferred by helicopter to ships waiting offshore. The RMs who were the first to occupy Aden in 1839 were also the last to leave after 128 years. On 30 November, the People's Republic of Southern Yemen (later renamed the People's Republic of Yemen) officially declared its independence. Before long, the new regime was supporting the overthrow of the neighbouring regime of the pro-British Sultan of Oman. In 1968,

2 Para was deployed to Hong Kong to counter illegal immigration from the People's Republic of China.

The Congo (1960–1965)

Hundreds of Western hostages held by rebels in the Congo in 1965 and 1978 were liberated in rescue operations carried out by parachute forces. For two of these operations paratroopers were flown in from Belgium to the Belgian former colony in USAF transport planes. Belgian paratroop units that were garrisoned in the African country long before it gained independence were also involved in hostage-rescue missions. These units were the 2nd, the 4th and the 6th Para-Commando Battalions, belonging to the Belgian Army's Para-Commando Regiment.[38] In the riots of 4 January 1959, when the Congo was still a colony of Belgium, the 2nd Para-Commando Battalion was dispatched urgently to Léopoldville, in the north-west of the country, for a whole month to maintain order. Léopoldville, renamed Kinshasa, later became the capital of the independent (Democratic) Republic of the Congo.

By 1960, a cadre of the battalion with new recruits had formed the 4th Para-Commando Battalion, which was deployed to Rwanda-Urundi (Urundi became independent as Burundi in 1962). From there, it was mobilized for operations in the nearby Congo. The 6th Para-Commando Battalion, garrisoned at Kitona in Bas-Congo, a north-western province, was raised in the same way. In July, the 4th Para-Commando Battalion was sent to Goma to seize an airfield. One company was parachuted into Bunia, another provincial capital in eastern Congo, to free hostages held by rebels. Three paratroopers were killed in the operation. In July, about 3,000 Belgian Para-Commandos intervened in a number of Congolese cities to facilitate the evacuation of Western nationals and the disarmament of mutineers from the newly-formed Congolese National Army (CNA). In January 1961, a company of the 4th Para-Commando Battalion repelled an attack of the CNA on the Goma airfield, losing one man. The battalion was disbanded on 10 October 1962.

The Congo was granted independence on 1 July 1960, without the benefit of a transitionary period which Belgium could use to prepare the Congolese for their future. For the next five years in the former Belgian colony, because of the civil war tormenting most parts of the country, hundreds of fleeing Europeans and Americans found themselves in extremely dangerous situations, if not in desperate need of protection. The Simba ('Lion' in Swahili) rebellion began in early 1964. By August, the rebels, who wanted the secession of eastern and western regions from the newly-independent (Democratic) Republic of the Congo, had captured Stanleyville (later to be renamed Kisangani). Later in the month, the Congolese Army, spearheaded by central government-hired English-speaking and French-speaking mercenary units, were making headway against the rebels.

The mercenary units involved in the fighting in Congo in 1964 were the '5th Commando' led by a British ex-colonel, Michael (Mike) Hoare, and the '6th Commando', led by a Belgian ex-colonel, Frederic Vanderland. Sensing defeat, the rebel militias took hostages from the local white population in areas under their control in Stanleyville, in Paulis and in other towns. Congolese authorities then turned to the Belgian and the United States governments for assistance. Years later, it became known that among the hostages in Stanleyville were three CIA and two State Department officials.[39] Combat rescue operations were then planned in Brussels by Belgian army, US Army and USAF staff officers, code-named Dragon Rouge, Dragon Noir, Dragon Blanc and Dragon Vert. The Belgian army would provide personnel for the airdrops and the United States Air Force in Europe (USAFE) the necessary planes. Of the four operations planned, two were finally carried out. The green light for Operations Dragon Rouge and Dragon Noir was given on 13 November, but a delay became necessary. The formation providing the paratroopers, the Para-Commando Regiment, had to parade in Brussels three days later, during the King's birthday celebrations.

Five hundred and forty-five paratroopers, eight jeeps and twelve motorized tricycles were transported to Congo in twelve Lockheed C-130 Hercules aircraft.[40] They arrived at Kamina airfield by way of Torrehon in Spain and Ascension Island, a British overseas territory in the Atlantic Ocean. At 16.00 on 24 November, 230 paratroopers, including a company from the Congo-based Belgian 2nd Para-Commando Battalion, were dropped from five C-130Es onto the Stanleyville airfield. They suffered four casualties during the jump. Two Congolese Air Force Martin B-26 Marauder light bombers were flying over the immediate area throughout the operation, tasked with rendering fire support on demand. Within 50 minutes, the paratroopers had captured the airfield, forcing the rebel forces to retreat, and had the runway cleared of obstacles. The planes transporting heavy equipment were then able to land. Meanwhile, the paratroopers, having left a platoon to guard the airfield, were advancing rapidly towards Stanleyville.

At the same time, Congolese army units as well as a mercenary force were heading from a different direction towards Stanleyville, where a total of 800 non-Congolese hostages were held by the rebels. Among them were twenty American nationals, including five consular officials.[41] Paratroopers were the first to arrive. The moment they became aware of the arrival of the paratroopers, the rebels murdered twenty-eight of the hostages and ran away – almost without a fight. In total, at least eighty Western nationals were killed by retreating rebels that day. After clearing Stanleyville of any Western national they could find, with the support of Congolese soldiers and many mercenaries, who had arrived in the meantime, the paratroopers withdrew to a stream west of the city to defend the airfield until the evacuation was completed. Seven C-130Es took off loaded with about a hundred of the liberated hostages. Among those transferred next were the wounded hostages and rescuers. One of the five wounded paratroopers died while being evacuated.[42] The evacuation phase of Operation Dragon Rouge went on for two days during which a total of 2,200 refugees, including 400 pro-Belgian Africans, were moved to safety.[43]

Two days later, US and Belgian armed forces cooperated in another operation to rescue nearly 400 Western hostages held near Paulis, about 240 miles (386km) from Stanleyville. Operation Dragon Noir was planned using the area's airfield as a drop zone. The force selected for the airborne assault were 240 men plus two radio jeeps and four armoured jeeps. They jumped from seven C-130Es and had captured and secured the airfield within 30 minutes. The paratroopers were lucky enough to quickly discover where the hostages were held. The rebels murdered nearly thirty detainees and disappeared before the rescuers' arrival. In three days, motorized patrols liberated 355 hostages at scattered locations in the Paulis area. They were flown out on eight USAF planes. During the operation, one paratrooper was killed and seven more were wounded. Then, in Washington the Johnson administration decided not to stage any more such operations.[44] In 1965, with the rebels having lost their effectiveness and after five years of turbulence, Major General Joseph D. Mobutu used his position as *Armée Nationale Congolaise* (ANC – Congolese National Army) chief-of-staff to seize power in a coup d'état. On 16 May 1968, Mobutu raised a parachute brigade of two regiments (each of three battalions).[45]

In October 1971, the country changed its name to the Republic of Zaire. In early May 1978, Marxist guerrillas stormed Shaba (later named Lualamba) in the south-east of the country. They were members of the Front for the National Liberation of the Congo (FNLC), who had been trained by Cuban and East German instructors in Mozambique and had invaded this ore-rich region by way of neutral Zambia. On 11 May, the rebels had captured Kolowezi, a mining town, where they took 3,000 Europeans, mostly Belgian and French nationals, hostage. The Congolese 311th Paratrooper Battalion was sent against the invaders but failed to repel them.[46] The battalion lost fourteen killed and eight wounded. After that, President Mobutu requested foreign assistance. Units of French Foreign Legion's 2e *Régiment Étranger de Parachutistes* (2e REP – 2nd Foreign Parachute Regiment) and the Belgian Army's Para-Commando Regiment were sent to the Congo for the rescue of the European nationals in a combined operation.

At 14.30 on 19 May, 381 French paratroopers jumped over Kolwezi from C-130 transport planes (Operation Bonite) and landed under enemy fire on the town's horse-racing track. Six men were wounded on landing with a seventh falling in the hands of the guerrillas, who killed him on the street and mutilated him before even removing his parachute.[47] At the initial stage of the operation, two teams from the 13e *Régiment de Dragons Parachutistes* (13e RDP – 13th Parachute Dragoon Regiment) and one team from the 1er *Régiment de Parachutistes d'Infanterie de Marine* (1er RPIMa – 1st Marine Parachute Infantry Regiment) were deployed on observation and reconnaissance missions. The drop of the rest of the regiment was cancelled with the C-130s landing in Lubumbashi, 155 miles (250km) south-east of Kolwezi. Three and a half hours later, the Congolese mining-town was under French control. The following morning at 07.00, the second jump was conducted with 250 Legionnaires landing east of Kolwezi. The rebels, sandwiched between the outskirts of the town and the 'second wave' of French paratroopers, had no option but to withdraw. Later in the day, Belgian paratroopers air landed at Kolwezi airfield, which had been secured by their French colleagues. They immediately marched towards the town 3.7m (6km) away, where 60 Europeans and about 100 Africans had been massacred by the rebels before their retreat. After the arrival of the Belgian paratroopers in Kolwezi, the evacuation of refugees started. Over 2,000 Europeans and about 3,000 pro-Western Congolese were eventually flown to safety. A total of 700 Africans and 170 Europeans lost their lives between 19 and 21 May. During the rescue operation, the French suffered five paratroopers killed, twenty wounded and six missing in action. The Belgians had one paratrooper killed. The rebel casualties in the Battle of Kolwezi were 250 killed and 160 captured.[48]

The Dominican Republic (1965–1966)

In April 1965, United States President Lyndon B. Johnson sent an expeditionary force to the Dominican Republic, including paratroopers and marines. He was concerned that Communists in this Caribbean island were about to take control. Having seen President Eisenhower criticized for 'losing' Cuba and Kennedy almost humiliated by the Bay of Pigs failure, Johnson seemed determined that no similar such disaster would befall him. There would be no second Cuba, he had stated.[49] It was the first US military intervention in Latin America in thirty years. In the Dominican Republic, the second-largest Caribbean nation (after Cuba), political instability was endemic since the assassination of dictator Rafael Trujillo four years earlier. Juan Emilio Bosch, the elected President, was overthrown after a military coup and two years later the growing dissatisfaction resulted another coup – this time by pro–Bosch military officers. Allegations of foreign support for the rebels, who had already controlled the capital, Santo Domingo, brought forward the US military intervention in the civil war-torn Dominican Republic. A 42,000-strong expeditionary force was mobilized by the Americans in the framework of Power Pack, as their involvement in the Dominican civil war was code-named.

On 26 April, a US naval task force arrived off the Dominican coast. Two days later, when the evacuation of American and other foreign nationals from Santo Domingo had been completed, more than 500 marines came ashore. On 29 April, 114 Lockheed C-130 Hercules, carrying paratroopers and equipment, took off from Pope Air Force Base in North Carolina.[50] They were to land at Ramey Air Base in Puerto Rico, but when it became known that St Isidro, a Dominican airfield, was controlled by 'Royalist' (friendly) forces, thirty-three of the planes, those carrying the 3rd Brigade of the 82nd Airborne Division, were sent to land there. The C-130s which were transporting equipment continued their flight to Puerto Rico. The paratroopers air landed at St Isidro airfield at 02.15. Meanwhile, in the United States the 101st Airborne Division and the rest of the 82nd Airborne Division were ready to intervene if necessary.[51] In the Dominican Republic, a further 1,500 marines had also come ashore. At St Isidro, the 1st Battalion of the 505th Infantry Regiment (Airborne), secured the airfield, while the 1st Battalion of the 508th Infantry Battalion (Airborne) moved in two columns towards the Duarte Bridge. In fifteen minutes, the paratroopers had made contact with 'Royalist' forces and by late afternoon had secured a power plant and both banks of the Ozama River. Meanwhile, a platoon from the 82nd Airborne was helicoptered to Embajador to assist marines defending a nearby landing zone. Departing from the eastern part of the river, paratroop units moved all the way south into San Souci. There they established positions upon an eight-storey silo overlooking the rebel forces' stronghold in downtown San Domingo. Sniper fire accounted for the majority of the US casualties throughout the intervention. At the same time, the marines were conducting their respective missions. They didn't use their tanks – the same applies to the paratroopers who had left their armour back at Fort Bragg.[52] There was also a prohibition on the use of artillery. The marines secured and held an area containing the buildings of most foreign embassies.

The rebel forces were estimated at 1,500 regular troops and 5,000 armed civilians, supported by at least five tanks. While 80 per cent of the rebels were trapped in Ciudad Nueva with no prospect of achieving a military victory, the Organization of American States (OAS) Council made a call for a truce. The first cease-fire agreement was agreed upon, the following day, by US officials, 'Royalists' and the 'Constitutionalist' rebels. The second ceasefire agreement was signed on 5 May. By that time, the US troop build-up in the Dominican Republic had reached its peak at 24,000. Under the pact of Santo Domingo, the OAS was tasked with overseeing the implementation of the peace deal. A day later, OAS member states established the Inter-American Peace Force (IAPF) to be serve as a peace-keeping formation in the Dominican Republic. The IAPF consisted of 1,748 Brazilian, Paraguayan, Nicaraguan, Costa Rican, Salvadoran and Honduran troops, commanded by Brazilian Army General Hugo Panasco Alvim. Lieutenant General Bruce Palmer was appointed deputy commander, as a 6,000-US force was to remain in the Caribbean country for some time.

The withdrawal of American troops from the Dominican Republic started on 26 May with the marines leaving by 4 June. Eleven days later, the rebels launched a desperate attempt to expand the boundaries of their Santo Domingo stronghold. It was the bloodiest battle of the entire intervention fought after the withdrawal of the US Marine forces from the country. Five killed and thirty-one wounded was the casualty rate for the paratroopers in two days of fierce fighting. In the end, the US forces seized and retained an area of thirty square blocks of rebel territory in downtown Santo Domingo. After that, the end of the civil war in the country was a matter of days. Of the 44,348 US personnel deployed during the conflict in the Caribbean island, 47 were killed and 283 were wounded.[53] Among the killed, thirteen were paratroopers and ten were marines. The 'Royalist' forces had 500 soldiers and 325 gendarmes killed. Six hundred was the estimated death rate for the rebels. Ten thousand Dominican civilians lost their lives during the conflict. Eleven wounded was the casualty rate for the IAPF. In the elections, held in July 1966, Joaquín Balaguer won and remained in power for the next twelve years. The Inter-American peacekeepers had left the country by 15 September.

Chad (1969–1993)

In 1965, civil war erupted in Chad – five years after this central African country became independent – with northern Muslim rebels fighting the (southern) central government.[54] The main rebel force was the *Front de Libération Nationale du Tchad* (Frolinat – National Liberation Front of Chad), which remained active until 1993. By 1968, the revolt had extended to most of the country. Chadian President François Tombalbay was eventually forced to ask for help from France. Some 3,000

French soldiers, including paratroopers, were deployed to Chad for an operation code-named Bison. Elements of French Foreign Legion's 2e REP arrived in the country in April 1969 to support the government forces. No combat jumps have been conducted during France's involvement in Chad – only a few parachute drops were performed, involving mostly small detachments. The main characteristic of the tactics applied by the French against the insurgents was the use of airpower for ground support. It was something similar to what the United States were doing at the time in Vietnam. This tactic helped the French to win every engagement with the rebels with their 20mm helicopter-mounted cannon.[55] In July 1971, the French ceased direct military involvement until 28 August 1972, when Operation Bison was officially considered over. The operation, which cost five lives among the servicemen deployed, did not succeed to destroying the insurgency which promptly took on new vigour when the French departed.

In 1976, Libya openly supported the Frolinat rebels and two years later a pro-Marxist insurgency movement became active in southern Chad. French troops, including paratroopers from the 2e REP, had to return to central Africa to protect French lives in an operation code-named Tacaud.[56] In May 1978, elements of the 2e REP captured and held a town called Ati, west of the country's capital, Ndjamena. In June 1978, a French Air Force Sepecat Jaguar attack aircraft was shot down, but the pilot ejected and was later recovered by a Search and Rescue (SAR) helicopter.[57] Throughout 1978, helicopters and fighters were deployed extensively to defend central Chad.[58] In December 1980, Libyan troops entered the country at the request of the then Chadian government.

On 6 January 1981, Libya and Chad decided to unite. The merger plan caused strong adverse reaction in Africa and was immediately condemned by France and other Western countries as a menace to African unity. Libyan troops were withdrawn from Chad in November 1981. In June 1982, rebel forces led by Hissene Habre, captured the capital N'Djamena and forced the pro-Libyan President Goukouni Queddei to flee the country in November 1981. Two years later, 3,000 troops were dispatched to Chad, including paratroopers, to assist Habre in opposing the Libyan-backed rebels. On 3 July, Zaire sent a paratrooper detachment to Libya, which was later increased to about 2,000 men. The Zairean paratroopers were deployed chiefly around N'Djamena. The deployment of the French and Zairean troops freed Chadian forces to fight the rebels.

In January 1984, the smouldering crisis became more acute when a French Air Force Jaguar was shot down by rebel forces using a SA-7 missile near the town of Zigey.[59] The pilot, Captain Michel Croci, was killed.[60] Until the end of the year, the French troops and aircraft were used only to defend N'Djamena.[61] France and Libya agreed to a simultaneous withdrawal of troops from Chad in September 1984, but the French had to return as Libyan troops chose to remain in the north of the country. French paratroopers were deployed to Faya-Largeau, a strategically important town with a nearby airfield, which had been the main objective of the Libyan forces ever since their invasion of the country.[62] The town was captured by the Libyans in 1975 and was retaken by government forces five years later. Libyan troops recaptured

Faya-Largeau in 1983 but had to withdraw three years later. On 18 February 1986, the 1st Company of the French Foreign Legion's 2e REP were dropped in a remote area between N'Djamena and the Aouzou Strip to search for the pilot of a Soviet-built Libyan Air Force Tu-22 fighter-bomber. The aircraft had crashed as a result of technical problems a day earlier on its return to base (Aouzou Strip), after having bombed the Chadian capital's airport. The following day, 200 French commandos took possession of a camp at Dubut near N'Djamena. The Libyan troops were driven from their last stronghold in Chad in 1987. France's military presence in the central African country went on until 2014.

Anguilla (1969)

British paratroopers were sent to Anguilla in March 1969 to restore order to the Caribbean island, whose population could not agree on an imposed decolonization decision. It all started in February 1967, when Britain, believing that federation was the right answer to Anguilla's problems as a mini-state, linked the 35-square-mile (91km²) island to its larger neighbour Saint Christopher and Nevis.[63] This led to revolts in this island lying east of Puerto Rico in the Caribbean Sea, as the English-speaking population preferred Anguilla to remain a British Overseas Territory.[64] In two referendums, on 11 July 1967 and on 6 February 1969, the Anguillans voted by a large majority against their island's incorporation to the unified dependency of St Christopher-Nevis-Anguilla.[65] Those objecting to the idea of Anguilla remaining under British rule, being organized and led by extremist politicians although they were proved by two referendums only to be a small minority, created an explosive situation across the island and particularly in its capital, The Valley. The goal of the revolution was not independence according to international law, but rather disassociation from the other two islands, although the rebels went as far as to declare the island the 'Republic of Anguilla'. Meanwhile, civil unrest had climaxed to armed insurrection. It forced British Prime Minister Harold Wilson to discuss 'military options' on 14 March 1969 in London during an emergency cabinet meeting.[66] The dispatch of a parachute battalion to the Caribbean island on a low-order mission was decided in that meeting – a decision criticized by most of the British and international press.

2 Para, minus 'B' Company, and other support units were prepared for deployment. The 'Anguilla Force' also included a half-squadron of Royal Engineers and detachments of the Royal Corps of Signals and Royal Army Medical Corps. Twenty-two members of London's Metropolitan Police were added to the force to assist with law enforcement. A proposition for an airborne assault was ruled out as the British did not want the operation to look like a military invasion. For the same reason, London started talking about a 'crisis' in Anguilla and not a revolution. To soften the political profile of the intervention, the paratroopers were to reach Anguilla on two Royal Navy frigates. They were prepared to find armed people ready to fight across the island. On 18 March 1969, a contingent of 300 paratroopers landed unopposed on Anguilla – a number of them were helicoptered ashore.[67] Moving inland simultaneously from Crocus and Road Bay, the British encountered some surprise and a good degree of

indignation among the locals. They met no resistance at all and the only weapon discovered was an old rifle. Civil unrest ceased in Anguilla and law and order were restored by the British without a single casualty. Two paratroopers were prosecuted for rape.[68] By mid-May, the paratroopers had withdrawn from the island. They were relieved by 2 Para's 'B' Company which remained in Anguilla until mid-September. The last British troops left the island in July 1971. The Anguilla crisis ended up as victory for the rebels, who succeeded in removing the island from the associated state. The Anguillans were formally allowed to secede from St Christopher and Nevis on 19 December 1988. While the other two islands went on to gain full independence from the United Kingdom, Anguilla preferred to remain a British Overseas Territory.[69]

Oman (1970–1976)

Elements of 22 SAS were deployed to this Arabian sultanate in 1970 to conduct a counter-insurgency against communist guerrillas. The revolt had been started by Muslim separatists in the western province of Dhofar eight years earlier. They were politically led by the Dhofar Liberation Front (DLF). The Omani army's two regiments, after deploying 1,000 soldiers to the province, were able to contain the rebellion. When the DLF were eventually influenced by the Marxist Peoples' Front for the Liberation of the Occupied Arabian Gulf (PFLOAG), things got out of hand for Sultan Said bin Taimur's repressive regime. In late 1967, the support to the rebels from the USSR and Red China had tipped the scales in their favour. Meanwhile, PFLOAG had taken control of the whole Jebel Dhofar, running parallel to the sea, where most Dhofaris lived. The Omani army had been driven from the mountains down to the coast and were restricted to four urban centres: Salalah, Rayzut, Taqa and Mirat. The Omani army did not have the manpower or training to wage an effective counter-insurgency campaign, so Sultan Said bin Taimur called on Britain for military aid. The first SAS detachments arrived in the sultanate in December 1969 and immediately started training the Omanis in counter-insurgency warfare. The detachments were officially named British Army Training Teams (BATTs) so that officials could deny that British combat units had been deployed to Oman. The first BATTs operated in Taqa and Mirbat. Seven months later, on 23 July 1970, the role of the British in Oman was upgraded when Sultan Said bin Taimur was deposed in a bloodless coup by his son Qaboos, who had been educated at the Royal Military Academy, Sandhurst. SAS men were assigned as bodyguards for the new sultan's protection.[70]

The new sultan asked the British to get more involved in the war against communism in his country, and in September, a full SAS squadron arrived in Oman. The SAS plans included also a 'hearts and minds' (propaganda) civil-aid programme, aiming at winning back the Dhofaris to the Sultan's cause. The Regiment realized that this was the key to winning the war rather than military might.[71] SAS personnel established and ran clinics in Dhofar for the local population and their animals. Advanced drilling equipment was brought from the United Kingdom to bore new wells and open up old ones that had been sealed on the former Sultan's orders. Qaboos bin Said Al-Said was persuaded by the British to declare a general amnesty in late summer. The amnesty granted by the new sultan, in combination with the SAS 'heart and minds' campaign, persuaded hundreds of rebels who were disillusioned with the communist interference in their cause or alienated by PFLOAG hardliners to surrender to the Omani authorities. Between September 1970 and March 1971, 200 *adoo* (guerrillas) gave themselves up. Furthermore, a vast number of Dhofaris, including former DLF fighters, volunteered for combat duties under the British. They eventually joined the *firqat*, irregular units, consisting of SAS-trained and -commanded ex-guerrillas.

Among them were former DLF chieftains like Salim Mubarak, whose idea it was to form these units. Each *firqat* had sixty-eight Dhofaris operating not like conventional infantry but usually as a reconnaissance formation. The units saw combat for the first time on 24 February 1972 in a combined operation, ending with the capture of Sudh, 19 miles (30km) east of Mirbat. By the end of the war, these units had a total strength of 2,000 men.[72] The counter-insurgency operations had started nearly four months earlier with an assault on Jebel Dhofar involving 800 men. The force, led by Lieutenant Colonel Johnny Watts, commanding officer of 22 SAS, included two SAS squadrons, two companies of the Omani Army and five *firqats*. Their mission was to drive the *adoo* off the Jebel Dhofar. On 2 October, one SAS squadron and two *firqats* captured and secured an old airfield at Lympne, 3.7 miles (6km) east of Jibjat. The airfield was used for reinforcements to be flown in. The following day, at Jibjat another enemy-held airstrip was taken by SAS and *firqat* elements after a fierce battle. The Watts' force was then ordered to advance down both the eastern and the western sides of the Wadi Darbat. Before long, the *adoo* were forced to clear off the plateau and take refuge into the wadis.

In March 1972, a joint SAS and *firqat* force mounted a probing operation during which the 'Eagle's Nest', a position of caves and ridges on the edge of the plateau, was taken despite heavy enemy attacks which lasted for a week.[73] This operation, code-named Jaguar, resulted in the Omani authorities establishing a stabilizing presence on Jebel Dhofar. It was a significant defeat for the *adoo*, as the coastal plain and its towns were left under government control. Other operations mounted at the time were Leopard in the west of Jebel Dhofar and Simba close to the border with Yemen. Then, barriers were constructed in four locations to cut off *adoo* supplies coming from the neighbouring People's Democratic Republic of Yemen.[74] The barriers consisted of barbed wire, booby traps, mines and ground sensors. In early summer, the *adoo* decided to mount an attack on Mirbat, a small town by the sea, in order to challenge the government's control of the coastal plains.[75] Mirbat was to be the scene of an epic battle between a handful of SAS men and several hundred communist guerrillas.

At 06.00 on 19 July, 250 *adoo* assaulted a BATT camp in Jebel Ali, outside the port of Mirbat. The camp was defended by nine SAS men, all from Eight Troop, 'B' Squadron. A 23-year-old captain, Mike Kealy, was the commanding officer. The attackers were armed with automatic rifles and a Carl Gustav rocket launcher. Although heavily outnumbered, the SAS men resisted stiffly. Staff Sergeant Talaiasi Labalaba was killed while operating a 25-pounder. Trooper Thomas Tobin replaced him only briefly in the gun-pit as he also received a fatal wound.[76] Meanwhile, Lance-Corporal

Harris was operating a mortar from the pit at the base of the building. The situation was desperate for the SAS men until *firqat* members who had been spending the night in Jebel Ali surprised the *adoo*. Almost at the same time, Omani aircraft appeared suddenly in the sky and helicopters landed on the shore, south-east of Mirbat, twenty-three men of 'G' Squadron, 22 SAS. The three CAC 167 Strikemaster light attack aircraft, flying low and strafing the enemy on the ground with their guns, provided badly-needed air support to the defenders. The *adoo* were eventually forced to retreat, leaving thirty of their fighters killed on the battlefield, although it is believed that many more later died of their wounds. The SAS losses were two killed and further two wounded. The Battle of Mirbat, as it went down in history, was the turning point of the war in Dhofar as its successful defence proved the worth of Sultan Qaboos bin Said Al-Said's policies and led to disagreements within the communist insurgency.[77] Though there would be another four years of fighting, PFLOAG was thereafter waging a losing battle.

After Mirbat, government agencies started to take over the duties of the BATTs. In 1973, an Iranian Special Forces battalion was deployed to guard one of the areas close to Oman's border with (communist) Yemen. The SAS cleared the area between Salalah and the Thamrait road. The following year, the *adoo* were cleared from all the valleys in central Dhofar by SAS troops and *firqat* teams. In October 1975, the Yemenis had withdrawn the regular troops they had deployed inside Oman to assist the *adoo*.[78] By 1975, the communist rebels had been pushed back to the Yemeni border. In September 1976, the SAS squadrons were withdrawn from Oman, signalling the successful end a war they had waged almost single-handedly.

East Timor (1975–1999)

Indonesia, after failing to incorporate Western New Guinea in the early 1960s, started to make claims on another of her neighbours: East Timor. On 7 October 1975, Indonesian forces, spearheaded by paratroopers, invaded this former Portuguese colony. The controversial occupation of East Timor by Indonesia lasted for nearly twenty-five years. *Operasi Seroja* (Operation Lotus) was the largest military operation carried out by Indonesian forces since their country's independence. Following a naval bombardment of Dili, the capital of East Timor, seaborne troops went ashore.[79] At the same time, 641 paratroopers jumped over Dili. Some 400 of them ended up casualties, after descending within the city or on top of retreating enemy militiamen.[80] Many were reported killed or wounded by friendly fire.[81] A total of 10,000 troops participated in the invasion.[82] By noon, Dili had been captured by the Indonesian forces and the heavily outnumbered East Timorese militiamen had fled to the mountains surrounding their country's coastal capital.[83] On 10 December, a second Indonesian invasion resulted in the capture of Baucau, East Timor's second-largest town. By Christmas Day, following an operation involving a 10,000-force, the towns of Liquisa and Maubara had also been seized. In April 1976, some 35,000 Indonesian soldiers were garrisoned in East Timor with a further 10,000 standing by in (Indonesian) West Timor. A large portion of these troops belonged to Indonesia's elite commands. The Indonesian occupation of East Timor was characterized by an extremely violent conflict between Indonesia's military and East Timorese guerrillas struggling for the liberation of their country. After nearly twenty-five years of brutal repression at the hands of the occupation forces, the East Timorese were able to vote overwhelmingly for independence from Indonesia in a referendum held in 1999 in East Timor under the auspices of the United Nations. Their country became an independent state on 10 May 2002 as the Democratic Republic of Timor-Leste.

Djibouti (1976)

In 1976 parachute-trained soldiers and gendarmes carried out the first overseas anti-terrorist operation in French history. On 3 February, a bus carrying thirty French schoolchildren was attacked and hijacked by four militants in Djibouti, the capital of French Somaliland, in the Horn of Africa. The kidnappers were members of the Somali Coast Liberation Front (SCLF), a guerrilla organization aiming at liberating French Somaliland and connecting it to neighbouring Somalia. The bus driver was forced to go to Loyada, 11 miles (18km) south-east of Djibouti, and stop within 197 yards (180m) of the Somali border. It was immediately surrounded by elements of the 13th Demi-Brigade of the French Foreign Legion (FFL), which was stationed to French Somaliland at the time. Another unit of the FFL, the 2nd Company of the 2e REP, deployed to the Horn of Africa since December 1975, also rushed to the area. The Legionnaires, including the paratroopers, entrenched themselves in a palm grove situated some 270 yards (250m) from the bus. Before long, the terrorists demanded the immediate release of all imprisoned SCLF members and the end of French rule in the area otherwise they would start killing the schoolchildren.

As negotiations between the local French commander and the terrorist were dragging on in the desert heat, a crack counter-terrorist unit, the *Groupe d'Intervention de la Gendarmerie National* (GIGN – National Gendarmerie Intervention Group), were on their way from France. This unit, which had been established two years earlier, was highly trained and expert in a wide range of military skills, including parachuting.[84] The French Foreign Legion's GOLE, a battalion-size intervention force that had been raised in Corsica four years earlier, was also deployed to Djibouti because of the school bus highjack. A team of GIGN snipers arrived in Djibouti in the morning of 4 February and immediately joined the French forces close to the hijacked bus. The team consisted of nine men – eight snipers and Lieutenant (later Major) Christian Prouteau, the founder and first commander of the GIGN. Meanwhile, Somali troops and armed SCLF militants had taken up positions behind the wire on the Somali side of the border, having their guns pointed at the French army and security forces personnel. At 14.00, a meal laced with tranquillizers was sent to the bus for the schoolchildren. Almost three hours later, when it was visible in the snipers' sights that the schoolchildren had fallen asleep inside the bus, the order for the assault was given. At 15.45, the snipers eliminated the kidnappers with coordinated shots. At once, a group of paratroopers ran and seized the bus while two more groups advanced and seized the border. The Somali soldiers and the SCLF militants, spotting the French assault, opened fire on the paratroopers, but it was too little and too late for the kidnappers and their cause.

By 16.05, the rescue operation was over. The children were safe except a schoolgirl who was wounded in an explosion and eventually died of her injuries. The driver and a female children's escort were wounded. In the firefight that erupted briefly between forces from both sides of the border several SCLF militants were killed or wounded. The French casualties included Lieutenant Doucet, commander of the 1st Platoon, 2nd Company, 2e REP, who was seriously wounded. When the GOLE force arrived in Djibouti, it was all over, but they were ordered to remain there for the next four months to strengthen France's military presence in the area. A few months later, GIGN's sister unit, the *Escadron Parachutiste d'Intervention de la Gendarmerie Nationale* (EPIGN – the National Gendarmerie Parachute Squadron), was deployed to Djibouti, where it provided security to the referendum that led to the independence of Afars and Issas (formerly French Somaliland).

Chapter 16

Airborne Forces and the Vietnam War

A few hundred combat jumps, most of which were medium or small scale, were conducted in South East Asia during the war in Vietnam and the civil wars in neighbouring Laos and Cambodia. South Vietnamese paratroopers carried out most of the airborne operations or missions in Indochina between 1960 and 1975, although the general opinion on this matter across the world is different because of the participation of two US airborne divisions in the war. Only four combat jumps were conducted in Vietnam exclusively by American paratroopers or marines. At least eight airborne operations or missions involved US, South Vietnamese and Australian troops. One combat jump is attributed to Australian paratroopers alone. Finally, fourteen missions involving American and South Vietnamese military personnel were sponsored by the CIA.

The civil war in South Vietnam, in which North Vietnamese troops were eventually involved, began in November 1955 and formally lasted nineteen years. This is the second of the Indochina Wars after the one that led in the withdrawal of French colonial forces from South East Asia in 1956. Vietnam had been divided into two, with a communist regime in the north under Ho Chi Minh and a pro-Western democracy in the south under Ngo Dinh Diem. Direct US military involvement in South Vietnam begun in 1965 and lasted until 1973. In August 1964, US Congress passed the South East Asia Resolution, which allowed President Lyndon B. Johnson to conduct military operations in the region without a declaration of war. It was in response to an alleged attack on a US warship in the Gulf of Tonkin by a North Vietnamese torpedo boat. On 2 March 1965, US aircraft commenced bombing targets in North Vietnam – coinciding with the deployment of ground forces in South Vietnam. The so-called 'Americanization' of the Second Indochina Conflict had begun. This conflict, which also including the Laotian and the Cambodian civil wars, ended in 1975 with all three countries of the Indochinese Peninsula becoming communist states.

It is little known that Ho Chi Minh, the victor of the Vietnam Wars, had briefly been a United States ally during the Second World War and that he reportedly owed his life to an American paratrooper. On July 1945, a seven-man OSS team, led by Major Allison Thomas, parachuted into Ho Chi Minh's jungle headquarters at Tan Trao area, north of Hanoi.[1] The US Army provided the Vietnamese communist guerrillas, who were called Viet Minh at that time, with small arms and explosives in their struggle against the Japanese occupation forces. Furthermore, the OSS team's medic, Lieutenant Paul Hoagland, treated the guerrilla leader, who was very ill at the time. According to historian Cecil B. Currey, Hoagland may have saved Ho Chi Minh's life.[2] In return, the guerrillas assisted the United States by rescuing downed American pilots. The collaboration between the Americans and Ho Chi Minh's communist forces lasted less than a month – until the Japanese surrender on 15 August 1945. In early 1956, the US 187th ARCT was considered for an airdrop onto Dien Bien Phu to relieve the French forces, who were under severe pressure there at the final stage of the first Indochina War, but Eisenhower's administration decided against the engagement of American troops in combat. In fact, the US involvement in Indochina had begun in 1955 with the arrival in Saigon, in southern Vietnam, of a military training mission.

The direct participation of US Army personnel in South Vietnam's struggle against the Moscow- and Peking-supported Vietnamese communist guerrillas, known as the Viet Cong (VC), did not start until 1961. The United States had already 50,000 troops stationed in South Korea. In 1957, a 12-man mission from the US Army's 77th Special Forces Group Airborne (SFGA), arrived in South Vietnam to train the country's Special Forces, called the *Luc Luong Dac Biet* (LLDB). The Airborne, the Ranger and the Marine Divisions had soon developed into the most effective formations of the South Vietnamese armed forces. In 1962, President Kennedy agreed on the deployment of 400 Special Forces troops in South Vietnam. Military assistance was also provided to Laos and Cambodia.

The first camp of the green-bereted troopers of the US Army was established in Buon Emayo in the south of the country. In 1962, four-or five-man US–South Vietnamese teams were parachuted into North Vietnam to gather intelligence. Two such missions, code-named Dido and Echo, were carried out in June 1961 and a third seven months later. These missions were sponsored by the CIA. The United States decided to intervene in South East Asia, because another failure on her part to stop communist expansion, after the fiasco of the CIA-sponsored Bay of Pigs invasion in Cuba, would seriously damage US credibility with its allies and harm the reputation of the US President as leader of the Western World.[3] Kennedy was interested in using the Special Forces for counter-insurgency warfare in Third World countries threatened by communist insurgents, although they were originally intended for use behind the front lines after a conventional invasion of Western Europe by Soviet forces. He believed that the guerrilla tactics employed by the newly-raised elite units of the US Army's Special Forces and US Navy's SEALs would be effective in South East Asia. It is believed that Kennedy was briefed in counter-insurgency warfare by one of his advisors, General Maxwell D. Taylor.[4] Taylor had commanded the 101st Airborne Division during the Second World War.

The Green Berets (Special Forces) and the SEALs, whose troopers were qualified paratroopers, were assigned missions behind enemy lines or in enemy-controlled territories in Indochina, mostly in South Vietnam. They were operating in three- or four-man teams, employing unconventional warfare tactics. In case of problems, a twelve-man heliborne detachment was ready to rush to the team's rescue. The first time Americans participated in major combat in Vietnam was on 12 January 1962, when US Army Piacecki H-21 helicopters transported over a thousand South Vietnamese paratroopers for an assault on a suspected VC stronghold about 10 miles (16km) west of Saigon. The guerrillas were surprised and defeated, with the paratroopers capturing a sought-after radio transmitter. The Americans had no casualties in this operation, while the Viet Cong had six of their men killed. The first US Special Forces trooper killed in Vietnam was Sergeant Jimmy Gabriel. His team was attacked by numerically superior Viet Cong forces near An Chau, a village located 360 miles (579km) west of Saigon. Gabriel, who was gunned down by the enemy while calling for support on a radio, belonged to the 1st SFGA.

Combat Jumps

The first combat jump of the Vietnam War was conducted on 5 March 1962, when elements of South Vietnamese army's Airborne Division were parachuted onto Boc Tuk to reinforce a garrison. The first Vietnamese paratroopers had been trained by the French, who raised the first airborne company in Indochina in 1948. Many of these paratroopers had fought against Viet Minh communist forces between 1948 and 1956. Some of them had even survived the Battle of Dien Bien Phu and their subsequent detention in Ho Chi Minh's prisoner-of-war camps. As of 1951, members of the South Vietnamese Army's Ranger Group could also volunteer for parachute training. As qualified paratroopers, they were then admitted to the 7th Ranger Group, which was a component of the Airborne Division. The South Vietnamese Airborne Division was garrisoned in Tan Son near Saigon and its strength was 13,000 men in 1967, split into twelve battalions.[5] The South Vietnamese airborne division was decimated at a later phase of the war, during the Hue-Da Nang campaign.[6] Twenty more combat jumps were conducted by South Vietnamese paratroopers, following that of 5 March 1962.

On 2 January 1963, nearly 1,200 men from the Airborne Group (a four-battalion component of the Airborne Division) landed on Tay Ninh, during an unspecified operation. The next drop involved a thousand paratroopers, also from the Airborne Group, who landed in Ba Ria twenty-six days later. Airborne operations involving 1,181 South Vietnamese paratroopers were carried out in various combat zones on 13, 21 and 24 March 1963. On 4 June 1963, a raid was conducted on Bien Hoa by a 232-strong South Vietnamese Special Forces unit. On 10 September 1963, 500 South Vietnamese Rangers were parachuted in during a combined operation in Ca Mav area. The next combat jump was conducted in neighbouring Cambodia. A thousand men, also from the Airborne Group, were dropped in a border area called Parrots Beak on 20 October. On 24 November 1963, a battalion of the Airborne Group parachuted onto Ce Mau Pen. Five months later, on 12 April 1964, 584 paratroopers were dropped in Kien Long to reinforce the South Vietnamese positions in the area. The next combat jump was conducted in Laos in 1965 by a (South Vietnamese) Special Forces group, which remained on Laotian soil from 24 June to 1 July on a reconnaissance mission. On 3 August 1965, the Airborne Group's 3rd Parachute Battalion was dropped in Duc Co for reinforcement. Three operations were conducted between September and November 1965, starting with a combat assault in Ben Cat by the Airborne Group's 3rd, 5th and 6th Parachute Battalions. On 14 September, a 1,125-strong force, comprising the Airborne Group's 3rd and the 8th Parachute Battalions, jumped over Lai Khe on an unspecified mission. A raid by units of the South Vietnamese Airborne Group was executed in An Khe in mid-November 1965.

There was an interruption in airborne missions on the part of South Vietnamese from that date until late December 1971. On Christmas Day, two four-man Special Forces teams, using HALO [7] parachutes, landed on Cambodian soil on a reconnaissance mission. Three days later, two more teams jumped over Laos in the same way on a similar mission. In May 1972, two airborne missions were carried out by South Vietnamese paratroopers – the first on 4 May at Pleiku and the second twenty-four days later at Quang Tri. The last combat jump of the Vietnam War was conducted in mid-November 1972 in Kom Pong Trach by two teams of Vietnamese Special Forces on a reconnaissance mission.

Meanwhile, CIA-sponsored drops in North Vietnam for intelligence gathering were being carried out by joint US-South Vietnamese military teams. Eleven such missions were conducted in addition to the ones that have already been mentioned. In 1962, two drops were recorded – one in April and one in May. Ten drops were conducted in 1963 – in April (one), May (one), June (two), July (two), August (one), September (one), October (one) and December (one). In 1964, CIA-sponsored missions were carried out in May (one), June (two), July (three), October (one) and November (one). One drop was conducted in September 1965.

Essentially, the war in Vietnam began on 2 January 1963 with a battle involving regular VC troops and South Vietnamese forces at Ap Bac, a village located 35 miles (56km) south-west of Saigon. The battle was to have been a routine heliborne operation into the rice-rich Mekong Delta, but ended up a major victory for the communist rebels. A South Vietnamese force was tasked with destroying a Viet Cong radio transmitter at Ap Tan Thoi in Dih Tuong province. The helicopters, ten banana-shaped CH-21 Shawnees, supported by five UH-1 Huey gunships, were to carry one company at a time in three waves. The Civil Guard Battalions, a total force of 1,500 men, were to reach the target on foot. The helicopters landed 328 yards (300m) from Ap Bac to avoid enemy gunfire. At 07.00 the first wave of CH-21s off loaded the first soldiers, elements the 11th Infantry Regiment. From camouflaged foxholes behind the trees, about 350 VC regulars loosed a deadly barrage of machine-gun fire.[8] The helicopters were also riddled by fire and were downed. The air-landed soldiers were pinned down under heavy fire. At 13.30, the South Vietnamese 4th Mechanized Rifle Squadron was ordered up to the downed helicopters to rescue the troops and US crews, which were trapped to the south-west of Ap Bac. The Squadron's M113 armoured personnel carriers (APCs) failed to reach them and were forced to withdraw.[9] The use of airborne forces at Ap Bac was then decided.

Three hundred men of the South Vietnamese 8th Airborne Battalion were dropped from Fairchild C-123 Provider transport planes late in the afternoon. Trying to avoid enemy gunfire, the pilots dropped the paratroopers in front of the entrenched enemy positions instead of behind the Mechanized Rifle Squadron.[10] Several paratroopers were shot at while descending to the ground by the VC and a few more were stuck in trees. The remnants were pinned down and couldn't break the enemy's line of defence. By the end of the day, nineteen paratroopers had been killed and another thirty-three wounded or injured. Two US Army personnel who parachuted with the South Vietnamese, Captain Fletcher Ware and Sergeant Russel Kopti, were also wounded.[11] On 3 January, the VC positions were hit hard by an artillery barrage before South Vietnamese reinforcements started arriving from three directions. During the night of 2/3 January, the VCs, although encircled by a few thousand enemy troops, had managed to slip away through the rice fields, taking with them their dead and wounded comrades.[12] On 3 January, Ap Bac was therefore captured unopposed. It is believed that Colonel Huynh Van Cao, commander of the South Vietnamese forces in the area, had deliberately left an escape route for the VC as he wanted to halt the costly fighting for political reasons.[13] Eighty-three South Vietnamese were killed in the battle and over a hundred were wounded. VC casualties were limited although their positions were hit by artillery and napalm bombing. Three killed and eight wounded were the US casualties.[14] Of the fifteen helicopters directly involved in the operation, only one escaped undamaged. Five were downed or damaged.[15] Of the ten Shawnee troop carriers, four were knocked out of the sky. Of the five heavily-armed Hueys, all were hit. For the VC the Battle of Ap Bac marked the first time they stood and fought a large South Vietnamese formation despite being outnumbered by almost five to one.[16] A 350-strong VC force checked approximately 3,000 South Vietnamese troops.[17]

Two airborne divisions, the 101st and the 82nd, were among the nine US divisions (or twenty-five US Army brigades) that became involved in the Vietnam War. Of the 82nd Airborne's three brigades only one – the 3rd – was deployed in Vietnam. The 82nd Airborne Division was kept as a strategic reserve in case of a war against Soviet forces in Western Europe. While the 3rd Brigade was deployed in Vietnam, the division created a provisional 4th Brigade consisting of the 4th Battalion, 325th Infantry Regiment (Airborne), the 3rd Battalion, 504th Infantry Regiment (Airborne) and the 3rd Battalion, 505th Infantry Regiment (Airborne). These units, like all the PIR of the 82nd and the 101th Airborne Divisions, had been renamed Infantry Regiments (Airborne) in September 1957. By November 1963, there were 16,000 US troops in Vietnam – up from Eisenhower's 900 military advisors. They were mainly involved in search-and-destroy operations. By 1965, the number of American forces in South East Asia had risen to nearly 190,000. In July 1965, mixed patrols, each made up from two or three US Green Berets and ten South Vietnamese Special Forces troopers, were assigned missions. On 7 May 1965 the first airborne unit arrived in Vietnam, which was the 3rd Battalion, 506th Infantry Regiment (Airborne), 187th Airborne Brigade.[18] The brigade was a component of the 101st Airborne Division. The division's 1st Airborne Brigade was deployed there later, on 29 July. Units of the 3rd Brigade, 82nd Airborne Division, arrived in Vietnam in 1966. The 1st and 2nd Battalions, 503rd Infantry Regiment (Airborne), 173rd Brigade (Airborne) of the 82nd Airborne Division arrived in Vietnam along with the division's famous 3rd Battalion, 319th Field Artillery Regiment. The brigade performed combat duties in the Huphu Bai area before moving south of Saigon. They fought in the Mekong Delta and along the Cambodian border for a period of twenty-two months. The 101st Airborne's 187th Brigade (Airborne) was deployed there in December 1967. The Vietnam War witnessed the world's largest and longest troop airlift directly into a combat zone. It brought 10,356 men from the 101st Airborne Division more than 10,000 miles from their base at Fort Campbell in North Carolina to Bien Hoa in South Vietnam on 13 December 1967.[19] For the transportation of the division's 2nd and 3rd Airborne Brigades a total of 373 C-141 Starlifter and 20 C-133 Cargomaster aircraft were used. Paratroopers took part in major campaigns and battles. They also conducted numerous air-assault operations and search-and-destroy missions. Every airborne unit had a tour of duty in southeast Asia. The 173rd Airborne Brigade, 82nd Airborne's 2nd Battalion, 503rd Infantry Regiment (Airborne), participated in the only combat jump conducted by US forces during the Vietnam War.[20] It was also one of the last units to leave the country after the Vietnamization of the war in 1971. The first operation involving US paratroopers was carried out north-east of Saigon between 31 May and 3 June 1965 by units of the 173rd Brigade (Airborne). The brigade was assigned seven more operations that year. The first combat operation assigned to a unit of the 101st Airborne Division (the newly arrived 1st Brigade) was carried out between 10 and 21 August 1965 south-west of Nha Trang, the capital of Khan Hoa Province.[21] Until the end of the year, the 1st Brigade, 101st Airborne Division, was involved in eight more combat operations.

In April 1966, a three-man US team parachuted in a remote area on a Combat Search and Rescue (CSAR) mission. It was the first drop conducted by the US military in the Vietnam War. Two months later, on 14 June, a 13-man team from the US Marines' 1st Reconnaissance Company landed by parachute near Chi Lai to establish an outpost. Another parachute drop was executed by US Marine paratroopers on 17 November 1969, when six men of Team-51 jumped over Nui Tran on a reconnaissance mission. The only combat jump involving exclusively US paratroopers was conducted on 22 February 1967, when 745 men from the 173rd Airborne Brigade landed in Ka Tum to reinforce ground forces. The operation saw three brigades comprising eight battalions being dropped by transport planes or being delivered by helicopter into War Zone 3 in Tay Ninh Province in the south-east of South Vietnam, close to the border with Cambodia.[22] During the battle, the brigade operated at the north-eastern part of the War Zone along with the US 196th Infantry Brigade. The operation, code-named Junction City, was a success and the battered enemy division was forced to retreat.[23]

A combat jump was also conducted by Australian paratroopers in Vietnam. On 15 December 1969, a ten-man pathfinder team of the Australian Army's 3rd SAS parachuted in Phuoc Tuy to prepare the dropping zone. The following morning, approximately 100 Australian SAS troopers were dropped in the area to participate in a raid. Australian SAS squadrons were rotated in Vietnam from 1966 to 1971.[24] Combat jumps involving US, South Vietnamese and Australian paratroopers have also been reported during the Vietnam War. On 27 December 1966, about 1,200 men from the South Vietnamese Airborne Group and thirty-three US military advisors landed by parachute in Chuong Thien. A jump involving 350 South Vietnamese paratroopers and twenty-nine American advisors was conducted four months later for the establishment of a Special Forces camp. On 5 October 1967, some 274 South Vietnamese and thirty-five US and Australian paratroopers were dropped in Bu Prang, participating in a raid code-named Blue Max. During 1970, four or six-man US–South Vietnamese teams, which were assigned reconnaissance missions, conducted static-line parachute jumps in Cambodia and Laos. These missions were carried out in Cambodia on 10 January, 21 January and 21 February and in Laos on 23 August, 9 September and 11 September. On 28 September 1970, a US–South Vietnamese team jumped over Laos using HALO parachutes. The reconnaissance missions in Laos and Cambodia went on throughout 1971. Static-line drops were conducted by US–South Vietnamese Special Forces teams in Laos on 10 February 1971 and in Cambodia in February, April and May 1971. HALO parachutes were used by the participants in a reconnaissance mission carried out by another US–South Vietnamese team in February 1971.

In June 1966, the Long-Range Reconnaissance Patrols (LRRPs or 'Lurps') were created by the 1st Cavalry Division (Airmobile), the 1st Brigade, 101st Airborne Division, and other formations. On 25 September 1967, 'E' Company and 'F' Company were activated as 20th Infantry (Airborne) and 51st Infantry (Airborne). These units penetrated deep into the jungle in their distinctive tiger-stripe uniforms to conduct reconnaissance, ambushes and more. The nucleus of these unit came from 1st Brigade, 101st Airborne Division's LRRP Platoon, and 173rd Airborne Brigade, 82nd Airborne Division's LRRP platoon.[25] On 15 December 1968, a LRRP was also created by the 82nd Airborne Division. On 1 February 1969, the LRRP companies and detachments were re-designated as lettered companies of the 75th Ranger Infantry Regiment.

In mid-1965, the US Army recognized the need for more unconventional warfare, following a proposal by the then Major David Hackworth, an officer of the 101st Airborne Division.[26] In November 1965, Hackworth raised the 50-strong Tiger Force, the most decorated platoon-sized unit in the US Army.[27] The unit was part of the 1st Battalion, 1st Brigade, 101st Airborne Division. By 1969, such units had been formed in the 75th Regiment, US Rangers. Tiger Force was initially assigned reconnaissance missions. By the end of the war, the unit had killed approximately 1,000 enemy soldiers.[28] In 1968, elements of the Tiger Force allegedly carried out atrocities such as torture and executions of prisoners, killing unarmed South Vietnamese villagers, including women and children, collecting the scalps of victims, etc. Those accused of committing such crimes were not tried but were allowed to resign from the army.[29] The journalist who disclosed these atrocities, Michael D. Sallah, of the *Toledo Daily Blade* in Ohio, was awarded the 2004 Pulitzer Price for investigative reporting.

Airborne Units in Air Assault and Ground Operations

The first air assaults of the Vietnam War were conducted by South Vietnamese paratrooper and Ranger forces on 5 January and 27 April 1964. On the first occasion, 115 helicopters carried over 1,000 elite troops to their objective. On the second, paratroopers and Rangers were deployed by helicopter west of Quang Ngai, close to the border with Kon Tum province. The first air assault involving US forces was carried out on 8 November 1965. It was during this operation that elements of the

173rd Airborne Brigade were ambushed by over 1,200 VC fighters near Hill 65, east of Saigon, during a search-and-destroy operation. The paratroopers belonged to the Brigade's 1st Battalion, 503rd Infantry Regiment (Airborne), which had been delivered by helicopter two days earlier north-east of the Don Nai River to support the 1st Royal Australian Regiment. The Americans fought back and managed to drive the VC fighters from Hill 65. The paratroopers held their positions against numerous attacks, being involved on several occasions in hand-to-hand fighting. The VC fighters were forced to disengage and withdraw, scattering into the jungle. Forty-nine paratroopers and 403 VC fighters were killed in the battle.

The first major battle between US and North Vietnamese Army (NVA) forces was fought in the Ia Drang Valley in South Vietnam's central highlands six days later. It was also the first large-scale air assault operation of the war. Air Cavalry units were involved in the battle, but several of their officers and non-commissioned officers were qualified paratroopers. Lieutenant Colonel (later Lieutenant General) Harold G. Moore had performed 300 parachute jumps although he had served in the 101st Airborne Division for only three years, from 1948 to 1951. Besides being a paratrooper, Moore was also a qualified jump master. In the Battle of Ia Drang Valley Moore led the 1st Battalion, 7th Cavalry Regiment (1/7th Cavalry). The unit was a component of the 1st Cavalry Division (Airmobile), commanded by Brigadier General Harry W.O. Kinnard, a Second World War paratrooper who had participated in combat jumps with the 101st Airborne Division in Normandy and in Holland in 1944.

The Battle of Ia Drang began on the morning of 14 November 1965, when helicopters delivered the 1,000-man force into the valley, using seven landing zones. Lieutenant Colonel Moore led the 1st Battalion, 7th Cavalry Regiment and Lieutenant Colonel Robert McDade was in charge of the regiment's 2nd Battalion. The soldiers rushed to establish three defensive perimeters, code-named X-Ray, Albany and Columbus. They soon found themselves under heavy fire by numerically superior North Vietnamese regular forces. They were completely surrounded and unable to retreat even if they wanted to. The Americans were able to hold out over three days of battle largely through the support of air power and heavy artillery bombardment. When reinforcements arrived in the afternoon of 18 November, the North Vietnamese troops conducted an orderly retreat. According to US sources, North Vietnamese casualties were between 1,070 and 1,753 (killed, wounded and captured).[30] The NVA announced 1,228 (including 559 killed) as their casualties against 1,500 to 1,700 for the enemy. The Americans gave their casualties as 499 killed, missing and wounded. Additionally, four US helicopters were shot down and fifty-five more were damaged. Despite the high casualties, both sides declared a victory. Moore's men, defending from the X-Ray perimeter, could claim a tactical victory, as they exacted an almost 10:1 kill ratio against the enemy. Ia Drang was the first time that North Vietnamese forces went head to head in their attempt to overrun the US positions. The battle also taught the Americans to stick to their superior air power in the later stages of the war.

In 1966, air assault operations were assigned to the 1st Air Cavalry Division (Airmobile). On 24 January at Kim Son Valley, on 16 May at Vinh Thanh Province and on 13 September units of the division were helicoptered almost up to their objectives.

The same happened in January 1966, when units of the 173rd Airborne Brigade became involved in a search-and-destroy operation 12.5 miles (20km) north of Binh Duong Province. Two infantry brigades, an American and an Australian, also took part in the operation.[31] The allied force was able to partially clear the area of enemy troops.[32] On 2 June 1966, units of the 101st Airborne Division were tasked to relieve the South Vietnamese 42nd Regiment which was under siege at Toumorong, north-east of Tak To, in South Vietnam's Central Highlands.[33] A battalion of the 1st Cavalry Division was also involved in the operation, which was under the overall command of Brigadier General Willard Pearson, commander of the 1st Brigade, 101st Airborne Division. The 1st Battalion, 327th Infantry Regiment (Airborne) was deployed by helicopter north-east of Toumorong, while the 2nd Battalion, 502nd Infantry Regiment (Airborne) was establishing control of the town. On 7 June, a North Vietnamese battalion attacked repeatedly the 1/327's and the 2/502's positions. On the afternoon of 7 June, the 1st Battalion, 5th Cavalry Regiment, was helicoptered in the area in support of 'C' Company, 2nd Battalion, 502nd Infantry Battalion (Airborne), having been encircled by enemy forces. The American units defended their positions until 11 June, when the North Vietnamese were hit by air and artillery bombardment. They were forced to withdraw, leaving behind 688 dead. A further twenty-one North Vietnamese soldiers were taken prisoner. The US casualties in this operation were 48 killed and 239 wounded.

On 8 March 1967, a massive search-and-destroy operation, spearheaded by the 173rd Airborne Brigade, was carried out in an area north-west of Saigon that had become a VC stronghold.[34] Two more US Army units participated in the operation, the 25th Infantry Brigade and the 11th Armored Cavalry Regiment. The casualties inflicted to the VC forces were 750 killed and 280 captured.[35] In comparison, the US forces lost 72 killed and 337 wounded. The operation failed to eradicate the enemy presence in the area, which was the primary objective for the forces involved. The VC swiftly re-established their dominant position in an area so close to the South Vietnamese capital. A month later, an operation was carried out in Kon Tum, Dar Lac and Pleiku provinces, involving two South Vietnamese heliborne battalions and two US infantry battalions. In the operation units of the US 173rd Airborne Brigade were employed as reinforcements. On 11 May 1967, the 1st Brigade, 101st Airborne Division, was involved in large-scale search and destroy operations in Quang Ngai Province. On 21 June, 'C' Company, 2nd Battalion, 503rd Infantry Regiment (Airborne), was ambushed by the NVA's 6th Battalion, 24th Regiment, near Hill 1338, located south of Dac To. Of the 137 men that comprised the unit 75 were killed and another 23 were wounded. A search of the battlefield revealed only fifteen North Vietnamese dead.[36]

In October and November 1967, the so-called 'Border Battles' erupted across South Vietnam's central highlands. When North Vietnamese troops attacked a border outpost in Kon Tum Province. The clashes, which began at a border outpost in Kon Tum Province, involved four regiments of the North Vietnamese 1st Division, fighting against the 173rd Airborne Brigade and a South Vietnamese force, made up of airborne and infantry troops. On 23 November 1967, two battalions of the 503rd

Infantry Regiment (Airborne), the 2nd and the 4th, captured Hill 875 in a combined operation with US Army's 1st Battalion, 12th Infantry Regiment. Eighty-seven killed and 130 wounded were the casualties for the 2/503rd and 28 killed and 123 wounded for the 4/503rd.[37] These clashes lasted twenty-two days. The US and South Vietnamese losses were 262 killed compared to the enemy's 1,200 to 1,600.[38]

On 30 January 1968, the enemy launched the Tet Offensive, including attacks on Saigon and Hue. Hue was even temporarily captured by communist forces. Saigon was defended mainly by South Vietnamese forces, including airborne and Ranger units. South Vietnamese paratroopers and Rangers fought also for the defence and the recapture of Hue in one of the longest and bloodiest battles of the war. Outside Hue, elements of the US 101st Airborne Division and the 1st Air Cavalry Division were tasked with cutting off access to Indochina's historic city and the enemy's lines of supply and reinforcement. Between 26 February and 30 April, two battalions of the 101st Airborne Division's 327th and 502nd Infantry Regiments (Airborne) were involved in a combined operation in Phuoc Tuy province.

By early April the North Vietnamese and the VC forces had suffered more than 40,000 casualties in two campaigns, the Tet Offensive and the attack on Khe Sanh. The Battle of Khe Sanh, a North Vietnamese attack on a US Marine combat base, began on 21 January and lasted for two months. After Khe Sanh, another US combat camp was attacked – this time successfully – by North Vietnamese troops.[39] On the night of 9/10 March, a 2,000-strong force from the enemy's 325th Division stormed a US Special Forces camp in A Shau Valley. The seventeen Green Beret troopers and the 400 South Vietnamese militiamen were eventually forced to abandon the camp, being heavily outnumbered. The Green Berets suffered five killed and twelve wounded in the battle. The North Vietnamese casualties were estimated to be 800. The US defenders of the camp, including 186 of the South Vietnamese militiamen, were evacuated by fifteen H-34 helicopters, supported by four UH-1B gunships. The militiamen who were left behind were listed as missing in action. Two US aircraft were shot down by the North Vietnamese during the battle and the consequent CSAR (Combat Search and Rescue) operation. Both pilots were also rescued. The Battle of A Shau was a strategic victory for the North Vietnamese, who were able to take control of the valley until the end of the war. At the same time, another battle involving Green Beret troopers was fought in Kham Duc, in Quang Tin province, in south-central South Vietnam. American airpower averted a massacre of the US troops in Kham Duc, but couldn't prevent the North Vietnamese from winning.[40] US casualties were thirteen killed, thirty missing, two captured and nine aircraft lost. North Vietnamese casualties were 345 killed.[41] South Vietnamese casualties were ten killed, ninety-five missing and 102 captured. General Creighton Abrams later described the battle as a 'minor disaster'.[42]

Between 1 April and 17 May, units of US Army's 101st and the 82nd Airborne Divisions were involved for the first time in a joint operation during the Vietnam War. Over 2,000 enemy soldiers were killed in the lowland of Quang Tri and Thua Thien Provinces, during the operation code-named Carentan II. US casualties were 195 killed. Nevada Eagle was the longest-lasting operation of the Vietnam War. From

May 1968 through February 1969, US and South Vietnamese forces, spearheaded by the 101st Airborne Division, were tasked with forcing the VC from the plains into the mountains and denying the control of rice crops to the enemy. US losses in the operation were 353 killed or missing in action.

On 11 June 1968, General William C. Westmoreland was replaced in the command of the US forces in South Vietnam by his classmate from the West Point military academy General Creighton W. Abrams, a tank officer. Westmoreland, an artillery officer, had been in favour of search-and-destroy operations against the communist forces in every scale (small, medium and large) throughout the four years of his command in South Vietnam.[43] He became a paratrooper after the Second World War, being assigned to the 82nd Airborne Division. During the Korean War, Westmoreland commanded the 187th Airborne Regimental Combat Team and later, in 1956, he was appointed commander of the 101st Airborne Division.

In 1968, US airborne units, all belonging to the 101st Airborne Division, participated in six search-and-destroy, five reconnaissances in force and one clear-and-search operations in various areas of South Vietnam. Three search-and-destroy operations were carried out in January by the 1st, the 2nd and the 187th Brigades, and a fourth in May by the 3rd Brigade. On 16 March, an operation of this type was assigned to the 3rd and the 187th Brigades. Two brigades, the 1st and the 2nd, were involved in 27 September in another search-and-destroy operation. Reconnaissance-in-force operations were carried out by the 173rd Airborne Brigade in January and March, and by the 1st Brigade in June. Such operations were also assigned to the 1st and 3rd Battalions, 503rd Infantry Regiment (Airborne) in June and the 506th Infantry Regiment (Airborne) in December. A clear-and-search operation was carried out in December by the 2nd Brigade. On 10 May 1969, a joint US–South Vietnamese military operation was carried out in A Shau Valley to prevent the enemy from mounting an attack against neighbouring coastal provinces. In the operation participated units of the 101st Airborne Division (including the 187th, the 501st and the 506th Airborne Regiments) and the US 9th Marine Regiment. In May 1969, when the 7th and 8th Battalions of the North Vietnamese 29th Regiment had entrenched themselves on Hill 937, also known as Hamburger Hill, a US–South Vietnamese force was ordered to remove them.[44] The assault began on 10 May, involving units of the 101st Airborne Division, the 9th Marine Regiment, the 5th Cavalry and the South Vietnamese 3rd Infantry Regiment. After ten days of fighting and eleven consequent assaults up the hill, the mission was carried out. Those who reached the top of the hill first were paratroopers – elements of the 3rd Battalion, 187th Airborne Brigade. Despite heavy losses, the captured hill was later abandoned. Seventy-two Americans and thirty-one South Vietnamese were killed in the battle, compared to the enemy's 1,500 killed and wounded. According to North Vietnamese claims, the US losses were 630 killed.

Units of the 101st Airborne Division were involved in twelve clear-and-search operations in various areas of South Vietnam during 1969. Two of them were carried out in January by the 1st Battalion, 503rd Infantry Regiment (Airborne), and the 3rd Battalion, 506th Infantry Regiment (Airborne). Also in January, an operation of this type was assigned to the 173rd Airborne Brigade, which was deployed in Lam Dong

Province along with the 1st Battalion, 503rd Infantry Regiment (Airborne). Clear-and-search operations were carried out also in February by the 3rd Battalion, 503rd Infantry Regiment (Airborne), in March by the 173rd Airborne Brigade, the 1st Battalion, 503rd Infantry Regiment (Airborne) and the 3rd Battalion, 506th Infantry Regiment (Airborne). Five more operations were also assigned to the Division's 1st, 2nd and 3rd Brigades in the provinces off Thua Thien and Quang Tri, including the valleys of A Shau and Da Krong, between June and September 1969. Clear-and-search operations were carried out also in October and November, mostly in Binh Dinh Province, by the 173rd Airborne Brigade and the 506th, Infantry Regiment. On 22 October, three US divisions, spearheaded by the 101st Airborne, fought in Quang Tri Province, killing 384 North Vietnamese and VC fighters. In the operation, which lasted three months, the 5th Infantry and the 1st Marine Divisions also participated.

Between 7 December 1969 and 31 March 1970, about 670 North Vietnamese and VC fighters were killed in operations in Thua Thien Province involving units of the 101st Airborne Division and the South Vietnamese 1st Infantry Division. In December 1969, a search-and-destroy operation was assigned to the 2nd Brigade and a reconnaissance-in-force was carried out a month earlier by the 3rd Brigade, 101st Airborne Division. In mid-1969, the Vietnamization of the war began – a plan than enabled the withdrawal of 60,000 US troops from Vietnam by the end of the year. The major burden fell on the South Vietnamese Army's Special Forces. The 7th and the 8th Ranger Brigades were deployed west of Saigon, the 4th Airborne Brigade and the 951st Ranger Group east of Saigon. The 1st Airborne Brigade in Ba Ria, south-east of Saigon, the 9th Ranger Brigade in Lai Thieu, north of Saigon, and the 2nd Marine Division in Bien Hoa, north-east of Saigon. In 1970, operations involving airborne units were also carried out. Between 1 March and 17 November, the 2nd Battalion, 503rd Airborne, was deployed in Pleiku Province to operate alongside the 1st Squadron, 10th Cavalry Regiment. In April and May, the 1st Brigade, 101st Airborne Division, conducted a reconnaissance-in-force operation south of Phu Bai and in August the Division's 3rd Battalion was assigned a clear-and-search operation in Thua Thien Province. Between 4 and 5 May, US and South Vietnamese forces, including the 3rd Battalion, 506th Infantry Regiment (Airborne), raided eastern Cambodia during Phase I of the Cambodian incursion. Between 20 May and 28 July, the 3rd Battalion, the 506th Infantry Regiment (Airborne), was involved in clear-and-search operations in South Vietnam – Dak Lak Province, the Khe Sanh Plateau and Binh Dinh Province.

In the United States, the protests against the war forced President Nixon to decide the Vietnamization of the war by withdrawing US troops and building up the South Vietnamese so that they could do the fighting for themselves. The protests were intensified after bloody battles of questionable value, such as the capture of Hamburger Hill in 1969, and the invasion of Cambodia in 1970. By the end of 1970, 122,000 US troops had been withdrawn from Vietnam. Between 1 January and 13 March 1971, the 173rd Airborne Brigade carried out operations in Binh Dinh, Phu Bon and Pleiku Provinces. On 30 January, units of the 101st Airborne Division participated in a combined operation (also involving the US 1st Brigade, 5th Infantry Division, and the

2nd Squadron, 17th Cavalry Regiment) for the control of an area between Khe San and the Laotian border. US losses in the operation, code-named Dewey, were seventy-five killed. The last operation involving US paratroopers in the Vietnam War was carried out between 1 April and 5 September 1970 in Quang Tri and Thua Thien Provinces. A combined force of the 101st Airborne Division and the South Vietnamese 1st Infantry Division were involved in a search-and-destroy operation code-named Texas Star. The US Army claimed that 1,782 North Vietnamese soldiers and VC fighters were killed in the operation. US losses were 386 killed and 1,978 wounded.[45]

On 1 December 1971, the withdrawal of the 101st Airborne Division from South Vietnam began. It was completed with the arrival of the last units in the United States on 31 January 1972. The US military involvement in the war included a spectacular air-assault in North Vietnam. On 21 November 1970, fifty-six Special Forces troopers, led by Colonel Arthur D. Simons, landed from helicopters in Son Tay 23 miles (37km) west of Hanoi, the North Vietnamese capital. The objective was the recovery and rescue of sixty-one US prisoners of war who were supposedly detained in a local camp. The Green Berets didn't rescue anybody, due to an intelligence failure.[46] The raid planners had not been notified that the prisoners had been transferred. The raiders found the camp empty of POWs, when they stormed in heavily armed, during the night.[47] They killed forty-two guards and destroyed infrastructure before being extracted by five helicopters. According to Hanoi, the North Vietnamese casualties in this raid were six soldiers and seven civilians killed. Two of the raiders were wounded and one of their helicopters was damaged during the operation that was code-named Ivory Coast.

After the US military withdrawal, the South Vietnamese forces proved ineffective in combat. The 2nd Airborne Brigade participated in operations on 30 March 1972 and the 1st Airborne Brigade, along with the (South Vietnamese) 18th Ranger Commando, in the Battle of An Loc on 13 April 1975. Fifteen months earlier, a peace accord was signed in Paris ending the conflict. The withdrawal of the last US combat troops from South Vietnam had been completed in March 1974, but hostilities had been resumed by the end of the year. North Vietnamese forces were advancing southward almost at ease. On 30 April 1975, communist forces entered Saigon, forcing South Vietnam to surrender and uniting the country. In Vietnam, the US casualties were 58,000 dead, 153,303 wounded and 1,948 missing in action. The South Vietnamese casualties were 230,000 killed and 1,169,763 wounded (estimated). Vietnamese communist forces had approximately 1,100,000 killed and an unknown figure of wounded.

Chapter 17

Airborne Operations and
Air Assaults, 1972–2018

After the Second World War, airborne deployments tended to be limited to battalion-size drops rather than brigade- or divisional-size operations, with combat jumps themselves eventually becoming a rarity. It is characteristic that US 82nd Airborne Division's first operational jump since 1944 was conducted as late as 1989, when the unit was deployed to Panama. The small number of combat jumps by paratroops in post-war conflicts (Korea, the Middle East and Algeria in particular) in comparison with the ones conducted during the Second World War can be attributed to the emphasis given to helicopter operations. The earliest helicopters, being fragile, small and having a limited load-carrying capacity, were used mostly for reconnaissance as well as casualty evacuation. Larger models were then built and, beginning in Vietnam, where the Americans fielded an entire division as 'airmobile cavalry', helicopters provided unprecedented mobility to small bodies of lightly-armed troops. Since helicopters can get men and equipment out of the battlefield as well as into it, they have largely replaced the paratroopers and gliders of the Second World War without however fundamentally changing the general considerations pertaining to airborne versus ground warfare.[1]

This particular development brought about changes in the structure and the operational role of certain units, initially in the United States. Gliders, which had been used by the belligerents on several occasions between 1941 and 1945, were abandoned as soon as the war ended. The US Army's 101st Airborne Division was the first formation to be affected by these changes. In 1968, during the Vietnam War, the division adopted the structure and equipment of an air-mobile formation.[2] Six years later, the 101st Airborne was re-organized as an air assault unit in the light of US Army's new battlefield doctrine called AirLand Battle. Even airborne units, like the US 82nd Airborne Division, have an attached helicopter section because it makes them far more useful. Helicopters give them mobility, mobile fire support and (extra) anti-armour capability.

It all started in 1946, when the US Marine Corps (USMC) experimented with helicopters in order to allow a dispersed attack on enemy-occupied shores. Two years later, the USMC School came out with Amphibious Operations – Employment of Helicopters (Tentative) or Phib-31, which was the first manual on air-mobile operations.[3] Air-mobile units were designed and trained for insertion and vertical envelopment, air supply and – if necessary – air extraction. The first vertical envelopment mission was performed by the USMC on 20 September 1951, during the Korean War, when helicopters delivered 224 combat-equipped troops to secure 'Hill 884'. Five years later, during the Suez crisis, a (British) Royal Marine force was helicoptered from a naval vessel to the shore near Port Said in Egypt. Between 1956 and 1961, the French army in Algeria introduced air mobility in their operations against the nationalist guerrillas. The Israeli army, after the 1956 War during which they conducted the first combat jump of their history, concentrated on re-organizing and training their airborne and Special Forces units with the emphasis on helicopter operations. Following the successful vertical envelopment in Korea, these techniques were put into effect by the US forces in Vietnam with air assault being one of them. The term derived from the combination of two types of operations known as air mobility and vertical envelopment. Air assault is specifically a combat insertion rather than transportation to an area in the vicinity of combat. The US Army Field Manual describes an air-assault as an operation in which assault forces (combat, combat support and combat service support), using firepower, mobility and total integration of helicopter assets, manoeuvre on the battlefield under control from the ground under an air manoeuvre commander to engage and destroy enemy forces or to seize and hold key terrain, usually behind enemy lines.

On 15 April 1963, USMC helicopters were used to insert a South Vietnamese force behind enemy lines in an operation code-named Shuffy. Two months earlier, on 15 February, an Army battalion-size unit specially trained in helicopter operations was activated at Fort Benning, Georgia. The unit grew fast, within two years becoming the 11th Air-Assault Division. Major General Harry Kinnard, a legendary paratroop commander during the Second World War, became commander of the formation. In Vietnam, where it was deployed on 25 August 1965, the formation was re-named the 1st Cavalry Division (Air Mobile). They were trained to combine operations with UH-1A attack helicopters. The US Army's air cavalry fulfilled the traditional cavalry reconnaissance and raiding roles. Another formation that was transformed into an air-assault unit was the 101st Airborne Division. Following their return from Vietnam, the division was reorganized with only one brigade in a paratroop role. Four battalions of the briefly de-activated 173rd Airborne Brigade were absorbed into the 101st Division's 3rd Brigade in 1972. The remaining two brigades and supporting units were organized and trained as an air-mobile force. On 26 March 1974, an air-assault school was established at the division's base at Fort Campbell, Kentucky. The 101st Air-Assault Division with a strength of 27,000 personnel is the US Army's larger formation. In February 1991, during the First Gulf War, the division struck 155 miles (249km) behind enemy lines – in the deepest air-assault operation in history. Also in 1991 in Iraq, approximately 400 helicopters transported 2,000 soldiers to destroy, as they did, a large concentration of enemy troops. In that war, the 101st Air-Assault Division had lost sixteen soldiers but captured thousands of enemy troops. The division was involved ten years later in military operations in Afghanistan and in Iraq again.

Air-mobile operations proved to be invaluable on the modern battlefield, allowing the landing of soldiers with increased control and precision close to their objective. Landing a battalion-size force covertly wherever operation planners want to represents a worthwhile advantage. Instead of having the troops scattered over a wide area as often happens in parachute drops, planners achieve a greater concentration of force close to an objective. This is the same benefit conferred by tactical helicopters but there is much less risk of ground fire bringing down a transport aircraft. The restructuring of the airborne forces and the raising of air-assault units in the United States has not affected the number of paratroopers, however. The US Army runs forty-six parachute-training classes a year with the average class numbering about 400 trainees, producing 18,500 new paratroopers every year. Massive jumps are also conducted by the US Army, not only in combat but also in exercises at home and abroad, in which foreign paratroopers are often invited to participate. On 16 May 1996, the US and the British armies conducted the biggest parachute drop since the Second World War, 6,000 men jumping from 144 Hercules transport planes over Fort Bragg in North Carolina. Two thousand of them were from the British 5th Airborne Brigade. On 17 March 2015, 2,100 paratroopers jumped over Fort Bragg during bilateral exercises, 900 of whom were from the British 16th Air-Assault Brigade's 3 Para. The British Army's first move toward air mobility was the reorganization of the 24th Infantry Brigade as an airportable formation in the summer of 1970. Britain's 16th Air-Assault Brigade was formed in 1999, after an amalgamation of elements of the 5th Airborne Brigade and the 24th Airmobile Brigade, which brought together the agility and reach of airborne forces in the potency of the attack helicopter. The United Kingdom maintains the 16th Air-Assault Brigade as a rapid-reaction force that can be quickly sent to trouble spots across the world. The formation, headquartered and based in Colchester, is made up of three battalions and numerous supporting units, including a field artillery regiment.

A common disadvantage when it comes to either a combat jump or an air assault is the fact that troop-carrying aircraft and helicopters can easily be heard (and seen in case of a daylight operation) from quite a distance. The troops are also easily spotted on arrival in case of an unsecured drop zone or landing zone. When US forces invaded Grenada in 1983, they lost a number of Black Hawk helicopters to a single enemy machine-gunner. The planes are susceptible to surface-to-air missiles and the troops can only land by parachute or disembark from helicopters with limited supplies. The amount of weaponry, equipment and ammunition that airborne and heliborne troops can carry in combat is limited to around 77lbs (35kg). It means that these forces are heavily depended on re-supply drops. They are also without armour or artillery.[4] It means that the airborne or heliborne troops can be assigned only short-term operations as they can hold positions for no more than two days before being relieved by ground forces, including tanks. The normal price to be paid for the deployment of troops by air during the Second World War was horrendous casualties and the results in many operations, despite a number of spectacular successes achieved, never quite fulfilled the most sanguine expectations of the interwar period.[5] In case of a combat jump, landing zone dispersion, owing either to unexpected winds or to a pilot's or a jumpmaster's miscalculation, can be a serious problem. Parachute delivery can scatter forces over a large area and to reassemble them into coherent units might require hours.[6] Sometimes the outcome was even worse, as during the 1943 Allied invasion of Sicily, when numbers of paratroopers fell into the sea and were drowned. An off-target drop disorientates the soldiers and as it increases the distance between the drop zone and their objective, it therefore increases the time required to secure it. Dispersion can cost the element of surprise and may result in mission failure should a determined enemy be able quickly to mount a counter-attack. The limited number of strategic transport aircraft available reduces the level of immediate armoured support that can be delivered. Although it is now possible for armies like the American, the Russian and the Chinese to airdrop a variety of light tanks, heavy weapons and support vehicles, the availability of sufficient aircraft for such operations was still an issue in 2015.

Since the Second World War, most armies operate parachute troops for one role or another. Many have argued that since the advent of helicopters, paratroopers have become obsolete, while others still argue that there is still no better way of landing a large unit of troops in the one place so quickly and efficiently. The advantages of the employment of airborne troops in combat have kept paratroopers as an important factor in modern warfare. There is still no faster way, for example, to put a thousand or more elite troops on the ground more or less simultaneously. Airborne is still the perfect technique for initial seizure of objectives during a forced-entry operation. Modern transport aircraft enable paratroops to reach objectives well beyond the reach of heliborne forces. A single Airbus A400M, for instance, can carry 116 fully equipped paratroopers (or 37,000kg/81,600lb of cargo) and a single C-295 ninety-one paratroopers to any part of the world within eighteen hours. The four-engine turboprop A400M went into service in 2013 and by 2018 had become the main transport plane of several air forces, including the French, the German, the Spanish and the British. That's why these transport planes are valued as strategic assets. Modern transport aircraft, such as the C-17, can drop much heavier equipment than any modern helicopter can. Furthermore, helicopters, having to land, take off or hover, are much more vulnerable to enemy small arms or RPGs than fixed-wing aircraft cruising at 500ft and 125 knots over the drop zone. A tilt-rotor aircraft, the V-22 Osprey, on the other hand, can easily replace the helicopter in an air assault, as it also takes off and lands vertically, but can also go as far as a cargo plane, having a range that far exceeds that of a traditional helicopter

Since the raising of air-assault units, paratroopers have been used in mass drops in Afghanistan by the Soviets, in Grenada by the Americans, in the wars in Angola and South Rhodesia by South Africa, in Panama by the Americans and in Iraq and Afghanistan by the US and the British Armies.

Northern Ireland

Between 1970 and 1996, British parachute units were rotated in Northern Ireland in a counter-terrorist role or to support the security forces in their duties. On a number of occasions, they were helicoptered into action. The first paratroopers arrived in Northern Ireland in February 1970. They were members of the 2nd Battalion (2 Para), Parachute Regiment, which spent more time in Northern Ireland than any other unit of the British army.[7] British paratroopers, members of the 1st Battalion (1 Para), were involved in the 'Bloody Sunday' incident on 30 January 1972, when thirteen Irish Catholic protesters were shot dead in Derry during an anti-interment rally.[8] Between 9 and 11 August 1972, eleven innocent civilians were shot dead at Ballymurphy, Belfast, following action involving men of 1 Para. Between 1971 and 1996, fifty-one Parachute Regiment members were killed while serving in Northern Ireland. On 27 August 1979, sixteen paratroopers, all members of 2 Para, were killed by two remote-controlled explosions at Warren Point, County Down, while travelling in a three-vehicle convoy.[9] One of them was their commanding officer, Lieutenant Colonel David Blair. 22nd SAS's units were involved in anti-terrorist operations in Northern Ireland from 1969 until 1996. The deployment of the regiment in Northern Ireland was formally admitted by the British government in January 1976, although there was an SAS presence in the Province prior to that, having had a proxy intelligence role through the 14th Intelligence Company.[10]

The first SAS unit to arrive in Northern Ireland was 'D' Squadron.[11] It was initially deployed to South Armagh to counter the IRA activity in the area. By 1977, there were two squadrons in situ, with the result that the terrorist threat temporarily declined. The role of the SAS in Ulster was to run agents, conduct surveillance and intelligence-gathering missions and to carry out ambush operations. Throughout the 1970s, the patient observation-post work in rural areas, couple with plainclothes work in the towns and cities, began to pay off. Between 1976 and 1989, thirty-seven IRA and INLA terrorists were killed in gun battles with the SAS. At the same period, the SAS lost four men.[12] The regiment also conducted controversial cross-border raids to arrest wanted terrorists, like Sean McKenna, Kevin Burne and Patrick Mooney, who were captured in 1976. Peter Cleary was the first IRA official to be killed by the SAS in Northern Ireland. A leading member of the Provisional Irish Republican Army's South Armagh Brigade, Cleary was arrested near Forkhill, County Armagh. According to the SAS, he was shot after trying to disarm his guard in a bid to escape.[13] In May 1977, Captain Robert Nairac, was captured by the IRA, while operating undercover in the village of Dromintee in South Armagh. His body has never been found and the nature of his mission in the Province has never been disclosed by the British authorities.[14] Nairac had been present when Cleary was killed.[15]

Cyprus, Uganda, and England

On 20 July 1974, 120 paratroopers were dropped in Mia Milia, near Nicosia, during the Turkish invasion of Cyprus with more jumping near Kyrenia in the north of the island the following day. On 4 July 1976, a hundred Israeli commandos air-landed at Entebbe airport in Uganda, where 102 Israeli passengers from a hijacked French airliner were held hostage by seven Palestinian and two German terrorists. All the hijackers and forty-five Ugandan soldiers were killed by the commandos, who also destroyed eleven MiG-17s and MiG-21s of the Ugandan air force.[16] A hundred and three of the 106 hostages were rescued. One Israeli commando (Lieutenant Colonel Yonatan Netanyahu) was killed during the operation and five more were wounded.

The British SAS conducted a rescue operation on 5 May 1980 in London, when the Iranian embassy was seized by seven armed terrorists and twenty-six people were being held as hostages.[17] Elements of the SAS's Special Projects Team burst in the building killing of six terrorists and the capture of the seventh. They were all members of the Democratic Revolutionary Front for the Liberation of Arabistan (a region of Iran). Twenty-five of the hostages were rescued – two of them wounded. The SAS soldiers suffered no casualties. The operation was over in seventeen minutes.

The Soviet Army in Afghanistan

Several airborne and air-assault units were deployed to Afghanistan by the Red Army even prior to the Soviet military intervention in that country. The fact that Afghanistan is a mountainous country was a challenge for operation planners as they could make extensive use of helicopters. At the time of the Soviet-Afghan War, the Red Army could field thirteen air-assault brigades and nineteen separate air-assault battalions. On 14 April 1979, eight months before the Soviet invasion, the Afghan President Nur Mohammad Taraki made an appeal for Soviet military assistance following an anti-government uprising in Herat province a month earlier. Moscow obliged by sending an airborne battalion, which arrived in the capital Kabul on 7 July, commanded by Lieutenant Colonel A. Lomakin. When Taraki was murdered on the orders of his deputy, Hafizullah Amin, Moscow decided to intervene because Afghanistan's new strongman seemed ready to adopt a non-aligned (if not pro-Western) policy, thus hurting Soviet interests in the region. On 24 December, a 30,000-strong Red Army force invaded Afghanistan. On the morning of 27 December, the Soviet 103rd Guards 'Vitemsk' Airborne Division landed at the airport at Bagram. After occupying Kabul, the invaders staged a coup. On 17 December, 700 Soviet troops, some of them dressed in Afghan uniforms, occupied governmental, military and media buildings. The Presidential Palace was attacked by twenty-four KGB operatives, 520 men from a Spetsnaz unit, the 154th Battalion and eighty-seven paratroopers from the 345th Guards Airborne Regiment. The 154th Spetsnaz was also known as 'the Muslim Battalion' because it consisted exclusively of soldiers from the southern republics of the Soviet Union. Amin was killed during the assault and Babrak Karmal, a communist politician, was installed as head of state by the Soviets.[18] Within two weeks, five Red Army divisions, including the 105th Airborne, had been deployed in Kabul and other regions of Afghanistan. A sixth division, the 56th Air-Assault, arrived shortly. The Soviet invasion and presence exacerbated nationalistic sentiments causing the rebellion to spread further.[19] It was also bitterly resented by the devoutly Muslim and largely anti-communist population.

The Afghan resistance, identified collectively as the Mujahideen, was strongly supported by foreign countries like the United States, Pakistan, Saudi Arabia, Iran and Egypt. Helicopters were deployed extensively in support of the Soviet troops, including the Special Forces, in their missions. It is characteristic that of the 750 Soviet aircraft destroyed from all causes between 1980 and 1985 in Afghanistan, nearly 640, or 85 per cent, were helicopters.[20] The Soviet troops, both heliborne and mechanized, were supposed to actively seek out and engage insurgent groups rather than wait for them to strike. They were supposed to detect movement in advance of an attack and move troops rapidly enough to intercept and engage the enemy. They were also supposed to reduce the flow of outside aid to the Mujahideen. The most publicized mission of the war involving Soviet Special Forces was the defence of Hill 3234 by Soviet paratroopers. Members of the 9th Company of the 345th Independent Guards Airborne Regiment, commanded by Colonel Valery Vostrotin, were helicoptered on the hilltop on 7 January 1988, during a large-scale operation in the Paktia province close to the Pakistani border. In the operation, code-named Magistral, the 56th Separate Air-Assault Brigade was also involved. The seventy-two paratroopers were attacked by a force of 200–250 Mujahideen. After fierce fighting that lasted continuously for almost twenty-four hours, the Mujahideen were forced to retreat. Thirty-nine of the paratroopers were killed in the battle and a further twenty-eight were wounded. Only five men were unwounded when friendly troops arrived on Hill 3234 by helicopter. From time to time, the Soviet Army undertook multi-divisional offensives into Mujahideen-controlled areas – particularly in the strategically-important Panjshir Valley and the cities of Herat and Kandahar. Throughout their deployment in Afghanistan Soviet forces were unable to establish their authority outside Kabul. They could only conduct search and destroy operations with heliborne troops and supported by Mil Mi-24 Hind gunship helicopters. By 1986, the Soviets found themselves bogged down in an endless guerrilla war – bleeding in their own Vietnam. The Mujahideen started to mount sabotage raids even across the border on Soviet soil. In the end, the Mujahideen prevailed and the Soviet Army was forced to withdraw from Afghanistan on 15 February 1989, having paid a heavy price for their intervention. Their total losses were 14,453 dead, 53,753 wounded and 312 missing in action, according to Soviet sources, in a 10-year war, involving a total of 620,000 troops. Kabul fell to the Mujahideen three years later.

The Iran-Iraq War

Airborne operations took place during the Iran-Iraq War (1980–8), but there were few actual combat jumps, because the belligerents employed their airborne units mostly as heliborne forces or elite infantry. At the time, Iraq could field one airborne (the 23rd) and nine Special Forces brigades. An Iranian airborne formation, the 23rd Airborne Special Forces Brigade, had been a component of the 23rd Commando Division in 1979, following the Islamic Revolution in that country. The first Iranian paratroopers were ten officers who were sent to France for parachute training in 1953. Two years later a paratroop battalion was raised in the Army. By 1970, the paratroop battalions had increased to six, comprising the 23rd Airborne Special Forces Brigade. In 1991, the airborne brigade was separated from the 23rd Commando Division. It was named 65th Airborne Special Forces Brigade, but it is also called NOHED Brigade. NOHED is the acronym for '*Niruhaye Vizheye Havabord*', meaning 'Airborne Special Forces' in Farsi (Persian). Iran also possesses two commando divisions, the 23rd and the 58th, and three independent commando brigades, the 25th, the 35th and the 45th. The 23rd Commando Division and the 65th NOHED are headquartered in Tehran. The first Iraqi paratroopers were trained in Britain in April 1954 and two years later a paratroop squadron was raised in the Iraqi army.[21]

In 1959, a parachute training establishment was created in Iraq and a year later, on 9 March 1960, the paratroop squadron was enlarged to a battalion. The 2nd Parachute Battalion was raised on 2 July 1967 and the 17th Independent Parachute Brigade came into being on 1 December 1969. The 1st Commando Battalion was formed in May 1965 and the 2nd two years later. The eight–year conflict begun with a full-scale invasion of Iran by Iraqi forces on 22 September 1980 and gradually developed into a bloody war of attrition. The main reasons for the invasion was a long-lasting dispute over the 124-mile (200km) long Shatt al-Arab (Arvand Rud in Persian) waterway, which forms a partial boundary between the two countries, and three Iranian islands in the Straits of Hormuz and part of Iran's Khuzestan province, called Arabistan by the Iraqis.[22] The Iraqis were also alarmed by the influence on their country's long-suppressed Shia majority by the Iranian revolution. During the war, the Iranian 23rd Commando Division participated in various operations under the direct command of the Defence Minister Mostafa Chamran Save'ei, a US-educated physicist, who had been trained in guerrilla warfare in Cuba and Egypt.[23] On 22 September, Iraqi commandos were among the forces that crossed the Karun River and reached the Abadan City in south-west Iran. Abadan, defended by paramilitary forces, remained under siege for ten months and three weeks. On 7 November, Iranian commando units attacked Iraqi oil export terminals at Mina al-Bakr and al-Faw. On 22 March 1982, Iranian heliborne troops landed behind Iraqi lines close to Shustar in south-western Iran, during an operation involving also Revolutionary Guard and regular army units. On 24 February 1984, Iranian forces carried out an air assault on the oil-producing island of Majnoon, severing communications between Amareh and Basra. The island was captured by 27 February. The victory was overshadowed for the Iranians by the loss of hundreds of soldiers. They were killed when Iraqi jets shot down nearly fifty helicopters transporting troops to Majnoon that day.

By 1986, Iran began training troops in infiltration, night-fighting and mountain warfare at the insistence of generals like Ali Sayad Shirazi. As a junior officer during the Shah era, Shirazi, an artillery officer, had been sent for further military education in the United States. He commanded the Iranian ground forces from 1980 until 1986. On 10 October 1986, Iranian commandos who were dropped by parachute on Iraqi territory destroyed an oil pipeline. On 24 April 1987, Iranian commandos swept through minefields and penetrated as deep as 6 miles (10km) into north-eastern Iraq, capturing 300 square miles (777km²) of Iraqi territory.[24] On 18 April 1988, a 40,000-strong Iraqi force including commando units liberated the Faw Peninsula that had been occupied by Iranian troops.[25] On 25 June 1988, Iraqi paratroopers were dropped to the east of Majnoon Island during a large-scale operation involving two Iraqi Armies, the 3rd and the 6th, about 2,000 tanks and units of the elite Presidential Guard.

The Gambia

On 31 July 1981, Senegalese troops, spearheaded by paratroopers, invaded the Gambia in west Africa to put down a coup that had been attempted by leftist guerrillas against the country's president Dawda Kairaba Jawara.[26] Senegal was asked to intervene by Jawara, who was in London at the time for the Royal Wedding between His Royal Highness The Prince of Wales and Lady Diana Spencer.[27] Four hundred French-trained Senegalese paratroopers landed at Jambour village in the Gambia. They captured and held Yundum airport before advancing towards Banjul, the Gambian capital and largest city. Before long, nearly 3,000 Senegalese soldiers were deployed to the Gambia, one of Africa's smaller countries, which is geographically enveloped on three sides by Senegal. In the meantime, three British SAS men, assisted by a patrol of Senegalese paratroopers, managed to rescue Jawara's family, being held hostage in a Banjul hospital.[28] Major Ian Crook and two sergeants from 'B' Squadron, 22nd SAS Regiment, had slipped into the Gambia from Senegal, dressed in jeans and T-shirts and carrying their guns and ammunition in rucksacks. On 1 August, Jawara announced from Dakar, Senegal's capital, that the rebellion in his country had been crushed.[29]

The Falklands

The Falklands War began on 2 April 1982, when Argentine forces invaded the British Depended Territories of the Falkland Islands and South Georgia in South Atlantic some 8,000 miles (13,000km) from Great Britain. Among the British troops dispatched to carry out the repossession of the Falklands and South Georgia were the 2nd and the 3rd Battalions (2 Para and 3 Para) of the Parachute Regiment. Some troops sailed to the South Atlantic in Royal Navy ships including HMS *Hermes* (the flagship). Others were flown direct to Ascension Island, a staging post located approximately half way between Britain and the Falklands. On 5 April, sixty-six men of 'D' Squadron SAS and support personnel flew to Ascension without waiting for official approval.[30] The next day, 'G' Squadron and Regimental HQs were on their way there. The Regiment undertook a number of missions during the conflict, including infiltration, surveillance, intelligence gathering, diversionary actions and raids. They often cooperated with the Royal Marines' SBS. In the Falklands the SAS conducted more traditional tasks like raiding and patrolling behind enemy lines. Troopers also conducted covert surveillance of Argentine positions prior to the British landings. By 27 April, a 75-man RM force, including a troop of the SAS Regiment led by SAS Major Cedric Delves, recaptured the island of South Georgia some 746 miles (1,200km) east of the Falklands. During the landings, two days earlier two helicopters were crushed at the mouth of Cumberland Bay. On the night of 14/15 May, the SAS carried out a raid on Pebble Island on the Falklands, where the Argentine Navy had taken over an airstrip. The SAS men destroyed eleven enemy T-34 and Pucara aircraft. Two days later, a Westland Sea King helicopter dropped a three-man SAS team onto Chilean soil. They crossed the border and penetrated into Argentina to destroy enemy aircraft on an airfield but the mission was called off because of the presence of 2,000 enemy troops in the area. The SAS men were able to return to Chile and take a civilian flight back to the UK. From the beginning of May, SAS and SBS parties were put ashore of East and West Falkland to undertake a number of missions. The most important of these missions was to determine which sites would be most suitable for a large-scale landing. The teams were inserted by Sea King helicopters from HMS *Hermes*. SAS activity was concentrated around Bluff Cove, the capital (Port Stanley), Berkeley Sound, Cow Bay, Port Salvador, San Carlos Water, Goose Green and Lafonia on West Falkland around Port Howard and in Fox Bay. The SAS established many observation posts on east and west Falkland throughout the conflict. Vital, timely intelligence were reported to the command cell established by Admiral John F. Woodward on HMS *Hermes*. A reconnaissance was undertaken on East Falkland by a four-man patrol from 'G' Squadron led by Captain Aldwin Wight to report on enemy movements around Stanley. They established a camouflaged observation post on Beaver Ridge overlooking Stanley.

On the night of 20 May, forty men of 'D' Squadron, led by Major Delves, mounted a diversionary raid in Darwin/Goose Green area to support the main landings, which were to take place the next day at San Carlos. Landing north of Darwin by helicopter, the men engaged the enemy garrison. Simultaneously, a group of SBS men, supported by an SAS mortar team, attacked and seized Fanning Head. On their way back from Darwin, the SAS bought down a Pucara aircraft with a Stinger missile, a successful end to what had been a textbook diversion. During the Battle of Goose Green, 2 Para (fielding approximately 500 men) attacked enemy positions on East Falkland. The commander of 2 Para, Lieutenant Colonel Herbert Jones, was killed at the head of his battalion, while charging the well-defended Argentine positions.[31] He was posthumously awarded the Victoria Cross. During the night of 21 May, 4,000 men of 3 Commando Brigade were put ashore at San Carlos on the west shore of East Falkland. The plan was to establish a strong beachhead at San Carlos and then launch an attack across east Falkland to take Port Stanley. On 21 May, the 2 Para was the first unit to land in the Falklands, south of San Carlos, on the eastern side of San Carlos Water. Two paratrooper battalions, the 2nd and the 3rd, also landed from the sea. After the Argentine defeat at Goose Green, Venezuela and Guatemala offered to send paratroopers to the Falklands.[32] The weeks after the landing saw the SAS and SBS supporting conventional forces by conducting deep-penetration patrols to locate enemy forward positions and drive in their outposts. On the night of 30 May, the SAS assisted 42 Commando in taking Mount Kent. Five patrols were landed on West Falkland on 5 June. On the night of 13 June, a combined SAS, SBS and RM party raided Stanley harbour as a diversion for 2 Para's attack on Wireless Ridge. Earlier, on 2 June, advancing elements of 2 Para moved to Awan Inlet house in a number of Army Westland Scout helicopters. A contingent of 2 Para was transferred unopposed by a RAF Chinook helicopter to Fitzroy, a settlement on Mount Pleasant, and Bluff Cove, a settlement at Port Fitzroy. During the battle at Mount Longdon on 13 June, Sergeant Ian McKay of 3 Para died in a grenade attack on an Argentine bunker, which earned him a posthumous Victoria Cross.[33]

Earlier, on 10 June, Argentinian troops surrounded an SAS observation post near Port Howard in West Falkland. The occupants, Captain Hamilton and his signaller, both from 'D' Squadron, decided to shoot their way out. Hamilton was killed as he covered the escape of his comrade who was captured. SAS teams led by Major Delves mounted missions in the vicinity of Port Stanley before the Argentinian surrender. The same day, a ceasefire was declared and later the commander of the Argentine forces in Stanley, General Mario Menéndez, surrendered to Major General Jeremy Moore. Seven water jumps were conducted by British paratroopers during the Falklands War. There was no other way for British military personnel to reach their units, particularly after the task force's departure for the campaign. On 19 April 1982, a SAS man was dropped by parachute near HMS *Hermes* in South Atlantic. On 18 May, eight Special Forces men were dropped near HMS *Antelope* and three days later, elements of 22 SAS were parachuted near HMS *Andromeda*. On 31 May, elements of the Parachute Regiment were dropped next to HMS *Penelope*. On 7 and 13 June, a total of thirty-two troopers of 22 SAS were parachuted next to HMS *Andromeda*. On 9 June, elements of 22 SAS were dropped to HMS *Glamorgan*. In the seventy-four days of the war 649 Argentinians and 255 British servicemen were killed. Eighteen men of 'D' Squadron were killed on 19 May, when a Sea King helicopter transferring them from *Hermes* to HMS *Intrepid* inexplicably crashed into the sea. Some 1,880 Argentine and 777 British were wounded. Twenty-one of the dead were from 3 Para, eighteen from 2 Para and nineteen from the SAS. The losses of the two paratroop battalions, thirty-nine dead and ninety-three wounded, were the highest dead toll of any British regiment on land in that conflict.

The Lebanon

On 6 June 1982, while the British were about to capture Port Stanley in the Falklands, a 60,000-strong Israeli force with more than 800 tanks invaded southern Lebanon, supported by artillery, aircraft and attack helicopters. The 35th Paratrooper Brigade, the elite Golani Brigade, the Na'Thal Paratrooper Battalion and two groups of naval commandos from *Sayeret-13* were attached to the invading 91st Division. The operation was launched after a Palestine gunman's attempt to assassinate Israel's ambassador to the United Kingdom, Shlomo Argov. In charge of the troops that stormed into Lebanon was Defense Minister Ariel Sharon, an emblematic figure in the history of the Israeli airborne forces. Paratroopers, operating as elite infantry or heliborne troops, captured Sidon after a three-day battle. In Jezzine they also repulsed a counter-attack by Syrian commandos after a firefight that lasted all night. On 14 July, the siege of Beirut begun. A month later, an agreement was reached, according to which more than 14,000 Palestine Liberation Organization (PLO) combatants were forced to evacuate the city and be relocated to other Arab countries. Israeli forces remained in Sidon until February 1985.

Grenada

Airborne and air-assault missions were carried out in October 1983 during the invasion of Grenada – the first major operation conducted by the US military since Vietnam. In fact, the decision for a low-altitude airborne assault was taken while the aircraft transporting the Ranger battalions were approaching the Caribbean island nation, located 99 miles (160km) north of Venezuela. The men were supposed to air land but when information came that the runway of Grenada's Point Salines airport was obstructed, they were ordered to don parachutes. It had all started on 16 October, when Grenada's legitimate government was overthrown by pro-Cuban military officers. Following the condemnation of Grenada's military junta by the Organization of American States (OAS), a military intervention was decided in Washington, involving 7,000 US troops and 300 soldiers from Caribbean countries, including Barbados, Jamaica and Dominica, christened the Caribbean Peace Force. The main objectives of the operation, code-named Urgent Fury, were the capture of the (under construction) Point Salines airport by the 75th Ranger Regiment to permit the 82nd Airborne Division to land reinforcements on the island, the capture of Pearls airport by the 8th Marine Regiment and the rescue of US students studying at the local university. The intervention force included three regiments (325th, 505th and 508th) and supporting units of the 82nd Airborne Division, the 1st and 2nd Battalions of the 75th Ranger Regiment and the 8th Marine Regiment. The invaders would have to face about 1,500 Grenadian soldiers and about 700 armed Cuban nationals, manning defensive positions.[34]

Grenadian forces possessed eight Soviet-made BTR-60 PB armoured personnel carriers and two BRDM-2 scout vehicles. Their arsenal also included a number of Soviet-made ZU-23-2 anti-aircraft guns. On 23 and 24 October, US Navy SEALs were airdropped at the sea on a reconnaissance mission. Due to bad weather, resulting in the drowning of four men, both assignments were eventually aborted. At 05.30 on 25 October, 500 Rangers from the 1st and 2nd Ranger Battalions along with thirty-five Delta Force operatives descended on the southern portion of the island of Grenada in the Caribbean. The Rangers captured and secured the airfield of Point Salinas. The drop began in the face of moderate resistance which was suppressed by AC-130 gunships, providing support for the landing. By 10.00, the airstrip had been cleared of obstructions and transport planes were able to land and unload reinforcements including vehicles. By 14.00, units of the 82nd Airborne Division had landed at Point Salines. The transport planes carrying the paratroopers had taken off from Grantley Adams International Airport in the Caribbean island of Barbados. Meanwhile, the 2nd Battalion, 8th Marine Regiment, had landed south of Pearl Airport using CH-46 Sea Knight and C-53 Sea Stallion helicopters. They encountered only light resistance. At 05.30, elements of the 8th Marine Regiment mounted an air assault and captured Pearls airport encountering only light resistance. Later in the morning SEAL Team 6 operators made an unsuccessful air assault to seize the island nation's radio station. One MH-60 helicopter crash-landed because of anti-aircraft fire and a pilot was killed, during an air assault against Richmond Hill Prison by Delta Force elements. A raid on Fort Rupert by 'C' Company of the Ranger Regiment was successful in capturing officials of the so-called People's Revolutionary Government. On the morning of 26 October, the 2nd Battalion, 325th Infantry Regiment (Airborne), was ambushed by Cuban forces near the village of Calliste, suffering two killed and six wounded. On the afternoon, Rangers of the 2nd Battalion were helicoptered by CH-46 Sea Kings as far as the university campus and rescued 233 US students. St George, the capital of Grenada, was captured on 27 October. By November, hostilities were declared to be at an end with all US objectives met. On 1 November, two companies from the

22nd Marine Amphibious Unit made a combined sea and helicopter landing on the island of Carriacou, 17 miles (27km) north-west of Grenada. The US forces sustained nineteen killed and 116 wounded during the Grenada intervention. The Grenadian military suffered forty-five dead and 358 wounded. The Cuban casualties were twenty-five killed, fifty-nine wounded and 638 captured. After the defeat of the pro-Cuban regime, Governor-General Paul Scoon, who had been under house arrest since the overthrow of Grenada's legitimate government, headed a caretaker administration until free elections were held. US forces remained in Grenada until December.

Kashmir

On 13 April 1984, Indian heliborne troops (a full battalion of the elite Kumaon Regiment) landed and took control of the entire Siachen Glacier in the Kashmir region close to the Himalayas.[35] It was a tactical and strategic victory for India, which captured and has held ever since 985.71 square miles (2,553km²) of territory claimed by Pakistan in the northernmost geographical region of the Indian subcontinent. It was also the first air-assault conducted in the highest battlefield in the world.

Honduras and Panama

In March 1988 a force of 3,000 US combat troops, including paratroopers, were deployed to Honduras in Central America in March 1988 in response to Nicaraguan Sandinista attacks on Contra opposition bases on Honduran soil.[36] Among the US Army units arriving at Palmerola (now known as Soto Cano) air base on 18 March was the 504th Infantry Regiment (Airborne) of the 82nd Airborne Division.[37] The Regiment's two battalions involved in the operation, code-named Golden Pheasant, were dropped by parachute as a show of force. The 1st Battalion jumped onto Palmerola on 17 March and the 2nd Battalion parachuted into the La Paz DZ a day later. These were the division's first operational jumps since the Second World War.

Twenty-one months later, in the early hours of 20 December 1989, the entire 75th Ranger Regiment (1,300 men) followed by the reinforced Division Ready Brigade of the 82nd consisting of the 1st and 2nd Battalions, 504th PIR (2,700 men) and supporting units, conducted combat jumps to secure the Rio Hato and Torrijos-Tecumen airports in Panama. In the days that followed the Rangers and paratroopers continued combat operations in conjunction with other forces of Task Force Pacific. This marked US Army's first combat parachute deployment of armoured vehicles.[38] Ten M551 Sheridan tanks were dropped by air with two of them being destroyed on landing.

The Gulf Wars

Airborne and air-assault operations were conducted mostly by US forces during the two Gulf Wars. Iraq was also the largest deployment of US Special Forces since Vietnam.[39] Following the invasion of Kuwait by Iraqi troops on 2 August 1990 and the subsequent Saudi plea for assistance, the US 82nd Airborne Division was airlifted from Fort Bragg, North Carolina, nonstop to Dhahran, Riyadh and Thummam aboard C-5 Galaxies and C-41 Starlifters. The division's 4th Battalion, 325th Infantry Regiment (Airborne) was assigned to guard the Saudi Royal family. On 10 August, the 17,000-strong 101st Air-Assault Division was deployed to the north-west region of Saudi Arabia, close to the Iraqi border. The division's aviation assets included AH-64A Apache, AH-IF Cobra, UH-60 Black Hawk, OH-58C/D Kiowa and the CH-47 Chinook helicopters.[40] On 15 January 1991, twelve men of the US Special Forces Delta Team parachuted HAHO (High Altitude High Opening) into Iraq to identify air attack targets. The first unit to move into Iraq were three patrols of the British 'B' Squadron SAS in late January 1991. These eight-man patrols landed behind enemy lines to gather intelligence on the movements of Scud mobile ballistic missile launchers, which could not be detected from the air as they were hidden under bridges and camouflage netting during the day.[41]

On 17 January, the 101st Air-Assault Division's Aviation Regiment fired the first shots of the war. Eight AH-64 helicopters destroyed two Iraqi early warning radar sites. On 24 February, the US XVIII Airborne Corps launched a sweeping attack across Southern Iraq's largely undefended desert, led by the US 3rd Armored Cavalry regiment and the 24th Infantry Division (Mechanized). The 101st conducted a combat air assault into enemy territory. It advanced as far as 155 miles (250km) behind enemy lines in what is considered the deepest air assault in history. By nightfall, the division had cut off Highway 8 – a vital supply line between Basra and the Iraqi forces. The 101st lost sixteen men in action during the 100-hour ground war and captured thousands of prisoners of war. Meanwhile, the 2nd Brigade, 82nd Airborne Division, had been deployed in an airfield near Abqaiq in Saud Arabia in the vicinity of the Aramco oil facilities. The other brigades, the 1st and the 3rd, were stationed near Dhahran. On 23 February the 82nd protected the XVIII Airborne Corp's flank in its move inside south-western Iraq. In the 100-hour ground war the 82nd drove deep into Iraq and captured thousands of enemy soldiers. Two British battalions, the 1st and the 3rd (1 Para and 3 Para) of the Parachute Regiment, were tasked with securing the Rumayalah oil fields before heading north to secure the main supply route north of Basra. By the end of the month, 3 Para had entered Basra almost unopposed – the other two battalions, after crossing the Euphrates River, captured El Qurna. As the fighting ended, 1 Para occupied Maysan province and Al Amarah.

Airborne and Special Forces units from the United States, the United Kingdom, Australia and Poland participated in the second Gulf War – the 2003 invasion of Iraq. On the night of 17 March, the majority of 'B' and 'D' Squadrons of the SAS crossed the border from Jordan to conduct a ground assault on a suspected chemical munitions site in the city of al-Qa'im. The sixty men of 'D' Squadron were flown 80 miles (129km) into Iraq in MH-47Ds (Boeing CH-47 Chinook) helicopters in three waves. Following the insertion, 'D' Squadron established a patrol laager and awaited the arrival of 'B' Squadron, who had driven overland from Jordan. The plant was destroyed in an airstrike.[42] 'B' Squadron Delta Force was the first US Special Operations Force (SOF) to enter western Iraq crossing the border from At'ar in fifteen vehicles. Their role was to conduct selected high-priority site exploitation in suspected chemical weapons facilities.[43] On 18 March, 'A' Squadron of the Australian SAS Regiment infiltrated Iraq and headed toward H-3 Air Base to set up observation posts. On 18 March, H-2 Air Base was captured by British and Australian SAS troopers. On 21 March, elements of 2nd Battalion, 5th SFGA crossed the border to support the Rumaylah oilfields along with US Marine units. On 22 March, the majority of the 2nd and 3rd Battalions of 10th SFGA flew in six MC-130H Combat Talons from Romania to a location near Irbil. On 24 March 2003, the 3rd Battalion, 75th Ranger Division, and twenty-four men from the USAF Combat Control Team were dropped at Al Qaim in Iraq. Two days later 'B' Squadron, 22 SAS was parachuted near Mosul. On 24 March, during the Battle of Nasiriyah, the 101st Air-Assault Division attacked north in support of the 3rd Infantry Division. On 25 March, H-3 Air Base was captured by elements of Delta Force and a battalion of the 5th SFGA. The base was handed over to a company of Royal Marines (45 Commando), who were flown in from Jordan. After Turkey denied access for American forces to attack Iraq from the north through its territory, the US 173rd ARCT was alerted for a massive insertion onto Bashur airfield to establish an airhead and allow the build-up of armoured forces in the north of the country. Some 945 men from the 173rd and twenty operators from the USAF 786th Security Force Squadron (SFS) were involved in the jump conducted on 26 March 2003. The area was controlled by elements of the 10th SFGA and pro-Western Kurdish guerrillas (Peshmerga). The following day, 200 men of the 173rd ARCT's 2nd Battalion, 508th Infantry Regiment (Airborne), were dropped as reinforcements. The airdrop held numerous Iraqi divisions in the north rather than allowing them to be diverted south to oppose the main effort. The jump by the 786th SFS marked the first and only combat jump by conventional USAF personnel. The 3rd Battalion, 75th Ranger Regiment, then conducted a combat parachute drop onto H-1 Air Base securing the site as a staging area for operations in the west. On 29 March, elements of the 75th Ranger Regiment and the USAF Tactical Squadron were parachuted to seize the Haditha Dam in Iraq. On 1 April, units of Britain's 16th Air-Assault Brigade secured the oil fields in South Iraq, while Polish commandos captured offshore platforms near Rumaila, preventing their destruction. On 6 April, British paratroopers (3 Para) fought their way into Iraq's second-largest city, Basra, after two weeks of fierce fighting. They then cleared the old quarter of the city. Iraq was the largest deployment of the US Special Forces since Vietnam. Baghdad fell on 4 April – three weeks into the invasion.

Somalia

The US Army's 3rd Ranger Battalion, 75th Ranger Regiment, and elements of Delta Force were assigned in October 1993 to seize Somali National Alliance (SNA) rebel officials during a meeting in downtown Mogadishu, the capital of the civil war-torn Somalia. The US forces had been deployed to the eastern African country between March 1993 and March 1995 as part of a peacekeeping intervention under the auspices of the United Nations. On 3 October, Delta Force operators roped down from hovering MH-60L Black Hawk helicopters close to the target, while the Rangers who had arrived in the area in twelve Humvee vehicles established a four-corner defensive perimeter. The operation was carried out under heavy fire by SNA combatants who controlled the area. The captured SNA officials were finally transferred to a US base in the outskirts of the city. It was a Pyrrhic tactical victory for the US/UN forces, as nineteen of the participants in the operation were killed in the battle or shortly after and another seventy-three were wounded.[44] Two Black Hawk helicopters were shot down during the operation by rocket-propelled grenade launchers.

Sierra Leone

Air-assault operations were conducted in Sierra Leone in south-west Africa in 2000 for the rescue of military peacekeeping personnel who had been threatened or captured by local rebels at the late stages of the country's civil war. In July, two companies of the 5th Battalion, 8th Gurkha Rifles Regiment, on a United Nations' assignment in Sierra Leone, were under siege in Kailahun by armed cadres of the Sierra Leonean Revolutionary United Front (RUF). A rescue party, led elements of 'D' Squadron, 22 SAS and Indian Parachute Regiment's 2nd Battalion (Special Forces), was inserted in the area by helicopter on 13 July and managed to extract their blue-helmet colleagues in an operation code-named Khukr. Weeks later, five British soldiers on patrol were overpowered and captured by rebels. British forces had been deployed to Sierra Leone to protect the evacuation of British and Commonwealth nationals. An operation was organized for the rescue of the British soldiers, all members of the Royal Irish Regiment, in which 150 men were involved. They were elements of 'D' Squadron, 22 SAS and elements of 1 Para.[45] While heliborne paratroopers were conducting a diversionary assault in the village of Magbeni, the SAS stormed the nearby Occra Hills, where the five soldiers were held hostage. All five were rescued by the SAS who also liberated twenty-one Sierra Leonean civilians being held by the rebels. One British soldier and twenty-five rebels were killed during the operation.

US and Coalition Forces in Afghanistan

The second invasion of Afghanistan started with the seizure of a desert landing strip 100 miles (160km) south of Kandahar, the spiritual birthplace and home of the Taliban movement. On 15 October 2001, a recce party from USN SEAL Team 8 were inserted in the area on a reconnaissance mission and four days later the 3rd Battalion, 75th Ranger Regiment landed by parachute almost unopposed and captured the airfield, which was upgraded at no time and was used for operations in north Afghanistan.[46] Before long, battalions of the 101st Air-Assault Brigade and the 15th Marine Expeditionary Unit were stationed at Forward Operating Base (FOB) Rhino, as it was christened. On 2 November, elements of the US Special Forces and CIA operatives from the Special Activities Division inserted into the Dari-a-Balkh Valley. Seven days later, of Mazar-i-Sharif, in Balkh Province, was captured in the first major offensive by US and Afghan Northern Alliance forces. It was the first major defeat for the Taliban, who lost 400–600 combatants in the battle. A thousand US Army Rangers were airlifted into the city to defend it in case of a counter-attack by Taliban forces.

On 11 November, a US Special Forces detachment was inserted by helicopter near Herat.[47] The same day, an uprising erupted in the city with groups of people attacking Taliban with sticks, knives and hidden guns. The Taliban were forced to flee toward the mountains across the Iranian border. Herat was liberated by Northern Alliance troops on 12 November. Kabul, the capital of Afghanistan, fell to US–Northern Alliance forces two days later. On 14 November, elements of the 3rd Battalion, 5th SFGA and a Northern Alliance force averted the re-capture of Tarikot by Taliban combatants. Eleven days later, a few thousand Taliban prisoners-of-war, who were held in Qala-i-Jangi fortress in Balkh Province in north Afghanistan, revolted. It took six days for Northern Alliance fighters to quell the revolt. All but eighty-six of the Taliban POWs were killed. The Northern Alliance fighters were supported in the operation by nine US Green Berets and eight British SBS troopers. Kandahar, the last major city under Taliban control, was captured on 7 December by a force consisting of 750 US, 150 Australian and 1,600 Northern Alliance soldiers. The Australians were from their Army's Special Air Service Regiment. Meanwhile, an operation involving US, British and German Special Forces was under way in the mountainous area of Tora Bora in eastern Afghanistan against the headquarters of Osama bin Laden, the founder and leader of al-Qaeda, responsible for the 11 September terrorist attack. Elements of the US 5th SFGA, the US Delta Force, the British SBS (Special Boat Section) and the German *Kommando Spezialkräfte* (KSK) participated in the operation either as airborne or heliborne troops. They attacked fortified positions in caves and bunkers scattered throughout the mountainous region. Although 200 al-Qaeda militants were killed during the eleven-day battle, the strategic objective of the operation was not achieved as the Allied troops failed to capture or kill bin Laden who managed to escape to Pakistan.

Another Coalition operation was carried out between 1 and 18 March 2002 in the Shahikot Valley and the Arma Mountains, in Paktia Province. Two battalions, the 1st and the 2nd, of the 187th Airborne Combat Team, 101st Air-Assault Division, were inserted in the designated areas by CH-47D Chinook helicopters, supported by six orbiting AH-64A Apache helicopters. They were supported in the process by Teams 2, 3 and 8 US Navy SEALs, the US Army's 3rd SFGA and elements of Canadian Joint Task Force 2, the German KSK, the Australian SAS Regiment, the New Zealand SAS Regiment, the Norwegian *Forsvarets Spesialkommando* (FSK), the Dutch *Korps Cammandotroepen* and the Danish *Jaegerkorpset*. It resulted in a victory for the Coalition forces as the Taliban were forced to evacuate these regions having suffered heavy casualties.

On 17 May, an Australian SAS patrol was ambushed by Taliban combatants in south-eastern Afghanistan, while participating in an operation code-named Condor. They were rescued by a heliborne force from the British 45 Commando. On 28 January 2003, elements of the 82nd Airborne Division, supported by Apache helicopters and Norwegian Air Force F-16 fighters, cleared seventy-five caves of Taliban combatants in various regions of Kandahar Province. Between 9 and 28 February, the 2nd Battalion, 7th SFGA, a sniper team of the US Navy SEALs and elements of the 82nd Airborne Division carried out mopping-up operations in Bahgran Valley, Helmand Province, in south-east Afghanistan. Eighteen Taliban combatants were killed, during the operation. It was a Coalition victory as the Taliban were forced to evacuate these regions, having suffered heavy casualties.

On 27 January 2003, the 2nd Battalion, 504th Infantry Regiment (Airborne), 82nd Airborne Division, carried out a cave-clearing operation in the Adi Ghar Mountain, Kandahar Province. They were supported by the division's AC-130 Spectre gunships and Norwegian Air Force F-16 fighter jets. Five hundred Italian paratroopers were involved in a US-led operation carried out between 2 and 6 July in the Paktia and Khost Provinces in eastern Afghanistan. On 29 July, elements of the 82nd Airborne Division participated as heliborne troops in an operation in Ayubkhei Valley in Paktia Province. About two years later, on 14 June 2007, elements of the 82nd Airborne Division mounted an air assault against a Taliban compound south-west of the town of Kajaki, in southern Helmand Province. One of the Chinook helicopters participating in the operation was hit by an RPG round and crashed, killing five Americans, one Briton and one Canadian on board. On 27 June 2005, four US Navy SEALs were ambushed by a large number of Taliban combatants after being inserted by helicopter on Sawtalo Sar Mountain, Kunar Province, in north-east Afghanistan. Two MH-47 helicopters with eight troopers on board each were sent to support the SEALs who were fighting hard and were in a desperate situation. The first of the helicopters, when it was approaching, was brought down when a Taliban combatant fired an RPG-7. It crashed, killing the eight SEALs aboard and the crew. The second helicopter, which carried eight men from the 160th Army Special Operations Aviation Regiment, was ordered to leave the area and return to base. Three of the ambushed and outnumbered SEALs were killed during the firefight. The fourth managed to escape, although wounded. He was helped by a nearby villager until his rescue by friendly forces.

On 1 April, over 1,000 Coalition troops were deployed to relieve Sangin, Helmand Province, in south Afghanistan. An air assault was mounted against Taliban combatants south of the city by 82nd Airborne Division's 508th Infantry Regiment (Airborne). Two hundred and fifty British Royal Marine Commandos participated in the operation, supported by Danish and Estonian Special Operations units. Air support was provided by Royal Dutch and US Air Force fighter jets. On 16 July 2007, 200 British paratroopers were inserted by Chinook helicopters into Sangin, breaking the siege of the city by the Taliban. They were supported in the operation by 700 coalition troops, including American, Canadian and Estonian forces. Four days later, a twenty-man detachment from the British 3rd Battalion, the Parachute Regiment, were outnumbered by attacking Taliban combatants near Sangin. Belfast-born Corporal Bryan Budd, who was killed during the firefight, was posthumously awarded the Victoria Cross for heroism in the battlefield as he had killed three enemies single-handed. The remnants were rescued by friendly troops rushed to the area in helicopters. Four hundred and four soldiers, mostly from the airborne and Special Operations units, were killed during the re-deployment of British forces in Afghanistan to the Taliban stronghold of Helmand Province. Only five men had been killed in action during the previous deployment of the British Army in the region. By February 2010, the British death toll in Afghanistan had exceeded that of the Falklands War.

Meanwhile, a tactic applied by the US Special Forces in Afghanistan during counter-insurgency (COIN) missions combined air drops and helicopter extraction. The raiders parachuted in, stormed the objective and then helicopters arrived to retrieve the airborne troops. In another tactic, tested by the US Special Forces in Afghanistan, the paratroopers were dropped and secured the landing zone. Then, they were quickly reinforced by the main force arriving by helicopters and not overland as had previously been the standard practice in warfare.

A Kill-or-Capture Mission

On the night of 1/2 May 2011, Osama bin Laden was killed in Abbotabad, 34 miles (55km) from Islamabad, the capital of Pakistan, during an air assault involving two dozen US Navy SEALs and one Belgian Malinois military working dog.[48] Two Black Hawk helicopters delivered the SEAL Team 6 men to the compound, where the leader of al-Qaeda was residing with combatants and members of his family. Twenty-five more SEALs were standing by in three Chinook helicopters just across the border in Afghanistan in case reinforcements were needed.[49] One of the helicopters crash-landed but without any of the SEALs or crew on board being seriously injured. The raiders, wearing night vision goggles, stormed the compound, killing five people, including bin Laden, and capturing seventeen more. The SEALs suffered no casualties, although they came under enemy fire. The kill-or-capture mission was over in fifteen minutes although it was scheduled to last less than forty.[50] The SEALs destroyed the crash-landed helicopter with explosives before leaving the area. They were helicoptered to Bagram airfield, the largest US military base in Afghanistan, taking with them bin Laden's body. The killing of al-Qaeda's founder and leader is regarded a major strategic victory by the West in the US-led war against global terrorism.

Sumatra, the Central Africa Republic and Mali

The emphasis given by war planners to air-assault operations in the past few decades doesn't mean that the days of combat jumps are over. On 19 May 2003, 600 Indonesian paratroopers were dropped in Aceh, Sumatra to attack insurgents. On 5 March 2007, fifty-eight French paratroopers were dropped at Biayo, in the Central Africa Republic to seize an airfield. One of the major jumps conducted since 2000 was the drop of French paratroopers (11th Parachute Brigade) to capture Timbuktu in Mali from rebel insurgents. On 28 January 2013, 250 men from two companies of the 2e REP were parachuted onto north Timbuktu to block an enemy force. Five years later, on 27 September 2018, 120 French Legionnaires of the 2e REP were parachuted into the Ménaka region of north-eastern Mali near the Niger border. Forty jumped from an Airbus A400M Atlas and eighty from two Transall F-160s. This was the first time an A400M had been used in an operational parachute drop since its adoption by the French Air Force in 2013. Ménaka was at the time one of the most unstable area in Mali because of the activity of the Islamic State fighters in Greater Sahara.

Notes

Preface

1. *The Times of Israel*, 18 January 2015.

Chapter 1: The Origins of Military Parachuting

1. Gene Eric Salecker, *Blossoming Silk Against the Rising Sun: US and Japanese Paratroopers at War in the Pacific in World War II*, Stackpole, 2010, p. xiii.
2. A static line is a cord attached to an aerial platform. It is still in use for the automatic deployment of parachutes.
3. Bryan R. Swopes, *This Day in Aviation*, 1 March 2016.
4. Associated Press, 1 March 1912.
5. Tony Reichhardt, *Berry's Leap* [in: https://bit.ly/2WMcDnP; accessed: 06 June 2019].
6. Robert Jackson, *Bailing Out: Amazing Dramas of Military Flying*, Pen & Sword, 2006, p. 11.
7. Ibid., p. 21.
8. Ibid., p. 28.
9. Lee B. Kennett, *The First Air War 1914–1918*, Free Press, 1998.
10. Jackson, *Bailing Out*, p. 22.
11. Ibid., p. 22.
12. Jon Guttman, *Heinecke Parachute: A Leap of Faith for World War I German Airmen* [in: https://bit.ly/2Io6pkL; accessed: 06 June 2019].
13. C.G. Sweeting, *US Army Aviators' Equipment 1917–1945*, McFarland, 2015, p. 116.
14. Jackson, *Bailing Out*, p. 33.
15. Ibid., p. 23.
16. Ralf Barker, *The Royal Flying Corps in France*, Constable, 1995.
17. Jackson, *Bailing Out*, p. 30.
18. Sweeting, *US Army Aviators' Equipment*, pp. 120–1.
19. Ibid., p. 121.
20. *Popular Science Monthly*, November 1929, p. 65.
21. Salecker, *Blossoming Silk*, p. xi.
22. Diana G. Cornelisse, *Splendid Vision, Unswerving Purpose: Developing Air Power for the US Air Force During the First Century of Powered Flight*, USAF Publications, pp. 128–9.
23. Richard Stimson, *History of Flight: The Parachute* [in: https://bit.ly/2WUTgsY; accessed: 06 June 2019].
24. Sweeting, *US Army Aviators' Equipment*, p. 122.
25. Jackson, *Bailing Out*, p. 22.
26. IRVIN is the founder's surname and IRVING is the name of his company. The difference has to do with a typing error made accidentally on a legal document.
27. Scott A. Berg, *Lindbergh*, G.P. Putman's Sons, 1998, p. 73.
28. Leonard Moseley, *Lindbergh: A Biography*, Doubleday and Company, 1976, p. 56.
29. Jackson, *Bailing Out*, p. 33.

30. Amelia Mary Earhart was the first female aviator to fly solo across the Atlantic. She disappeared on 2 July 1937 near Lae, an island in Papua New Guinea, while attempting to make a circumnavigational flight of the globe in a Lockheed Mode 10-E Electra aircraft.

Chapter 2: The Four Pioneer Nations

1. Martin van Creveld, *Technology and War, From 2000 B.C. to the Present*, Brassey's, 1991, p. 188.
2. Franz Kurowski, *Jump Into Hell: German Paratroopers in World War II*, Stackpole, 2010, p. 2.
3. David M. Glantz, *The Soviet Airborne Experience, Research Survey No. 4*, Combat Studies Institute, 1984, p. 8.
4. Ibid., p. 6.
5. Jackson, *Bailing Out*, p. 36.
6. Hilary St. George Saunders, *The Red Beret*, New English Library, 1973, p. 21.
7. Kurowski, *Jump Into Hell*, p. 2.
8. Mircea Tănase, 'Collaboration Under the Canopy of the Parachute Within the Socialist Camp', *Annals of the Academy of Romanian Scientists* 4 (2012), p. 48.
9. Glantz, *The Soviet Airborne Experience*, p. 22.
10. Ibid., p. 132.
11. *Warfare History Network*, 6 July 2016.
12. Ibid.
13. *The Aeronautical Journal*, Volume 32, Issue 209, May 1928, pp. 340–1.
14. https://bit.ly/2WWieIt, accessed: 20 January 2018.
15. Nino Arena, *Folgore: Storia del Parachutismo Militare Italiano*, Centro Editoriale Nationale Divulgazioni Umanistiche Sociologiche Storiche, 1966, pp. 50–4.
16. BBC, 11 November 1942.
17. Angelo Pirocchi and Velimir Vuksic, *Italian Arditi: Elite Assault Troops 1917–1920*, Osprey Publishing, 2004, pp. 3–4.
18. Albert N. Garland and Howard McGaw Smyth, *Sicily and the Surrender of Italy*, Washington DC: Office of the Chief of Military History. Department of the Army, 1965, pp. 534–5.
19. Carlos Caballero Jurado, *Foreign Volunteers of the Wehrmacht 1941–1945*, Osprey Publishing, 1983, pp. 8–9.
20. Emmanuele Sica and Richard Carrier, *Italy and the Second World War. Alternative Perspectives*, Brill, 2018, p. 117.
21. https://bit.ly/2HXOp1C, accessed: 08 December 2017.
22. William Mitchell, *Memoirs of World War I*, Random House, 1960, p. 268.
23. Isaac Devine, *Mitchell: Pioneer of Air Power*, Duell, Sloan and Pearce, 1943, p. 151.
24. Franz Kurowski, *Deutsche Fallschirmjäger 1939–1945*, Aktuell, 1990, p. 12.
25. Gerald Devlin, *Paratrooper! The Saga of Paratroop and Glider Combat Troops During World War II*, Robson, 1979, p. 32.
26. H. H. Arnold, *Winged Warfare*, Harper and Brothers, 1941, p. 56.
27. Salecker, *Blossoming Silk*, p. xii.
28. Volkmar Kuhn, *German Paratroopers in World War II*, Ian Allen, 1978, p. 8.
29. G.W. Bush (Speech), 14 August 2002.
30. For more details, see: www.paradata.org.uk
31. Jerry Autry, *General William C. Lee, Father of the Airborne: Just Plain Bill*, Airborne Press, 1995.
32. For more details, see: www.airbornepress.com
33. Lieutenant Colonel John T. Ellis, *Paper on the U. S. Army Ground Forces, 1946*, Study No. 25, Washington DC: Historical Section, Army Ground Forces, p. 11.
34. Bart Hagerman, *USA Airborne: 50th Anniversary 1940–1990*, Turner Publishing, 1990, p. 31.
35. *The Atlanta Georgian*, 2 April 1917.
36. David Doyle, *M551 Sheridan*, Signal Publication, 2008, pp. 44–6.
37. Tim Cooke, *US Airborne Forces*, Powerkids Press, 2013, p. 6.

38. Jackson, *Bailing Out*, p. 40.
39. Hauptman Piehl, *Ganze Männer*, Verlagshaus Bong, 1943, p. 41.
40. Peter Darman, *A-Z of the SAS*, Sidgwick and Jackson, 1992, p. 19.
41. Ibid., p. 42.
42. Ibid., p. 91.
43. Ibid., p. 170.
44. Ibid., p. 58.

Chapter 3: The German Paratroopers

1. John Strawson, *Hitler as Military Commander*, Sphere Books Limited, 1973, p. 38.
2. Kurowski, *Jump into Hell*, p. 3.
3. Christopher Aisly, *Hitler's Sky Warriors: German Paratroopers in Action 1939–1945*, Spellmount Limited, 2000, p. 18.
4. Bruno Bräuer was the first German officer to complete parachute training. He fought in Crete in May 1941 and later served as a commander of the island. After the war, he was convicted of war crimes and was executed in Athens on the sixth anniversary of the German invasion of Crete.
5. Martin Pöppel, *Παράδεισος και Κόλαση, Το Πολεμικό Ημερολόγιο ενός Γερμανού Αλεξιπτωτιστή [Paradise and Hell, The Combat Diary of a German Paratrooper]*, Eurobooks, 2008, p. 10.
6. Richard Rule, 'Fallschirmjäger: The German Paratrooper Corps', *Warfare History Network*, 24 November 2018.
7. Generalmajor Hellmuth Reinhardt, *Airborne Operations. A German Appraisal*, Office of the Chief of Military History, Special Staff Department of the Army (Washington), 1989, p. 51.
8. Ibid.
9. Ibid., pp. 12, 13 and 52.
10. Ibid., p. 3.
11. Chris McNab, *German Paratroopers: The Illustrated History of the Fallschirmjäger*, MBI Publishing Company, 2000, p. 39.
12. Jeremy Black, *Introduction to Global Military History, 1775 to the Present Day*, Routledge, 2005, p. 121.
13. Owen Booth, *The Illustrated History of the Second World War*, Chartwell Books, 1998, pp. 44–9.
14. Bruce Quarrie, *German Airborne Troops 1939–1945*, Osprey Publishing, 2007, p. 7.
15. Peter Halclerode, *Wings of War: Airborne Warfare 1918–1945*, Weidenfeld and Nicolson, 2005, p. 48.
16. McNab, *German Paratroopers*, p. 50.
17. Reinhardt, *Airborne Operations*, p. 18.
18. McNab, *German Paratroopers*, p. 55.
19. Ibid., p. 52.
20. Ibid., p. 57.
21. Williamson Murray and Allan R. Millett, *A War to be Won, Fighting the Second World War*, The Belknap Press of Harvard University Press, 2000, p. 105.
22. McNab, *German Paratroopers*, p. 59.
23. Ibid.
24. Murray and Millett, *A War to be Won*, p. 105.
25. Andrew Roberts, *The Storm of War, A New History of the Second World War*, Allen Lane, 2009, pp. 125–6.
26. Murray and Millett, *A War to be Won*, p. 107.
27. Ibid., p. 106.
28. Ibid., p. 107.
29. Black, *Introduction*, p. 123.
30. Roberts, *The Storm of War*, p. 126.
31. Murray and Millett, *A War to be Won*, p. 106.
32. R. C. Mowat, *Ruin and Resurgence 1939–1945*, Blandford Press, 1966, p. 26.
33. Major Thomas J. Sheenan, *World War II Vertical Envelopment, The German Influence on US Army Airborne Operations*, US Army Command and General Staff College, 2003, p. 34.

34. Murray and Millett, *A War to be Won*, p. 107.
35. Roberts, *The Storm of War*, p. 126.
36. Mark Mazower, *Hitler's Empire: How the Nazis Ruled Europe*, Penguin, 2008, p. xiii.
37. Correlli Barnett, *Hitler's Generals*, Grove Press, 1989, p. 472.
38. Chris Mason, *Falling from Grace: The German Airborne in World War II*, US Marine Corps Command and Staff College/Marine Corps University, 2002, p. 30.
39. Roberts, *The Storm of War*, p. 127.
40. Reinhardt, *Airborne Operations*, pp. 20–1.
41. Mason, *Falling from Grace*, p. 30.
42. Murray and Millett, *A War to be Won*, p. 107.
43. Bonner F. Fellers, *Military Attaché Report, Airborne Invasion of Crete*, Military Intelligence Division, War Department General Staff, Egypt, 9 August 1941, p. 1.
44. David Polk, *World War II Airborne Carriers and Technology Engineering*, Turner Publishing Company, 1991, p. 8.
45. Reinhardt, *Airborne Operations*, p. 22.
46. Ibid.
47. Mason, *Falling from Grace*, p. v.
48. Reinhardt, *Airborne Operations*, p. 25.
49. Sheenan, *World War II Vertical Envelopment*, p. 48.
50. Reinhardt, *Airborne Operations*, p. 25.
51. Ibid., p. 33.
52. Peter Smith and Edwin Walker, *War in the Aegean*, William Kimber Publishing, 1974, pp. 116–17.
53. The German II Parachute Corps was created in 1943 from the 3rd and 5th Parachute Divisions and a division that had been raised in the Russian Front a year earlier by the then Generalmajor Eugen Mendl.
54. Martin Blumenson, *Breakout and Pursuit*, Washington Center of Military History, 1961, p. 655.
55. Derek Mallett, *Hitler's Generals in America, Nazi POWs and Allied Military Intelligence*, University Press of Kentucky, 2013, p. 43.
56. Cornelius Ryan, *A Bridge Too Far*, Hamish Hamilton, 1974, p. 49.
57. Peter Caddick-Adams, *Snow and Steel: The Battle of the Bulge 1944–1945*, Oxford University Press, 2014, p. 354.
58. Donald M. Goldstein, *Nuts! The Battle of the Bulge: The Story and Photographs*, Potomac Books, 1994, p. 191.
59. T.B.H. Otway, *The Second World War 1939–1945, Army Airborne Forces*, Imperial War Museum, 1990, p. 298.
60. Toby Thacker, *The End of the Third Reich*, Tempus Publishing, 2006, pp. 92–3.

Chapter 4: The British Paratroopers

1. Jackson, *Bailing Out*, p. 37.
2. Saunders, *The Red Beret*, p. 19.
3. Ibid., p. 44.
4. *The Telegraph*, 25 October 2015.
5. Saunders, *The Red Beret*, p. 131.
6. H.F. Joslen, *Orders of Battle. Second World War 1939–1945*, Naval and Military Press, 2003, p. 85.
7. Peter Harclerode, *Wings of War. Airborne Warfare 1918–1945*, Cassel, 2007, p. 223.
8. Ken Ford, *D-Day 1944. Sword Beach and the British Airborne Landings*, Bloomsbury Publishing, 2011, pp. 18–20.
9. Saunders, *The Red Beret*, p. 49.
10. Ibid., p. 56.
11. *The London Gazette* (Supplement), 15 May 1942.
12. Saunders, *The Red Beret*, p. 71.
13. Ibid., p. 75.

14. Ibid., p. 89.
15. Ibid., p. 109.
16. Otway, *The Second World War*, p. 70.
17. Richard Wiggan, *Operation Freshman*, William Kimber, 1986, p. 64.
18. Otway, *The Second World War*, p. 3.
19. R.C. Mowat, *Ruins and Resurgence 1939–1965*, Bradford Press, 1966, p. 132.
20. Howard N. Cole, *On Wings of Healing. The Story of the Airborne Medical Services 1940–1960*, William Blackwood, 1963, p. 67.
21. Gregory Ferguson, *The Paras 1940–1984*, Osprey Publishing, 1984, p. 14.
22. Saunders, *The Red Beret*, p. 274.
23. Dominique Eudes, *Οι Καπετάνιοι. Ο Ελληνικός Εμφύλιος Πόλεμος [The Greek Civil War 1943–1949]*, Εκδόσεις Εξάντας, 1975, p. 268.
24. Cole, *On Wings of Healing*, p. 72.
25. Saunders, *The Red Beret*, p. 274.
26. Ibid., p. 275.
27. Foreign and Commonwealth Office Archives, FCO 371/48245, R. 486.

Chapter 5: Other Allied Paratroopers

1. Steven J. Zaloga and Richard Hook, *The Polish Army 1939–1945*, Osprey Publishing, 1982, p. 21.
2. A covert operation's aim is to secretly fulfil a mission's objective without anyone knowing who sponsored or carried out the operation.
3. Edward T. Russell, *Leaping the Atlantic Wall. Army Air Forces Campaigns in Western Europe 1942–1945*, Air Force History and Museum Programme, 1999, p. 21.
4. Jan M. Cichanowski, *The Warsaw Rising*, Cambridge University Press, 2002, p. 67.
5. Ibid.
6. George Iranek-Osmecki, *The Unseen and Silent. Adventures from the Underground Movement Narrated by Paratroops of the Polish Home Army*, Sheed and Ward, 1954, p. 350.
7. The cap badge of the Belgian paratroopers was designed by Corporal Robert Tait, of the London (Scottish) Regiment.
8. Darman, *A-Z of the SAS*, p. 160.
9. Ibid., p. 181.
10. Bern Horn, 'A Question of Relevance. The Establishment of a Canadian Parachute Capability', *Canadian Military History*, Vol. 8, 1999, pp. 27–8.
11. Ibid.
12. *Toronto Daily Star*, 31 March 1945.
13. *Report Number 139*, Directorate of History, National Defence Headquarters, Ottawa, July, 1986.
14. Ιερός Λόχος (Ierôs Lôhos) in Greek means Sacred Company. The name did not change even when the unit grew to the size of a regiment.
15. Phillippe Dean (Philippe Dean-Gigantes), *I Should Have Died*, Hamish Hamilton, 1976, p. 141.
16. Darman, *A-Z of the SAS*, p. 156.
17. *Πόλεμος και Ιστορία (War and History)*, Vol. 41, Athens, March 2001, p. 15.
18. *A History of the Hellenic Army 1821–1997*, Hellenic Army General Staff, Army History Directorate, 1999, p. 223.
19. Peter Dennis, Jeffrey Gray, Ewan Morris, Robin Prior and Jean Bou, *The Oxford Companion to Australian Military History*, Oxford University Press, 2008, p. 410.
20. Gavin Long, *The Final Campaigns. Australia in the War of 1939–1945*, Australian War Memorial, 1963, p. 554.
21. Ibid.
22. Peter Dennis and Jeffrey Gray, *The Foundations of Victory. The Pacific War 1943–1944*, Army History Unit of Australia, 2004, p. 113.
23. *Australian Army, History in Focus*, 4 December 2016.

24. Ronald McNicoll, *The Royal Australian Engineers 1919–1945. Teeth and Tail. History of the Royal Australian Engineers*, Vol. 3, The Corps Committee of the R.A.E., 1982, p. 363.
25. Long, *The Final Campaigns*, p. 554.
26. Cliff Lord and Julian Tennant, *ANZAC Elite: The Airborne and Special Forces Insignia of Australia and New Zealand*, IPL Books, 2000, p. 16.
27. Ossie Baker, *These Were the First of the Spring. Paras in Home Front*, June 1990, pp. 6–7.
28. South African National Defence Forces, Archives File 'UDF Paratroop Company', Directorate of Documentation Services and Personnel Records Section, 23 July 1943.
29. Trooping the Colour (Brochure), 1 Parachute Battalion, Bloemfontein, 1 April 1982.
30. Nick van der Bijl, *No. 10 Inter-Allied Commando 1942–1946*, Osprey Publishing, 2006, p. 6.
31. Ibid., p. 8.
32. Ken Ford and Howard Gerrard, *D-Day 1944. Sword Beach and British Airborne Landings*, Osprey Publishing, 2002, p. 75.
33. David Horner, *SAS Phantoms on the Jungle. A History of the Australian Special Air Service*, Allen and Unwin, 1989, p.26.
34. G.B. Courtney, *Silent Feet. The History of Z Special Operations 1942–1945*, P.J. and S.P. Austin, 1993, p. 14.
35. Ian McGibbon, *The Oxford Companion to New Zealand Military History*, Oxford University Press, 2000, p. 627.

Chapter 6 Allied Airborne Operations in Europe (I)

1. M.J. Alexander and John Sparry, *Jump Commander. In Combat with the 505th and 508th Parachute Infantry Regiments, 82nd Airborne Division in World War II*, Casemate, 2010, p. 43.
2. Peter Harclerode, *Wings of War, Airborne Warfare 1918–1945*, Weidenfeld and Nicolson, 2005, p. 256.
3. Ferguson, *The Paras*, p. 11.
4. Clay Blair, *Ridgway's Paratroopers. The American Airborne in World War II*, Dial Press, 1985, p. 85.
5. Saunders, *The Red Beret*, p. 11.
6. Alexander and Sparry, *Jump Commander*, p. 80.
7. Brigadier C.J.C. Molony et al, *The Mediterranean and Middle East, The Campaign in Sicily 1943. History of the Second World War*, Naval and Military Press, 1973, pp. 81–2.
8. Guy LoFaro, *The Sword of St Michael. The 82nd Airborne Division in World War Two*, 2011, p. 141.
9. Samuel Mitcham and Friedrich von Stauffenberg, *The Battle of Sicily. How the Allies Lost their Chance for Total Victory*, Stackpole, 2007, p. 45.
10. Maurice Tugwell, *Airborne to Battle, A History of Airborne Warfare 1918–1971*, Kimber, 1971, p. 162.
11. Saunders, *The Red Beret*, p. 119.
12. Alfred Nigl, *Silent Wings Savage Death*, Graphic Publishers, 2007, p. 67.
13. David Reynolds, *Paras, An Illustrated History of Britain's Airborne Forces*, Sutton, 1998, p. 37.
14. Allen L. Langdon, *Ready, A World War Two History of the 505th PIR*, Western, 1986, p. 28.
15. *General Harold Alexander's dispatches, The Conquest of Sicily, The London Gazette* (Supplement), 10 February 1948, p. 1018.
16. E.M. Flanagan, *Airborne. A Combat History of American Airborne Forces*, Random House Publishing, 2005, p. 98.
17. James A. Huston, *Out of the Blue, United States Army Airborne Operations in World War II*, Purdue University Press, 1998, p. 137.
18. Victor Dover, *The Sky Generals*, Cassel, 1981, p. 82.
19. Saunders, *The Red Beret*, p. 267.
20. Antony Beevor, *D-Day. The Battle of Normandy*, Viking, 2009, pp. 51–2.
21. Darman, *A-Z of the SAS*, p. 179.
22. Barry Gregory, *Airborne Warfare 1918–1945*, Phoebus, 1979, p. 101.
23. Ken Ford and Steven J. Zaloga, *Overlord: The D-Day Landings*, Osprey, 2009, p. 207.
24. Harclerode, *Wings of War*, p. 309.

25. Will Fowler, *Pegasus Bridge Bénouville. D-Day 1944*, Osprey, 2010, p. 49.
26. William F. Buckingham, *D-Day. The First 72 Hours*, Tempus, 2005, p. 119.
27. Ibid., p. 123.
28. Otway, *The Second World War*, p. 178.
29. Stephen E. Ambrose, *Pegasus Bridge*, 2003, pp. 155–68.
30. Buckingham, *D-Day*, pp. 142–3.
31. Harclerode, *Wings of War*, p. 318.
32. Robert Johns had volunteered for army service at 14 having lied about his real age. When he died, Private R. Johns, of the 13th Parachute Battalion, was two years below the minimum age for active service (*MailOnline*, 22 May 2016).
33. Harclerode, *Wings of War*, p. 363.
34. Otway, *The Second World War*, p. 91.
35. R.N. Gale, *With the 6th Airborne Division in Normandy*, Sampson Low, 1948, p. 95.
36. Julie Guard, *Airborne. World War Two Paratroopers in Combat*, Osprey, 2007, p. 184.
37. Chester Wilmot, *The Struggle for Europe*, Wordsworth Editions, 1997, p. 243.
38. George E. Koskinaki, *D-Day with the Screaming Eagles*, Casemate, 1970, p. 250.
39. Alexander and Sparry, *Jump Commander*, p. 197.
40. Blair, *Ridgway's Paratroopers*, p. 295.
41. Robert J. Kershaw, *It Never Snows in September. The German View of Market-Garden and the Battle of Arnhem*, Ian Allen, 2004, p. 14.
42. John C. Warren, *Airborne Missions in the Mediterranean 1942–1945*, Maxwell A.F.B, 1955, p. 82.
43. Saunders, *The Red Beret*, p. 270.
44. Ibid.
45. Ibid., p. 271.
46. Jeffrey J. Clark and Robert Ross Smith, *Riviera to the Rhine. The United States Army in World War II, European Theater of Operations*, Center of Military History, US Army, 1993, pp. 118–25.

Chapter 7: Allied Airborne Operations in Europe (II)

1. Donald R. Burgett, *The Road to Arnhem*, Dell, 2001, p. 14.
2. Christopher Hibbert, *Arnhem*, Phoenix, 2003, pp. 29–30.
3. Henry Kreisler, *A Life in Peace and War. Conversation with Sir Brian Urquhart*, Institute of International Studies, University of California, Berkley, 19 March 1996, p. 2.
4. John Frost, *A Drop too Many*, Cassell, 1980, p. 198.
5. Cornelius Ryan, *A Bridge Too Far*, Popular Library, 1974, p. 258.
6. John C. Warren, *Airborne Operations in World War Two*, USAF Historical Division, 1956, p. 98.
7. Ferguson, *The Paras 1940–1984*, p. 21.
8. Flanagan, *Airborne*, p. 245.
9. Robert Urquhart, *Arnhem*, Pen & Sword, 2007, pp. 5–10.
10. Tugwell, *Airborne for Battle*, p. 239.
11. Kershaw, *It Never Snows in September*, p. 23.
12. Harclerode, *Wings of War*, p. 460.
13. Darman, *A-Z of the SAS*, p. 51.
14. Burgett, *The Road to Arnhem*, p. 41.
15. Ibid., pp. 233–6.
16. John Waddy, *A Tour of the Arnhem Battlefields*, Pen & Sword, 1999, p. 42.
17. Saunders, *The Red Beret*, p. 217.
18. Tugwell, *Airborne for Battle*, p. 258.
19. Martin Evans, *The Battle for Arnhem*, Pitkin, 1998, p. 6.
20. Lloyd Clark, *Arnhem. Jumping the Rhine 1944 and 1945*, Headline, 2008, p. 170.
21. Martin Middlebrook, *Arnhem 1944. The Airborne Battle*, Viking, 1994, pp. 195–6.
22. *The London Gazette* (Supplement), 23 November 1944, pp. 5375–6.

23. Middlebrook, *Arnhem 1944*, pp. 267–70.
24. Zaloga and Hook, *The Polish Army*, p. 21.
25. *The London Gazette* (Supplement), 2 November 1944, pp. 5015–16.
26. Middlebrook, *Arnhem 1944*, pp. 282–6.
27. Frost, *A Drop too Many*, p. 229.
28. Middlebrook, *Arnhem 1944*, p. 321.
29. William F. Buckingham, *Arnhem*, Tempus, 2002, p. 79.
30. *Private Papers of Major-General R. E. Urquhart*, CB DSO, Imperial War Museum, Documents: 15783 (07/64/1-12).
31. Ferguson, *The Paras 1940–1984*, p. 26.
32. Nigl, *Silent Wings Savage Death*, p. 75.
33. Frost, *A Drop too Many*, p. 198.
34. Ibid., p. 12.
35. Burgett, *The Road to Arnhem*, p. 23.
36. Ibid.
37. James Gavin, *Airborne Warfare*, Infantry Journal Press, 1947, p. 121.
38. Frost, *A Drop too Many*, p. 242.
39. Flanagan, *Airborne*, p. 265.
40. Philip Nordyke, *Four Stars of Valor. The Combat History of the 505th PIR in World War II*, Zenith, 2006, pp. 329–31.
41. James Gavin, *On to Berlin. Battles of an Airborne Commander 1943–1946*, Viking Press, 1978, p. 239.
42. Guy LoFaro, *The Sword of St. Michael. The 82nd Airborne Division in World War II*, Hachette UK, 2011, p. 481.
43. Gary F. Evans, *The 501st PIR at Bastogne, Belgium, December 1944*, US Army Center of Military History, Historical Manuscripts Collection 8-3.1 BB2, 22 June 1972.
44. *The New York Times*, 10 January 2009.
45. Flanagan, *Airborne*, p. 268.
46. Bart Hagerman, *17th Airborne Division*, Turner, 1999, p. 28.
47. Burgett, *The Road to Arnhem*, p. 134.
48. Saunders, *The Red Beret*, p. 279.
49. Otway, *The Second World War*, p. 304.
50. Barry Gregory and John Bacheler, *Airborne Warfare 1918–1945*, Exeter Books, 1979, pp. 83–4.
51. Tugwell, *Airborne to Battle*, p. 273.
52. Devlin, *Paratrooper!*, p. 624.
53. Saunders, *The Red Beret*, p. 90.
54. Harclerode, *Wings of War*, pp. 559–61.
55. Cole, *On Wings of Healing*, p. 166.
56. Saunders, *The Red Beret*, p. 289.
57. Devlin, *Paratrooper!*, p. 617.
58. *The London Gazette*, 31 July 1945, p. 3965.
59. Saunders, *The Red Beret*, p. 289.
60. Huston, *Out of the Blue*, p. 215.
61. G. G. Norton, *The Red Devils. The Story of the British Airborne Forces*, Pan Books, 1973, p. 93.

Chapter 8: Japanese, Indian, Gurkha and Chinese Paratroopers

1. *The London Gazette*, 6 May 1919, p. 5652.
2. Air Vice Marshal Alan Johnson, 'The Evolution of Parachutes for Aircrew', *Royal Air Force Historical Society Journal* 37 (2006), p. 28.
3. Gordon L. Rottman and Akira Takizawa, *Japanese Paratroop Forces of World War II*, Osprey Publishing, 2005, p. 4.
4. Salecker, *Blossoming Silk*, p. 11.

5. Ibid., p. 10.
6. Maurice Tugwell, *Assault from the Sky. The History of Airborne Warfare*, Kimber, 1978, p. 279.
7. Salecker, *Blossoming Silk*, pp. 5–6.
8. Ibid., p. 8.
9. Ibid., p. 7.
10. Donald Miller, *The Story of WWII*, Simon and Schuster, 2001, p. 422.
11. Imperial Japanese Navy, Sixth Air Army Report, Confidential Telegram No. 121340, 12 June 1945.
12. Luis Allen, *Burma: The Longest War 1941–1945*, Dent, 1984, p. 220.
13. More information about the airborne forces of India and Pakistan that were raised after the two countries became independent from Britain can be found in Chapter 14.
14. Wang Zen, Chinadaily.com, 19 May 2015.
15. Alexander and Sparry, *Jump Commander*, p. 248.
16. Ibid., p. 256.

Chapter 9: Allied Airborne Operations in the Pacific

1. Ronald H. Spector, *Eagle against the Sun*, Vintage Books, 1985, p. 143.
2. Matthew A. Sweeney, *American Operations in the Pacific Theater. Extending Operational Reach and Creating Operational Shock*, School of Advanced Military Studies, United States Army Command and General Staff College, Monograph, 2014, p. 1.
3. Salecker, *Blossoming Silk*, p. 318.
4. Library of Congress, *Reports of General Douglas MacArthur*, p. 124.
5. Salecker, *Blossoming Silk*, pp. 125–6.
6. Dennis and Gray, *The Foundations of Victory*, p. 113.
7. Library of Congress, *Reports of General Douglas MacArthur*, p. 124.
8. Samuel Eliot Morison, *History of US Naval Operations in World War II. New Guinea and the Marianas, March 1944–August 1944*, University of Illinois Press, 1953, p. 139.
9. Library of Congress, *Reports of General Douglas MacArthur*, p. 124.
10. Dennis and Gray, *The Foundations of Victory*, p. 113.
11. Michael Calvert, *Chindits. Long Range Penetration*, Pan/Ballantine, 1975, p. 159.
12. Dwight Jon Zimmerman, 'Wingate, the Chindits and Operation Loincloth', *Defence Media Network*, 24 March 2015.
13. Calvert, *Chindits*, p. 159.
14. Brian Bond and Kyoichi Tachikawa, *British and Japanese Leadership in the Far Eastern War 1941–1945*, vol. 17 of a Military History and Policy series, Routledge, 2004, p. 122.
15. Field Marshal William Slim, *Defeat into Victory*, Pan Military Classics, p. 506.
16. General Woodburn Kirby, *The War Against Japan, vol. 4*, Her Majesty's Stationery Office, London, 1962, p. 394.
17. Allen, *Burma*, p. 479.
18. Tugwell, *Assault from the Sky*, p. 279.
19. Devlin, *Paratrooper!*, p. 562.
20. Library of Congress, *Reports of General Douglas MacArthur*, p. 266.
21. Devlin, *Paratrooper!*, p. 566.
22. William Bruer, *Retaking the Philippines. America's Return to Corregidor and Bataan, October 1944–March 1945*, Saint Martin's Press, 1986, p. 137.
23. Harclerode, *Wings of War*, pp. 613–14.
24. Devlin, *Paratrooper!*, p. 566.
25. Salecker, *Blossoming Silk*, p. 237.
26. Marvin Miller, *The 11th Airborne Brick*, Miller, 2011, p. 54.
27. Salecker, *Blossoming Silk*, p. 241.
28. *Axis History Forum*, 7 June 2004.
29. Devlin, *Paratrooper!*, p. 571.

30. Salecker, *Blossoming Silk*, p. 241.
31. Devlin, *Paratrooper!*, p. 573.
32. Robert L. Eichelberger, *Our Jungle Road to Tokyo*, Viking Press, 1950, p. 195.
33. Harclerode, *Wings of War*, p. 21.
34. Ibid., p. 624.
35. Salecker, *Blossoming Silk*, p. 221
36. Edward Flanagan, *The Rock Force Assault*, Presidio Press, 1945, p. 23.
37. Salecker, *Blossoming Silk*, p. 250.
38. Flanagan, *The Rock Force Assault*, p. 174.
39. Ibid., p. 178.
40. Flanagan, *The Rock Force Assault*, p. 211.
41. Ibid., pp. 261–5.
42. Ibid., p. 291.
43. Salecker, *Blossoming Silk*, p. 280.
44. 'Rescue at Dawn. The Los Baños raid': A documentary hosted by Will Lyman; *The History Channel*.
45. Harclerode, *Wings of War*, pp. 623–4.
46. Patrick K. O'Donnel, *World War Two's Pacific Veterans Reveal the Heart of Combat*, Free Press, 2010, p. 197.
47. Harclerode, *Wings of War*, p. 636.
48. *Army Battle Casualties and Nonbattle Deaths*, Statistics and Accounting Branch, Office of the Adjutant General, Final Report, 1 June 1953, pp. 88–9.
49. *The 188 GIR, Unit History*: [https://www.ww2-airborne.us/units/188/188.html]
50. Flanagan, *The Rock Force Assault*, p. 345.
51. Huston, *Out of the Blue*, p. 231.
52. Flanagan, *The Rock Force Assault*, p. 345.

Chapter 10: Second World War Special Operations Units

1. Darman, *A-Z of the SAS*, p. ii.
2. Ibid., p. 46.
3. Ibid., p. 174.
4. Leroy Thompson, *SAS. Great Britain's Elite Special Air Service*, Zenith Imprint, 1994, p. 48.
5. Darman, *A-Z of the SAS*, p. 127.
6. Michael E. Haskew, *Encyclopedia of Elite Forces in the Second World War*, Pen and Sword, 2007, p. 40.
7. Darman, *A-Z of the SAS*, p. 127.
8. Haskew, *Encyclopedia of Elite Forces*, p. 40.
9. Darman, *A-Z of the SAS*, pp. 9 and 178.
10. Ibid., p. 127.
11. Andrea Molinari, *Desert Raiders: Axis and Allied Special Forces 1940–1943*, Osprey Publishing, 2007, p. 75.
12. James Short and Angus McBride, *The Special Air Service*, Osprey Publishing, 1981, p. 9.
13. Ibid., p. 9.
14. *Daily Mail*, 21 February 2008.
15. Darman, *A-Z of the SAS*, p. 114.
16. Ibid., p. 142.
17. Ibid., p. 42.
18. Haskew, *Encyclopedia of Elite Forces*, p. 54.
19. Molinari, *Desert Raiders*, p. 75.
20. Darman, *A-Z of the SAS*, p. 163.
21. Ibid., p. 49.
22. Short and McBride, *The Special Air Service*, p. 11.
23. Haskew, *Encyclopedia of Elite* Forces, p. 42.
24. Mike Morgan, *Daggers Down: Second World War Heroes of the SAS and the SBS*, Sutton, 2000, p. 15.

25. Darman, *A-Z of the SAS*, p. 34.
26. Ibid., p. 18.
27. Ibid., p. 170.
28. Ibid., p. 114.
29. Ibid., p. 61.
30. Ibid., p. 37.
31. *The Times*, 6 June 2006.
32. Short and McBride, *The Special Air Service*, p. 14.
33. Darman, *A-Z of the SAS*, p. 130.
34. Ibid., p. 81.
35. Ibid., p. 30.
36. Ibid., p. 153.
37. Ibid., p. 48.
38. Ibid., p. 175.
39. Ibid., p. 62.
40. Shortt and McBride, *The Special Air Service*, p. 15.
41. Darman, *A-Z of the SAS*, p. 131.
42. C.N. Trueman, 'The History Learning Site', 25 May 2015.
43. Darman, *A-Z of the SAS*, p. 11.
44. Ted Kemp, *A Commemorative History: First Special Service Force*, Taylor Publishing, 1995, p. 15.
45. Bret Werner and Michael Welply, *First Special Service Force*, Osprey Publishing, 2006, p. 5.
46. https://www.sfa28.org/frederick-award; accessed: 10. 12. 2017.
47. Kemp, *A Commemorative History*, p. 64.
48. Shelby Stanton, *World War II Order of Battle. An Encyclopedic Reference to US Army Ground Forces from Battalion through Division, 1939–1946*, Stackpole Books, 2006, p. 191.
49. Robert H. Adleman and Colonel George Walton, *The Devil's Brigade*, Chilton Books, 1966, p. 19.
50. Kemp, *A Commemorative History*, p. 18.
51. Ibid., p. 21.
52. Ibid., p. 29.
53. Ken Joyce, *Snow Plough and the Jupiter Deception: The Story of the 1st Special Service Force and the 1st Canadian Special Service Battalion 1942–1945*, Vanwell Publishing, 2006, p. 118.
54. John C. Fredricksen, *American Military Leaders: From Colonial Times to the Present*, Volume 2, ABC-CLIO, 1999, p. 270.
55. Ibid.
56. Warren, *Airborne Missions in the Mediterranean*, p. 94.
57. Joyce, *Snow Plough*, p. 273.
58. M.R.D. Foot, *The Special Operations Executive 1940–1946*, Pimlico, 1999, p. 62.
59. David Stafford, *Mission Accomplished: SOE and Italy 1943–1945*, The Bodley Head, 2011, pp. 45–51.
60. Roderick Bailey, *Target Italy: The Secret War against Mussolini 1940–1943*, Faber and Faber, 2014, pp. 61–4.
61. S.B. Dyson, *Origins of the Psychological Profiling of Political Leaders: The US Office of Strategic Services and Adolf Hitler*, Intelligence and National Security, 29, 2014, pp. 654–74.
62. Peter Wilkinson and Joan Bright Astley, *Gubbins and S.O.E.*, Pen and Sword Military, 2010, p. 95.
63. David W. Hogan, *US Army Special Operations in World War II*, Center of Military History, Department of the Army, pp. 49–50.
64. Darman, *A-Z of the SAS*, p. 90.
65. Giles Milton, *The Ministry of Ungentlemanly Warfare*, John Murray, 2016, p. 282.
66. Anne-Marie Walters, *Moondrop to Gascony*, Moho Books, 2009, p. 219.
67. http://www.pegasusarchive.org/arnhem/war_1stbde.htm ; accessed: 29.10.2017
68. Heinze Hölne, *Canaris: Hitler's Master Spy*, Doubleday, 1979, p. 377.
69. Helmuth Spaeter, *Dier Brandenburger: Eine Deutsche Kommandotruppe*, Angerer, 1982, pp. 47–54.
70. Ibid., pp. 250–73.

71. Christopher Ailsby, *Hitler's Sky Warriors: German Paratroopers in Action 1939–1945*, Spellmount, 2000, p. 91.
72. Peter Smith and Edwin Walker, *War in the Aegean*, William Kimber Publishing, 1974, pp. 116–27.
73. Lieutenant Colonel Wayne D. Eyre, 'Operation RÖSSELSPRUNG and The Elimination of Tito, May 25, 1944: A Failure in Planning and Intelligence Support', *The Journal of Slavic Military Studies* 19 (2006), 343–76.
74. Antonio J. Munoz, *Forgotten Legions. Obscure Combat Formations of the Waffen-SS*, Paladin Press, 1991, p. 42.

Chapter 11: Parachutes and Pilots in the Second World War

1. Henry Sakaida, *Japanese Army and Air Force Aces 1937–1945*, Osprey, 1997, p. 33.
2. Ibid.
3. Colin D. Heaton, 'Luftwaffe Eagle: Johannes Steinhoff', *Military History Magazine* (February 2000).
4. Townsend was the first Allied flying officer to shot down a Luftwaffe aircraft. It happened on 2 February 1940, when two Hurricanes from RAF Acklington attacked a Luftwaffe Heinkel He 111 near Whitby in North Yorkshire
5. Robert Tate, *Hans-Joachim Marseille, An Illustrated Tribute to the Luftwaffe's 'Star of Africa'*, Schiffer Publishing, 2008, p. 16.
6. John Weal, *Jadgeschwader 2 'Richthofen'*, Osprey Publishing, 2000, p. 106.
7. *London Gazette*, 1 January 1945.
8. Gerhard Steinecke, *Ritterkreuzträger Profile Nr 11 Hans Philipp – Einer von Vielen*, Unitec-Medienvetrieb, 2012, p. 34.
9. Ernst Obermaier, *Die Ritterkreuzträger der Luftwaffe Jagdflieger 1939–1945 [The Knight's Cross Bearers of the Luftwaffe Fighter Force 1939–1945]*, Verlag Dieter Hoffman, 1989, p. 160.
10. *The Merseyside Few*, 10 September 2010.
11. Jerry Scutts, *Night Fighter Aces of WWII*, Osprey Publishing, 1998, pp. 54–6; Christopher Shores, *Air Aces*, Presidio, 1983, p. 152.
12. Reina Pennington, *Wings, Women and War: Soviet Airwomen in World War II Combat*, University of Kansas, 2001, p. 134.
13. Reina Pennington and Robin Higham, *Amazons to Fighter Pilots: A Biographical Dictionary of Military Women*, Vol. I, Greenwood Press, 2003, p. 172.
14. David P. Williams, *Hunters of the Reich: Night Fighters*, Spellmount, 2011, p. 177.
15. Andrew Johannes Matthews and John Foreman, *Luftwaffe Aces – Biographies and Victories Claimed*, Vol. 3, Red Kite, 2015, pp. 1065–9.
16. Raymond F. Toliver and J. Trevor Constable, *Fighter Aces of the Luftwaffe*, Schiffer Publishing 1996, p. 250.
17. Mike Spick, *Aces in the Reich*, Greenhill Books, 2006, pp. 231–2.
18. Ernst Obermaier, *Die Ritterkreuzträger der Luftwaffe Jagdflieger 1939–1945*, Verlag Dieter Hoffman, 1989, p. 244.
19. Ibid., p. 186.
20. *The Daily Telegraph*, 27 December 2011.
21. *The London Gazette* (Supplement), 3 September 1940, pp. 5343–4.
22. Ibid., 15 August 1941, p. 4726.
23. Lieutenant Adolf Pietrasiak resumed combat missions after parachuting to safety. On 9 November 1943, he took off from England in a Spitfire and never returned. His body was never found.
24. B.S. Northway (ed.), *A History of 107 Squadron*, Tuddenham, UK: No. 107 Squadron RAF, 1963, p. 22.
25. Jackson, *Bailing Out*, p. 44.
26. Charles Hoyt Watson, *DeShazer: The Doolittle Raider Who Turned Missionary*, The Light and Life Press, 1950, p. 20.
27. Carroll V. Glines, *The Doolittle Raid: America's Daring First Strike Against Japan*, Orion Books, 1988, pp. 166–8.

28. He had his legs amputated in 1931 following a plane crash he was involved in as an RAF pilot.
29. Laddie Lucas, *Flying Colours: The Epic Story of Douglas Bader*, Hutchinson Publishing Group, 1981, p. 187.
30. Matthew Parker, *Battle of Britain: July–October 1940 – An Oral History of Britain's 'Finest Hour'*, Headline, 2001, p. 292.
31. *The Times*, 29 June 2005.
32. *The London Gazette* (Supplement), No. 36,133, 27 July 1943, p. 3444.
33. Ιστορία της Ελληνικής Πολεμικής Αεροπορίας, Τόμος Γ ('History of the Hellenic Air Force, Vol. III'), Athens, 1990, p. 195.
34. Πρωία [Proia newspaper], 17 November 1940.
35. J.R. Smith and A. Kay, *German Aircraft of the Second World War*, Putnam, 1972, p. 492.
36. Gebhard Aders and Werner Held, *Jagdgeschwader 51 'Mölders' Eine Chronik – Berichte – Erlenisse – Dokumente (Fighter Wing 51 'Mölders', A Chronicle – Reports – Experiences – Documents)*, Motorbuch Verlag, 1993, pp. 181–2.
37. Martin Gilbert, *The Second World War*, Henry Holt, 2004, p. 504.
38. Gary Hyland and Anton Gill, *Last Talons of the Eagle*, Headline, 1999, p. 221.
39. Steven J. Zaloga and Jim Laurie, *V-1 Flying Bomb 1942–1952*, Osprey Publishing, 2005, p. 39.
40. *San Antonio Express*, 30 June 2006.
41. *The Times of India*, 24 April 2018.
42. Wilbur W. Mayhew, *Pictorial History of the 7th Bombardment Group*, Historical Foundation, 1988, p. 286.
43. Leroy Thompson, *The Colt 1911 Pistol*, Osprey Publishing, 2011, p. 42.
44. Ibid., p. 42.
45. Melton had been shot down over Rangoon on 25 November 1943.
46. John L. Frishbee, 'Valor: David and Goliath', *Air Force Magazine* (July 1966), p. 79.
47. Jackson, *Bailing Out*, p. 42.
48. Alexander Gillespie, *A History of the Laws of War*, Volume I, Hart Publishing, 2011, p. 56.
49. Patrick Bishop, *Fighter Boys: The Battle of Britain*, Penguin Books, 2004, p. 194.
50. Kristen Alexander, *Clive Caldwell: Air Ace*, Allen and Unwin, 2006, pp. xviii–xxii.
51. Ibid., p. 28.
52. *The London Gazette* (Supplement), 11 September 1946.
53. Davide Beretta, *Batterie Semoventi Alto Zero: Quelli di El Alamein*, Mursia, 1977, p. 190.
54. John Weal, *Fw 190, Defence of the Reich Aces*, Osprey Publishing, 2011, p. 70.
55. Obermaier, *Die Ritterkreuzträger*, p. 176.
56. Jay A. Stout, *Fighter Group: The 352nd 'Blue-Nosed Bastards' in WWII*, Stackpole Books, 2012, p. 128.
57. Stephen Darlow, *D-Day Bombers, The Veteran's Story: RAF Bomber Command and the US Eighth Force Support to the Normandy Invasion 1944*, Kindle, 2004, p. 271.
58. Protocol Additional to the Geneva Conventions of 12 August 1949 and relating to the Protection of Victims of International Armed Conflict (Protocol 1), 8 June 1977, International Committee of the Red Cross.

Chapter 12: Other Paratroopers

1. R H. Markham, *Tito's Imperial Communism*, Kessinger Publishing, 2005, p. 184.
2. Michael I (Mihai I) was the last king of Romania. He reigned from 1927 to 1930 and from 1940 until his abdication on 30 December 1947.
3. Otopeni airfield, located 10 miles (16km) north of Bucharest was used as an air base by the Germans during the Second World War. In 2018, Otopeni was one of the two airports serving the capital.
4. www.ww2f.com/Russia-war/21827-forgotten-eastern-front.html
5. Mircea Tănase, 'Collaboration Under the Canopy of the Parachute Within the Socialist Camp', *Annals of the Academy of Romanian Scientists, Series of History and Archaeology*, Vol. 4 (2012), 47.
6. Adrian Cioroianu, 'Atuurile Rui Georghe Georghiu-Dej', *Dosarele Istoriei* 3 (1997), 2.

7. This particular Junker Ju 52 plane belonged to the Norwegian Air Force. It had fled to Finland following the invasion of Norway by German troops in April 1940.
8. Axis History Forum, 15 February 2006.
9. A pair of Heinkel He 115 seaplanes, on loan from Luftwaffe, were flown by Finnish pilots.
10. Axis History Forum, 6 December 2010.
11. Axis History Forum, 14 July 2008.
12. Utti Jaeger Regiment, maavoimat.fi.
13. She was Katarina Matanović, Yugoslavia's first female parachutist.
14. Skopje is today the capital of Northern Macedonia, Batajnica is a town near Belgrade, the capital of Serbia and Cerklje is a town in north-western Slovenia.
15. Mexico started with the formation of an airborne unit in 1945 with Sweden and Indonesia to follow six years later. Norway and the Philippines acquired their first airborne force in 1962 with more countries to follow.
16. The name of Turkey's first Special Forces unit was *Hususi ve Yardimci Muharip Birlikleri*.
17. David Miller, *The Illustrated Directory of Special Forces*, Zenith Imprint, 2002, p. 98.
18. In 1993, with the rise of the Kurdish insurgency, the Hakkâri Mountain and Commando Battalion was upgraded into a brigade.
19. Peru's first parachutist was a civilian mechanic, Enrique Tavernie, who was dropped onto Las Palmas airfield, near Lima, on 27 March 1927 from an AVRO airplane.
20. General Alberto Thorndike Elmore, 1 December 2006: http://www.arribasiemprearriba.com/Articulos/ParacaidismoEnElPeru.htm
21. Alvaro de Souza Pinheiro, *Knowing Your Partner, The Evolution of Brazilian Special Operations Forces, Report 12-7*, Joint Special Operations University, 2012, pp. 40–1.

Chapter 13: Post-1945 Operations (I)

1. Cole, *On Wings of Healing*, pp. 196–7.
2. Martin Brayley, *The British Army 1939–1945: The Far East*, Osprey Publishing, 2002, p. 47.
3. M.C. Ricklefs, *A History of Modern Indonesia since 1300*, Stanford University Press, 1991, p. 224.
4. Anthony Reid, *The Indonesian National Revolution 1945–1950*, Longman, 1974, p. 152.
5. Ibid., p. 153.
6. Adrian Vickers, *A History of Modern Indonesia*, Cambridge University Press, 2005, p. 100.
7. J. De Moor, *Westerling's Oorlog* [in Dutch], Balans, 1999, pp. 437–512.
8. Owen Pearson, *Albania in the Twentieth Century: A History*, Vol. III, I.B. Tauris, 2006, p. 375.
9. Ibid., p. 377.
10. Terry White, *Swords of Lightning*, Brassey's, 1992, p. 122.
11. Darman, *A-Z of the SAS*, p. 109.
12. J. Paul de B. Taillon, *The Evolution of Special Forces in Counter Terrorism. The British and American Experience*, Greenwood, 2000, p. 29.
13. K.C. Slater, *Air Operations in Malaya, Anthology of Selected Topics on Counterinsurgency*, Vol. II, Lackland Military Training Center, 1963, p. 196.
14. Alastair MacKenzie, *Special Force: The Untold Story of 22nd Special Air Service (SAS) Regiment*, I.B. Tauris, 2011, p. 69.
15. Ibid., pp. 69–70.
16. Ibid., p. 71.
17. *New York Times*, 9 May 1948.
18. Robert O' Neil, *Australia in the Korean War 1950–1953, Combat Operations*, Vol. II, Australian War Museum, 1985, p. 706.
19. Darman, *A-Z of the SAS*, p. 96.
20. Shelby L. Stanton, *Rangers at War*, Ivy Books, 1993, pp. 8–9.
21. Thomas Taylor, *Rangers Lead the Way*, Turner Publishing, 1996, p. 102.
22. James L. Stokesbury, *A Short History of the Korean War*, Harper Perennial, 1990, p. 90.

23. Roy E. Appleman, *South to the Naktong, North to the Yalu: US Army in the Korean War, June–November 1950*, US Department of the Army, 1998, p. 654.
24. George Odgers, *Remembering Korea: Australians in the War of 1950–1953*, New Holland Publishers, 2009, p. 44.
25. Appleman, *South to the Naktong*, p. 656.
26. E.M. Flanagan, *The Rakkasans: The Combat History of the 187th Airborne Infantry*, Presidio, 1997, p. 161.
27. Ibid.
28. Jack Gallaway, *The Last Call of the Bugle: The Long Road to Kapyong*, University of Queensland Press, 1999, p. 74.
29. Norman Bartlett (ed.), *With the Australians in Korea*, Australian War Memorial, 1960, p. 30.
30. Appleman, *South to the Naktong*, p. 660.
31. Ibid., p. 658.
32. Flanagan, *The Rakkasans*, p. 166.
33. *US Airforce Magazine*, October 2000.
34. Michael F. Dilley and Lance Q. Zedric, *Elite Warriors: 300 Years of America's Best Fighting Troops*, Pathfinder Publishing, 1999, p. 202.
35. Michael Varhola, *Fire and Ice: The Korean War 1950–1953*, Da Capo Press, 2000, p. 114.
36. *The New York Times*, 14 November 1951.
37. Walter G. Hermes, *Truce Tents and Fighting Front: The Last Two Years*, Center of Military History, 1990, pp. 233–62.
38. Samuel Zaffrini, *Westmoreland: Biography of General William C. Westmoreland*, Morrow and Company, 1994, p. 81.
39. *Los Angeles Times*, 13 September 1998.
40. Martin Windrow and Wayne Braby, *French Foreign Legion Paratroops*, Osprey Publishing, 1985, p. 12.
41. George C. Herring and Bernard B. Fall, *Street Without Joy: The French Debacle in Indochina*, Stackpole Books, 2005, pp. 28–31.
42. Phillip Davidson, *Vietnam at War: The History 1946–1975*, Presidio Press, 1988, p. 49.
43. Harry Summers, *Historical Atlas of the Vietnam War*, Houghton Mifflin, 1995, pp. 28–31.
44. Qiang Zhai, *China and the Vietnam Wars 1950–1975*, University of North Carolina Press, 2000, p. 31.
45. Fredrik Logevall, *Embers of War: The Fall of an Empire and the Making of America's Vietnam*, Random House, 2012, p. 329.
46. Spencer C. Tucker, *Vietnam*, University Press of Kentucky, 1999, p. 65.
47. Logevall, *Embers of War*, p. 323.
48. Max Boot, 'The Consummate Warrior', *The Weekly Standard*, 5 July 2010.
49. Bernard Fall, *Street without Joy*, Schocken Books, 1989, pp. 97–103.
50. Logevall, *Embers of War*, p. 329.
51. Fall, *Street without Joy*, p. 171.
52. *The Times* (London), 31 July 1953.
53. James F. Humphries, *Through the Valley: Vietnam 1967–1968*, Lynne Rienner Publishers, 1999, p. 214.
54. Martin Windrow, *The Last Valley: Dien Bien Phu and the Last French Defeat in Vietnam*, Weidenfeld and Nicolson, 2004, p. 195.
55. Ibid., p. 245.
56. Andrew Wiest, *Rolling Thunder in a Gentle Land*, Osprey Publishing, 2006, p. 43.
57. Windrow, *The Last Valley*, p. 222.
58. Major Vincent J. Goulding, *Dien Bien Phu*, Marine Corps Command and Staff College, 1985, p. 37.
59. Windrow, *The Last Valley*, pp. 303–4.
60. Ibid., p. 416.
61. Fall, *Street without Joy*, pp. 176–9.
62. General Henri Navarre, *Le Temps des Vérités*, Plon, 1957, p. 354.
63. Andrew Roberts (ed.), *Great Commanders of the Modern World*, Quercus, 2011, pp. 381–2.
64. Claudine, Huguette, Liliane and Junon were the outposts still held by the French at Dien Bien Phu, when a ceasefire was arranged on 7 June 1954.

65. Kenneth Conboy, *South-East Asian Special Forces*, Osprey Publishing, 1991, p. 7.
66. Major Beau G. Rollie, *Helicopters in Irregular Warfare: Algeria, Vietnam and Afghanistan*, US Military Academy, 2001, p. 10.
67. Lieutenant Colonel John W. Towers, *The French in Algeria 1954–1962*, US Army War College, 2000, p. 1.
68. Edgar O' Balance, *The Algerian Insurrection 1954–1962*, Archon Books, 1967, p. 13.
69. Charles R. Shrader, *The First Helicopter War, Logistic and Mobility in Algeria 1954–1962*, Praeger, 1999, p. 3.
70. Alistair Horne, *A Savage War of Peace*, Viking Press, 1978, p. 118.
71. Walter J. Boyne, *How the Helicopter Changed Modern Warfare*, Pelican Publishing, 2011, p. 71.
72. Raphaël Branch, *L' Embuscade de Palestro [The Palestro Ambush]*, Armand Colin, 2010, p. 181.
73. Towers, *The French in Algeria*, p. 5.
74. Orville Menard, *The Army and the 5th Republic*, University of Nebraska Press, 1967, p. 44.
75. Memorandum by General Jacques E Massu, commander of the French army in Algiers, 29 March 1957, 1R 339/3* SHD.
76. P.R. Delarue, Réflections du Prêtre sur le Terrorism Urbain. A typed text under this title was attached as an appendix to General Massu's Memorandum of 29 March 1957, 1R 339/3* SHD.
77. Boyne, *How the Helicopter Changed Modern Warfare*, p. 72.
78. Horne, *A Savage War of Peace*, p. 337.
79. Samy Cohen (ed.), *Democracies at War Against Terrorism*, Palgrave Macmillan, 2008, p. 280.
80. Horne, *A Savage War of Peace*, p. 358.
81. Randolph Churchill and Martin Gilbert, *Winston S. Churchill*, Vol. 3, Houghton Mifflin, 1988, p. 647.
82. Ferguson, *The Paras*, p. 35.
83. John Newsinger, *British Counterinsurgency*, Palgrave Macmillan, 2016, p. 94.
84. David French, *Fighting EOKA, The British Counter-Insurgency Campaign in Cyprus 1955–1959*, Oxford, 2015, pp. 72 and 86.
85. Newsinger, *British Counterinsurgency*, p. 104.
86. Charles Foley (ed.), *The Memoirs of General Grivas*, Longman, 1964, p. 34.
87. Derek Varble, *The Suez Crisis*, Osprey, 2003, p. 26.
88. John Weeks, *Assault from the Sky: A History of Airborne Warfare*, Putnam, 1978, p. 139.
89. Richard J. Aldrich, *The Clandestine Cold War in Asia 1945–1965: Western Intelligence, Propaganda and Special Operations*, Routledge, 2013, p. 106.
90. *The London Gazette*, Issue 41172, 10 September 1957.
91. Varble, *The Suez Crisis*, p. 67.
92. *The London Gazette*, 10 September 1957.
93. J.L. Moulton, *The Royal Marines*, Sphere Books, 1973, p. 114.
94. David Chandler, *The Oxford Illustrated History of the British Army*, Oxford, 1994, p. 349.
95. Avi Shlaim, *The Iron Wall: Israel and the Arab World*, W.W. Norton, 2011, p. 181.
96. Dominic Sandbrook, *Never Had it so Good: A History of Britain from Suez to the Beatles*, Abacus, 2006, p. 18.
97. *The Collins Encyclopedia of Military History*, Harper Collins, 1994, p. 1343.
98. Zeev Schiff, *A History of the Israeli Army 1870–1974*, Straight Arrow Books, 1974, p. 40.
99. Gregory Pedlow and Donald E. Welzenbach, *The CIA and Overhead Reconnaissance: The U-2 and Oxcart Programmes 1954–1974*, CIA, 1992, pp. 181–6.
100. Norman Polmar, *Spyplane: The U-2 History Declassified*, Zenith Press, 2001, p. 137.
101. *American Heritage Magazine*, Vol. 51, Issue 5, September 2000.
102. 'Cold War', Episode 8, CNN, 15 November 1998.
103. Thomas Reed, *At the Abyss: An Insider's History of the Cold War*, Random House, 2007, p. 57.
104. Dino A. Brugioni and Doris G. Taylor, *Eyes in the Sky: Eisenhower, the CIA and Cold War Aerial Espionage*, Naval Institute Press, 2010, pp. 346–7.
105. Pedlow and Welzenbach, *The CIA and Overhead Reconnaissance*, pp. 177–81.
106. Ibid., pp. 181–6.
107. Peter B. Heller, *The United Nations Under Dag Hammarskjold, 1953–1961*, Scarecrow Press, 2001, p. 79.

108. International Commission of Jurists, Report of the Committee of Enquiry into Events in Bizerta, Tunisia between 18 and 24 July 1961, Geneva, 1961, p. 16.
109. Institute of Current World Affairs, The Bizerte Affair, 31 July 1961.
110. Alejandro de Quesada, *The Bay of Pigs: Cuba 1961*, Osprey Publishing, 2009, pp. 24–5.
111. Enrique Ros, *Girón la Verdadera Historia*, Ediciones Universales, 1994, pp. 287–98.

Chapter 14: The Arab-V and Indo-Pakistan Wars

1. Another combat jump was that of Israeli paratroopers into the Karameh area of Jordan in March 1968 to capture or kill high-ranking Palestinian militants.
2. Derek Varble, *The Suez Crisis 1956*, Osprey Publishing, 2003, p. 29.
3. Ibid., p. 33.
4. Michael Clodfelter, *Warfare and Armed Conflicts: A Statistical Encyclopedia of Casualty and Other Figures 1492–2015*, McFarland, 2017, p. 573.
5. Kenneth Michael Pollack, *Arabs at War: Military Effectiveness 1948–1991*, University of Nebraska Press, 2004, p. 59.
6. Eric Hammel, *Six Days in June: How Israel Won the 1967 Arab-Israeli War*, Simon and Schuster, 1992, p. 239.
7. Pollack, *Arabs at War*, p. 294.
8. Samir A. Mutawi, *Jordan in the 1967 War*, Cambridge University Press 2002, p. 42.
9. Al Jazeera, '1967 Arab-Israeli War Timeline,' 13 July 2009.
10. Ibid.
11. Mohamed Abdel Ghani el-Gamasy, *The October War*, The American University of Cairo Press, 1993, p. 79.
12. Chaim Herzog, *The Arab-Israeli Wars*, Arms and Armour Press, 1982, p. 165.
13. George W. Gawrych, *The Albatross of Decisive Victory: War and Politics between Egypt and Israel in the 1967 and 1973 Arab-Israeli Wars*, Greenwood Press, 2000, p. 3.
14. Alex Woolf, *Arab-Israeli Wars Since 1948*, Heinemann and Raintree, 2012, p. 27.
15. CIA Intelligence Report, *The 1973 Arab-Israeli War: Overview and Analysis of the Conflict, September 1975 (Released 29 August 2012)*, p. 10.
16. *Jewish Telegraph Agency*, 30 December 1968.
17. J. Bowyer and Irving Louis Horowitz, *Assassin: Theory and Practice of Political Violence*, Transaction Publishing, 2005, p. 137.
18. CIA Intelligence Report, *The 1973 Arab-Israeli War*, p. 67.
19. Abraham Rabinovich, *The Yom Kippur War: The Epic Encounter That Transformed the Middle East*, Random House, 2017, p. 171.
20. CIA Intelligence Report, *The 1973 Arab-Israeli War*, p. 67.
21. John Laffin and Mike Chappel, *The Israeli Army in the Middle East Wars 1948–1973*, Osprey Publishing, 1982, p. 19.
22. Gawrych, *The Albatross of Decisive Victory*, p. 103.
23. Rabinovich, *The Yom Kippur War*. p. 477.
24. *Al Ahram*, 22 March 1968.
25. Aharon Yaffe, 'The War of Attrition in the "Land of Pursuits": The 1968–1970 War in the Jordan Valley,' Ariel Center for Policy Research, pp. 1–7.
26. *The Times of Israel*, 19 January 2015.
27. Kameel B. Nasr, *Arab and Israeli Terrorism: The Causes and Effects of Political Violence 1936–1993*, McFarland, 1996, p. 40.
28. William J. Burns, *Economic Aid and American Policy Towards Egypt 1955–1981*, State University of New York Press, 1985, p. 24.
29. Spencer C. Tucker (ed.), *The Encyclopedia of the Arab-Israeli Conflict: A Political, Social and Military History*, ABC CLIO, 2008, p. 229.

30. Hasi Karmel, *Intelligence for Peace: The Role of Intelligence in Times of Peace*, Frank Cass Publishing, 1999, p. 56.
31. Michael Oren, *Origins of the Second Arab-Israeli War: Egypt, Israel and the Great Powers*, Frank Cass Publishing, 1992, p. 25.
32. *Defense News*, 7 January 2016.
33. Gal Perl Finkel, 'The Combat Ethos is Alive and Well,' *Israel Hayon*, 31 July 2014.
34. Ahramonline, 1 December 2016.
35. Simon Dunstan, *The Yom Kippur War 1973*, Osprey Publishing, 2003, p. 34.
36. Major Stephanie R. Kelley USAF, *Egypt's Air War in Yemen (Report)*, Air Command and Staff College / Air University, Alabama, March 2010, p. 6.
37. Pollack, *Arabs at War*, p. 49.
38. Asher Orkaby, *Beyond the Arab Cold War: The International History of the Yemen Civil War 1962–1968*, Oxford University Press, 2017, p. 62.
39. Ibid., p. 64.
40. Edgar O'Balance, *The War in the Yemen*, Hamden, 1971, p. 93.
41. Kelley, *Egypt's Air War in Yemen*, p. 6.
42. Gawrych, *The Albatros of Decisive Victory*, pp. 220 and 231.
43. Jeremy Bender, 'Jordan's Special Forces are some of the best in the Middle East', *Business Insider*, 4 February 2015.
44. Robert Stephens, *Nasser: A Political Biography*, Simon and Schuster, 1971, p. 340.
45. Benny Morris, *1948: A History of the First Arab-Israeli War*, Yale University Press, 2008, p. 251; Pollack, *Arabs At War*, pp. 448 and 459–60.
46. CIA Intelligence Report, *The 1973 Arab-Israeli War*, p. 67.
47. Joseph Holliday, 'The Syrian Army, Doctrinal Order of Battle', *Institute for the Study of War*, February 2013, p. 7.
48. Ibid., p. 8.
49. Patrick Seale, *Asad: The Struggle for the Middle East*, I.B Tauris, 1988, p. 430; Nikolaos van Dam, *The Struggle for Power in Syria: Politics and Society Under Asad and Ba'th Party*, I.B Tauris, 2011, p. 121.
50. Holliday, 'The Syrian Army', p. 8.
51. Ibid.
52. *International Institute for Strategic Studies, The Military Balance 2006*, pp. 208–9.
53. *The Telegraph*, 9 August 2011.
54. Joseph Holliday, 'The Assad Regime, Middle East Security Report 8,' *Institute for the Study of War*, March 2013, p. 9.
55. Ramachandra Guha, *India After Gandhi*, Harper Collins, 2007, p. 94.
56. *The Statesman* (India), 6 July 2006.
57. Kenneth Conboy, *Elite Forces of India and Pakistan*, Bloomsbury Publishing, 2012, p. 64.
58. Ibid.
59. *Time* magazine, 17 September 1965.
60. Brigadier Tariq Mehmood Shaheed was killed during a freefall parachute display at Rahwali in Punjab province on 29 May 1989.
61. *New Buzz India*, 30 July 2016.
62. *The Daily Star* (Bangladesh English-language newspaper), 25 March 2015.
63. Abdurrahman Siddiqi, *East Pakistan the End Game: An Onlooker's Journal 1969–1971*, Oxford University Press, 2004, p. 260.
64. *New Buzz India*, 30 July 2016.
65. *The Daily Star*, 25 March 2015.
66. Major General A.O. Mitha is considered the conceptual founder of his country's Special Forces. During the Second World War, he fought in Burma with airborne units of the British Indian Army.
67. Mandeep Singh Bajwa, 'Pakistan Special Service', 7 November 2013.

Chapter 15: Post-1945 Airborne Operations (II)

1. Message from UK Political Representative to the Foreign Office, 27 December 1961 (PREM 11/4359).
2. Darman, *A-Z of the SAS*, p. 28.
3. Ibid., pp. 35–6.
4. Christopher Tuck, *Confrontation, Strategy and War Termination: Britain's Conflict with Indonesia*, Routledge, 2016, p. 180.
5. Karl DeRouen and Uk Heo, *Civil Wars of the World: Major Conflicts Since World War II*, ABC-CLIO, 2007, p. 431.
6. Peter Dickens, *Special Air Service Secret War in South-East Asia: 22 SAS Regiment in the Borneo Campaign 1963–1966*, Greenhill Books, 2003, p. 153.
7. Darman, *A-Z of the SAS*, p. 24.
8. Ibid., p. 76.
9. J. Paul de B. Taillon, *The Evolution of Special Forces in Counter-terrorism: The British and American Experiences*, Greenwood, 2000, p. 30.
10. Darman, *A-Z of the SAS*, pp. 24 and 190.
11. Ibid., p. 23.
12. Christopher Pugsley, *From Emergency to Confrontation: The New Zealand Armed Forces in Malaya and Borneo 1949–1966*, Oxford University Press, 2003, p. 255.
13. Neil Smith, *Nothing Short of War: With the Australian Army in Borneo 1962–1966*, Unsung Military History, 1999, p. 41.
14. Darman, *A-Z of the SAS*, p. 25.
15. Pugsley, *From Emergency to Confrontation*, pp. 206–13.
16. Darman, *A-Z of the SAS*, p. 13.
17. Ibid., p. 25.
18. Emil Simpson, *War from the Ground up: Twenty-First Century Combat as Politics*, Oxford University Press, 2012, p. 167.
19. Charles Allen, *The Savage Wars of Peace: Soldiers' Voices 1945–1989*, Brown Book Group, 2016, pp. 155–6.
20. Ibid., p. 159.
21. Narayanan Ganesan and Sund Chull Kim (eds), *State Violence in East Asia*, University Press of Kentucky, 2013, pp. 155–6.
22. Peter Dickens, *Secret War in South East Asia*, Presidio Press, 1983, p. 72.
23. Darman, *A-Z of the SAS*, p. 25.
24. John Coates, *An Atlas of Australia's Wars*, Oxford University Press, 2006, p. 333.
25. Jonathan Walker, *Aden Insurgency: The Savage War in Yeman [sic] 1962–1967*, Pen and Sword, 2011, p. 102.
26. Darman, *A-Z of the SAS*, p. 133.
27. Walker, *Aden Insurgency*, p. 98.
28. Darman, *A-Z of the SAS*, pp. 9 and 150.
29. *The Canberra Times*, 4 May 1964 and 16 May 1964.
30. Walker, *Aden Insurgency*, p. 96.
31. Darman, *A-Z of the SAS*, p. 9.
32. Ibid.
33. Ibid., p. 150.
34. Ibid., p. 9.
35. Julian Paget, *Last Post: Aden 1964–1967*, Faber and Faber, 1969, p. 264.
36. J.E. Peterson, *Defending Arabia*, Croom Helm, 2017, p. 97.
37. Walker, *Aden Insurgency*, p. 127.
38. The 2nd Para-Commando Battalion men wear green berets, honouring their lineage to the British-raised and trained 4th (Belgian) Troop of British Army's No. 10 Commando, which distinguished itself

during the Second World War. The 1st Battalion of the Belgian Para-Commando Regiment, in memory of the unit's origins as part of the British SAS in the Second World War, wears a maroon beret with SAS wings: Darman, *A-Z of the SAS*, p. 18.

39. David Robarge, 'CIA's Covert Operations in the Congo 1960–1968: Insights from Newly Declassified Documents', *Studies in Intelligence* 58/3 (2014), pp. 1–9.
40. Lieutenant Colonel W.H. Glasgow, *Headquarters US Army Europe*, Historical Section (8–3.1 CW4/1965), p. 8.
41. *The New York Times*, 12 November 1964.
42. Glasgow, *Headquarters US Army Europe*, p. 34.
43. *Time Magazine*, 19 December 1965.
44. Robarge, 'CIA's Covert Operations', p. 3.
45. British Military Attaché Kinshasa, *Report for the Period Ending 30 June 1970*, Foreign and Commonwealth Office, 31/577.
46. *Raids* (Magazine), May 2006, p. 45.
47. The first dead Legionnaire in Kolwezi was officially identified as Richard Arnold. He was an English-born corporal, whose real name was Robert Guy Ashby: http://foreignlegion.info/Battle-of-Kolwezi/
48. http://foreignlegion.info/Battle-of-Kolwezi/
49. Laurence A. Yates, *Power Pack: US Intervention in the Dominican Republic 1965–1966*, Combat Studies Institute, 1988, p. 8.
50. Ibid., p. 68.
51. Ibid., p. 71.
52. Ibid., p. 141.
53. Bruce Palmer, *Intervention in the Caribbean: The Dominican Crisis of 1965*, University Press of Kentucky, 2015, p. 169.
54. Alain Rouvez (assisted by Michael Coco and Jean-Paul Paddack), *Disconsolate Empires: British and Belgian Military Involvement in Post-Colonial Sub-Saharan Africa*, University Press of America, 1994, p. 151.
55. Brian Ferguson, *The State, Identity and Violence: Political Disintegration in the Post-Cold War World*, Routledge, 2002, p. 267.
56. Braby and Windrow, *French Foreign Legion Paratroops*, p. 278; Jérôme De Lespinois, 'Emploi de la Force Aérienne, Tchad 1969–1987', *Journal Pencer les Ailes Françaises* 6 (2005), pp. 70–2.
57. De Lespinois, 'Emploi', pp. 65–74.
58. Millard Burr and Robert Collins, *Darfur: The Long Road to Disaster*, Markus Wiener Publishers, 2008, pp. 119–24.
59. Michael Brecher and Jonathan Wilkenfeld, *A Study of Crisis*, The University of Michigan Press, 1997, p. 92.
60. Haim Shaked and Daniel Dishion (eds), *Middle East Contemporary Survey*, Vol. 8, 1983–4, The Moshe Dayan Center, 1986, p. 589.
61. Brecher and Wilkenfeld, *A Study of Crisis*, p. 94.
62. Ibid., p. 88.
63. Guy Arnold, *Wars in the Third World since 1945*, Bloomsbury, 1991, p. 108.
64. Donald Westlake, *Under an English Heaven*, Simon and Schuster, 1972, pp. 78–9.
65. Vincent Hubbard, *A History of St Kitts*, Macmillan Caribbean, 2002, pp. 1479.
66. Arnold, *Wars in the Third World since 1945*, p. 108.
67. Hubbard, *A History of St Kitts*, pp. 147–49.
68. Shalini Puri and Lara Putnam (eds), *Caribbean Military Encounters*, Palgrave Macmillan, 2017, p. 162.
69. Hubbard, *A History of St Kitts*, pp. 147–9.
70. Darman, *A-Z of the SAS*, p. 148
71. Ibid., p. 47.
72. Ibid., p. 56.
73. Ibid., p. 138.
74. Ibid., p. 139.

75. Pete Scholey and Frederick Forsyth, *Who Dares Wins: Special Forces Heroes of the SAS*, Osprey Publishing, 2008, p. 104.
76. Darman, *A-Z of the SAS*, p. 120.
77. Ibid.
78. Ibid., p. 139.
79. Adam Schwarz, *A Nation in Waiting: Indonesia in the 1990s*, Westview Press, 1994, p. 204.
80. José Ramos-Horta, *Funu: The Unfinished Saga of East Timor*, The Red Sea Press, 1987, pp. 107–8.
81. Joseph Nevins, *A No-so-distant Horror: Mass Violence in East Timor*, Cornell University Press, 2005, p. 28.
82. *Cold War History*, Vol. 5, 2005, pp. 281–315.
83. James Dunn, *Timor: A People Betrayed*, ABC Books (Australian Broadcasting Corporation), 1996, pp. 257–60.
84. *The Independent*, 27 April 2016.

Chapter 16: Airborne Forces and the Vietnam War

1. The Office of Strategic Services (OSS) was an agency of the Joint Chiefs of Staff, which coordinated activities behind enemy lines for all branches of the US armed forces, during the Second World War.
2. *The New York Times*, 20 July 2005.
3. Stanley Karnow, *Vietnam: A History*, Penguin, 1997, p. 265.
4. *The New York Times*, 20 July 2005.
5. Gordon Rottman and Ron Volstad, *Vietnam Airborne*, Osprey Publishing, 1990, p 27.
6. George Veith, *Black April: The Fall of South Vietnam 1973–1975*, Encounter Books, 2013, pp. 197–203.
7. High Altitude Low Opening (HALO) is a parachute technique. The trooper, wearing an oxygen mask, exits the aircraft at an altitude of 33,000ft (10,000m) and is supposed to open his free-fall parachute no more than 2,550ft (760m) from the ground.
8. *The New York Times*, 10 January 1963.
9. Truong V. Truong, *Vietnam War*, The New Legion, 2010, p. 407.
10. Ibid., p. 416.
11. Ibid., p. 417.
12. Mark Moyar, *Triumph Forsaken: The Vietnam War 1954–1965*, Cambridge University Press, 2006, p. 194.
13. Historynet, 25 July 2006.
14. David M. Toczek, *The Battle of Ap Bac: They Did everything But Learn from It*, Naval Institute Press, 2001, p. 82.
15. Truong, *Vietnam War*, p. 419.
16. *Foreign Relations of the US 1961–1963*, Vol. III, Vietnam: January–August 1963, Doc. 1, p. 1.
17. Truong, *Vietnam War*, p. 419.
18. John McGrath, *History, Organization and Employment in the US Army*, Combat Studies Institute, 2004, p. 65.
19. *Airlift Tanker: History of US Air Lift and Tanker Forces*, Turner Publishing, 1995, p. 34.
20. Spencer C. Tucker, *Encyclopedia of the Vietnam War*, ABC-CLIO, 2000, p. 199.
21. Michael Clodfelter, *Mad Minutes and Vietnam Months*, Pinnacle, 1996, p. 37.
22. McGrath, *History, Organization and Employment in the US Army*, p. 67.
23. Ibid., p. 68.
24. Darman, *A-Z of the SAS*, 1992, p. 3.
25. James F. Gebhardt, *Eyes Behind the Lines: US Army Long-Range Reconnaissance and Surveillance Units*, Combat Studies Institute Press, 2005, pp. 45–110.
26. Gordon L. Rottman, *US Army Long-Range Reconnaissance Patrol Scout in Vietnam 1965–1971*, Osprey Publishing, 2008, p. 33.

27. Andrew Birtle, *US Army Counterinsurgency and Contingency Operations Doctrine: 1942–1976*, Government Printing Office, 2006, p. 375.

28. Rottman, *US Army Long-Range Reconnaissance Patrol Scout*, p. 33.

29. 'Vietnam War Crimes', Socialistworker.org, 14 November 2003.

30. Guenter Lewy, *America in Vietnam*, Oxford University Press, 1978, p. 450.

31. Paul Ham, *Vietnam: The Australian War*, Harper Collins, 2007, pp. 152–3.

32. Chris Coulthard-Clark, *The Encyclopedia of Australian Battles*, Allen and Unwin, 2001, p. 280.

33. David H. Hackworth and Julie Sherman, *About Face: The Odyssey of an American Warrior*, Simon and Schuster, 1989, pp. 534–46.

34. Larry Addington, *America's War in Vietnam: A Short Narrative History*, Indiana University Press, 2000, p. 100.

35. Bernard Rogers, *Vietnam Studies - Cedar Fall-Junction City: A Turning Point*, Department of the Army, 1974, pp. 17–24.

36. Edward F. Murphy, *Dak To: America's Sky Soldiers in South Vietnam's Central Highlands*, Ballantine, 2007, pp. 77–8.

37. Tucker, *Encyclopedia of the Vietnam War*, pp. 90–1.

38. James Willbanks, *The Tet Offensive: A Concise History*, Columbia University Press, 2008, p. 17.

39. Michael P. Kelley, *Where We Were in Vietnam*, Hellgate Press, 2002, p. 5.

40. Donald Mrozek, *Air Power and the Ground War in Vietnam*, University Press of the Pacific, 2002, p. 85.

41. James H. Hillbanks, *Vietnam War Almanac*, Infobase Publishing, 2009, p. 261.

42. Bruce Davies, *The Battle of Ngok Tavak: Bloody Defeat in South Vietnam*, Allen and Unwin, 2008, p. 6.

43. *New York Times*, 20 July 2005.

44. 'Battle of Dong Ap Bia—Hill 937, 10–21 May 1969 (Battle of Hamburger Hill),' e-history, Ohio State University [https://bit.ly/2ZoC10K; accessed: 12.05.2018]

45. James S. Wilbanks, *Vietnam War Almanac*, Checkmark Books, 2010, p. 332.

46. Benjamin F. Schemmer, *The Raid: The Son Tay Prison Rescue Mission*, Random House Publishing Group, 2002, p. 91.

47. John Cargus, *The Son Tay Raid: American POWs in Vietnam Were Not Forgotten*, Texas A. & M. University Press, 2010, p. 52.

Chapter 17: Airborne Operations and Air Assaults, 1972–2018

1. Van Creveld, *Technology and War*, p. 276.

2. *Handbook FY 2013*, Warrior Training Center, Air Assault School, p. 11.

3. Eugene W. Raulins, *Marines and Helicopters 1946–1962*, USMC History and Museum Division, 1976, p. 35.

4. *The Times of Israel*, 19 January 2015.

5. Van Creveld, *Technology and War*, p. 197.

6. Ibid., p. 195.

7. 'Life as a paratrooper', BBC, 23 August 2001.

8. Dermot Walsh, *Bloody Sunday and the Rule of Law in Northern Ireland*, Gill and Macmillan, 2000, p. 88.

9. Toby Harnden, *Bandit Country*, Hodder and Stoughton, 1999, p. 198.

10. *The Barron Report*, Dublin Monaghan Bombings, 2003, p. 221; Tony Geraghty, *The Irish War, The Hidden Conflict Between the IRA and British Intelligence*, Google Books, 1998, p. 129.

11. Darman, *A-Z of the SAS*, p. 129.

12. Ibid, p. 130.

13. Geraghty, *The Irish War*, p. 120.

14. Darman, *A-Z of the SAS*, p. 125.

15. Raymond Murray, *The SAS in Ireland*, Mercier Press, 1990, p. 170.

16. Michael Brzoska and Frederic S. Pearson, *Arms and Warfare, De-escalation and Negotiation*, University of South Carolina Press, 1994, p. 203.

17. Darman, *A-Z of the SAS*, p. 45.

18. Gilles Kepel, *Jihad: The Trail of Political Islam*, I. B. Tauris, 2002, p. 138.
19. Olivier Roy, *Islam and Resistance in Afghanistan*, Cambridge University Press, 1990, p. 118.
20. CIA, Directorate of Intelligence, Office of Soviet Analysts, Intelligence Assessment, SOV 87–10007, February 1987, p. 7.
21. *The Iraqi Army Sixtieth Anniversary, 6th January 1921–1981*, The Political Guidance Bureau, Ministry of Defense, Al-Adeeb Baghdad Press, 1981, p. 114.
22. Nicola Firzli (ed.), *The Iraq-Iran Conflict*, Institute of Studies and Research 'Editions du Monde Arabe', 1981, pp. 39 and 44–5.
23. Sepehr Zabih, *Aspects of Terrorism in Iran*, Annals of the American Academy of Political and Social Science, International Terrorism, September 1982, 463, pp. 84–94.
24. *The Imposed War, Defense vs Aggression*, Islamic Republic of Iran, War Information Headquarters, Supreme Defense Council, 1987, p. 16.
25. Rob Johnson, *The Iran-Iraq War*, Palgrave Macmillan, 2011, p. 160.
26. Hassan B. Jallow, *Journey for Justice*, Author House, 2012, p. 106.
27. James R. Davis, *Fortune's Warriors: Private Armies and the New World Order*, Douglas and McIntyre, 2000, p. 24.
28. Scholey and Forsyth, *Who Dares Wins*, p. 12.
29. Guy Arnold, *Wars in the Third World Since 1945*, Bloomsbury, 2016, p. 356.
30. Laurence Freedman, *The Official History of the Falklands Campaign*, Routledge, 2005, p. 224.
31. *The London Gazette* (Supplement), No. 49.134, 8 October 1982, pp. 12831–2.
32. Nick van der Bijl, *Nine Battles to Stanley*, Leo Cooper, 1999, p. 141.
33. *The London Gazette* (Supplement), No. 49.134, 8 October 1982, pp. 12831–2.
34. Peter Huchthausen, *America's Splendid Little Wars: A Short History of US Engagements from the Fall of Saigon to Baghdad*, Penguin, 2004, p. 69.
35. 'War at the Top of the World', *Time Magazine*, 4 July 2005.
36. Robert Kagan, *Twilight Struggle: American Power and Nicaragua 1977–1990*, Free Press, 1996, p. 585.
37. *New York Times*, 18 March 1988.
38. David Doyle, *M551 Sheridan*, Signal Publication, 2008, pp. 44–6.
39. Alexander Stillwell, *Special Forces in Action: Elite Forces Operations 1991–2011*, Amber Books, 2012, p. 199.
40. Frederick Stanwood, Patrick Allen and Lindsay Peacock, *Gulf War, A Day-by-Day Chronicle*, BCA, 1991, p. 13.
41. Jonathan Riley, *Decisive Battles: From Yorktown to Operation Desert Storm*, Continuum, 2010, p. 207.
42. Neville Leigh, *The SAS 1983–2004*, Osprey Publishing, 2016, pp. 34–6.
43. Ibid., pp. 93, 127–8.
44. Robert M. Cassidy, *Peacekeeping in the Abyss: Britain and American Peacekeeping Doctrine and Practice After the Cold War*, Greenwood Publishing, 2004, p. 157.
45. William Fowler, *Operation Barras: The SAS Mission – Sierra Leone 2000*, Weidenfeld and Nicolson, 2004, p. 126.
46. Neville Leigh, *Special Forces in the War on Terror*, Osprey Publishing, 2015, p. 43.
47. Dick Camp, *Boots on the Ground: The Fight to Liberate Afghanistan*, Zenith Imprint, 2012, p. 209.
48. *New York Times*, 11 May 2011.
49. *The New Yorker*, 8 August 2011.
50. Associated Press, 17 May 2011.

Sources

Books and Recommended Reading

Adams, James, Morgan, Robin, and Bambridge, Anthony, *Ambush. The War between the SAS and the IRA*, Pan Books Limited, 1988.

Addington, Larry, *America's War in Vietnam: A Short Narrative History*, Indiana University Press, 2000.

Adleman, Robert H., and Walton, Colonel George, *The Devil's Brigade*, Chilton Books, 1966.

Aisly, Christopher, *Hitler's Sky Warriors: German Paratroopers in Action 1939–1945*, Spellmount Limited, 2000.

Alexander, Mark J., and Sparry, John, *Jump Commander. In Combat with the 505th and 508th Parachute Infantry Regiments, 82nd Airborne Division in World War II*, Casemate, 2010.

Allen, Luis, *Burma: The Longest War 1941–1945*, Dent, 1984.

Ambrose, Stephen E., *Pegasus Bridge*, Simon and Schuster, 2001.

Arena, Nino, *Folgore: Storia del Parachutismo Militare Italiano*, Centro Editoriale Nationale Divulgazioni Umanistiche Sociologiche Storiche, 1966.

Arnold, Guy, *Wars in the Third World since 1945*, Bloomsbury, 1991.

Arnold, H.H., *Winged Warfare*, Harper and Brothers, 1941.

Arthurs, Ted G., *Land with no Sun. A Year in Vietnam with the 173rd Airborne*, Stackpole, 2006.

Autry, Jerry, *General William C. Lee, Just Plain Bill*, Airborne Press, 1995.

Bailey, Roderick, *Target Italy: The Secret War Against Mussolini 1940–1943*, Faber and Faber, 2014.

Barker, Ralf, *The Royal Flying Corps in France*, Constable, 1995.

Beevor, Anthony, *D-Day. The Battle of Normandy*, Viking, 2009.

Bennett, David, *A Magnificent Disaster*, Casemate, 2006.

Berg, Scott A., *Lindbergh*, G.P. Putman's Sons, 1998.

Bishop, Patrick, *Fighter Boys: The Battle of Britain*, Penguin Books, 2004.

Black, Jeremy, *Introduction to Global Military History: 1775 to the Present Day*, Routledge, 2005.

Blair, Clay, *Ridgway's Paratroopers. Airborne Warfare 1918–1945*, Weidenfeld and Nicolson, 2005.

Blumenson, Martin, *Breakout and Pursuit*, Washington Center of Military History, 1961.

Bond, Brian, and Tachikawa, Kyoichi, *British and Japanese Leadership in the Far Eastern War 1941–1945*, Military History and Policy Series, Routledge, 2004.

Booth, Owen, *The Illustrated History of the Second World War*, Chartwell Books, 1998.

Boyen, Walter J., *How the Helicopter Changed Modern Warfare*, Pelican Publishing, 2011.

Braby, Wane, and Windrow, Martin, *French Foreign Legion Paratroops*, Osprey Publishing, 1985.

Brayley, Martin, *The British Army 1939–1945: The Far East*, Men at Arms, Osprey Publishing, 2002.

Bridson, Rory, *The Making of a Para*, Guild Publishing, 1989.

Brown, Ashley, *Elite Forces. Israeli Paras*, Orbis, 1986.

Bruer, William, *Retaking the Philippines. America's Return to Corregidor and Bataan*, Saint Martin's Press, 1986.

Buckingham, William F., *Arnhem*, Tempus, 2002.

———, *The First 72 Hours*, Tempus, 2005.

Burgett, Donald R., *The Road to Arnhem*, Dell, 2001.

Burns, Dwayne T., and Burns, Leland, *Jump into the Valley of the Shadow. The World War II Memories of a Paratrooper in the 508th Parachute Infantry Regiment*, Casemate Publishers, 2006.

Caddick-Adams, Peter, *Snow and Steel: The Battle of the Bulge 1944–1945*, Oxford University Press, 2014.

Calvert, Michael, *Chindits. Long Range Penetration*, Pan/Ballantine, 1975.

Camp, Dick, *Boots on the Ground: The Fight to Liberate Afghanistan*, Zenith Imprint, 2012.

Cargus, John, *The Son Tay Raid: American POWs in Vietnam were not Forgotten*, Texas A. and M. University Press, 2007.

Cassidy, Robert M., *Peacekeeping in the Abyss: Britain and America Peacekeeping Doctrine and Practice after the Cold War*, Greenwood Publishing, 2004.

Cichanowsky, Jan M., *The Warsaw Rising*, Cambridge University Press, 2002.

Clark, Jeffrey J., and Smith, Robert Ross, *Riviera to the Rhine. The United States Army in World War II European Theater of Operations*, Center of Military History, US Army, 1993.

Clark, Lloyd, *Arnhem. Jumping the Rhine 1944 and 1945*, Headline, 2008.

Clodfelter, Micheal (*sic*), *Mad Minutes and Vietnam Months*, Pinnacle, 1996.

———, *Warfare and Armed Conflicts: A Statistical Encyclopedia in Casualty and Other Figures 1492–2015*, McFarland and Company, 2008.

Coates, John, *An Atlas of Australia's Wars*, Oxford University Press, 2006.

Coen, Samy (ed.), *Democracies at War Against Terrorism*, Palgrave Macmillan, 2008.

Cole, Howard N., *On Wings of Healing. The Story of the Airborne Medical Services 1940–1960*, Blackwood, 1963.

Collins, James L., and Simmons, Edwin H., *The SAS Elite Forces*, Orbis, 1986.

Conboy, Kenneth, *South-East Asian Special Forces*, Osprey Publishing, 1991.

Cooke, Tim, *US Airborne Forces*, Powerkids Press, 2013.

Cornelisse, Diana G., *Splendid Vision, Unswerving Purpose: Developing Air Power for the US Air Force During the First Century of Powered Flight*, USAF Publications, 2003.

Coulthard-Clark, Chris, *The Encyclopedia of Australian Battles*, Allen and Unwin, 2001.

Courtney, G.B., *Silent Feed. The History of Z Special Operations*, Austin, 1993.

Cull, Brian, *Wings over Suez*, Grub, 1996.

Darlow, Stephen, *D-Day Bombers, The Veteran's Story: RAF Bomber Command and the Normandy Invasion 1944*, Kindle, 2004.

Darman, Peter, *A-Z of the SAS*, Sidgwick and Jackson, 1992.

Davidson, P., *Vietnam at War*, Oxford University Press, 1991.

Davies, Bruce, *The Battle of Ngok Tavak: Bloody Defeat in South Vietnam*, Allen and Unwin, 2008.

Dean, Phillipe, *I Should Have Died*, Hamish Hamilton, 1976.

Dennis, Peter, and Gray, Jeffrey, *The Foundations of Victory. The Pacific War 1943–1945*, Army History Unit of Australia, 2004.

———, Morris Ewan, Prior, Robin, and Bou, Jean, *The Oxford Companion to Australian Military History*, Oxford University Press, 2000.

DeRoven, Karl, and Heo, Uk, *Civil Wars of the World: Major Conflicts since World War II*, ABC-CLIO, 2007.

Devine, Isaac, *Mitchell: Pioneer of Air Power*, Duell, Sloan and Pearce, 1943.

Devlin, Gerald, *Paratrooper! The Saga of Paratroop and Glider Combat Troops During World War II*, Robson, 1979.

Dickens, Peter, *Special Air Service Secret War in South-East Asia: 22 SAS Regiment in the Borneo Campaign 1963–1966*, Greenhill Books, 2003.

Dilley, Michael F., and Zedric, Lance Q., *Elite Warriors: 300 Years of America's Best Fighting Troops*, Pathfinder Publishing, 1999.

Edwards, Roger, *German Airborne Troops 1936–1945*, MacDonald and Janes, 1974.

Eichelberger, Robert L., *Our Jungle Road to Tokyo*, Viking Press, 1950.

El-Gamasy, Mohamed Abdel Ghani, *The October War*, The American University of Cairo Press, 1993.

Ellis, L.F., and Warhurst, A.E., *Victory in the West. The Defeat of Germany*, Naval and Military Press, 1968.

Eudes, Dominique, Οι Καπετάνιοι. Ο Ελληνικός Εμφύλιος Πόλεμος 1943–1949 *(The Chieftains. The Greek Civil War 1943–1949)*, Εξάντας, 1975.

Fall, Bernard, *Street without Joy*, Schocken Books, 1989.

Ferguson, Gregory, *The Paras 1940–1984*, Osprey Publishing, 1984.
Firzli, Nicola (ed.), *The Iraq-Iran Conflict*, Institute of Studies and Research 'Editions du Monde Arabe', 1981.
Flanagan, E.M., *Airborne. A Combat History of American Airborne Forces*, Random House Publishing, 2005.
———, *The Rakkasans: The Combat History of the 187th Airborne Infantry*, Presidio, 1997.
———, *The Rock Force Assault*, Presidio Press, 1945.
Foot, M.R.D., *The Special Operations Executive 1940–1946*, Pimlico, 1999.
Ford, Ken, *D-Day 1944. Sword Beach and the British Airborne Landings*, Bloomsbury Publishing, 2011.
———, and Gerrard, Howard, *D-Day 1944, Sword Beach and the British Airborne Landings*, Osprey Publishing, 2002.
———, and Zaloga, Steven J., *Overlord. The D-Day Landings*, Osprey Publishing, 2009.
Fraser, David, *And We Shall Shock Them: The British Army in the Second World War*, Phoenix, 1999.
Fredricksen, John C., *American Military Leaders: From Colonial Times to the Present, Vol. 2*, ABC-CLIO, 1999.
French, David, *Fighting EOKA, The British Counter-Insurgency Campaign in Cyprus 1955–1959*, Oxford University Press, 2015.
Frost, John, *A Drop Too Many*, Cassel, 1980.
Gale, R.N., *With the 6th Airborne Division in Normandy*, Sampson Low, 1948.
Gallaway, Jack, *The Last Call of the Bugle: The Long Road to Kapyong*, University of Queensland Press, 1999.
Gavin, James M., *On to Berlin. Battles of an Airborne Commander 1943–1946*, Viking, 1978.
Gawrych, George W., *The Albatross of Decisive Victory: War and Politics Between Egypt and Israel in the 1967 and 1973 Arab-Israeli Wars*, Greenwood Press, 2000.
Geraghty, Tony, *The Irish War. The Hidden Conflict between the IRA and British Intelligence*, Google Books, 1998.
———, *Who Dares Wins*, Fontana/Collins, 1981.
Gill, Rollan, and Groves, John, *Club Route in Europe. The History of 30 Corps from D-Day to May 1945*, MLRS, 1946.
Gillespie, Alexander, *A History of the Laws of War, Volume I*, Hart Publishing, 2011.
Glantz, David M., *The Soviet Airborne Experience*, Research Survey No. 4, Combat Studies Institute, 1984.
Glines, Carroll V., *The Doolittle Raid: America's Daring First Strike Against Japan*, Orion Books, 1988.
Goldstein, Donald M., *Nuts! The Battle of the Bulge: The Story and Photographs*, Potomac Books, 1994.
Gregory, Barry, *Airborne Warfare 1918–1945*, Phoebus, 1979.
———, and Bacheler, John, *Airborne Warfare 1918–1945*, Exeter Books, 1979.
Guard, Julie, *Airborne: World War II Paratroopers in Combat*, Osprey, 2007.
Hagerman, Bart, *USA Airborne: 50th Anniversary 1949–1990*, Turner Publishing, 1990.
Hammel, Eric, *Six Days in June: How Israel Won the 1967 Arab-Israeli War*, Simon and Schuster, 1992.
Harclerode, Peter, *Para! Fifty Years of the Parachute Regiment*, Arms and Armour Press, 1992.
———, *Wings of War: Airborne Warfare 1918–1945*, Weidenfeld and Nicolson, 2005.
Hartigan, Dan., *A Rising of Courage. Canada's Paratroops in the Liberation of Normandy*, Drop Zone Publishers, 2000.
Haskew, Michael E., *Encyclopedia of Elite Forces in the Second World War*, Pen and Sword, 2007.
Herring, George C., and Fall, Bernard B., *Street Without Joy: The French Debacle in Indochina*, Stackpole Books, 2005.
Herzog, Chaim, *The Arab-Israeli Wars*, Arms and Armour Press, 1982.
Hillbanks, James H., *Vietnam War Almanac*, Infobase Publishing, 2000.
Hoare, Mike, *Congo Warriors*, Robert Hale Limited, 1991.
Horn, Bern, 'A Question of Relevance. The Establishment of a Canadian Parachute Capability', *Canadian Military History*, Vol. 8, 1999.
Horne, Alistair, *A Savage War of Peace*, Viking Press, 1978
Horner, David, *SAS Phantoms of the Jungle. A History of the Australian Special Air Service*, Allen and Unwin, 1989.
Humphries, James F., *Through the Valley: Vietnam 1967–1968*, Lynne Rienner Publishers, 1999.

Huston, James A., *Out of the Blue. United States Army Airborne Operations in World War II*, Purdue University Press, 1998.

Hutchthausen, Peter, *America's Splendid Little Wars: A Short History of US Engagements from the Fall of Saigon to Baghdad*, Penguin, 2004.

Jackson, Robert, *Bailing Out: Amazing Dramas of Military Flying*, Pen and Sword Publishing, 2006.

Johnson, Rob, *The Iran-Iraq War*, Palgrave and Macmillan, 2011.

Jeapes, Colonel Tony, *SAS. Operation Oman*, William Kimber and Company Limited, 1983.

Joslen, H.F., *Orders of Battle. Second World War 1939–1945*, Naval and Military Press, 2003.

Joyce, Ken, *Snow Plough and the Jupiter Deception: The Story of the 1st Special Service Force and the 1st Canadian Special Service Battalion 1942–1945*, Vanwell Publishing, 2006.

Juell, Brian, *Over the Rhine. The Last Day of the War in Europe*, Spellmount, 1985.

Kagan, Robert, *Twilight Struggle: American Power and Nicaragua 1977–1990*, Free Press, 1996.

Kelley, Michael P., *Where We Were in Vietnam*, Hellgate Press, 2002.

Kemp, Anthony, *The SAS at War*, John Murray Limited, 1991.

Kemp, Ted, *A Commemorative History: First Special Service Force*, Taylor Publishing, 1995.

Kennett, Lee B., *The First Air War 1914–1918*, Free Press, 1998.

Kepel, Gilles, *Jihad: The Trail of Political Islam*, I.B. Tauris, 2002.

Kershaw, Robert J., *It Never Snows in September. The German View of Market-Garden and the Battle of Arnhem*, Ian Allen, 2004.

Koskinaki, George E., *D-Day with the Screaming Eagles*, Casemate, 1970.

Krott, Rob, *Desperate Jump in the Ardennes*, Herndon, 2003.

Kuhn, Volkmar, *German Paratroopers in World War II*, Ian Allen, 1978.

Kurowski, Franz, *Deutsche Fallschirmjäger 1939–1945*, Aktuell, 1990.

———, *Jump into Hell: German Paratroopers in World War II*, Stackpole, 2010.

Ladd, James D., *SAS Operations*, Robert Hale, 1986.

Laffin, John, and Chappel, Mike, *The Israeli Army in the Middle East Wars 1948–1973*, Osprey Publishing, 1982.

Langdon, Allen L., *Ready. A World War II History of the 505th Parachute Infantry Regiment*, Western, 1986.

Leulliette, Pierre, *St Michael and the Dragon. A Paratrooper in the Algerian War*, Heinemann, 1964.

Lewy, Guenter, *America in Vietnam*, Oxford University Press, 1978.

LoFaro, Guy, *The Sword of St. Michael, The 82nd Airborne Division in World War II*, Hachette Books, 2011.

Logevall, Frederik, *Embers of War: The Fall of an Empire and the Making of America's Vietnam*, Random House, 2012.

Long, Gavin, *The Final Campaigns, Australia in the War of 1939–1945*, Australian War Memorial, 1963.

Lord, Cliff, and Tennant, Julian, *ANZAC Elite: The Airborne and Special Forces Insignia of Australia and New Zealand*, IPL Books, 2000.

Lucas, James, *Kommando. German Special Forces of World War II*, Crafton Books, 1995.

Lucas, Laddie, *Flying Colours: The Epic Story of Douglas Bader*, Hutchinson Publishing Group, 1981.

MacDonald, Peter, *The SAS in Action*, Sidgwick and Jackson, 1991.

MacKenzie, Alastair, *Special Force: The Untold Story of the 22nd Special Air Service (22nd SAS) Regiment*, I.B. Tauris, 2011.

MacNab, Chris, *German Paratroopers: The Illustrated History of the Fallschirmjäger*, MBI Publishing Company, 2000.

Mallet, Derek, *Hitler's Generals in America, Nazi POWs and Allied Military Intelligence*, University Press of Kentucky, 2013.

Markham, R.H., *Tito's Imperial Communism*, Kessinger Publishing, 2005.

Marshall, S.L.A., *Night Drop. The American Airborne Invasion of Normandy*, Jove Publications, 1984.

Matthews, Andrew Johannes, and Foreman, John, *Luftwaffe Aces – Biographies and Victories Claimed*, Red Kite, 2015.

Megellas, James, *All the Way to Berlin. A Paratrooper at War in Europe*, Presidio Press, 2003.

Menard, Orville, *The Army and the 5th Republic*, University of Nebraska Press, 1967.

Middlebrook, Martin, *Arnhem 1944. The Airborne Battle*, Viking, 1994.

Miller, David, *The Illustrated Directory of Special Forces*, Zenith Imprint, 2002.

Milton, Giles, *The Ministry of Ungentlemanly Warfare*, John Murray, 2016.

Mitcham, Samuel, and Von Stauffenberg, Friedrich, *The Battle of Sicily. How the Allies Lost their Chance for Total Victory*, Stackpole, 2007.

Mitchell, William, *Memoirs of World War I*, Random House, 1960.

Molinari, Andrea, *Desert Raiders: Axis and Allied Special Forces 1940–1943*, Osprey Publishing, 2007.

Molony, Brigadier C.J.C. et al, *The Mediterranean and Middle East. The Campaign in Sicily 1943, History of the Second World War*, Naval and Military Press, 1973.

Morison, Samuel Eliot, *History of US Naval Operations in World War II, New Guinea and the Marianas March 1944–August 1944*, University of Illinois Press, 1953.

Morris, Benny, *1948: A History of the First Arab-Israeli War*, Yale University Press, 2008.

Moseley, Leonard, *Lindbergh: A Biography*, Doubleday and Company, 1976.

Mortimer, Gavin, *Stirling's Men*, Weidenfeld and Nicolson, 2004.

Moulton, J.L., *The Royal Marines*, Sphere Books, 1973.

Mowat, R.C., *Ruin and Resurgence 1939–1945*, Blandford Press, 1966.

Moyar, Mark, *Triumph Forsaken: The Vietnam War 1954–1964*, Cambridge University Press, 2006.

Mrozek, Donald, *Air Power and the Ground War in Vietnam*, University Press of the Pacific, 2002.

Muñoz, Antonio J., *Forgotten Legions. Obscure Combat Formations of the Waffen-SS*, Paladin Press, 1991.

Murray, Raymond, *The SAS in Ireland*, The Mercier Press, 1990.

Murray, Williamson, and Millett, Allan R., *A War to be Won, Fighting in the Second World War*, The Belknap Press of Harvard University Press, 2000.

Murphy, Edward F., *Dak To: America's Sky Soldiers in South Vietnam's Central Highlands*, Ballantine, 2007.

Nasr, Kameel B., *Arab and Israeli Terrorism: The Causes and Effects of Political Violence 1936–1993*, McFarland, 1996.

Neville, Leigh, *Special Forces in the War on Terror*, Osprey Publishing, 2015.

———, *The SAS 1983–2004*, Osprey Publishing, 2015.

Newsinger, John, *British Counterinsurgency*, Palgrave Macmillan, 2016.

Nigl, Alfred, *Silent Wings Savage Death*, Graphic Publishers, 2007.

Nordyke, Philip, *All American All the Way, The Combat History of the 82nd Airborne Division in World War II*, Zenith Press, 2005.

———, *Four Stars of Valor. The Combat History of the 505th Parachute Infantry Regiment in World War II*, Zenith Press, 2006.

O'Balance, Edgar, *The Algerian Insurrection 1954–1962*, Archon Books, 1967.

———, *The War in the Yemen*, Hamden, 1971.

Odgers, George, *Remembering Korea: Australians in the War of 1950–1953*, New Holland Publishers, 2009.

O'Donnel, Patrick K., *Beyond Valor. World War II's Ranger and Airborne Veterans Reveal the Heart of the Combat*, The Free Press, 2001.

———, *World War II's Pacific Veterans Reveal the Heart of Combat*, Free Press, 2010.

O'Neal, N.C., *History of the Second World War*, Odhams Press, 1951.

Otway, T.B.H., *The Second World War 1939–1945, Army Airborne Forces*, Imperial War Museum, 1990.

Palmer, Bruce, *Intervention in the Caribbean: The Dominican Crisis of 1965*, University Press of Kentucky, 2015.

Pearson, Owen, *Albania in the Twentieth Century: A History, Vol. III*, I. B. Tauris, 2006

Pennington, Reina, *Wings, Women and War: Soviet Airwomen in World War II Combat*, University of Kansas, 2001.

———, and Higham, Robin, *Amazons to Fighter Pilots: A Biographical Dictionary of Military Women, Vol. 1*, Greenwood Press, 2003.

Peterson, J.E., *Defending Arabia*, Croom Helm, 2017.

Philpott, Bryan, *Eject Eject*, Ian Allan, 1989.

Pirocchi, Angelo, and Vuksic, Velimir, *Italian Arditi: Elite Assault Troops 1917–1920*, Osprey Publishing, 2004.

Polk, David, *World War II Airborne Carriers and Technology Engineering*, Turner Publishing Company, 1991.

Pollack, Kenneth Michael, *Arabs at War: Military Effectiveness 1948–1991*, University of Nebraska Press, 2004.

Polmar, Norman, and Allen, Thomas B., *World War II: The Encyclopedia of the War Years 1941–1945*, Dover, 2012.

Pöppel, Martin, *Παράδεισος και Κόλαση: Το Πολεμικό Ημερολόγιο Ενός Αλεξιπτωτιστή (Paradise and Hell: The War Diary of a German Paratrooper)*, Eurobooks, 2008.

Pugsley, Christopher, *From Emergency to Confrontation: The New Zealand Armed Forces in Malaya and Borneo 1949–1966*, Oxford University Press, 2003.

Quarrie, Bruce, *German Airborne Troops 1939–1945*, Osprey Publishing, 2007.

Qesada, Alejandro de, *The Bay of Pigs: Cuba 1961*, Osprey Publishing, 2009.

Rabinovich, Abraham, *The Yom Kippur War: The Epic Encounter that Transformed the Middle East*, Random House, 2017.

Reid, Anthony, *The Indonesian National Revolution 1945–1950*, Longman, 1974.

Reynolds, David, *Paras. An Illustrated History of Britain's Airborne Forces*, Sutton, 1998.

Riley, Jonathan, *Decisive Battles: From Yorktown to Operation Desert Storm*, Continuum, 2010.

Roberts, Andrew, *The Storm of War, A New History of the Second World War*, Allen Lane, 2009.

Rottman, Gordon L., *US Army Long-Range Reconnaissance Patrol Scout in Vietnam 1965–1971*, Osprey Publishing, 2008.

———, *US Airborne Units in the Pacific Theater 1942–1945*, Osprey Publishing, 2007.

———, and Takizawa, Akira, *Japanese Paratroop Forces of World War II*, Osprey Publishing, 2005.

———, and Volstad, Ron, *Vietnam Airborne* (Elite), Osprey Publishing, 1990.

Roy, Olivier, *Islam and Resistance in Afghanistan*, Cambridge University Press, 1990.

Ruggero, Ed, *Combat Jump. The Young Men Who Led the Assault into Fortress Europe, July 1943*, Harper Collins, 2003.

———, *US Paratroopers and the Fight to Save D-Day*, Harper Collins, 2006.

Ryan, Cornelius, *A Bridge too Far*, Popular Library, 1974.

Sakaida, Henry, *Japanese Army and Air Force Aces 1937–1945*, Osprey Publishing, 1997.

Salecker, Gene Eric, *Blossoming Silk Against the Rising Sun: US and Japanese Paratroopers at War in the Pacific in World War II*, Stackpole, 2010.

Saunders, Hilary St. George, *The Red Beret*, New English Library, 1973.

Schemmer, Benjamin F., *The Raid: American POWs in Vietnam were not Forgotten*, Harper and Row, 1976.

Schiff, Zeev, *A History of the Israeli Army 1870–1974*, Straight Arrow Books, 1974.

Scholey, Pete, and Forsyth, Frederick, *Who Dares Wins: Special Forces Heroes of the SAS*, Osprey Publishing, 2008.

Scutts, Jerry, *Night Fighter Aces of World War II*, Osprey Publishing, 1998.

Seymour, William, *British Special Forces*, Sidgwick and Jackson, 1985.

Shores, Christopher, *Air Aces*, Presidio Press, 1983.

Shortt (*sic*), James, and McBride, Angus, *The Special Air Service*, Osprey Publishing, 1981.

Shrader, Charles R., *The First Helicopter War. Logistics and Mobility in Algeria 1954–1962*, Praeger, 1999.

Sica, Emmanuele, and Carrier, Richard, *Italy and the Second World War, Alternative Perspectives*, Brill, 2018.

Slim, Field Marshall William, *Defeat into Victory*, Pan Military Classics, 2009.

Smith, Neil, *Nothing Short of War: With the Australian Army in Borneo 1962–1966*, Unsung Military History, 1999.

Smith, Peter, and Walker, Edwin, *War in the Aegean*, William Kimber Publishing, 1974.

Spector, Ronald H., *Eagle against the Sun*, Vintage Books, 1985.

Spick, Mike, *Aces in the Reich*, Greenhill Books, 2006.

Stafford, David, *Mission Accomplished: S.O.E. and Italy 1943–1945*, The Bodley Head, 2011.

Stanton, Shelby L., *Rangers at War*, Ivy Books, 1993.

———, *World War II Order of Battle, An Encyclopedic Reference to US Army Ground Forces from Battalion through Division 1939–1946*, Stackpole Books, 2006.

Stanwood, Frederick, Allen, Patrick, and Peacock, Lindsay, *Gulf War, A Day-by-Day Chronicle*, BCA, 1991.

Stout, Jay A., *Fighter Group, The 352nd 'Blue-Nosed Bastards' in World War II*, Stackpole Books, 2012.

Steer, Frank, *Battleground Europe. Market-Garden: The Bridge*, Leo Cooper, 2003.

Stokesbury, James L., *A Short History of the Korean War*, Harper Perennial, 1990.

Strawson, John, *Hitler as Military Commander*, Sphere Books Limited, 1973.

Sweeting, C.G., *US Army Aviators' Equipment 1917–1945*, McFarland, 2015.

Taillon, J. Paul de B., *The Evolution of Special Forces in Counter-Terrorism: The British and American Experiences*, Greenwood, 2000.

Tate, Robert, *Hans-Joachim Marseille, An Illustrated Tribute to the Luftwaffe's 'Star of Africa'*, Schiffer Publishing, 2008.

Taylor, Thomas, *Rangers Lead the Way*, Turner Publishing, 1996.

Thacker, Toby, *The End of the Third Reich*, Tempus Publishing, 2006.

Thompson, Leroy, *SAS. Great Britain's Elite Special Air Service*, Zenith Imprint, 1994.

Thompson, Timothy J., *The Ardennes on Fire. The First Day of the German Assault*, Xlibris Corporation, 2010.

Toczek, David M., *The Battle of Ap Bac: They did Everything but Learn from It*, Naval Institute Press, 2001.

Toliver, Raymond F., and Constable, J. Trevor, *Fighter Aces of the Luftwaffe*, Schiffer Publishing, 1996.

Truong, V.T., *Vietnam War*, The New Legion, 2010.

Tuck, Christopher, *Confrontation, Strategy and War Termination: Britain's Conflict with Indonesia*, Routledge, 2016.

Tucker, Spencer C., *Vietnam*, University Press of Kentucky, 1999.

——— (ed.), *The Encyclopedia of the Arab-Israeli Conflict: A Political, Social and Military History*, ABC CLIO, 2008.

Tugwell, Maurice, *Airborne to Battle. A History of Airborne Warfare 1918–1971*, Kimber, 1971.

———, *Assault from the Sky. The History of Airborne Warfare*, Kimber, 1978.

Van Creveld, Martin, *Technology and War, From 2000 B.C. to the Present*, Brassey's, 1991.

Van der Bijl, Nick, *Nine Battles to Stanley*, Leo Coopers, 1999.

———, *No. 10 Inter-Allied Commando 1942–1946*, Osprey Publishing, 2006.

Varble, Derek, *The Suez Crisis*, Osprey Publishing, 2003.

Varhola, Michael, *Fire and Ice: The Korean War 1950–1953*, Da Capo Press, 2000.

Veith, George, *Black April: The Fall of South Vietnam 1973–1975*, Encounter Books, 2013.

Vickers, Adrian, *A History of Modern Indonesia*, Cambridge University Press, 2005.

Waddy, John, *A Tour of the Arnhem Battlefields*, Pen and Sword, 1999.

Walker, Jonathan, *Aden Insurgency: The Savage War in Yeman [sic] 1962–1967*, Pen and Sword, 2011.

Walmer, Max, *Modern Elite Forces*, Salamander Books, 1984.

Walsh, Dermot, *Bloody Sunday and the Rule of Law in Northern Ireland*, Gill and Macmillan, 2000.

Walters, Anne-Marie, *Moondrop to Gascony*, Moho Books, 2009.

Warner, Philip, *The SAS*, Sphere Books Limited, 1988.

Warren, John C., *Airborne Missions in the Mediterranean 1942–1945*, Maxwell A.F.B., 1955.

———, *Airborne Operations in World War II*, USAF Historical Division, 1956.

Weeks, John, *Assault from the Sky: A History of Airborne Warfare*, Putnam, 1978.

———, *The Airborne Soldier*, Blandford Press, 1986.

White, Terry, *Swords of Lightning*, Brassey's, 1992.

———, *The Making of the World's Elite Forces*, Sidgwick and Jackson, 1992.

Wiggan, Richard, *Operation Freshman*, William Kimber, 1986.

Willbanks, James, *The Tet Offensive: A Concise History*, Columbia University Press, 2008.

———, *Vietnam War Almanac*, Checkmark Books, 2010.

Wilkinson, Peter, and Astley, Joan Bright, *Gubbins and S.O.E.*, Pen and Sword Military, 2010.

Williams, David P., *Hunters of the Reich: Night Fighter*, Spellmount, 2011.

Wilmot, Chester, *The Struggle for Europe*, Wordsworth Editions, 1997.

Windrow, Martin, *The Last Valley: Dien Bien Phu and the Last French Defeat in Vietnam*, Weidenfeld and Nicolson, 2004.

Wolf, Marion, *Posttraumatic Stress: Disorder, Phenomenology, and Treatment*, American Psychiatric Publications, 1990.

Woolf, Alex, *Arab-Israeli Wars Since 1948*, Heinemann and Raintree, 2012.

Wurst, Spencer F., and Wurst, Gayle, *Descending from the Clouds. A Memoir of Combat in the 505th Parachute Infantry Regiment, 82nd Airborne Division*, Casemate Publishers, 2004.

Zaloga, Steven J., *Inside the Blue Berets. A Combat History of Soviet and Russian Airborne Forces 1930–1995*, Presidio, 1995.

———, and Hook, Richard, *The Polish Army 1939–1945*, Osprey Publishing, 1982.

Zhai, Qiang, *China and the Vietnam Wars 1950–1975*, University of North Carolina Press, 2000.

Official Publications, Reports, Essays, Papers, Articles, etc

A History of the Hellenic Army 1821–1997, Hellenic Army General Staff, Army History Directorate, 1999.

Airborne Operations, An Illustrated History of the Battles, Tactics, and Equipment of the World's Airborne Forces, Salamander Books, 1988.

All American, The Story of the 82nd Airborne Division, Star and Stripes (Paris), 1944.

Appleman, Roy E., *South to the Naktong North to the Yalu: US Army in the Korean War, June–November 1950*, Department of the Army, 1998.

Bartlett, Norman (ed.), *With the Australians in Korea*, Australian War Memorial, 1960.

British Airborne Forces 1940–1990, The Golden Jubilee, The Parachute Regiment Association, 1991.

Brugioni, Dino, and Taylor, Doris G., *Eyes in the Sky: Eisenhower, the CIA and Cold War Aerial Espionage*, Naval Institute Press, 2010.

CIA, Directorate of Intelligence, Office of Soviet Analysts, *Intelligence Assessment, SOV 87–10007*, February 1987.

CIA Intelligence Report, *The 1973 Arab-Israeli War: Overview and Analysis of the Conflict*, September 1975 (Released 29 August 2002).

Dentay, Ted, 'Tactical Personnel Parachutes: The Next Leap', *International Defense Review*, 3/1995.

Dyson, S.B., 'Origins of the Psychological Profiling of Political Leaders: The US Office of Strategic Services and Adolf Hitler', *Intelligence and National Security* (29), 2014.

Ellis, Lieutenant Colonel John T., *The Airborne Command and Center*, Army Ground Forces Study No. 25, Historical Section, Army Ground Forces, Washington D.C., 1946.

Evans, Gary F., *The 501st Parachute Infantry Regiment at Bastogne Belgium in December 1944*, Center of Military History, Historical Manuscripts Collection 8–3.1. BB2, 22 June 1972.

Fellers, Bonner F., *Military Attaché Report, Airborne Invasion of Crete*, Military Intelligence Division, War Department General Staff, Egypt, 9 August 1941

Foreign Relations of the United States 1961–1963, Vol. III, Vietnam: January–August 1963.

Handbook FY 2013, Warrior Training Center, Air Assault School.

History of Military Operational Jumps, Special Forces (PDF).

Hoffman, Jon (*sic*) T., *Silk Chutes and Hard Fighting. USMC Parachute Units in World War II*, Historical Division, 1992.

Goulding, Major Vincent J., *Dien Bien Phu*, Marine Corps Command and Staff College, 1985.

Hogan, David W., *US Army Special Operations in World War II*, Center of Military History, Department of the Army, 1992.

Holliday, Joseph, *The Syrian Army. Doctrinal Order of Battle*, Institute for the Study of War, February 2013.

Institute of Current World Affairs, *The Bizerte Affair*, 31 July 1961.

International Commission of Jurists, *Report of the Committee of Enquiry into Events on Bizerta [sic] Tunisia between 18 and 24 July 1961*, Geneva, 1961

Ιστορία της Ελληνικής Πολεμικής Αεροπορίας, Ελληνική Πολεμική Αεροπορία, Τμήμα Ιστορίας, Τόμος Γ (*History of the Hellenic Air Force*, Hellenic Air Force, History Department, Volume III), 1990.

Johnstone, John H., *USMC Parachute Units*, Marine Historical Series, Number 32, Historical Branch, 1961.

Kelley, USAF Major Stephanie R., *Egypt's Air War in Yemen (Report)*, Air Command and Staff College / Air University, Alabama, March 2010.

Kreisler, Henry, *A Life in Peace and War. Conversation with Sir Brian Urquhart*, Institute of International Studies, University of California Berkley, 19 March 1996.

McGrath, John, *History, Organization and Employment in the US Army*, Combat Studies Institute, 2004.

Margelletti, Andrea, 'US Special Warfare Forces: Structure and Missions', *Military Technology*, 10/1989.

Mason, Chris, *Falling from Grace: The German Airborne in World War II*, US Marine Corps Command and Staff College/Marine Corps University, 2002.

Medal of Honor Recipients, US Army Center of Military History.

Memorandum by General Jacques E. Massu, Commander of the French army in Algiers, 29 March 1957 (1R 339/3* SHD).

Mircea, Tănase, 'Collaboration Under the Canopy of the Parachute within the Socialist Camp', *Annals of the Academy of Romanian Scientists, Series of History and Archaeology* (Vol. 4), 2012.

O'Neal, Robert, *Australia in the Korean War 1950–1953, Combat Operations, Vol. II*, Australian War Museum, 1985.

Pictorial History of the 7th Bombardment Group, Historical Foundation, 1988.

Pinheiro, Alvaro de Souza, *Knowing Your Partner, The Evolution of Brazilian Operational Forces*, Report 12-7, Joint Special Operations University, 2012.

Private Papers of Major-General R. E. Urquhart, CB DSO, Imperial War Museum. Documents: 15783 (07/64/1-12).

Protocol additional to the Geneva Conventions of 12 August 1949 and Relating to the Protection of Victims of International Armed Conflict (Protocol I), 8 June 1977, International Committee of the Red Cross.

Ramsay III, Lieutenant Colonel Robert, *Seizing and Holding the German Bridges at Arnhem*, Combined Arms Research Library (Kansas), 1992

Raulins, Eugene W., *Marines and Helicopters 1946–1962*, USMC History and Museum Division, 1976.

Reinhardt, Generalmajor Hellmuth, *Airborne Operations. A German Appraisal*, Office of the Chief of Military History, Special Staff Department of the Army (Washington), 1989.

Robarge, David, 'CIA's Covert Operations in the Congo 1960–1968: Insights from Newly Declassified Documents', *Studies of Intelligence*, Vol. 58, No. 3, September 2014.

Rogers, Bernard, *Vietnam Studies: Cedar Fall-Junction City: A Turning Point*, Department of the Army, 1974.

Rollie, Major Beau G., *Helicopters in Irregular Warfare: Algeria, Vietnam and Afghanistan*, US Military Academy, 2001.

Sheenan, Major Thomas J., *World War II Vertical Envelopment, The German Influence on US Army Airborne Operations*, US Army Command and General Staff College, 2003.

Slater, K.C., 'Air Operations in Malaya', *Anthology of Selected Topics on Counter-Insurgency, Vol. II*, Lackland Military Training Center, 1 March 1963.

South African National Defense Forces, Archive File 'UDF Paratroop Company', Directorate of Documentation Services and Personnel Records Section, 23 July 1943.

Starr, Barbara, 'Crucial Role for USA Special Forces', *Jane's Defence Weekly*, 16 December 1989.

Stern, Abraham, 'Parachute Pioneers', *Flying and Popular Aviation*, September 1952.

Sweeney, Matthew A., *American Operations in the Pacific Theater. Extending Operational Reach and Creating Operational Shock*, School of Advanced Military Studies, US Army Command and Staff College, Monograph, 2014.

The Imposed War, Defense versus Aggression, Islamic Republic of Iran, War Information Headquarters, Supreme Defense Council, 1987.

The Iraqi Army Sixtieth Anniversary, 6th January 1921–1981, The Political Guidance Bureau, Ministry of Defense, Al-Adeeb Baghdad Press, 1981.

Tolson, Lieutenant General John J., *Airmobility 1961–1971*, Department of the Army, Center of Military History, 1989.

Towers, Lieutenant Colonel John W., *The French in Algeria 1954–1962*, US Army War College, 2000.

Training Handbook on Parachute Jumping, Jumpmaster, Drop Zone, Airborne Operations, Military Team, Aircraft and Combat Equipment Loads, Field Manual, US Army, Reference Guide ASIN B0006FHA5W.

US Army Field Manual FM 1-02 (FM 101-5-1).

Warren, John C., *Airborne Missions in the Mediterranean 1942–1945*, USAF Historical Study (No. 74), 1955.

Wilson, Bob, *The Evolution of Iranian Warfighting during the Iran-Iraq War: When Dismounted Light Infantry Made the Difference*, US Army Foreign Military Office (PDF).

Yaffe, Aharon, *The War of Attrition in the 'Land of Pursuits': The 1968–1970 War in the Jordan Valley*, Ariel Center for Policy Research (PDF).

Yates, Laurence A., *Power Pack: US Intervention in the Dominican Republic 1965–1966*, Combat Studies Institute, 1988.

Zabih, Sepehr, 'Aspects of Terrorism in Iran', *Annals of the American Academy of Political and Social Science, International Terrorism*, September 1982 (463).

Zimmerman, Dwight Jon, and Gresham, John, *Beyond Hell and Back. How America's Special Operations Forces Became the World's Greatest Fighting Unit*, St Martin's Griffin, 2008.

Index